CW01184130

WARSHIP 2013

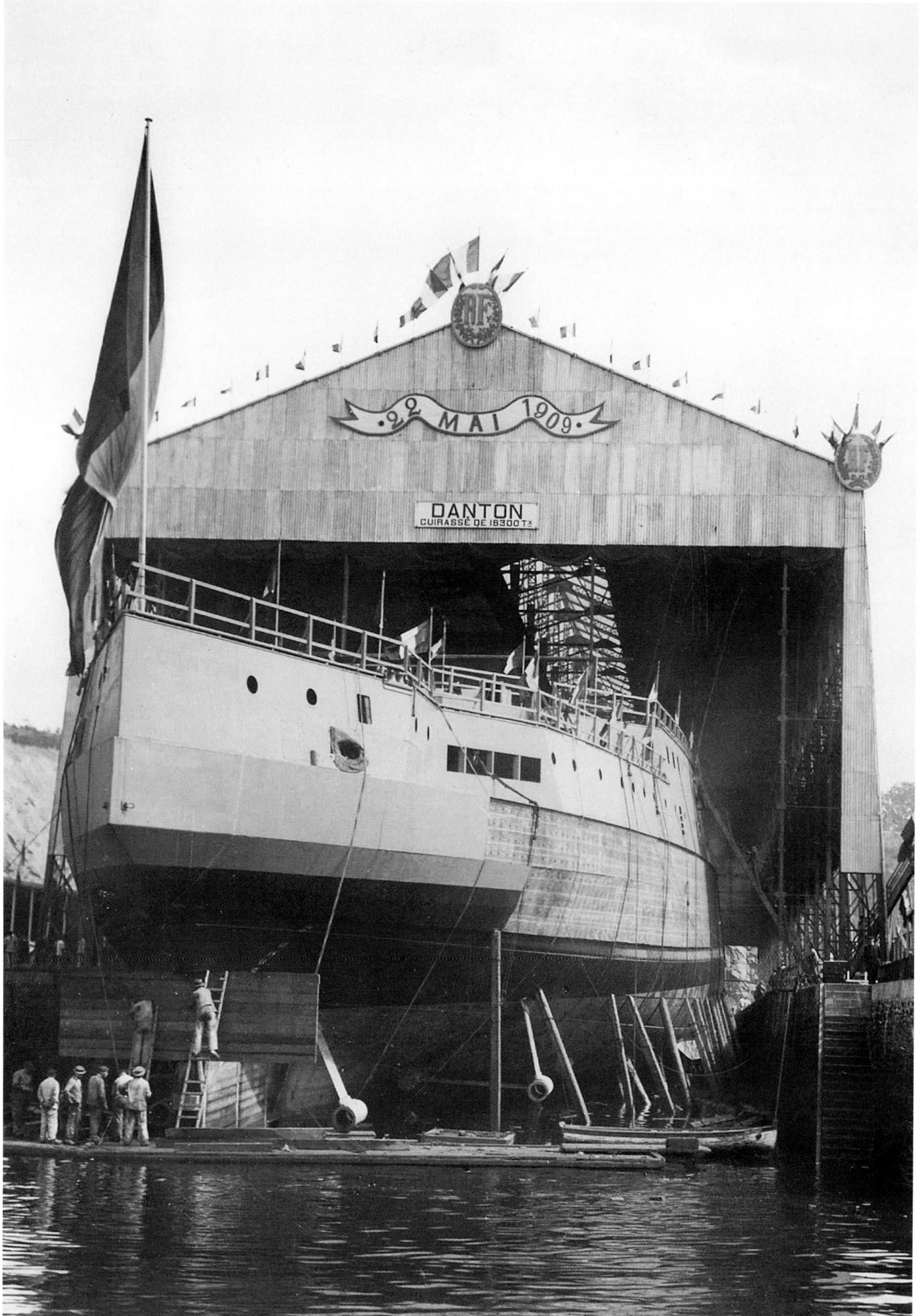

22 MAI 1909
DANTON
CUIRASSÉ DE 18300 Tx

WARSHIP 2013

Editor: **John Jordan**

Assistant Editor: **Stephen Dent**

CONWAY

Frontispiece:
The stern of the French battleship Danton *protruding from the Point-du-Jour slipway following her aborted launch. The slipway had been specially built for the ship, hence the commemorative plaque above the entrance. The Editor's article on the Danton class is on pp.45-64 of this year's annual. (Philippe Caresse collection)*

NEW TITLES FROM CONWAY

Elizabeth's Sea Dogs
How the English Became
the Scourge of the Seas
Hugh Bicheno
9781844861743 £25.00

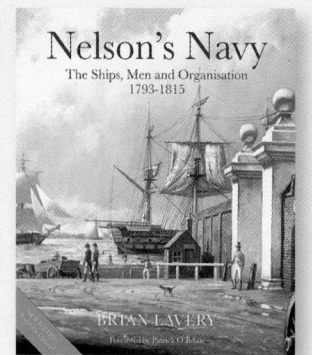

Nelson's Navy
The Ships, Men and
Organisation 1793-1815.
Revised Edition
Brian Lavery
9781844861750 £40.00

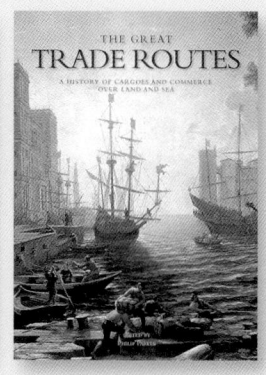

The Great Trade Routes
A History of Cargoes
& Commerce Over Land
and Sea
Edited by Philip Parker
9781844861415 £40.00

All Hands
The Lower Deck of the Royal
Navy Since 1939
Brian Lavery
9781844861552 £25.00

For further information relating to these titles and many other books on military, naval and maritime history please visit www.conwaypublishing.com

The *Warship* team are very pleased to receive suggestions for articles and contributions to the annual for consideration. If you are interested in contributing please send an outline, together with details of proposed illustrative matter, via post to the Anova Books London address (see below) clearly marked 'Warship Annual' or send an email to: conwaymaritime@anovabooks.com. We cannot guarantee to return posted material so please only send copies for initial consideration.

© Conway 2013

First published in Great Britain in 2013 by Conway,
an imprint of Anova Books, 10 Southcombe Street, London W14 0RA
www.conwaypublishing.com

All rights reserved. No part of this publication may be reproduced, stored in a retrieval system, or transmitted in any form or by any means, electronic, mechanical, photocopying, recording or otherwise, without the prior permission of the publisher.

British Library Cataloguing in Publication Data
A record of this title is available on request from the British Library.

ISBN: 9781844862054

Printed and bound in China by 1010 Printing International Ltd.

CONTENTS

Editorial	6

FEATURE ARTICLES

Rebuilding the Australian Cruiser Squadron 1930-1939 — 8
Peter Cannon looks at the transfer of three light cruisers to the Royal Australian Navy during the 1930s.

The Fourth Fleet Incident and the *Fubuki* Class — 30
Hans Lengerer examines one of the disasters which struck the Imperial Japanese Navy during the mid-1930s.

The 'Semi-Dreadnoughts' of the *Danton* Class — 46
John Jordan looks at how these ships, which on completion in 1911 formed the core of the French fleet in the Mediterranean, came to be built, and why their construction was so protracted.

The Battle Cruisers *Lion* and *Tiger* at Dogger Bank: The View of the Ships' Medical Officers — 67
Matthew Seligmann uses the Medical Officers' Journals of *Lion* and *Tiger* for 1915 to shed light on *Tiger*'s notably poor performance during the battle as well as on the treatment of casualties during the period in question.

Modern European Offshore Patrol Vessels — 78
Conrad Waters looks at four key OPV designs which have entered service in the last few years.

The Unlucky Destroyer *Espingole* — 94
Philippe Caresse tells the story of one of France's first destroyers.

The Soviet Aircraft Carrier: the Interwar Projects — 107
Richard Worth and Vladimir Yakubov take a detailed look at the various projects proposed during the period 1918-1944, including both conversions of existing ships and new-build carriers.

Securing 'The Ripest Plum': Britain and the South American Naval Export Market 1945-1975 — 119
Jon Wise looks at the attempts of British shipbuilders to secure warship orders in South America during the postwar era.

Toulon: The Self-Destruction and Salvage of the French Fleet — 134
Enrico Cernuschi and Vincent P. O'Hara look at the scuttling of the French Fleet in November 1942, and the efforts of the Italian *Regia Marina* to bring some of the key units back into service.

Russia's Coles 'Monitors': *Smerch*, *Rusalka* and *Charodeika* — 149
Stephen McLaughlin describes the origins, design and construction of three vessels that marked a major step forward in Russian shipbuilding, introducing a number of important innovations.

Warship Notes	164
Naval Books of the Year	182
Warship Gallery	200

Stephen Dent and Ian Johnston present a series of photographs depicting the activities of the Royal Navy's 1st Submarine Flotilla during the early 1920s.

EDITORIAL

In my editorial last year I emphasised how much we welcome contact from prospective contributors, and that policy has borne fruit once again this year with two of this year's ten feature article authors new to *Warship*, and a third contributing a substantial Warship Note.

Matthew Seligmann, Reader in History at Brunel University and author of a number of books on the Royal Navy during the early part of the 19th century, was introduced to me by one of our established authors, Stephen McLaughlin. During his research in the British archives – in this case the Admiralty Library at Portsmouth – Matthew had discovered the journals of the Medical Officers of the battlecruisers *Lion* and *Tiger* covering the period 1915-16. There has been considerable uninformed speculation by naval historians on the reasons for the poor performance of HMS *Tiger* at the Battle of Dogger Bank in late January 1915, which appears to have been largely fuelled by the claim from the vice-admiral commanding the Battle Cruiser Squadron, David Beatty, that the crew was 'very mixed', with a large number of recovered deserters and other miscreants and malcontents among their number. However, a close inspection of the Medical Officer's Journal (MOJ) for the ship reveals serious and widespread health problems, which were almost certainly due to 'overcrowding, overwork, damp, dirt and poor ventilation', conditions which the ship's Medical Officer of the time, Staff Surgeon John Reid Muir, attributes to the ship's rushed entry into service. The MOJs also have much to say about the nature of the casualties sustained in the two battlecruisers at Dogger Bank, and about the difficulties involved in treating them while the battle was still proceeding. Matthew's article will hopefully bring a new perspective to the evaluation of the performance of ships in battle by shifting the focus away from the ability of the big guns to deal out punishment and the ability of protection systems to absorb it to the equally important human element.

Our second new feature author is Peter Cannon, a Petty Officer serving in the RAN and lecturer in Australian naval history at the Royal Australian Naval College. As part of his academic research Peter has investigated the procurement process for the three light cruisers of the interwar Modified *Leander* type from the British Royal Navy. A brief developmental history by Keith McBride of these ships and their half-sisters of the *Leander* class was previously published in *Warship 1997-98*. Peter's article, while providing more comprehensive technical detail about *Sydney*, *Perth* and *Hobart* during their service with the Australian Navy, focuses more closely on the strategic background to their purchase, and on the infrastructure issues and financial arrangements involved in their acquisition. In the process Peter delivers insights into the difficult choices which have to be made by the smaller navies which, lacking the large-scale defence infrastructure or the budgetary resources of the major naval powers, have to weigh the benefits of local construction and technology transfer against affordability.

Peter Marland has been working on a major review which looks at the Technical Evolution of Weapon Engineering in the Royal Navy (TEWERN) during the post-war era. At the point when Peter approached me with a view to publishing the results of some of this work in *Warship*, we had agreed to publish Jon Wise's article on defence sales to South American navies (q.v.), which among other classes of warship featured the two 'Admiral' class destroyers built by Vickers for Chile during the late 1950s. The main armament of these ships was a Vickers-designed 4-inch gun designated Mk N(R), which after being turned down by the RN was cleared for export. This ingenious 62-calibre weapon, which featured a robust automatic feed system, proved particularly successful, but only ever entered service with the Chilean Navy. As the 4-inch Mk N(R) gun was one of the projects featured in Peter's original submission, we asked him to expand the entry into a fully-fledged Warship Note. It is hoped that this will be the first of a number of contributions from Peter featuring post-war RN weapons projects.

To refer to the remainder of our authors this year as 'the usual suspects' would be discourteous. As usual, each has produced a thoughtful contribution which hopefully will add to our knowledge and understanding of international warship development over the past 150 years.

In a departure from the interwar period which has been his customary focus, the Editor steps back into the pre-dreadnought era with an article on the six French battleships of the *Danton* class. Often described in modern reference sources as obsolete even before their completion some five years after HMS *Dreadnought*, the *Dantons* are far more interesting ships than a cursory glance at their 'vital statistics' would suggest, and their design was underpinned by considered theories of naval combat which emerged from a careful analysis of the lessons of the Russo-Japanese War. Late modifications to the design – and others which it was decided could not be incorporated without serious delays in completion – reveal a surprising degree of technical influence from the Royal Navy in the period which followed the Entente Cordiale of 1904.

Stephen McLaughlin continues his series on the early Russian ironclads with an article about the Coles monitors *Smerch*, *Charodeika* and *Rusalka*. Designed by an Englishman, Charles Mitchell, an experienced Tyneside shipbuilder who had been invited by the Russian Naval Ministry to modernise its shipyard on Galernyi Island, the ships were completed during the late 1860s and continued to serve in the coast defence role into the 1890s. *Charodeika* and *Rusalka* have the distinction of being the first Russian ironclads to be built using almost exclusively components of local manufacture.

In the second and final part of his series of articles on

Artists impression of CVA-01, *one of the designs which will be featured in* Warship 2014.

the disasters which struck the Imperial Japanese Navy during the mid-1930s, Hans Lengerer gives a full account of the 'Fourth Fleet Incident', in which the main body of the fleet was struck by a typhoon of unprecedented force during the summer manoeuvres of 1935. Although damage was widespread, the typhoon highlighted particular structural weaknesses in the recently-completed destroyers of the 'Special Type', two of which lost their bows in the storm. The draconian measures taken in the wake of the incident resolved the problems, but at the expense of the ships' performance; the increase in weight which resulted from the modifications reduced speed and endurance, and the application of modern construction techniques such as electric welding to new classes of warship was halted in its tracks, to the detriment of Japan's wartime shipbuilding effort.

To follow their articles on some of the major warships built for the Soviet Navy during the interwar period, Richard Worth and Vladimir Yakubov turn their attention to Soviet naval aviation and the attempts of the Navy to build aircraft carriers in the face of the indifference or outright hostility of the Soviet political establishment. Even when the Navy was permitted to make its case for these ships, successive plans for converted or purpose-built carriers ran into serious funding and infrastructure problems.

Jon Wise looks at the attempts by the British shipbuilding industry to secure orders for ships from South America during the post-war period, when orders from the Royal Navy were no longer capable of sustaining the multitude of shipyards which had built for victory during the Second World War. This drive for foreign orders was only partially successful; designs derived from ships in service with the RN were becoming less attractive, in part because of the increasing cost and sophistication of first-line warships, but also because the high-performance weapons and electronics with which it was proposed to equip them needed a licence from the MoD, which was reluctant to sanction the export of the latest technology.

The scuttling of the French Fleet at Toulon in November 1942 was an event which shook the world; all but a handful of France's most powerful modern warships were sunk. Less well known are the Italian attempts to salvage some of the cruisers and destroyers which had sustained the least damage from sabotage and which were simply resting in an upright position on the bottom of the harbour. Vince O'Hara and Enrico Cernuschi recount these efforts, which although extensive were ultimately of limited success, from an Italian perspective.

Diving on sunken warships is a hobby of regular French contributor Philippe Caresse. In this year's annual Philippe writes about his dive on the *Espingole*, one of the first destroyers built for the Marine Nationale, which foundered on rocks off the south of France in early 1903, shortly after her completion. His story includes an account of the ineffectual attempts to salvage the ship, much of which remains intact on the sea bottom to this day.

Our feature articles are rounded off by the customary survey of the latest trends in warship design and construction by Conrad Waters. The policing of territorial waters has become a key role for modern navies, and Conrad looks in detail at the latest offshore patrol vessel (OPV) designs from Britain, France, Spain and the Netherlands. These vary in size and capability from the relative cheap patrol vessel built to mercantile standards to the sophisticated small frigate capable of operating a helicopter and monitoring the surrounding sea- and air-space.

The line-up of feature articles for *Warship 2014* is already almost complete. We are very much looking forward to publishing a long-awaited article by Ian Sturton on the Royal Navy's abortive CVA-01 carrier project of 1965, which will be accompanied by line drawings based on the original plans. Other major features include articles by Kathrin Milanovich on the eight powerful armoured cruisers purchased from abroad for the Imperial Japanese Navy during the late 1890s, by new contributor Aidan Dodson on the German pre-dreadnoughts of the *Braunschweig* and *Deutschland* classes, by Luc Feron on the French armoured cruisers of the *Chanzy* class, and by Michele Cosentino on the recently-completed Italian aircraft carrier *Cavour*.

John Jordan
January 2013

REBUILDING THE AUSTRALIAN CRUISER SQUADRON 1930-1939

In his first article for *Warship*, **Peter Cannon** looks at the strategic thinking and the procurement process which saw the transfer of three light cruisers of the Modified *Leander* class to the Royal Australian Navy during the 1930s.

In the early 1930s Australia found herself needing to update the Royal Australian Navy's (RAN) cruiser force in order to retain its quota of ships allowed to the British Empire under existing naval arms limitation treaties, as well as meet its own defence requirements. This issue was addressed by the purchase of the British built Modified *Leander* class cruiser HMAS *Sydney*. The failure of the naval disarmament treaties and the worsening security outlook later in the decade made a further increase in cruiser numbers imperative for Australia's maritime security. The acquisition of a further two existing ships of this class represented the most expedient and cost-effective avenue for augmenting the RAN's surface warfare capability before the onset of the conflict many saw as inevitable.

During the early years of the twentieth century Australia, alone among the dominions of the British Empire, had made serious provision towards her own naval defence with the creation of a blue water force modelled upon, and greatly supported by, the world's most respected sea service, Britain's Royal Navy (RN). The RAN was formally established in 1911 and three years later successfully sent its modest, but nonetheless modern and effective forces to war under British Admiralty control.

In many ways the Navy of the inter-war period could be viewed as a semi-independent squadron of the RN as regards equipment, personnel training and administration. Post-First World War British Empire policy, implemented with varying degrees of success, strove to maintain Dominion naval forces with ships and personnel interchangeable with the RN in order to create a world-wide Imperial navy in time of war. While at first heavily reliant upon British personnel, particularly officers, over the years Australian officers and sailors were trained both at home and overseas as part of a large professional navy.[1] These farsighted policies, in which the young service derived invaluable benefit from the assets, facilities and tactical doctrine of the RN, eventually resulted in the mature, balanced and independent RAN of the 1950-60s and beyond.

This success could not have been achieved in such a time frame without the unique relationship exercised between the British Admiralty in London and the Australian Commonwealth Naval Board based in Melbourne, which facilitated the development of a first-class professional naval force. While the Australian government looked to the United Kingdom (UK) for naval guidance, political control of the navy was exercised through the Naval Board by the Minister for Defence. Admiralty organisation was widely regarded as a successful administrative arrangement, and the relationship between the Minister and the Naval Board was precisely the same as that between the British First Lord and the Board of Admiralty.

The Board itself was predominantly staffed by RN officers, headed by a flag officer as Chief of Naval Staff (CNS), who would gradually be replaced with Australian personnel of sufficient seniority. The Board exercised executive command of naval forces, and was supported by a Naval Staff. It was in no way subservient to the Admiralty, but its British officers took careful note of Admiralty policy and advice. However, they identified remarkably well with Australian interests and did an exceptional job for the Commonwealth. This was the organisation with which Australia built the navy that was to be the only force in the country trained, equipped and battle ready when war came in 1939.

Australian defence policy of the inter-war period was based upon the concept of Imperial Defence; British Empire interests would be defended by a partnership of UK, Dominion and Colonial forces. The Pacific was viewed as the potential future flashpoint, particularly by an insecure Australia, with an expansionist Japan the likely threat. Both Australia and New Zealand were reliant in an emergency upon a British fleet being despatched from European waters to a new base under construction at Singapore. The RAN was tasked with contributing units to this fleet along with being completely responsible for the protection of shipping and local defence of the Australia Station. Despite being placed well ahead of the other two services for the resources required to effect this forward-looking maritime policy, the post-First World War Navy struggled against a backdrop of technological obsolescence, political prevarication and popular lack of interest, as well as crippling financial constraints.

It was considered that in the event of war, the Japanese would not risk heavy forces with their attendant supply

Following Hobart *and* Perth's *pre-delivery refits, HMAS* Sydney *could easily be distinguished from her two sisters through the aerial spar projecting from the upper bridge roof to port as well as her retention of the original four Mk IV 4in gun mountings.* Sydney *is shown here arriving in Melbourne for a three-day visit on 24 September 1938.* (Allan C. Green Collection, State Library of Victoria)

complications as far south as Australia with a British fleet threatening their lines of communication from Singapore. The envisaged scale of attack would therefore involve armed merchant raiders along with regular cruisers. The ideal type of ship to protect Australia's vital shipping lanes was the long range cruiser, and it was in the RAN's interest to maintain a force of the most effective ships of this type available. Hence the priority of the Naval Board, struggling to maintain a professional service capable of future expansion in an emergency, was the RAN's cruiser squadron. Everything else was subordinate to that end and ruthlessly cut.

Australia, as a part of the British Empire, was a signatory to the naval disarmament treaties of the 1920s and 1930s, with its naval forces considered a component of Royal Navy strength. Both the Washington Naval Limitation Treaty of 1922 and the London Naval Treaty of 1930 placed restrictions upon certain categories of warship. The Washington conference saw any ship over a 10,000 tons standard displacement classified either as a capital ship or as an aircraft carrier, and the numbers and displacement of both types were limited. Any ship up to this limit was classed as an 'auxiliary vessel' and prohibited from mounting guns larger than 8in. Cruisers fell into this category, and there were no restrictions imposed upon the numbers any signatory could build.

The London conference introduced two categories of cruiser: category (a) cruisers armed with guns over 6.1in in calibre and category (b) cruisers with guns of 6.1in or under. It also imposed strict limits upon the total tonnage of cruisers a country could build. Both treaties saw a quota system imposed whereby the US gained parity with Britain, but Japan, France and Italy were restricted to reduced percentages. The RN, leading the world in the construction of 8in gun 'treaty' cruisers, had found them unaffordable in the numbers required and London would see an agreement to terminate their construction.

In light of the worldwide commitments it was entrusted with, Admiralty policy of the time maintained that the RN required a minimum of seventy cruisers, 45 for trade protection and 25 for battlefleet duties, despite the fact that the politicians would never fund such a force. At London, the Admiralty had pushed to end the international competition in the prohibitively expensive 'treaty cruisers' in order to pursue its preference for smaller cruisers that could be built in larger numbers. However, the UK Government imposed a limit of fifty cruisers upon the Navy to ensure the success of the conference. Cruisers operated by Australia, the only dominion navy operating the type, would count towards this new total as a quota of British Empire strength, and it is against this background that Australian efforts at strengthening its cruiser force during the 1930s need to be considered. Australian decisions would have an impact upon overall Empire security.

Replacing Brisbane

The RAN entered the 1930s with a force of four cruisers, all either built in Britain or British designed, as was the case will all RAN warships until the 1960s. The financial strain that came with the Great Depression in 1929-30 saw the Navy reduced to two new *Kent* class heavy cruisers, *Australia* and *Canberra*, one destroyer and a seaplane carrier in full commission.[2] Two older light cruisers, *Brisbane* and *Adelaide*, of the *Chatham* and

Birmingham classes respectively, were in reserve along with various smaller vessels.[3] The issue of replacing obsolescent Australian ships was first raised by the British government in 1930. They enquired whether the Australian Labor Government would be willing to lay down a new cruiser in 1933 to replace *Brisbane* as part of ongoing British construction programmes.

With her design dating from 1910, *Brisbane* was laid down at Cockatoo Island Dockyard in Sydney in January 1913 and completed in October 1916. She was a coal-burning ship of 5400 tons with a radius of action of around 4000 nautical miles and a maximum speed of 25 knots. She was armed with eight 6in Mark XI guns in single open gun shields, one single 3in anti-aircraft gun and two 21in torpedo tubes. Under the terms of the London treaty, cruisers were deemed to be overage 16 years after completion if they had been laid down prior to 1920, which meant that *Brisbane* would be overage in 1932.

The Australian Cabinet agreed with advice provided by the Naval Board that it was morally obligated to replace *Brisbane*. It was in the best interests of overall Empire cruiser capability to replace obsolescent ships with new construction, therefore the onus was upon Australia to pay for a new vessel. To make matters worse, according to the same treaty she had to be scrapped by 31 December 1936; if not, another ship would have to be disposed of in order to keep the overall Empire cruiser tonnage within its limits. This would mean that the RN would be forced to lose a ship more modern and capable than *Brisbane* to allow Australia to forego the expense of a replacement. Of course Australia could simply scrap the ship and accept a reduced quota of Empire cruiser numbers, along with the likely political repercussions. Whilst a replacement for *Brisbane* was agreed in principle, the parlous state of the country's finances saw the decision deferred pending improved financial conditions.

By 1933 the worst of the depression was over and a new United Australia Party Government, led by Joseph Lyons until his death in 1939, readdressed the question. An Australian proposal to increase its cruiser quota, through the Commonwealth paying the maintenance costs of new ships owned by the UK government while simultaneously retaining *Brisbane*, was firmly rejected by the Admiralty. There was no desire to increase the Australian proportion of the already dangerously low Empire cruiser strength. This was due to the fact that despite agreements with the Commonwealth Government, the Admiralty could never be certain that Australian warships would be placed under their control in time of war.[4]

It was suggested that a replacement for *Brisbane* be included in the next British naval construction programme. This programme represented the final instalment of new tonnage to be completed under the 1930 treaty which expired at the end of 1936. Britain was entitled to lay down four cruisers that year, all replacements for old ships. The new cruiser would be built in the UK for approximately £1,800,000 Sterling, or £A2,250,000, the cost in Australian pounds being 25% greater.

The Australian Cabinet replied that it wished to replace the cruiser but was still unable to commit due to ongoing financial pressures and other defence commitments, as well as the need to look into the question of whether to build such a ship in Australia as opposed to the UK. It suggested that it be announced that the new ships would be built, but that negotiations were still proceeding with the Commonwealth. Britain for its part went ahead

HMAS Brisbane *as a front-line cruiser. She is shown here in November 1923.* (Allan C. Green Collection, State Library of Victoria)

and ordered four cruisers, later amended to three, announcing that one of the ships was a replacement for HMAS *Brisbane* for the purposes of the London Treaty. It was however understood that a cruiser could be made available for purchase by Australia in 1935, and that provision might be found in the 1934-35 naval estimates to begin paying for the ship in instalments.

The Naval Board in the meantime was prepared to offer advice to the government as to what type of ship should replace *Brisbane* when the money did finally become available. The Board was in direct communication with the Admiralty through an RAN naval liaison officer at the Australian High Commission in London. This liaison was essential for the development of the RAN but at times annoyed their Australian political masters as they often found themselves out of the loop. Official government to government correspondence was effected between the Governor General in Melbourne and the Dominion Office in London.

The New Cruiser

The Board had written to the Admiralty in December 1931 requesting information on the first British post-Washington Treaty designed light cruiser, the *Leander* class, in order to frame a prospective policy around this type of ship. The British considered a ship of 7000 tons to be the most efficient all-round design for service on the trade routes and the *Leander* design, approved in 1929, was used as a template for the future size of cruisers at the London conference. The British were only partially successful in that whilst it was accepted to limit main armament to 6.1in, the US Navy would not agree to a reduction in maximum displacement.

Following London, the RN originally decided upon a programme of *Leanders* to succeed the suspended programme of heavy cruisers. However, internal opinion resulted in another, slightly smaller design tailored towards the requirements of operations with the battlefleet. This had the additional potential to allow for more hulls within the allocated tonnage cap. Hence the larger *Leander* would be built to police the trade routes, while the 5250-ton *Arethusa* class would satisfy fleet requirements and allow the total of fifty ships to be reached.

The Admiralty's reply to the Naval Board in March 1932, accompanied by the requested technical data, acquainted the RAN with these developments and laid open the option of either type of new cruiser. The *Arethusa* class ships were admirable fleet cruisers, but only met the minimum requirements consistent with seaworthiness and armament for trade route vessels. The larger *Leander* class were considered superior fighting units having eight 6in guns (*vice* six), eight torpedo tubes (*vice* six), and were steadier gun platforms. Another most important consideration from Australia's point of view was the larger ship's superior endurance. The first batch of four *Leander* class ships were under construction for the RN, but the lead *Arethusa* would not be ordered until September 1932.

The Board's views on the long term needs of the cruiser squadron were laid out in a memorandum by CNS, Admiral Sir George Hyde RAN, to the Minister for Defence, Senator Sir George Pearce, in March 1933. After outlining the desperate Empire cruiser situation and Australia's strategic concerns in the Pacific, Hyde went on to make his case based on the classes of ship currently under construction for the RN. He stated that, having built her full quota of 8in cruisers, Britain was replacing its outdated ships with 6in-gunned light cruisers, and that it had been found necessary to build two different types of light cruiser because the total tonnage of the class of ships had been capped.

The attributes of *Australia* and *Canberra*, with eight 8in guns, high speed and superb endurance, made them ideal for the commerce protection role in Australia's vast Pacific and Indian Ocean areas of interest. They had been built for the RAN to counter similar Japanese construction; Australia believed that the Japanese would employ their long-range cruisers against the trade routes, and that there was no point in building smaller vessels unable to defeat them in action. In 1933 the Imperial Japanese Navy (IJN) possessed twelve heavy cruisers with four 8500-ton light cruisers under construction or on order. This made it imperative that Australia replace *Brisbane*, and later *Adelaide*, with the most powerful 6in gun ships available, hence the recommendation for *Leander* class ships.

An improvement in government finances saw the replacement of *Brisbane*, now virtually a guaranteed death trap in action against a modern adversary, re-examined in early 1934. A defence paper outlining a minimum build time of two and a half years advocated an early decision by the government in the light of *Brisbane's* looming compulsory retirement date. The Admiralty was also anxious for an Australian decision as it formulated its own 1934 naval estimates. The RN remained constrained by the fifty ship limit until the end of 1936, but was being compelled to add a new and larger class of 6in cruiser to its own building programme to match the latest foreign

TABLE 1: *LEANDER* CLASS BUILDING DATA

	Ordered	Builder	Laid Down	Launched	Completed
Leander	18.02.30	Devonport Dockyard	08.09.30	24.09.31	23.03.33
Achilles	16.02.31	Cammell Laird, Birkenhead	11.06.31	01.09.32	10.10.33
Neptune	02.03.31	Portsmouth Dockyard	24.09.31	31.01.33	22.02.34
Orion	24.03.31	Devonport Dockyard	26.09.31	24.11.32	18.01.34
Ajax	01.10.32	Vickers-Armstrongs, Barrow	07.02.33	01.03.34	15.04.35
Amphion	01.12.32	Portsmouth Dockyard	26.06.33	27.07.34	06.07.36
Phaeton	10.02.33	Swan Hunter, Wallsend	08.07.33	22.09.34	24.09.35
Apollo	01.03.33	Devonport Dockyard	15.08.33	09.10.34	13.01.36

HMS Leander *in Melbourne January/February 1938 while serving with the New Zealand Division of the Royal Navy. She has been refitted with twin Mk XIX 4in gun mountings on the forecastle deck adjacent to the single funnel.* (Allan C. Green Collection, State Library of Victoria)

construction.[5] Remaining within the tonnage cap, set at 339,000 tons for the British Empire, would now deliver only 49 hulls, despite the fact that the Admiralty still considered its requirements to be seventy; moreover, this figure was based upon fighting only a one-ocean war.

The Local Construction Dilemma

The question of building cruisers in an Australian shipyard had been vigorously debated prior to the decision to order *Australia* and *Canberra* from John Brown's Clydebank yard in Scotland. The overriding concerns were those of cost and value for money. The Australian shipbuilding industry was inherently unstable and inefficient due to the unpredictable nature of government orders. This told against making the effort to be self-sufficient in this area of industry. Therefore, there was great reluctance to place orders for sophisticated modern cruisers in a local shipyard due to the potential for significant time and cost overruns.

Aside from this, Australian industry was only capable of 'assembling' a ship like *Leander* as opposed to building it from the keel up. Equipment for such a ship, including all armament and fire control systems, would have to come from the UK and the requisite plant to roll high tensile steel plates did not exist in the country.[6] No firm could be expected to pay for its installation for work that would last a few weeks, and the skills and capacity acquired through such expense would soon be dissipated and require rebuilding when a future armoured ship was laid down.

The £2,352,000 estimate to build a *Leander* class light cruiser in the UK was set against a minimum £A2,950,000 to build the same ship at Cockatoo Island Dockyard in Sydney, the only capable naval shipbuilding yard in the country.[7] Of this total, £A1,250,000 would have to be spent in the UK in order to import the steel and equipment unable to be manufactured locally, leaving £A1,700,000 to be spent at home. The time taken to build a ship in a British yard would be two and a half years, but was likely to be three and a half to four years if built in Australia. The RAN would be looking at an in-service date in the vicinity of at least 1937-38 even if the ship were ordered immediately, well past the cut-off date for *Brisbane* to go to the breakers.

The argument against a local build seemed overwhelming; especially when the suggestion was made that the £A700,000 saved by buying from the UK be used to pay for two new sloops the Navy needed. This would satisfy the vocal local shipbuilding advocates both within and outside Parliament. If these two much less sophisticated warships were built at Cockatoo Island, it would keep the dockyard and its work force fully occupied. Exactly the same thing had been done ten years previously during the last cruiser acquisition. On that occasion the government had, without even consulting the Navy, decided to build the seaplane carrier *Albatross* at Cockatoo with the savings made by ordering the two heavy cruisers in the UK. At least this time the RAN would get extra ships it actually wanted.

TABLE 5: COSTINGS

Comparison of Cost and Construction Times for UK and Australian Build Options: 1933

	Cost – UK	Cost – Australia	Time – UK	Time – Australia
Leander class cruiser	£2,352,000	£2,950,000	2.5 years	3.5 – 4 years
Arethusa class cruiser	£1,811,500	£2,274,000	2 years	3.5–4 years
Grimsby class sloop	£215,000	£275,000	1 year	1.5 years

Note: All figures are in Australian Pounds (= Sterling plus approximately 25%).

Choosing a Suitable Design

With the prospect of now going ahead with an acquisition, information was officially sought from the Admiralty through the Prime Minister's Department as to the most suitable type of cruiser that could be transferred to the Australian squadron in order to facilitate the debate in Cabinet. Interestingly, the Naval Board's advice to government now advocated the transfer of either HM Ships *York* or *Exeter*, both 8250-ton cruisers armed each with six 8in guns and already in commission, with a view to possessing a homogenous force of three heavy cruisers.

However, the Admiralty firmly rejected the idea. As pointed out to the Australian High Commissioner in London, Stanley Bruce, by the First Sea Lord Admiral Alfred Chatfield in February 1934, the Empire had only 15 heavy cruisers which were distributed around the world in support of their more numerous 6in gunned counterparts. This included five in the Pacific on the Hong Kong-based China Station. If three such ships were operated by the RAN there would be a disproportionate allocation to the Australia Station. The advice was to acquire a new-construction light cruiser, either a *Leander* or the new, larger 'M' type.

The Japanese had announced the 8500-ton *Mogami* class armed with fifteen 6.1in guns which prompted the Americans to reply with the 10,000-ton *Brooklyn* armed with fifteen 6in guns. Both seriously outgunned *Leander* and the resulting 'M', later known as the *Southampton*, or 'Town' class, was larger and more powerful than the predecessors upon which they were based.[8] They mounted twelve 6in guns arranged in four triple turrets along with much improved armour protection; improvements that could be afforded with their displacement of 9100 tons. As much as Australia, which had originally requested a ship with 8in guns in order to match the latest IJN construction, appreciated this latest British design, the problem remained that the Navy now required a cruiser immediately.

The first two ships of the *Southampton* class, which eventually ran to ten units, were ordered only on 1st May 1934, two and a half months after Bruce's discussion with Chatfield. This pair of ships was not due for completion until 1st April 1937, and following that an appreciable amount of time would be required in UK waters until the new type was thoroughly evaluated. Admiralty advice to the Australian government, in light of the pressing need to replace *Brisbane* before the end of 1936, was therefore to request the transfer of a ship belonging to the most powerful class of light cruiser then entering British service, the *Leander*.

The first batch of four *Leander* class ships, *Leander*,

Sketch of Rig plans provided by the Admiralty to the Naval Board in March 1932 of the Leander *class then building for the RN. The large single funnel is the prominent identification feature of the original class. The profile view shows a Fairey Seafox floatplane on the catapult along with a second aircraft stowed, whereas the plan view shows a Seafox in the latter position but the larger Fairey IIIF floatplane atop the catapult.*

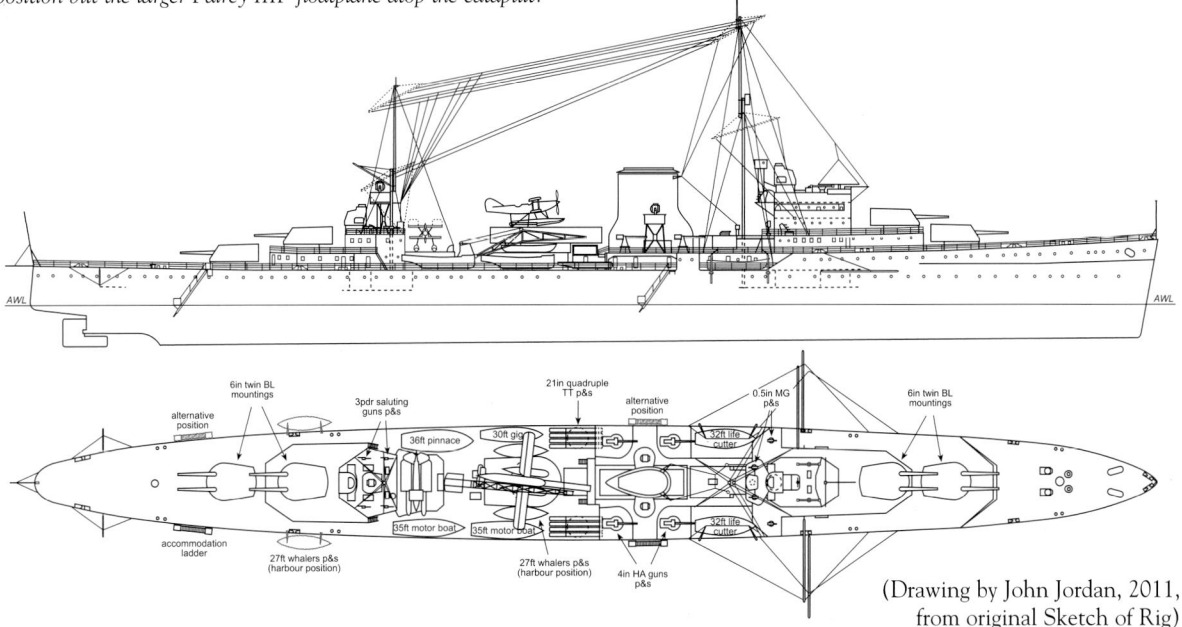

(Drawing by John Jordan, 2011, from original Sketch of Rig)

WARSHIP 2013

Sydney *on the slipway at Wallsend-on-Tyne prior to launching, 22 September 1934.* (H.J. Watson Collection)

Sydney *being launched into the River Tyne 22 September 1934. The 'E' Class destroyer HMS* Express *is fitting out in the background.* (Argus Newspaper Collection, State Library of Victoria)

Achilles, *Neptune* and *Orion*, were in commission by the end of February 1934 with a second batch of four on the stocks. Of this second group the first ship, *Ajax*, was being completed to the original design while the final three, *Amphion*, *Phaeton* and *Apollo*, were being built to a modified design and would be known as Modified *Leanders*. The Admiralty was prepared to transfer one of this second group of ships to the RAN. All four were due to complete in 1935: *Ajax* in April, *Amphion* in July, *Phaeton* in August and *Apollo* in November. The willingness of the British Government to agree to this arrangement was confirmed through the High Commissioner soon after.

A New *Sydney*

Based upon the information obtained from London, CNS advised the Minister for Defence that, due to the impossibility of transferring another 8in cruiser to the RAN for strategic reasons, the government should aim to take over a *Leander* class cruiser. The Admiralty suggested that either *Phaeton* or *Apollo*, due to be launched in August that year and completed in August and November of 1935 respectively, should be allocated to the Commonwealth. They wished to know which ship was preferred and whether her name was to be changed before the launch ceremony. The Naval Board met on 28 March and recommended to the Minister that *Phaeton* be allocated to the RAN and that she be renamed HMAS *Sydney (II)*.[9] Cabinet, meeting on 20 April, voted to replace *Brisbane* with the 7250-ton *Phaeton* as part of a three-year defence plan and rename her *Sydney* '...in order to perpetuate the distinguished war service of the first ship of this name.' And then came the bombshell:

> In view of the difference in tonnage and cost of replacement, and the necessity for considering provision for the programmes of the other Services as well as the remainder of the Naval items, the new cruiser will also be the substitute for H.M.A.S. "Adelaide" which becomes over age in 1938.[10]

It is not clear from the surviving correspondence as to whether the Naval Board was aware of this simplistic and short-sighted proposal prior to its adoption. So, despite the fact that the country was beginning to rearm, the long-term outlook for the RAN was a reduction in the cruiser squadron from four ships to three, not to mention the same decrease in Australia's quota of Empire warships.

The 1934 Defence Equipment Bill allocated a total of £A4,160,000 towards recovering from the drastic cuts to defence during 1930-32. £A2,800,000 of this outlay was to go towards naval construction, namely the purchase of the cruiser as well as laying down the suggested *Grimsby* class escort sloop, to become HMAS *Swan*, at Cockatoo Island.[11] In addition to the funds required to buy new ships, the Navy also needed to find the sailors to man them. Recruiting had virtually ceased during 1930-31, with permanent numbers sinking to 366 officers and 2776 ratings when recruiting was resumed in 1932. Six hundred men would need to be recruited and trained to man *Sydney*.

The new ship was much more capable than the one she was to replace. The final design for *Phaeton* and her sisters had been approved on 10 November 1932, with the ship being ordered on 10 February 1933 as part of the Admiralty's 1932 estimates. In the same programme were her two sister ships and the *Arethusa* class *Galatea*. The ships of the 1933 estimates, one of which had been announced as *Brisbane's* replacement, originally consisted of one Modified *Leander* and three *Arethusa* class but was revised to two of the larger *Southamptons* and one *Arethusa*. These ships did not complete until late 1936/early 1937.

At the time the Australian government decided to take her over, *Phaeton* was still on the slipway at Swan Hunter and Wigham Richardson's shipyard at Wallsend on the River Tyne in the north of England. Once completed, she would turn out to be the lightest of the Modified *Leanders*, coming in at 6830 tons standard displacement, rising to 8815 tons at full load. She was 555 feet long overall, 56.75 feet in the beam and had a draught of 20 feet fully laden. Her main armament consisted of eight of the latest model Mark XXIII 6in guns in four twin enclosed gunhouses: A & B turrets forward of the bridge and X & Y aft. The secondary armament was made up of four single Mark V 4in high-angle guns either side of the after funnel uptake. Close range anti-aircraft weaponry consisted of twelve 0.5in Vickers machine guns in three quadruple mountings; one either side abaft the bridge on the forward superstructure deck and another on a dedicated platform on the after superstructure abaft the searchlight platform. She was also fitted with two sets of quadruple 21in torpedo tubes on the upper deck below the 4in guns as well as four single 3pdr

Two gunners man HMAS Perth's *port Vickers 0.5in Mk II machine gun mounting on the forward superstructure deck abaft the bridge during 1940-1941. (Argus Newspaper Collection, State Library of Victoria)*

TABLE 2: ARMAMENT COMPARISON (AS DESIGNED)

Leander	8 x 6in/50 calibre BL Mk XXIII guns	4 x Mk XXI twin turrets
	4 x 4in QF Mk V guns	4 x single Mk IV HA mountings
	8 x 21in torpedo tubes	2 x QR Mk VII quad mountings
	1 x Director Control Tower, 1 x HACS Mk II	
Arethusa	6 x 6in/50 calibre BL Mk XXIII guns	3 x Mk XXI twin turrets
	4 x 4in QF Mk V guns	4 x single Mk IV HA mountings
	6 x 21in torpedo tubes	2 x TR Mk VII triple mountings
	1 x Director Control Tower, 1 x HACS Mk III	
Southampton	12 x 6in/50 calibre BL Mk XXIII guns	4 x Mk XXII triple turrets
	4 x 4in QF Mk V guns	4 x single Mk IV HA mountings
	6 x 21in torpedo tubes	2 x TR Mk VII triple mountings
	1 x Director Control Tower, 2 x HACS Mk III	

Hotchkiss saluting guns on the after superstructure deck.

With the building of the first four *Leanders* underway, the early 1932 decision to adopt unit a unit system of machinery layout in the *Arethusas* was applied to *Phaeton* and her two sisters. This redesign required the development of new upgraded boilers to deliver the same 72,000shp with four units as opposed to six in the previous ships. Alternating boiler and engine rooms created two self-contained machinery units powering separate pairs of shafts. This greatly reduced the chance of a complete loss of power due to action damage, particularly a single underwater hit, and led to the ships being built with two funnels instead of the single large trunked uptake of the original *Leander* design. The revised layout led to a symmetry that made these ships the most handsome cruisers ever built by the Royal Navy. Four Admiralty three-drum boilers provided steam for Parsons geared turbines driving four shafts for a maximum designed speed of 32.5 knots. The ship had an endurance of 7000nm at 14 knots or 10,700 miles at 12 knots.

Sydney was launched by Mrs Ethel Bruce, wife of the High Commissioner, on 22 September 1934 and

HMAS Sydney *alongside at Portsmouth prior to departure for Australia, September/October 1935. She would not arrive in Australia until August 1936 after initially being diverted to operate with the Mediterranean Fleet's Second Cruiser Squadron during the Abyssinian Crisis.* (Argus Newspaper Collection, State Library of Victoria)

commenced fitting out.[12] It was decided to bring *Brisbane* out of reserve, for the first time since 1929, for a one-way commission to transport *Sydney's* crew to England. She would be disposed of as soon as her crew transferred to the new ship, but would provide valuable training on passage as well as fetch a higher scrap metal price than was likely in Australia. As *Sydney* progressed towards completion on the Tyne, *Brisbane* was recommissioned and sailed for England on 2 May 1935, arriving at Portsmouth on 12 July. The 24 September saw the old cruiser pay off for the last time and her replacement commission into the RAN.

A detailed estimate of *Sydney's* overall cost made by the Admiralty in August 1934 totalled £1,675,000, or approximately £A2,093,750. For this Australia received the ship complete with a first outfit of guns, torpedoes, ammunition, sea stores, medical stores and equipment, mess gear, reserve guns, a gun mounting, reserve ammunition and torpedoes. Negotiations between the British Treasury and the Australian Government saw an agreement to pay for the ship in five instalments. Adjustments were apparently made over the life of the repayment schedule, with Australia contributing £30,000 towards design and building supervision costs as well as a £50,000 deduction following a decision not to proceed with delivery of the reserve gun mountings. The final payment was made in March 1939; an August 1938 estimate put the total expenditure at £A2,100,400.[13]

Following the handover of *Sydney*, the 19 year old *Brisbane* was disposed of through the Admiralty on behalf of the Commonwealth. Despite work being suspended during the Abyssinian crisis, it was resumed in January 1936; guns and ammunition were returned to Australia for coastal defence works along with other equipment and stores, while the stripped hull, lying at Portsmouth, was sold in June to Thomas Ward and Co. for £19,125 for breaking up. As it turned out, the five old RN cruisers that also came up for disposal in 1936, two 4290-ton *Ceres* class and three 4180-ton *Caledon* class ships, were retained when Britain decided to cite the deteriorating European political situation to invoke the 'Escalator' clause of the 1930 treaty late in 1936.[14] Despite being only one year younger than *Brisbane*, they were of more modern design, and were eventually employed on the trade routes as sufficient counters to enemy armed merchant cruisers.

A Deteriorating International Situation

As the three-year defence programme that procured *Sydney* came to an end, the political outlook for the British Empire around the world continued to deteriorate,

HMAS Sydney *with HMAS* Brisbane *alongside at Portsmouth, September/October 1935. This photo shows 'A' and 'B' Mk XXI turrets.* (Argus Newspaper Collection, State Library of Victoria)

HMAS Adelaide *served between 1922 and 1928 before being placed in reserve for a decade. Despite a 1938-1939 modernisation she could no longer be considered a front-line unit. She is shown here in Port Phillip Bay as completed some time between November 1922 and late 1923.* (Allan C. Green Collection, State Library of Victoria)

and funding for defence steadily increased. The 1936 London Naval Treaty, succeeding the 1930 arrangement, saw an end to quantitative restrictions upon light cruisers but instead limited them to 8000 tons. With the tonnage cap abolished Britain could now build as many ships as it wished. Thus the restrictions on Australia's quota of Empire cruisers were no longer relevant.

However, the Japanese had, after reluctantly agreeing to their inferior 5:5:3 quota vis-à-vis the UK and the US in 1930, refused to be restricted again. The 1936 treaty was therefore only ratified by Britain, France and the United States. British rearmament, though still hampered by political and financial concerns, gathered pace as the politicians recognised the possibility of having to face multiple enemies in both Europe and the Pacific. The Admiralty's priority regarding cruisers was to increase their numbers to seventy, and later 100, as fast as possible through an accelerated building programme. The new treaty restrictions forced a shift from the 9100-ton *Southamptons* to the slightly smaller *Fiji* class.

In Australian political circles, international events saw focus turn away from financial considerations towards naval preparedness. An expensive modernisation programme, including much-needed extra armour and anti-aircraft upgrades, had already been approved for the two heavy cruisers. In late 1937 it was also decided to retain *Adelaide*, still in reserve, as a trade protection cruiser following an extensive refit in which she would be converted from coal to oil firing. Because the 15-year-old ship was no longer required to be scrapped in accordance with any treaty, the RAN was inadvertently saved from the earlier decision that *Sydney* was to replace both older ships. The Admiralty, already in the process of rescuing older ships from the breaker's yard to undertake the same role envisaged for *Adelaide*, supported the decision.

However, *Adelaide* was no longer considered a front-line unit, as despite being more than capable of handling an enemy armed merchant raider, she was neither powerful enough to win a gunnery duel with, nor fast enough to run away from a modern cruiser. At best, the squadron tasked with the government's policy of defence against isolated raids, while Singapore shielded the country from direct invasion, consisted of only *Sydney* and the two heavy cruisers, with at least one of the latter being in dockyard hands at any one time until July 1941. The government was prepared to follow Britain's lead and build on the steady progress of the preceding defence programme and CNS, Admiral Sir Ragnar Colvin RN, had been investigating a plan to substantially augment the RAN in time for a war the Admiralty now saw as inevitable and potentially not all that far off.[15]

In late 1937/early 1938, CNS had been unofficially informed by the Admiralty that the two remaining Modified *Leander* class cruisers, HM ships *Apollo* and *Amphion*, could be made available for transfer to the RAN. Pricing figures had even been approved by the

British Treasury. Both ships required a refit prior to being handed over, and the option of scheduled anti-aircraft armament improvements could be completed in the UK as opposed to Australia. As part payment for the two cruisers, CNS had also managed to convince the Admiralty to take *Albatross*, in reserve since 1933 and practically useless to the RAN, off his hands.

At a meeting of the Council of Defence on 24 February 1938, CNS proposed that one cruiser should be purchased immediately. Purchase as opposed to local build was again preferred in order to secure economy and delivery in the shortest possible time frame. Building in Australia would cost roughly £A3,000,000, whereas a second-hand cruiser from the UK would cost around £A1,750,000. A second cruiser should then be purchased under similar conditions over the next two years. *Albatross* would be sold to the Admiralty, as this seemed acceptable to the British.

There was concern at the time that the Japanese, released from treaty restrictions, would build very large cruisers which could be countered only by British battle-cruisers. Australia could not hope to match such ships, and should therefore concentrate upon providing more cruisers for her own squadron within her financial capabilities as opposed to worrying about acquiring heavy ships.[16] If this were done, the RAN might even potentially supply one or even two cruisers to general trade protection duties on overseas stations during hostilities if the threat of raids on the Australian coast were deemed to be negligible. On Admiralty advice, CNS also advocated the building of two more sloops at Cockatoo Island at a cost of £A350,000 per unit. Personnel numbers would need to be increased by a maximum 2500 to cover these and other proposals.

The Naval Board's recommendations could be implemented by the end of 1939 with the exception that the cruiser would be in commission but not fully paid for. The Council agreed to recommend that the government commit the funds required for the expansion and improvement of defences that could be achieved by 30 June 1939. The ensuing report led to the Cabinet authorising the purchase of one new cruiser as part of a general expansion of all three services. A decision on a second cruiser was deferred until the views of CNS could be obtained. At the Council of Defence meeting of 18 March, CNS naturally recommended that, with no possibility of obtaining an 8in cruiser, the RAN should take over *Apollo* and *Amphion*. The first ship would be available that year and the second in 1939. He advocated waiting on the second ship as the RAN could not man her before that point.

Two Sisters for Sydney

Basing their stance upon Admiralty advice, the Naval Board considered that five modern cruisers were required to satisfy the government's trade protection strategy. Australia was unable to compete with Japan in the type of cruiser it was feared the IJN would build, but if she acquired more 6in ships it would strengthen the Australia Station and leave the Admiralty free to build bigger ships to counter potential Japanese construction. Moreover, the *Leanders* were considered more than a match for the majority of IJN cruisers in current service. This theory did not, however, take into account the fact that British ship-yards were already working to full capacity.

At this point the Federal Treasurer, Richard Casey, expressed concern at the delay in obtaining the two ships, reinforcing the theory that when danger looms politicians cannot spend the money fast enough. CNS stated that the Admiralty could possibly make the second ship available but the Navy's manning shortfall would be difficult to overcome. *Apollo* was serving out her first commission in the West Indies, while *Amphion* was a squadron flagship based in Simonstown, South Africa. The Council recommended the acquisition of the two ships and the govern-

HMAS *Albatross* in Port Phillip Bay during her one and only commission as an Australian warship between 1929 and 1933. She was not fitted with a catapult until 1936 (while in reserve), and originally relied upon her three onboard cranes to launch and recover Seagull III amphibians. (Allan C. Green Collection, State Library of Victoria)

Profile and plan of HMAS Perth at the time of her handover to the RAN in June 1939, showing the handsome symmetry of the class. Of note is her post-refit arrangement of twin Mk XIX 4in gun mountings on the after deckhouse arranged port and starboard with a crew shelter between each pair; note also the empty catapult support structure between the funnels. (Paul Webb, 1970)

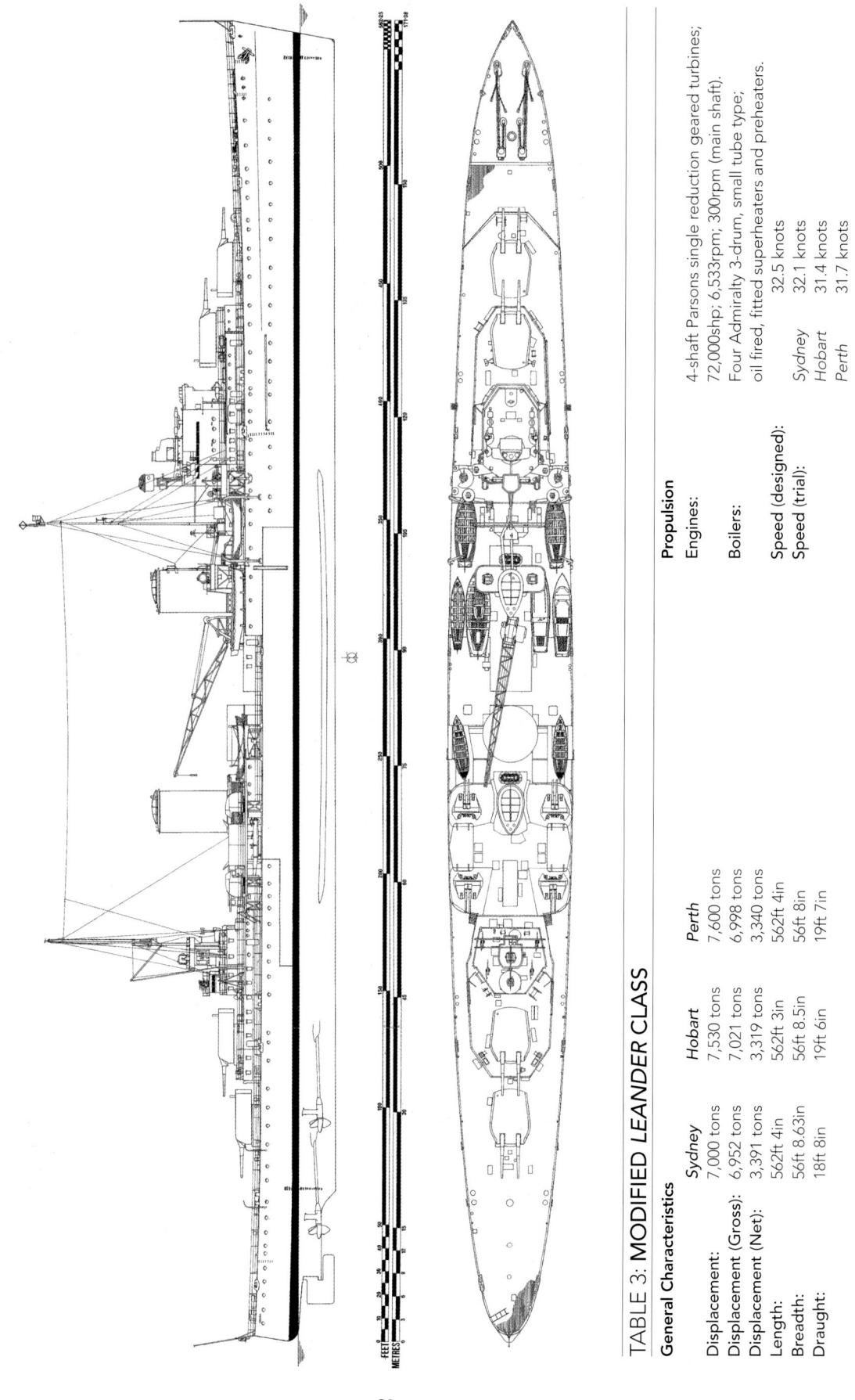

TABLE 3: MODIFIED LEANDER CLASS

General Characteristics

	Sydney	Hobart	Perth
Displacement:	7,000 tons	7,530 tons	7,600 tons
Displacement (Gross):	6,952 tons	7,021 tons	6,998 tons
Displacement (Net):	3,391 tons	3,319 tons	3,340 tons
Length:	562ft 4in	562ft 3in	562ft 4in
Breadth:	56ft 8.63in	56ft 8.5in	56ft 8in
Draught:	18ft 8in	19ft 6in	19ft 7in

Propulsion

Engines:	4-shaft Parsons single reduction geared turbines; 72,000shp; 6,533rpm; 300rpm (main shaft)
Boilers:	Four Admiralty 3-drum, small tube type; oil fired, fitted superheaters and preheaters.
Speed (designed):	32.5 knots
Speed (trial):	Sydney 32.1 knots
	Hobart 31.4 knots
	Perth 31.7 knots

Armament Warrant (1939)

8 × 6in/50 calibre BL Mk XXIII guns	200rpg
4 × 4in QF Mk V guns (Sydney)	250rpg (+ 200 star shell)
8 × QF Mk XVI guns (Hobart, Perth)	250rpg (+ 200 star shell)
4 × 3pdr Hotchkiss Saluting Guns	64rpg (saluting only)
12 × 0.5in Vickers Mk III machine guns	2,500 rounds per barrel
2 × 0.303in Vickers machine guns	
9 × 0.303in Lewis machine guns	
206 × 0.303in No. 1 Mk III SMLE rifles	
70 × Webley revolvers	
20 × swords	
8 × 21in torpedo tubes	8 × 21in Mk IX torpedos
1 × depth charge rail	7 × Mk VII depth charges (5 on rail, 2 stowed)
4 × Mk XXI twin turrets	
4 × single Mk IV HA mountings	
4 × Mk XIX HA mountings	
4 × single Mk 1 mountings	
3 × Mk II quad mountings	
2 × QR Mk VII quad mountings	
rail and hydraulic trap	

Protection

Magazines	Sides	Crowns
Engine & Boiler Rooms	3.5in NC	2in NC
Turret Roofs	3in NC on 1in DI	1.25in DI
	1in NC	

ASDIC
Type 132

Complement

Designed:	632:	46 officers, 586 men
Sydney, 1937:	596:	34 Officers, 560 men
Perth, 1941:	646:	35 officers, 611 men
Hobart, 1941:	648:	36 officers, 612 men
Hobart, 1945:	937:	47 officers, 890 men

REBUILDING THE AUSTRALIAN CRUISER SQUADRON 1930-1939

ment agreed the next day. Once again Australian shipbuilders were looked after with the approval of two further sloops, later to become *Parramatta* and *Warrego*.

The Admiralty was prepared to transfer *Apollo* in September 1938 for the price of £1,366,000 and *Amphion* in July 1939 for £1,360,000, these prices being based upon the building cost of the ships with a 12% per annum depreciation on the diminishing value. They also agreed, albeit with an understandable lack of enthusiasm, to the Australian proposal to transfer *Albatross* to the RN for the sum of £275,000. It was reasoned, at least in Australia, that the RN would be better able to employ the ship; Australian planning envisaged the Royal Australian Air Force providing air reconnaissance of local waters, whereas the British had requirements that could not be filled from shore bases and a seaplane carrier could be an asset. Payment for all three ships would be made in three annual instalments beginning when each ship was handed over.

HMS *Amphion* had been ordered as the lead Modified *Leander* on 1 December 1932 before being laid down in the Royal Dockyard in Portsmouth on 26 June 1933. She commissioned into the RN on 6 July 1935. Her sister ship *Apollo* was ordered from the Royal Dockyard, Devonport on 1 March 1933, laid down five months later on 15 August and completed on 13 January 1936.

Each cruiser now required a refit costing approximately £35,000 prior to handing over, for which the Commonwealth would be liable. The anti-aircraft armament upgrade the ships were programmed for would also cost around £100,000 per vessel. Admiralty approval had been given for a general increase in the anti-aircraft armament for capital ships and cruisers in November 1936, with delivery of the equipment to be made during 1937-38. The *Leander* and Modified *Leander* classes were to have their four 4in Mk V guns on Mk IV single mountings replaced by Mk XVI guns in twin Mark XIX mountings, effectively doubling the firepower of the secondary armament and providing gun shields and shelters for the gun crews.

The Admiralty strongly recommended that this work be done; *Australia* and *Canberra* were already to be refitted with the twin mountings, close range weapons and improved fire control arrangements as part of their modernisations. New mounts for *Sydney* were also funded during the current programme, although the equipment was not expected to arrive in Australia until November 1939, when her re-armament would be carried out in Sydney.[17] The Australian government advised that it was desirable for the two ships to undergo their scheduled refits and rearmaments in the UK prior to sale, along with the fitting of ASDIC (Sonar) and heavy 12,000lb catapults with appropriate cranes to handle the Seagull V amphibians operated by Australia.[18] £A169,257 had been included in the programme for each ship to cover the refit and the anti-aircraft upgrade. As was already customary for RAN cruisers, the government also decided to rename the ships after state capital cities; *Apollo* to become HMAS *Hobart* and *Amphion* HMAS *Perth*.

As for the additions and alterations to be made to the two ships before they were taken over, a new ASDIC set, Type 132, had been developed especially for cruisers (*Sydney* had already been so fitted) but was not immediately available for the two ships. Preliminary work was

The port 4in HA guns of HMAS Sydney in action during 1939-1940. (Argus Newspaper Collection, State Library of Victoria)

TABLE 4: PERFORMANCE BASED ON TRIAL DATA

	SHP	Speed	Endurance	Consumption	Harbour Consumption per 24 hrs (Clean)
Sydney	72,000shp	32.1kts	n/a	n/a	
	58,000shp	31.7kts	1,960nm	600 tons	5.5 tons (Not distilling)
	43,000shp	29.0kts	2,575nm	414 tons	11.5 tons (Distilling)
	24,100shp	26.3kts	3,510nm	277 tons	
	3,900shp	20.2kts	6,370nm	117 tons	
	3,200shp	13.9kts	9,000nm	57 tons	
Hobart	72,000shp	31.4kts	1,830nm	629 tons	7.5 tons (Not distilling)
	58,000shp	31.0kts	2,600nm	454 tons	12 tons (Distilling)
	43,000shp	29.6kts	3,260nm	340 tons	
	24,000shp	23.9kts	4,650nm	210 tons	
	10,000shp	20.0kts	7,180nm	104 tons	
Perth	72,000shp	31.7kts	1,780nm	615 tons	6.5 tons (Not distilling)
	58,000shp	30.6kts	2,450nm	462 tons	16 tons (Distilling)
	43,000shp	28.6kts	3,070nm	345 tons	
	15,000shp	22.7kts	6,060nm	138 tons	

Fuel and Fresh Water

	Sydney	*Hobart*	*Perth*
Oil Fuel	1,767.91 tons	1,771.7 tons	1,768 tons
Fresh Water (Tanks)	129.34 tons	130.4 tons	131.4 tons
Fresh Water (Feed)	45.11 tons	29.08 tons	48.8 tons
Fresh Water (RF)	139.91 tons	163.02 tons	158 tons

HMAS Sydney's EIIIH catapult extended to launch Seagull V A2-18 in 1939. (Argus Newspaper Collection, State Library of Victoria)

carried out on *Apollo* during her refit in order for her to be fitted at a later date. However, the set was not fitted until the ship was modernised at Cockatoo Island following serious action damage between 1943 and 1945. *Amphion* was fitted with the equipment during her pre-handover docking.

There were also no heavy 53ft catapults available, and with an eighteen-month lead time on orders, the Commonwealth was offered the ship's current outfit of two Seafox floatplanes per ship, which had inferior performance to the RAN's Seagull, and a 46ft light catapult. The Naval Board decided to stick with the Seagull V and to order a new model EIVH ('Extending, Heavy') catapult for *Amphion* and heavy cranes for both ships, while transferring the older EIIIH model from *Albatross* to *Apollo* when the former was handed over to the RN.[19] *Apollo*'s existing crane was modified to allow it to work the Seagull V, and although this was found not to be entirely satisfactory the same work was later approved for *Amphion*. The cost of rearming and refitting *Apollo* was

TABLE 5: AMOUNTS PROVIDED IN DEFENCE DEVELOPMENT PROGRAM 1938

HMAS *Hobart*	1938-39	1939-40	1940-41	Total	
Cost of Purchase	£570,874	£570,874	£570,874	£1,712,622	
Modernisation & Refit	£169,257			£169,257	
First Outfit Medical & Victualling Stores	£50,150			£50,150	
Reserve Stores	£9,850	£1,600		£11,450	
Totals	£800, 131	£572,474	£570,874	£1,943,479	
HMAS *Perth*	1938-39	1939-40	1940-41	1941-42	Total
Cost of Purchase		£568,370	£568,370	£568,360	£1,705,100
Modernisation & Refit	£169,257				£169,257
First Outfit Medical & Victualling Stores		£50,150			£50,150
Reserve Stores		£3,600	£8,000		£11,600
Totals	£169,257	£622,120	£576,370	£568,360	£1,936,107

Note: The two cruisers would cost £3,879,586 over 4 years.

HMS Apollo *coming alongside at Devonport carrying the body of former British Prime Minister Ramsay MacDonald on 25 November 1937. MacDonald had died at sea aboard the passenger liner* Reina del Pacifico *on 9 November and* Apollo, *serving in the West Indies, was tasked to repatriate his body from Bermuda.* (Leo van Ginderen Collection)

greatly reduced, as the Admiralty deducted the value of the returned single 4in guns, ammunition, light catapult and aircraft which were all included in the quoted sale price. However the loss of *Albatross*' catapult to the RN resulted in her sale price being lowered to £266,500 following negotiations in January 1939.

With the Admiralty insisting that *Albatross* be delivered to England, the ship was recommissioned from reserve to sail from Sydney on 11 July 1938 with a crew to man the first new cruiser at Devonport, where she arrived on 8 September. *Apollo* recommissioned as HMAS *Hobart* on 28 September 1938, eight days ahead of schedule, as the entire RN mobilised due to the Munich Crisis. She sailed for Australia with an inoperable catapult because the work could not be completed before her required departure date. By the time the ship's refit and modernisation, first outfit of reserve stores along with medical and victualling stores were added to the cost of the ship herself, the sail-away price for *Hobart* amounted to £A1,943,479. The extra costs were paid in 1938, while the capital value of the ship was paid off as three instalments of £A570,874 between 1938 and 1940, adjusted against the proceeds from *Albatross* over the same period.

By 15 May 1939, a crew had been scraped together with some difficulty to man the second cruiser, and they left Australia that day in the Blue Funnel Line ship SS *Autolycus*. *Amphion* recommissioned as HMAS *Perth* at Portsmouth on 29 June 1939, two months before the outbreak of war. Various significant delays with the manufacture of her new catapult resulted in her commissioning and operating without one. A catapult was finally fitted during the ship's August-November 1941 refit in Sydney.[20] *Perth*'s overall price tag ended up at £A1,936,107, paid between 1939 and 1941, although it is likely a final price adjustment was undertaken following the Admiralty decision to cancel delivery of the £21,305 spare 6in twin Mark XXI turret for *Perth* in March 1941.

When war came on 3 September 1939 the Royal Australian Navy had three modern cruisers, *Canberra*, *Sydney* and *Hobart*, ready for deployment in defence of

The former HMAS Albatross, *flying the Union Flag from the jack after transferring to the RN, lies alongside the newly commissioned HMAS* Hobart *at Devonport during September/October 1938. Note that the seaplane carrier has surrendered her EIIIH catapult, formerly mounted on the forecastle, to the cruiser.* (Royal Australian Navy)

HMAS Hobart in her post-refit configuration with twin Mk XIX 4in gun mountings and their crew shelter visible. She is shown at Malta in November 1938 during her delivery voyage to Australia. (Peter Cannon)

HMAS Hobart alongside in Sydney in 1939, with the Scott class destroyer leader Stuart and 'V' class destroyer Vampire outboard. (Sea Power Centre – Australia)

Australian waters and interests. *Australia* was hurriedly completing the final phase of her modernisation at Cockatoo Island and would soon rejoin the squadron, while *Perth*, not yet having made it to her new home from the UK, was already deployed on the RN's Americas and West Indies Station, providing an Australian contribution to the protection of British Empire trade at sea. The total number of Empire cruisers in service was 58, of which only 32 were of modern design: five of the latter were provided by the RAN. Added to this, *Adelaide* was fresh from her modernisation refit and soon at sea on escort and patrol duties.

Conclusion

The Naval Board had succeeded in providing Australia with a cruiser force capable of achieving what the government had asked of it during peacetime. The fortunes of war would ensure that the scenarios envisaged never quite came to pass, but the Navy's strength in the early days of the Second World War was its cruisers, which served in every ocean against all of the King's enemies. Of all the Dominions and British dependencies, only Australia attempted to provide for its own naval requirements as a component of a global Empire strategy.

The arguments used at the time to arrive at the purchase of the three Modified *Leanders* are difficult to challenge even with the benefit of hindsight. If there were doubts then, there appears to be no trace of them now. With the RAN unable to acquire another heavy cruiser in 1934, some may look at the powerful *Southampton* class and wonder what might have been. However, the fact remains that when Australia needed to replace an obsolescent ship lest the British Empire be disadvantaged further than it already was, the *Leander* class was the most modern and powerful light cruiser afloat.

The eight ships of the *Leander* and Modified *Leander* classes served in the British, Australian and New Zealand navies during the war. They emerged from the conflict with a successful reputation in battle, being able to withstand severe punishment and still make it home. Despite *Arethusa* offering a less ideal but cheaper option, so complete was Australia's faith in the Admiralty that no debate appears to have occurred over its advice towards the more expensive ship.

When the political will to acquire two more ships materialised during 1938, the time factor was the prevailing consideration. The option of local construction was again raised, but when two modern ships could be bought for the price of one being built in Australia, and in a fraction of the time, the choice was reasonably clear to the decision makers of the day. There was no discussion of attempting to obtain a more powerful new-construction

HMAS Perth *had her delivery voyage to Australia via the east coast of the United States and the Panama Canal interrupted by the outbreak of war, and was allocated to the Americas and West Indies Station on patrol and escort duties. She is shown arriving in Australia for the first time; the photo was taken at Sydney on 31 March 1940.* (Sea Power Centre – Australia)

HMAS Hobart *with Seagull V A2-7 on her ex-*Albatross *EIIIH catapult in 1939.* (Allan C. Green Collection, State Library of Victoria)

Southampton or *Fiji* class ship. Not only did *Apollo* and *Amphion* provide a significant boost to the combat power of a navy with only 5440 personnel, they were exceptional value for money, with the added advantage of being a type already in service with existing logistical and training support.[21] Throughout both cruiser acquisitions the government's determination to retain a viable and fully employed naval shipbuilding capacity was amply demonstrated by the construction of three escort sloops. It had been proved that these ships could be efficiently constructed in Australia, despite the fact that they too would have been cheaper to build in a British yard.

Furthermore, the RAN would have found it exceedingly difficult, if not impossible to dramatically reinforce the cruiser squadron over this period without the unstinting support of the RN. Indeed anyone familiar with the years of bureaucratic effort required to acquire and bring into service even the most insignificant piece of military equipment in the twenty-first century would be amazed at the simplicity of the acquisition processes for these three ships during the 1930s.

HMA Ships *Sydney*, *Perth* and *Hobart* saw extensive combat during the Second World War; gaining an enviable battle record but losing two of their number during the darkest days of the RAN's history. Following the stunning defeat of the Italian light cruiser *Bartolomeo Colleoni*, and the putting to flight of her sister *Giovanni Della Bande Nere* at the Battle of Cape Spada, *Sydney* was tragically – and controversially – lost with her entire complement of 645 officers and men in action with the German disguised merchant raider *Kormoran* off Western Australia on 19 November 1941.

Perth, along with USS *Houston*, was overwhelmed by the heavy escort of a Japanese invasion convoy during one of the most desperate cruiser actions of the war on the night of 28 February–1st March 1942. She lost 357 of her 681 crew in the narrow waters of the Sunda Strait, between Java and Sumatra, fighting against three Japanese cruisers and nine destroyers; a further 106 men died as prisoners of the Japanese. Alone of the class, *Hobart* survived to be decommissioned on 20 December 1947 and spent the remainder of her life in reserve. Various plans to refit her came to nothing, and she was sold to a Japanese shipyard in Osaka for scrap, arriving to be broken up on 2 April 1962. She had the privilege of being the last surviving cruiser to have served in the RAN. The enduring interest the exploits of the three Modified *Leander* class cruisers and their crews continue to enjoy sees these ships remain an important chapter in Australian Naval History.

Acknowledgments:

A version of this article was published by the Naval Historical Society of Australia's *Journal of Australian Naval History*, Volume 5, No. 2, September 2008. Thanks must go to John Jordan, who provided excellent advice regarding the processes of British cruiser design and policy through his original research into the inter-war period of naval disarmament treaties. Chief Petty Officer Imagery Specialist Damien Pawlenko RAN is also thanked for his photographic assistance.

The only Modified Leander to survive the war, HMAS Hobart is shown as she appeared in 1946 following major repairs and modernisation undertaken at Cockatoo Island in Sydney during 1943-1945. (Allan C. Green Collection, State Library of Victoria)

Sources:

Papers held at the Naval Historical Section, Seapower Centre-Australia, Canberra:
Ship's Files: HMA Ships *Sydney* II, *Perth* I and *Hobart* I.
Ship's Movement Files: HMA Ships *Brisbane* I and *Sydney* II.
H.M.A. Ships, Construction Branch, Navy Office, Melbourne, 1936, 1937 & 1941.

Papers held at the National Archives of Australia, Canberra and Melbourne:
A1608, Item C15/1/10, Council of Defence. Summary of Proceedings, Council of Defence Meeting 24th February 1938.
A1608, Item C51/1/6, RAN Cruisers.
A1608, Item M51/1/6, Defence – Purchase of New Cruisers.
A5954, Item 800/23, Purchase of New Cruisers and Sale of 'Albatross' – Financial arrangements.
A5954, Item 840/12, RAN Building Policy. Replacement of HMAS Brisbane.
A5954, Item 1006/2, Additional Cruisers for Royal Australian Navy.
A5954, Item 1720/37, CID (Committee of Imperial Defence) Secret Document. The retention of over-age cruiser tonnage due to be scrapped under the London Naval Treaty 1930.
A9787, Item 51, Council of Defence meeting 18th March 1938 agenda – no 4 – a programme for the further development of Australian Defence.
A9787, Item 55, Council of Defence meeting 18th March 1938 – Summary of Proceedings and agenda.
A9787, Item 83, Council of Defence meeting 26th August 1938 – agendum no 17/1938 – report on progress of the current defence development program 1937/8 to 1940/41.
MP151/1, 524/204/168, Cruisers for RAN – transfer of ALBATROSS to RN [Royal Navy] and transfer of APOLLO to RAN.
MP981/1, Item 463/201/956, Naval Defence Expansion.
MP981/1, Item 490/201/962, Anti-aircraft armaments – Increase (Cruisers).
MP981/1, Item 603/247/976, LEANDER Class cruisers.
MP1049/5, Item 1829/2/546, Armament list – CB 1773.
MP1049/5, Item 1903/2/157, APOLLO & AMPHION (HOBART & PERTH) – Fitting with A/S.
MP1049/5, Item 2026/3/83, Sale & replacement of HMAS 'Brisbane'.
MP1049/5, Item 2026/3/109, HMAS Adelaide – conversion to repair ship.

Publications:
D.K. Brown, *Nelson to Vanguard* (Chatham Publishing, 2000).
N. Friedman, *British Cruisers: Two World Wars and After* (Seaforth Publishing, 2010).
G.H. Gill, *The Royal Australian Navy 1942-1942* (Collins – Australian War Memorial, 1985).
R. Gillett & C. Graham, *Warships of Australia* (Rigby Ltd., 1977).
R. Hyslop, *Australian Naval Administration 1900-1939* (Hawthorn Press, 1973).
R. Hyslop, *Aye, Aye, Minister: Australian Naval Administration 1939-1959* (Australian Government Publishing Service, 1990).
J. Jeremy, *Cockatoo Island* (University of New South Wales Press, 1998).
R. Jones, *Seagulls, Cruisers and Catapults* (Pelorus Productions, 1989).
J. Jordan, *Warships after Washington: The Development of the Major Fleets 1922-1930* (Seaforth Publishing, 2011).

H.T. Lenton, *British and Empire Warships of the Second World War* (Greenhill Books, 1998).

L.J. Lind & M.A. Payne, *HMAS Hobart* (Naval Historical Society of Australia, 1979).

J. McCarthy, *Australia and Imperial Defence 1918-39* (University of Queensland Press, 1976).

Nicholls, Bob, *War to War: Australia's Navy 1919-1939* (Australian Military History Publications, 2012).

I. Pfennigwerth, *The Australian Cruiser Perth, 1939-1942* (Rosenberg Publishing, 2007).

A. Raven, & J. Roberts, *British Cruisers of World War Two* (Naval Institute Press, 1980).

M.J. Whitley, *Cruisers of World War Two* (Arms & Armour Press, 1996).

Footnotes:

[1] Whilst 25% of RAN personnel were on loan from the RN, this had fallen to 4% by 1931.

[2] By fiscal year 1932, naval expenditure had been reduced to a third of its 1927 level. During 1931 the Navy had also survived a serious Defence committee proposal, actually supported by CNS, to disband the force altogether and return to the old system of paying a subsidy to the RN.

[3] The pre-war *Birmingham* design was chosen by Australia over more recent construction due to its larger size and hence greater endurance and seaworthiness. *Adelaide* was laid down in 1917 and only completed in 1922 due to substantial difficulties procuring equipment from the UK as well as design alterations whilst under construction.

[4] The Australian Government reserved the right to decide upon releasing sea-going forces to Admiralty control in time of war, whilst local defence forces would remain under Australian control. A 1931 Admiralty War Memorandum concerning a naval war in the Far East pragmatically directed that Dominion forces should not be taken into account but regarded as extra assets should they materialise.

[5] The limit for individual ships following the 1930 London Treaty still stood at 10,000 tons.

[6] Over 95% of naval stores were imported from UK sources through the Admiralty.

[7] As a comparison, it had cost £405,000 to build the *Chatham* class HMAS *Melbourne* in the UK prior to the First World War.

[8] The lead ship of the class was originally to be named *Minotaur*, but was changed to *Newcastle* after a decision to name the ships after British cities. *Southampton*, ex-*Polyphemus*, ended up becoming the lead ship.

[9] The first HMAS *Sydney*, a sister ship of *Brisbane*, completed in Scotland in 1913 and was scrapped in Sydney during 1929. She had engaged in the RAN's first action at sea when she destroyed the German commerce raiding cruiser *Emden* off the Cocos Islands.

[10] National Archives of Australia: MP1049/5, Item 2026/3/83, Sale & replacement of HMAS 'Brisbane', Minute from Minister for Defence to the Naval Board, 20 April 1934.

[11] *Swan* would be the second Australian *Grimsby* class sloop; HMAS *Yarra* was then under construction at Cockatoo having been approved under the 1933–34 estimates.

[12] The Australian Prime Minister was not informed that the First Lord of the Admiralty had organised Mrs Bruce to launch *Sydney*. He subsequently requested the Duchess of York, later to become Queen Mary then the Queen Mother, to officiate. The King embarrassingly had to rule that it was then too late to change the arrangements.

[13] The Admiralty paid Swan Hunter £939,755 Sterling for the construction of *Sydney*. This did not include armament and armour, all of which was supplied to the shipyard. Swan Hunter's accounts show an actual cost of £749,769 resulting in a £189,986, or 25.33% profit.

[14] The Escalator Clause of the 1930 London Naval Treaty (Part 3, Article 21) allowed a signatory to depart from the terms of the treaty if it was considered that their national security was threatened by the naval construction of a foreign power that was not a signatory. The British invoked the clause to retain these five ships, due to the deteriorating political situation in Europe, in December 1936. It appears a rather moot point by that stage as the restrictions of the 1930 tonnage cap lapsed on 31 December 1936, thereby allowing for a generous interpretation of a signatory's obligations.

[15] Admiral Colvin had been appointed as CNS following the death of Sir Francis Hyde in July 1937, taking over in November of that year.

[16] A proposal to acquire a battleship, estimated at approximately £A20,000,000, foundered upon a prospective in-service date of 1943 as well as the pressing need for cruisers. Aside from this, the entire RAN expenditure for 1938 was only £A4,696,000.

[17] With the coming of war, *Canberra*, with the work on *Australia* having taken 17 months, was not taken in hand for her modernisation. For the same reason, *Sydney* never received the shielded twin mountings and their crew shelters. Her 4in gunners found themselves exposed to murderous German close range automatic weapon fire during the ship's final battle and were cut down to a man without being able to bring their guns into action.

[18] First flying on 21 June 1933, the Seagull V was designed by Supermarine in the UK to an Australian specification of the mid-1920s to operate from *Albatross* and the *Kent* class cruisers. The RN had opted for float fitted aircraft as opposed to seaplanes but later produced the Seagull as the virtually identical Walrus.

[19] *Sydney* had been fitted with an EIIIH catapult during construction and operated the Seagull V from commissioning. 1935 saw *Australia* fitted with the same type of catapult in the UK; *Canberra* and *Albatross* embarked theirs the following year. It was not possible to fit *Adelaide* to carry Seagulls and she never operated aircraft.

[20] *Perth* operated a seaplane in Australian waters without a catapult during late 1940. Thus equipped, she sailed for a deployment with the Mediterranean Fleet (December 1940-July 1941) but landed the aircraft after arrival. By this time it was preferred that cruisers ship additional anti-aircraft guns in lieu of aircraft in those waters and the catapult support structure was utilised first to fit two single Italian 20mm Breda guns, and later to install a quadruple Mk VII 2-pdr mounting (ex-HMS *Liverpool*) between 5 May and 16 July 1941. *Perth* transported an inoperable EIIIH catapult landed by HMS *Ajax* back to Australia with the long-awaited EIVH then being allocated to the British ship. *Perth* was fitted in Australia with *Hobart*'s ex-*Albatross* EIIIH, landed in June 1941 before that ship's deployment to the Mediterranean. *Ajax*'s original catapult was refurbished in Australia.

[21] There were 430 officers and 5,010 men on the active (seagoing) list in September 1939.

THE FOURTH FLEET INCIDENT AND THE *FUBUKI* CLASS

In the second part of his article on the disasters which struck the Imperial Japanese Navy during the mid-1930s, **Hans Lengerer** looks at the impact of the 'Fourth Fleet Incident'.

The mid-1930s brought severe trials for Japanese warship designers and shipbuilders. In 1934 the torpedo-boat *Tomozuru* capsized, and in the following year two destroyers of the *Fubuki* class lost their bows in a typhoon of hitherto unrecorded force. These incidents shook the Imperial Japanese Navy's confidence in its current design practices and the new construction techniques increasingly employed in the shipyards, which had previously been claimed to give IJN warships an edge over contemporary foreign designs. Both incidents resulted in enquiries which recommended fundamental changes in design and construction practices as they affected new construction, and many recently-completed warships had to be completely rebuilt, resulting in delays in new construction programmes.

The impact of the *Tomozuru* incident was the subject of the author's article published in *Warship 2011*. The present article deals with the Fourth Fleet Incident and its consequences.

The Great Manoeuvre of 1935

The Great Manoeuvre of FY1935 took place in three phases from 20 July to 7 October. In the first two phases the 1st and 2nd Fleets (1F & 2F) operated as the Combined Fleet (CF), but for the final phase of late September a Fourth Fleet (4F) was temporarily organised at Hakodate (Hokkaidô), as the exercise was due to end with a decisive battle between the Blue Fleet (CF = own forces) and the Red Fleet (4F = enemy forces) in the NW Pacific in an area between Japan and the Kurile Islands.

The ships sortied from Hakodate in three groups in the early morning of 25 September. Destroyer Squadrons 3 and 4 led off at 06.00 followed by the attached force, and finally the Main Body some four hours later. The units headed east and entered the Pacific through the Tsugaru Strait, whereupon they proceeded on a general course of 105° with a mean speed of about 10 knots. The destroyer squadrons preceded the Main Body some 100nm to the

THE ORGANISATION OF THE FOURTH FLEET

Main Body	Crudiv 2	CA Ashigara (flag), CL Sendai, AR Taigei
	Crudiv 5	CAs Myôkô, Nachi, Haguro
	Crudiv 7	CLs Mogami, Mikuma
	Crudiv 9	CLs Tenryû, Kitakami, Kiso, Oi
Desron.3		CL Kinu (flag)
	Desdiv 4	DDs Hakaze, Akikaze, Hokaze
	Desdiv 23	DDs Kikuzuki, Mikazuki, Mochizuki, Yûzuki
	Desdiv 30	DDs Mutsuki, Kisaragi, Yayoi, Uzuki
Desron 4		CL Naka (flag)
	Desdiv 7	DDs Akebono, Oboro, Ushio
	Desdiv 8	DDs Amagiri, Yûgiri
	Desdiv 11	DDs Shirayuki, Hatsuyuki
	Desdiv 12	DDs Murakumo, Usugumo, Shirakumo
Subron 3		AS Jingei (flag) with four Subdiv (11 SS)
Carrier Force	Cardiv 1	CVs Ryûjô, Hôshô
	Desdiv 5	DDs Asakaze, Harukaze, Matsukaze, Hatakaze
Attached Force		AV Kamui, CM Itsukushima,
		AOs Tsurumi, Sunosaki

Notes:
1. The three ships of Crudiv 2 played the role of battleships.
2. The torpedo forces comprised eight divisions with a total of 25 destroyers. Among them seven belonged to the '*Kaze*' (wind), eight to '*Tsuki*' (moon) and ten to the *Tokkei* (*Fubuki*) classes. The ships of the '*Kaze*' class were the oldest ones, completed between 1920 and 1924. The '*Tsuki*' class ships were commissioned between 1925 and 1927, those of the *Fubuki* class between 1929 and 1931. The most heavily damaged destroyers *Hatsuyuki* and *Yûgiri* were built at Maizuru Naval Dockyard. and commissioned in 1929 and 1930 respectively.

Source: *Shôwa Zôsen-shi*, Vol. 1, p.650

east. They passed a typical tropical storm advancing in the general direction of Hokkaidô in the afternoon without occurrence. On the night of 25/26th another typhoon approached from the direction of Ogasawara Island with rapidly increasing force. The Central Meteorological Observatory forecast that it would reach the Bosô peninsula in the morning, and warned that it was moving on a northerly course at 70 to 80km/h. Should the 200nm wide front maintain its general direction the Fourth Fleet would be on its outer edge. However, this assumption proved to be wrong, because at 10.00 the typhoon changed its course from NNW to NNE. This change made it almost certain that the Fourth Fleet would meet it about 250nm east of Iwate prefecture.

The Fourth Fleet was ordered to return to port, but the order could not be executed for various reasons[1] and the ships encountered an extraordinarily strong typhoon, with hitherto unrecorded wave heights and also ferocious irregular triangle waves. Most of the ships were damaged between 14.10 and 17.29, and the two *Fubuki* class destroyers *Yûgiri* and *Hatsuyuki* lost their bows as far as the bridge. The bulkheads of the forward boiler rooms held, and both destroyers were towed, stern first, into Ominato naval port on the next day, *Yugiri* by the light cruiser *Oi* and *Hatsuyuki* by the heavy cruiser *Haguro*.

The exercise was continued – albeit without the damaged Fourth Fleet ships – and the decisive battle fought off Sanriku.[2] After that the ships gathered off Shinagawa in Tôkyô Bay and the Great Manoeuvre ended on 7 October after the customary formal review aboard the training battleship *Hiei*, in the presence of Prince Fushimi, the chief of the Naval General Staff.

An investigation committee was established on 10 October and expressed reservations concerning hull strength, particularly that of the *Fubuki* class.[3] On 31 October a committee was set up to clarify the causes and propose remedial measures. After investigating the incident and discussing the problems experienced by each warship type, a report was submitted in April 1936 which included proposals for a number of structural modifications. By that time the structural defects of the 'Special Type' destroyers had already been dealt with, and the treatment of other ships begun.

The causes of this catastrophe, the second which had befallen the IJN within 18 months, were attributed to insufficient hull strength highlighted by a typhoon of unprecedented force, but the investigation was enlarged to cover the entire structure of contemporary IJN warships, and in particular the influence of electric welding upon hull strength. The formula for hull strength calculation which had been adopted world-wide proved to be insufficient when confronted with the unprecedented ratios of wave height to wave length, and had to be revised. In addition, the strength calculation of the inclined hull was introduced into the design process. The range of remedial measures grew larger and larger, and covered not only hull strength problems but also weight increase and the increase in the centre of gravity (CG). The cutting up of the hull of welded ships (eg the submarine depot ship *Taigei*) and the subsequent jointing by riveting were novel procedures. The reinforcement measures embraced many ships, and there were considerable knock-on effects which delayed new construction. In the end, the budget for new construction had to be used in part for repair and reconstruction.

When this incident happened, Rear-Admiral Fujimoto, who had been responsible for the design of the destroyers of the 'Special Type', was already dead.[4] The remedial measures were executed under his successor, the then-Captain Fukuda Keiji, with Dr. Hiraga Yuzuru as chief adviser. Like the stability improvement measures after the *Tomozuru* Incident the structural modifications were generally successful and no ship type, with the exception the 2nd class transports, suffered from insufficient strength in the period 1935-1945. On the other hand, speed and endurance were adversely affected, the application of electric welding was suppressed and delayed, the introduction of new materials and production processes seldom considered, and the progressive style of Fujimoto turned into the very conventional one of Dr. Hiraga. These essentially regressive changes, which affected not only ships already in service but the design and construction of new types, had a negative effect on fighting power.[5]

Outline of the Damage

The principal damage was as follows:

- Destroyer *Asakaze* (Main Body): cracks appeared in the bridge structure at 14.45.
- Destroyer *Harukaze* (Main Body): bridge windows broken and window-frames bent at 16.30.
- Destroyers *Mutsuki* and *Mochizuki*: bridges collapsed under the impact of huge waves at 14.10 and 16.20 respectively (*Mochizuki* recorded triangle waves) There was other damage as shown in the drawing of *Mutsuki*.
- Destroyers *Yûzuki*, *Mikazuki*, *Hokaze*, *Kikuzuki*: bridge windows broken and window-frames bent at 15.30, 16.30, 16.40, and 17.25 respectively.
- Destroyer *Oboro*: bridge windows broken, and cracks in the forecastle caused by water hammer at 15.45 and 15.47 respectively
- Destroyer *Shirayuki*: exceptional damage was a dent in the outer plating of the bottom at Frame 9.
- Destroyers *Yûgiri* and *Hatsuyuki*: bows broke off in front of the bridges at 16.02 and 17.29 respectively.
- Other destroyers of the *Fubuki* class: buckled plates in the forecastle deck fore and aft of the main gun (some ships like *Murakumo*, *Akebono*, *Ushio* also had them abaft the after deckhouse). The buckling in some cases

The capsized and drifting bow section of Hatsuyuki *at 14.45 on the following day, three and a quarter hours after discovery. It was sunk by gunfire at 19.10 to prevent the capture of secret documents.*

WARSHIP 2013

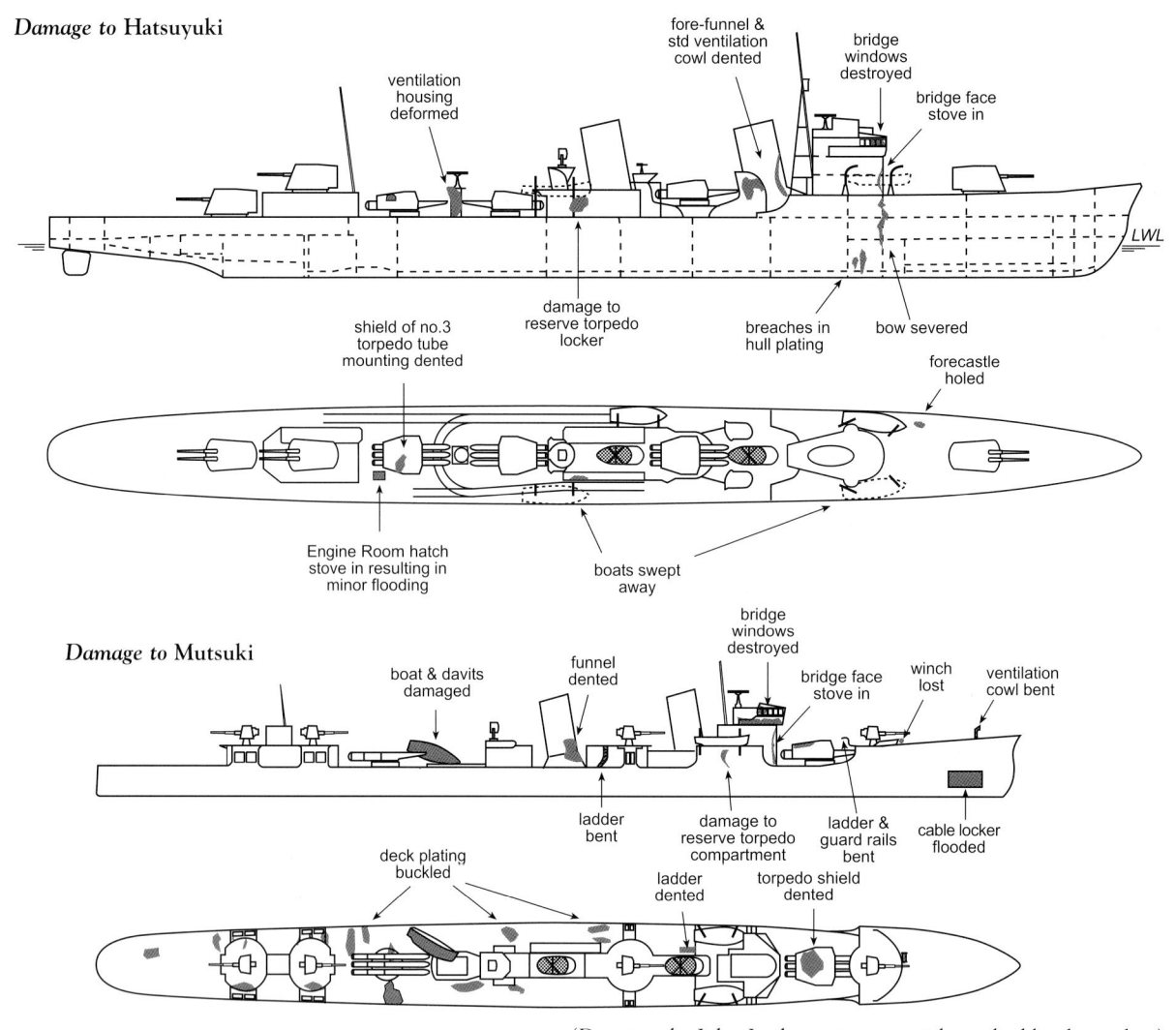

Damage to Hatsuyuki

- ventilation housing deformed
- fore-funnel & std ventilation cowl dented
- bridge windows destroyed
- bridge face stove in
- shield of no.3 torpedo tube mounting dented
- damage to reserve torpedo locker
- breaches in hull plating
- bow severed
- forecastle holed
- Engine Room hatch stove in resulting in minor flooding
- boats swept away

Damage to Mutsuki

- boat & davits damaged
- funnel dented
- bridge windows destroyed
- bridge face stove in
- winch lost
- ventilation cowl bent
- ladder bent
- damage to reserve torpedo compartment
- ladder & guard rails bent
- cable locker flooded
- deck plating buckled
- ladder dented
- torpedo shield dented

(Drawings by John Jordan using material supplied by the author)

extended to the sheer strake and outer shell plating. Some ships developed cracks in the deck plating at the same point (Frames 45/46) where the hulls of *Yûgiri* and *Hatsuyuki* had fractured.
- All destroyers of the *Mutsuki* class: loosened rivets by cracking of the caulking at the angles connecting the upper deck to the sheer strake amidships, some ruptured joints.
- All destroyers of the *Kamikaze* class (3rd Destroyer Division and Main Body): similar to *Mutsuki* class but generally less severe.
- Light carrier *Ryûjô*: damaged anchor deck and bridge (part of the front stove in and part of the compass platform bent outwards). Steering from the bridge had to be suspended temporarily.
- Light carrier *Hôshô*: fore part of the flight deck collapsed with one part resting on the anchor deck. Steering from the bridge became impossible because of lack of forward vision.
- Heavy cruisers of the *Myôkô* class (Main Body): loosened (and sometimes also severed) rivets and cracks in the caulking of the outer hull strakes, particularly the sheer and bilge strakes amidships. Hatchways and doors on the upper deck damaged. Ventilation cowls damaged and slight ingress of water.
- Light cruisers of the *Mogami* class: the outer hull plates were welded to the frames and the buckling already present was greatly increased fore and aft. Numerous hairline cracks appeared in the welded parts. The sound of cracking was heard in the vicinity of the forward main gun turrets, and the vibration of the bow became so extreme that the crew feared the forward section would break away altogether. The roller paths and barbettes of turrets 3 & 4, which were connected to the superstructure deck, were bent. Cracks also appeared in the welded parts in the vicinity of the shaft brackets and outer plating. The after oil tanks also developed cracks, with subsequent leakage of oil and water contamination. Multiple cracks also developed in the welded parts of the superstructures.
- Submarine depot ship *Taigei*: the electric welded shell plating close to the bow was deeply wrinkled, and there were cracks in the upper strakes forward of the bridge and near the waterline amidships. Large waves striking from aft damaged the hatchway to the hold, and a 50° list resulted in flooding of the steering compartment

THE FOURTH FLEET INCIDENT AND THE *FUBUKI* CLASS

Hatsuyuki was towed stern first by the cruiser Haguro to Ominato Naval Repair Facility for investigation and repair. This starboard close-up view of the position of the fracture directly in front of the bridge structure was taken in Ominato military port on 29 or 30 September 1935. Note the dented lower part of the bridge structure (also shown in the damage drawing) and the bent boat davit.

This close-up view of the port side shows the ship's boat resting upon the forecastle deck with the forward davit gone. The torn and buckled plating with its two scuttles is on the left of the picture. The dent in the front side of the funnel (see drawing) is not visible. Hatsuyuki belonged to the first group of the Fubuki class which can be easily distinguished by the large ventilation cowls on both sides of the funnels. Note the large shield of the forward triple torpedo mounting to protect the crew against spray. The voice tubes connecting the bridge with the torpedo tubes and the after deckhouse are clearly visible; they were later removed. Note the prominent curved galley pipe emerging from the lower part of the bridge structure and running along the upper half of the funnel.

Another view from port looking forward.

A port bow view which gives a more impressive view of the damage. The dent in the front of the bridge structure, the davits of the lost ship's boat to starboard (the boat to port appears undamaged, even though the forward davit is lacking), and the torn and deformed plates are more clearly in evidence than in the previous photo.

and caused the temporary breakdown of the rudder engine. The ship was steered manually until the emergency repair was completed.

Almost all ships had damage to external fittings and boats; numerous hatch covers and exposed doors were damaged and sometimes wrecked. Ventilation cowls were crushed and there was some water ingress. However, this damage was of a minor nature compared to the loss of the bows in *Yûgiri* and *Hatsuyuki*.

The Typhoon

When the Central Meteorological Observatory issued the warning at 04.30, the eye of the typhoon was about 150nm east of Inubô-Saki (Chiba prefecture) and the Fourth Fleet about 100nm east of Shimokita peninsula

The C-in-C 4F ordered the destroyer squadrons and the submarine squadron to steer a course that would them take away from the eye of the typhoon, and later the Main Body and other forces adopted a southerly course, intending to take the storm and the waves from about 20° to starboard. The Fourth Fleet adopted a formation almost 200nm wide from east to west. The destroyer squadrons were about 80nm east of the Main Body, which passed through the eye of the typhoon later, while the submarine squadron was about 100nm west of the main force. This meant that the eye of the typhoon was to starboard for the destroyer squadrons, while for the submarine squadron it was to port (see accompanying track chart).

The typhoon developed from what had for the past ten days been a typical tropical storm, and was of unexpected severity. In the centre the atmospheric pressure fell to 957mbar and at about 100nm from the centre there was a rain storm with high wind speeds. On the right of the typhoon, where the destroyer squadrons were steaming, a line of discontinuity was formed with different wind directions on both sides. The wind, with an average speed of 25m/s, and the typhoon, whose speed was about 22m/s, circled, seen from a bird's eye perspective, in an anti-clockwise direction, so that to the left wind speed and typhoon speed were set against each other with a corresponding reduction in speed, while to the right the contrary phenomenon was observed, with an aggregate wind speed of more than 40m/s. Ironically, the destroyer squadrons, which had been positioned in order to avoid the worst of the typhoon, were exposed to average wind speeds of 35m/s and sudden gusts up to 55m/s.

According to observers on the ships of the Main Body, the eye of the typhoon passed through at about 250nm west of Shiriyazaki[6] between 14.00 and 15.00. The minimum atmospheric pressure was measured at 957mbar, the average wind speed was 32.5m/s at the centre and 25m/s 100nm at the forward edge, and within this area huge waves were whipped up. The surface conditions changed very suddenly when the wind speed rose to 25m/s at 12.00 when the typhoon was about 100nm away. At 13.00 the height of the waves was about 10m and their length about 180m; between 13.00 and 14.00 wave heights of 15m and even 18m were recorded.

At about 10.00 the torpedo forces were about 100nm to

The Typhoon and the Course of the Ships

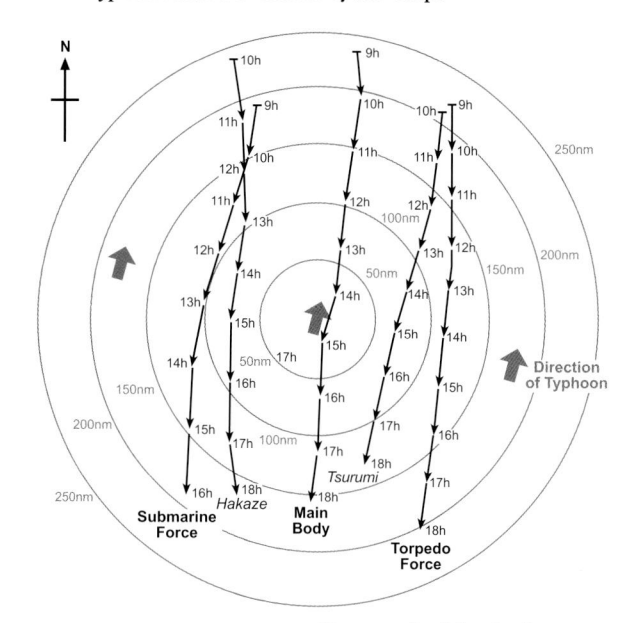

(Drawing by John Jordan using material supplied by the author)

the right of the eye (then still about 200nm off); the wind was from the east with a speed of about 20m/s but increasing in power. At 12.00 the barometer showed 968mbar and dropped further. The navigation officer of the destroyer *Yayoi*, Lieut. Kengo Tominaga, recorded the wind speed at 93.5km/h, the height of the waves as 7m and the colour of the ocean as 'very dark'. Even though 6 knots had been ordered, the destroyers had to make 9 knots to hold their course. Shortly after 14.00 visibility worsened rapidly, and the distance between the ships was increased to about 1,000m. By that time wind speed had increased to 35-40m/s (up to 144km/h) and the height of the waves often exceeded 20m. The destroyers were rolling 50°, occasionally 70°. At about 15.30 the dark clouds disappeared and the bridge personnel of *Yayoi* could see the eye of the typhoon passing at high speed. Lieut. Kengo had the impression that the wind slowed down,[7] but his observation was shared by only a few people. Within 30 minutes 'mountainous high waves' rolled on, followed by very high triangular waves formed by a strong wind which changed its direction frequently within the next 90 minutes: from E to SE, then S and finally SW. After 17.00 the first signs of the storm abating were observed, and at about 20.00 wind speeds between 8m/s and 10m/s from the SW were recorded and the height of the waves was significantly lower. The clouds began to disperse and stars were occasionally visible.

The bridge personnel of *Yugiri* and other ships observed that waves from different directions crashed into each other to form still higher crests. Under such conditions giant triangle waves as high as 20m to 30m rose at distances from 1-3km. The waves which hit *Yugiri* were higher than 15m and their length was from 150m to 200m, a ratio of 1:10 to 1:13. Three triangle waves piled up in front of the destroyer. The first crest hit the forecastle from starboard, the next was a head-on wave which

THE FOURTH FLEET INCIDENT AND THE FUBUKI CLASS

The destroyer Yugiri *as completed. The photo was taken on 30 August 1932 off Yokosuka. Note the mushroom-like ventilation cowls around both funnels which distinguished the ships of the second group from those of the first. Note also the different shape of the gun houses; ships of the second group mounted DP guns instead of the low-angle guns of the first group. Despite the increase in the angle of elevation there was no HA fire control system or specially-developed AA projectiles. The Fubuki class differed completely from earlier types of destroyer and was known as the 'Special Type' (Tokkei) due to their superior capabilities. The long forecastle, the mounting of the main guns in enclosed gunhouses, the roomy and enclosed bridge structure situated at the end of the forecastle, and three triple banks of torpedo tubes on the centre-line were features which laid the foundation for subsequent classes of IJN destroyer.*

buried the bow, and the crest of the third one hit from port and severed the bow in front of the bridge. It was 16.02, only 9 minutes after her bridge windows had been destroyed. In *Yugiri's* log the calamity is described laconically as follows:

Rainy, fog patches, wind speed (S) 35m/s, gusts 42m/s, long waves and triangular waves with a height of more than 15m, maximum rolling 50°, average 40°; position of the disaster 40°20'N/146°52'E'.

The report of the CO of the 11th Destroyer Division (*Hatsuyuki* and *Shirayuki*) has survived, and gives a more detailed account:[8]

Date and Position of the Incident:
Date: 26 Sep 1935; 17.29
Position: Estimated 40°0'N / 147°0'E
Sea Condition:
(A) At the Time of the Accident:
Weather: cloudy; type of clouds: Nimbus stratus; number of clouds: 8; wind direction: S
Wind speed: 28m/s; atmospheric pressure: 741.1 [mmHG]; wave force: 10 [highest]; wave direction: SE to S; visibility: 3,000m
Sea Condition: long waves and triangular waves; roll of the ship: 70° maximum; average port 50°, starboard 40°
(B) Sea Condition Before and After the Accident:
The wind force increased gradually from the morning of the 26th. At 13.00 it was 27m/s and at about 15.30 the maximum was measured at 30m/s. From 14.00 the wind force was measured every 15 mins. At about 17.00 the wind force decreased a little to 28m/s, the weather improved slightly and visibility became a little better. The atmospheric pressure rose and we thought we were coming out of the low pressure area. But the waves became gradually higher, and irregular triangle waves were formed. The waves were unusually high compared to the wind force, and the sea was rougher than we had ever experienced before.
Circumstances Surrounding the Loss of the Ship's Bow:

We left Hakodate at 06.00 on 25 September. *Hatsuyuki* was the lead ship of Destroyer Division 11 of the 4th Squadron. At about 11.00 on the 26th the wind strength and the rain increased. We knew by flag signal that an area of abnormally low atmospheric pressure was approaching, and completed preparations for the storm… At that time wind speed was 27m/s and the atmospheric pressure 746.5mb… At 13.20 visibility worsened… and from 14.05 the wind and waves became stronger: wind speed 28m/s, atmospheric pressure 742.0mb. Green seas rolled over the ship and there was some flooding…[9] At 14.25 the ship steered 140°, with frequent changes of between 5° and 10° in order to keep the ship between 20° and 30° against the strong wind. Speed was 7-8 knots[10]… At about 16.30 the wind was still strong and the waves high. The ship was subject to slamming by the crests of high waves and could only be steered at half speed; when speed fell to 7 knots the ship drifted off course. The rolling was sometimes 60° to 70°… At 16.42 a big wave hit the starboard side and tore away cutter no.1, the anemometer, and the electric depth meter. Part of the forward side of the fore-funnel was pushed in, and the ventilation cowling for Boiler Room 1 (BR1) was also damaged. A crack 6.5m in length appeared in the deck extending from the base of the fore-funnel. At about 17.00 friendly ships were sighted…,[11] and the course was changed to 210° to 230° to avoid collision with the ship to starboard, but at 17.15 the heading was changed to 150°. During this time we continuously encountered long waves with huge crests. We could escape them at first, but afterwards steep triangular waves hit the bow and a particular 'sharp headed' wave caused the bow to separate. The time was 17.29. The CO ordered 'All hands to the after part of the ship; original speed!' immediately, and then 'Flooding alert!' and the ship drifted… The bow section turned over to starboard and exposed the bottom. It drifted slowly, carried by the wind and waves and soon disappeared from view.[12]
Condition after the Accident and Countermeasures:
Reinforcement of the bulkhead of BR1 (completed at 18.45) and preparation for pumping in BR1. Launching of

Yugiri's bow separated at the same point as that of Hatsuyuki. She was also hit by huge triangle waves coming from all directions. The following photos were taken after she entered Ominato military port under tow of the light cruiser Oi, either at the end of September (like those of Hatsuyuki) or in early October.

This bow view shows the extent of the damage to Yugiri, which appears slightly greater than in the case of Hatsuyuki. Note how the plating to port has been completely torn away; the frames are visible, as are the bent boat davits to port.

This close-up of the port side of the bridge structure of Yugiri closely resembles photo no.2 of Hatsuyuki (but taken from the opposite side), and shows a clean fracture line except in the uppermost part. The fracture was between Frames 45 and 46 in both ships. After a new bow was fitted and numerous structural reinforcements carried out, resulting in a significant reduction in speed, Yugiri served until sunk by the gunfire of US destroyers off Cape St. George, New Ireland, on 25 November 1943. Her sister Hatsuyuki had been sunk four months earlier by air attack (a combined attack by US Navy, USMC, and USAAF planes) at Buin, Bougainville, Solomon Islands on 17 Jul 1943.

This almost broadside port view shows that the outer plating of the upper strake of the bow was completely torn away. The purpose of the canvas structure on the forecastle alongside the bridge structure was probably to protect the inspection party and possibly also men conducting repairs rather than concealment of the damage.

nine torpedoes and pumping out of water from motorboats 1 and 2[13] (completed at 18.00). At 18.15 Compartment no.6 was flooded via the ventilation ducts. The ducts were closed and the water pumped out. Between 18.17 and 18.45 heavy oil tanks nos.3&4 were emptied for trim control. At 18.24 flooding to BR1 but pumped out by using bilge ejector and transportable pumps.[14] At 19.05 sea water was reported in boiler no.1 and reserve water tank no.1; pumping went on until 22.00. Between 20.15 and 21.00 162 shells of main gun mounting no.3 were thrown overboard... At 18.00 cloudy; wind direction S (SW);[15] wind speed 24m/s (10m/s); atmospheric pressure 754.0mbar (755.0mb); wave force 9 (6); wave direction S; visibility 1,000m (500m); roll to port 45° (40°), to starboard 50° (40°); bow drifting to N. At 00.30 on the 27th the 5th Cruiser Division stood by, and at 04.25 the light cruiser Naka passed. From 06.30 personnel with equipment from the cruiser Nachi boarded, and reinforcement measures were executed in three areas until 08.00, the party from Nachi working with the ship's own damage control groups. Towing preparations were begun at 06.30 and the cruiser Haguro started towing, initially slowly but with speed rising to about 8 knots in the afternoon, with Hatsuyuki's astern turbines in operation. On the 28th it became foggy in the afternoon, but towing was continued until the ships entered Ominato port.

The Navy Ministry established an Enquiry on 10 October with Admiral Nomura Kichisaburô in the chair and, among others, two future C-in-Cs of the Combined Fleet as members: Vice-Admiral Yamamoto Isoroku and Rear-Admiral Koga Mineichi. It concluded that the cause of the accident was not to be attributed to failings by the ship's company, and expressed doubts about the longitudinal strength of the ships, particularly the *Fubuki* class.[16] The members of the committee agreed that *Yugiri* and *Hatsuyuki* had pitched very strongly in the high waves, generating very high bending stresses. Exceeding the designed strength, the deck plating of the forecastle had buckled and suffered deformation and subsequently cracks before the bow was separated at the weakest point (Frames 45/46) by the impact of several hundred tonnes of seawater hitting at a speed of about 70km/h as a solid mass. Both ships also had deformation to the plating of upper deck aft, which would have developed into cracks as in their sister-ships.

The Temporary Warship Property Investigation Committee

The *Rinji Kantei Seino Kaizen Chosa Iinkai* was appointed on 31 October with Admiral Kobayashi Seizô as chairman and Dr. Hiraga as adviser. Naval architects from the Navy Technical Department (NTD), naval dockyards and even some private shipyards investigated the strength of all ship types for more than five months, discussed the key issues, and proposed measures to eliminate defects and improve properties in close co-operation with tacticians also appointed to the committee. In the end the whole field of warship design, particularly hull structure, was in the dock.

A look into the composition of the Fourth Fleet reveals that the four *Myôkôs* and two *Mogamis* were new cruisers, the latter the most modern ones, while the three *Kuma*, one *Nagara*, and one *Naka* light cruisers were comparatively old ships. The latter had riveted hulls and superstructures, and their damage was marginal compared to the newer group, particularly the *Mogami* class, whose hull and superstructures were mainly welded and which experienced catastrophic damage to the hull structure.[17] Consequently the influence of electric welding upon the strength members of the hull became an important issue. Welding had been adopted primarily for weight saving, so the discussion naturally included deliberations about how to avoid an increase of the cente of gravity, with consequent negative effects on stability.

The principal results of the enquiry may be summarised as follows:

– The causal reason for the loss of the bow was the insufficient longitudinal strength of the *Fubuki* class. This defect could not be attributed solely to the considerable difference between the designed and the completed weights, nor to the weight increases after commissioning which had also affected strength. It extended to the particular method of calculating longitudinal strength. However, if ships which had been operating for perhaps seven years without incident suddenly revealed defective hull strength, it was certain that all ships designed according to the same principle had the same defect. This may also have been true of ships designed before the *Fubuki* class, where there was a similar disproportion between designed and completed weights, or where there had been a weight increase due to extensive reconstruction.
– The ratio between wave height and wave length as standard for the longitudinal strength calculation differed considerably from the world-wide accepted 1:20 ratio (wave height 1/20 of the wave length). Therefore a revised calculation method needed to be adopted and the calculations expanded to the inclined hull. Also, careful thought needed to be given to the allowable stress, and to the most favourable longitudinal stress distribution curve.
– The comparison of the damage between riveted and electric welded ships showed huge differences. Even though the incident was not caused directly by electric welding, the structural strength of the electrically welded ships was lower than that of the riveted ships. The range of application of welding and the techniques used needed to be revised.

The report of the committee was submitted on 5 April 1936. On 11 April Navy Minister Nagano Osami wrote an open letter to all C-in-Cs and heads of other organisations. In it he acknowledged that the disaster had occurred because the quest for superior fighting power had led the IJN to exceed technical limits and to neglect basic design principles. He regretted his embarrassment at having to inform the Emperor of these failings, and urged both the constructors and the tacticians to work together to resolve these issues and to ensure that the Imperial Japanese Navy was a credit to the nation.

After this enquiry, the pressure upon the constructors to meet over-ambitious tactical requirements was considerably relaxed.

The Longitudinal Strength of the Fubuki Class

When the 'Special Type' was first designed under the direction of Captain Fujimoto, great efforts were made to reduce weight without impairing strength. In KZGG Vol. 2, p.401/02, the principal measures are listed as follows:[18]

– Changes were made to the distribution of the longitudinal stress by making the permissible stress fore and aft higher. The dimensions of the longitudinal strength members and the number of frames were reduced compared to amidships in order to obtain a comparatively flat stress curve. [The effect of this departure from traditional methods was not subjected to rigorous calculations, and it became one of the principal causes of the Fourth Fleet Incident.]
– The thickness of the frames and their spacing were reduced in order to permit the use of thinner plates for the deck and sides. In the machinery spaces the frame spacing was increased from 600mm to 800mm and even 900mm to save weight.
– The diameter of the rivets was made smaller to correspond to the reduced plate thicknesses, and weight was thereby saved despite the significant increase in their number.
– The longitudinal strength members were reinforced but the thickness of the outer hull plating was reduced too drastically, particularly amidships.
– The number of stays and posts was reduced.
– The engine and boiler foundations were constructed in continuity with longitudinal strength members to

COMPARISON: WEIGHT DISTRIBUTION OF THE *FUBUKI* AND *MUTSUKI* CLASSES IN THE OFFICIAL TRIAL CONDITION

	Mutsuki	%	*Fubuki*	%	*Akatsuki*	%
Hull	494.6	27.9	585.0	26.5	609.3	27.9
Fittings	70.3	4.0	77.0	3.5	73.1	3.4
Fixed Equipment	25.1	1.4	32.6	1.5	40.1	1.8
Consumables	56.0	3.2	60.6	2.8	61.4	2.8
Guns	151.1	8.5	137.6	6.2	146.1	6.7
Torpedo	(incl. in guns)		129.0	5.8	122.6	5.6
Electric	27.4	1.5	35.6	1.6	43.8	2.0
Navigation	0.8	0.1	(incl. in ?)		2.5	0.1
Machinery	621.3	35.0	793.5	35.9	721.1	33.0
Heavy oil	305.1	17.2	334.2	15.1	317.5	14.5
Lubrication oil	6.9	0.4	?		7.2	0.3
Reserve feed water	11.8	0.7	23.7	1.7	39.9	1.8
Margin (Unknown)	2.5		-		1.2	0.1
Total	1,772.9	100	2,208.8	100	2,185.8	100

Sources: *Weight and Centre of Gravity Data for Miscellaneous Warships*, p. 25-34, KZGG, Vol. 2, p.398

Notes:
1. All weights are in metric tons (tonnes).
2. Note the differences between *Fubuki* and *Akatsuki*, particularly in machinery weight (72t was saved by mounting three instead of four boilers), hull (indicating slightly increased thicknesses of scantlings), guns, torpedoes and reserve feed water.
3. The official *Weight and Centre...* states the full load, normal, and light load conditions as 1,951.5, 1,548.8, and 1,292.6 tonnes for *Mutsuki*; 2,403.1, 1,948.7, and 1,659.5 tonnes for *Fubuki*; and 2,388.5, 1,919.3 and 1,623.0 tonnes for *Akatsuki*.

LONGITUDINAL STRENGTH BEFORE AND AFTER RECONSTRUCTION

Strength	Hogging						Sagging					
	Midship		Bow		Stern		Midship		Bow		Stern	
	TT	BC	TT	BC	TT	BC	TC	BT	TC	BT	TC	BT
Designed	8.35	8.00	7.14	7.20	5.56	6.55	5.33	5.85	5.60	7.45	5.78	6.68
	6.88	7.05	7.61	8.50	3.84	6.65	4.66	7.28	5.33	6.90	7.00	8.10
Actual	9.24	7.67	7.90	6.92	6.15	4.92	5.90	3.93	6.20	6.89	6.40	6.16
	7.61	7.35	8.42	8.87	4.25	6.69	5.15	6.91	5.90	7.35	7.75	8.62
Reinforced	8.21	7.35	6.06	5.74	5.29	3.02	3.77	2.57	5.57	5.42	4.43	4.56
	6.74	7.09	6.63	7.44	3.51	3.53	3.32	3.86	5.42	5.75	5.59	6.39

Sources: *Shôwa Zôsen-Shi* Vol.1, p.654, Fukuda, *op. cit.* p.129

Notes:
1. Stress is given in tons/in^2 (1,016kg/645.2mm^2).
2. TT = Top tension, BC = Bottom compression, TC = Top compression, BT = Bottom compression.
3. Bow is the first ¼ of the length, midship is ½ and stern is the after ¼ of the length.
4. The long forecastle is included in the strength calculation
5. Upper values are for *Mutsuki* class, lower ones are for *Fubuki* class.

contribute to the prevention of hull vibrations.
- The double bottom was adopted for the first time in a destroyer.
- Instead of the standard single plate bilge keel a broad, two-sheet, built-up type like that of the light cruiser *Yubari* was adopted

The total weight of the *Fubuki* class in the official trial condition was about 125% that of the *Mutsuki* class. By comparison the weight of armament increased by 76% (*Mutsuki* 151.1t, *Fubuki* 266.6t). The increase in machinery was roughly proportional at 28% (*Mutsuki* 621t, *Fubuki* 794t), but the proportion of the displacement allocated to the hull actually declined in relative terms, being only 20% greater (*Mutsuki* 495t, *Fubuki* 585t).

However, the difference between the designed weight and the weight at completion already exceeded 11%, and since the construction of these ships lasted for a period of seven years, from 1926 to 1932, various modifications were incorporated to take account of progress in weapon technology (especially fire control, radio and optical equipment, which necessitated an increase in the size of the bridge). In consequence fighting power increased but hull strength declined. Because of the pressure to reduce weight to a minimum, the safety reserve had been kept particularly low (according to Hori, 5% to 8% amidships), and was quickly consumed by the weight additions. The reduction in the strength members meant that they were subject to almost the same stress as those amidships.

According to the observations of the Hydrographic

THE FOURTH FLEET INCIDENT AND THE *FUBUKI* CLASS

Bureau the height of the waves in the northern Pacific was typically between ⅕₅ to ⅕₅ of the length. Waves of 15m height and 350m to 400m length were considered to be the maximum ratio.[19] Yet the wave the navigation officer of the cruiser *Nachi* had observed at 15.00 was more than 14m high and the length was about 120m, corresponding to a ratio of about 1:9. At around the same time the navigation officer of the destroyer *Amagiri* recorded wave heights of 25m with a length of 300m – a ratio of 1:12. Even though there existed uncertainties as to a definite ratio, the standard of 1:20 previously adopted for warship design proved totally insufficient, and the longitudinal strength of the *Fubuki* class (and all other ships) had to be re-calculated on the basis of a 1:10 ratio. Moreover, the stress was not distributed evenly, but depended on factors like hull form, height of freeboard fore and aft, reserve buoyancy, etc. The increase in compression stress was particularly large in ships like the *Fubuki* class which featured a long forecastle with considerable flare, because buoyancy amidships in the sagging condition was reduced while the compression stress at the ends increased. In the case of the *Fubuki* class a hull form adopted primarily to improve seaworthiness was particularly disadvantageous. When calculated on the basis of a 1:10 ratio the stress increased by 69% in the bow, where the dimensions of the strength members had been reduced, and by only 45% amidships.

The investigating committee concluded that the great compression stress acting upon the bow caused the buckling of deck plates which, with the excessive stress load and the constant pounding, developed cracks until the longitudinal strength members could no longer resist the overstress and broke at the point exposed to the greatest stress. It cited as the two key factors in the loss of the destroyers' bows i) the reduction in the thickness of the steel plates in the forecastle area, and ii) the unprecedented height of the waves, for which the height/length ratio was much lower than assumed.

The Measures to Improve Hull Strength

The longitudinal strength of the typical ships within each category were newly calculated with the ratios 1:20 and 1:10 and 30° inclination to each side, applying not only

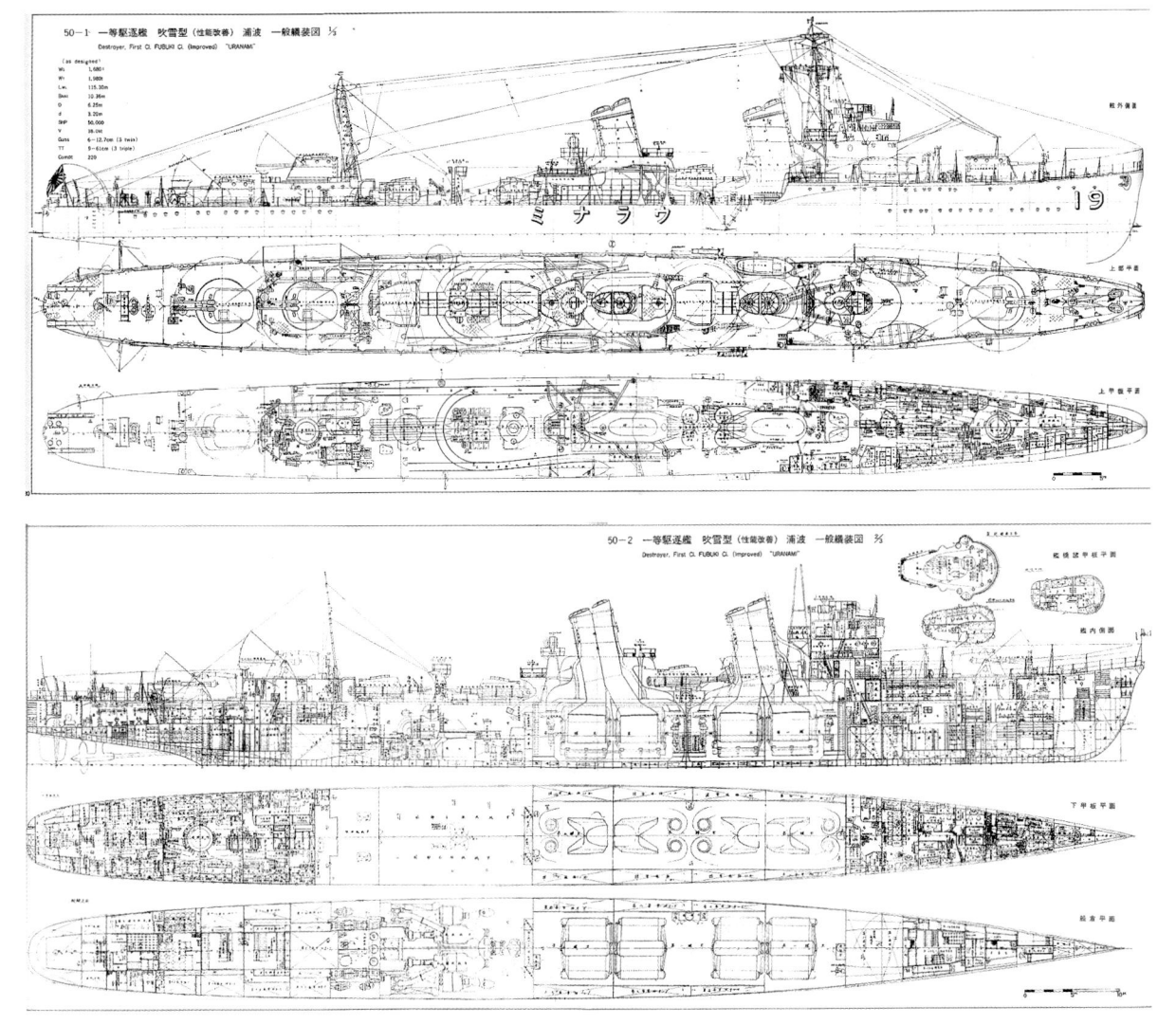

Official plans of the destroyer Uranami, *last ship of the first group of* Tokkei.

the Brian formula previously used but also Saito Shichigorô's revised formula to obtain the stress in every section of the hull (BM curve) and to determine the allowable stress accordingly; this dictated the dimensions of the longitudinal strength members. If unusually large differences between the results were obtained, the allowable stress was checked again and changed if necessary.

These calculations were straightforward in the case of ships at the design and early construction stages, but were more difficult to implement when deciding the reinforcement of the structure of completed ships. The key considerations were (i) to minimise the influence upon other ship characteristics, (ii) to avoid long reconstruction times in view of the international situation,[20] and (iii) to keep the cost of reconstruction as low as possible. The measures differed depending upon the class of ship, but can be generally characterised as precisely defined, effective and comparatively quickly executed. About 90% of the work was finished within one year, but work lasted until the end of 1938 for a few ships which required unusually extensive repairs and reconstruction.[21]

Comparison of Forecastle Deck Plating

Forecastle of *Mutsuki* at Frames 45/46
[Frame spacing 533mm]

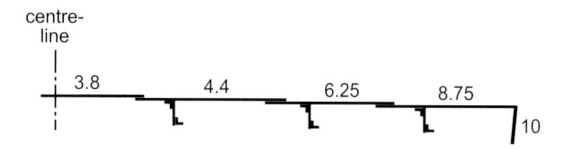

Forecastle of *Hatsuyuki* at Frames 45/46 as built
[Frame spacing 550mm]

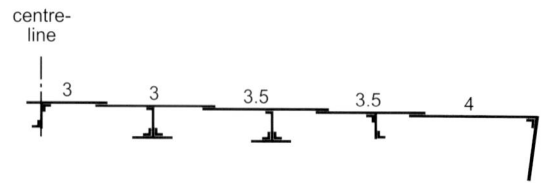

Forecastle of *Hatsuyuki* at Frames 45/46 after reconstruction

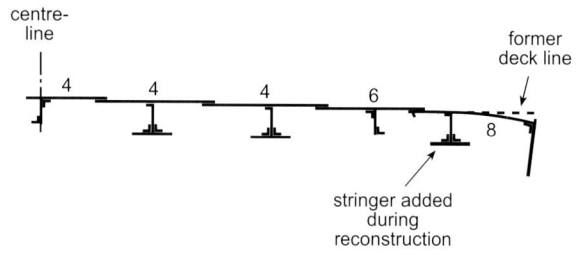

Notes:
1. As completed the outer strake of *Haysuyuki* was less than half that of *Mutsuki*.

2. During reconstruction the outer plate of the forecastle was curved downwards to meet the sheer strake, as in the older Japanese torpedo-boats, in order to avoid a concentration of stress at the deck edge.

Sources: Fukuda Keiji, op. cit., p.129
Matsumoto Kitarô, op. cit., p.203

(Drawn by John Jordan using material supplied by the author)

The strength and stability of Japanese warships was never again an issue. The findings from the study of waves and their influence upon the ship, the shift of the BM value to the forward part of the ship when underway, the new calculation methods for determining the allowable stress distribution curve and the dimensions and arrangement of the strength members, the jointing methods and related construction details were kept secret and used for the design of later ships. In this way design techniques and construction methods progressed. Electric welding of the principal strength members was prohibited and the IJN reverted to using riveting as before. However, electric welding was not only a means of saving weight but it also improved watertightness. After some bitter war experiences the application was gradually expanded, but it proved difficult to regain lost ground due to the lack of research in the four to five years following the incident.

The general principles adopted were as follows:

– The allowable stress distribution curve was defined, with the maximum value amidships and values at the fore and after ends which kept the curve as low as possible.
– The maximum permissible stress load was set at 10 tons per square inch.[22]
– The strength against buckling in the deck plating belonging to the strength members was to be more than doubled in relation to the compression stress calculated by the longitudinal strength calculation using the Brian formula.

Comparison of Buckling Stress at the Strength Deck

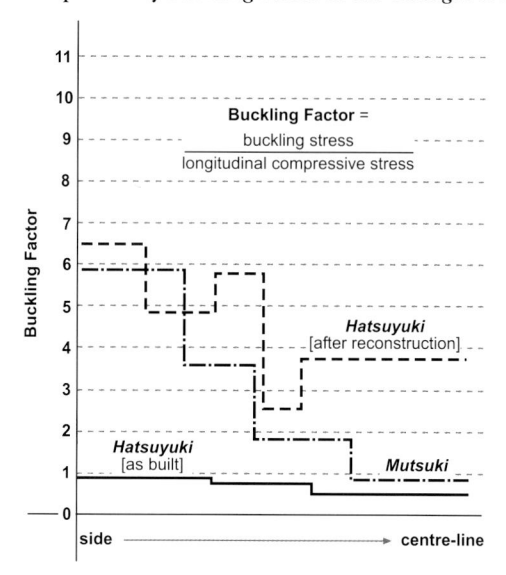

Notes:
1. Buckling stress is calculated with regard to rectangular plate surrounded by girders and beams. The stress on the fixed structure is calculated by applying the Brian formula.

2. Compressive stress assumed a wave height of 1:20 with the ship upright.

3. The graph shows the buckling factor between the plating at the side of the ship and the centre-line plating at Frames 45/46. Note the marked improvement in *Hatsuyuki* following reconstruction

Sources: Fukuda Keiji, op. cit., p.129
Matsumoto Kitarô, op. cit., p.203

(Drawn by John Jordan using material supplied by the author)

- In general double plates were used in the areas necessitating reinforcement. However, the consequent weight increase had to be considered; hence in the *Fubuki* class large areas of the fore and after hull sections had their original plates replaced by thicker ones.
- Double butt strap connections were used in the bilge strake instead of the single one.[23]

For the *Fubuki* class the remedial measures were as follows:

- The ships were docked and the bridge was cut away from the hull and supported on pillars. The deck plating of the bow was replaced by thicker plates (see drawing) and the bridge was then re-secured to the hull.
- The strength of the first bridge deck was reinforced.
- The number of girders in the forecastle was increased (see drawing).
- The deck plating in the vicinity of no.3 main gun was replaced by thicker plates, particularly at the sides.
- The connection between the deck plating and the sheer strake was rounded (similar to the turtleback deck of the early torpedo boats and destroyers – see drawing).
- The sheer and bilge strakes, which were particularly stressed when the ship rolled, were reinforced correspondingly.
- The plates in the waterline strake were replaced by thicker plates amidships.

In the same area (amidships) a second but thicker plate was fixed at the bilge strake and continued to the bow. Even though the same purpose could have been accomplished by using thicker plates, double plates were used to compensate for the weight increase in the upper part. Even this measure was insufficient to compensate for the weight increase, which was about 80 tonnes. Therefore the fourteen ships up to *Amagiri* were given 65 tonnes of ballast, and the later ships were fitted additionally with a ballast keel of 168mm height and filled with lead; in these ships the total weight of ballast increased to up to 110 tonnes. The stability of these ships had been found wanting at the time of the investigation which followed the *Tomozuru* Incident, and the Fourth Fleet Incident occurred before countermeasures were executed; the strength and stability improvement works were therefore carried out in combination. The ballast keel had the additional benefit of contributing to the improvement of the longitudinal strength.

As part of the reconstruction the opportunity was taken to reinforce the watertight doors, shutters, ventilation cowls and storm covers. Ventilators for the living accommodation of special construction were fitted in high posi-

STABILITY

		Fubuki /Akatsuki as completed			Hatsuyuki before/after reinforcement			Yugiri before/after reinforcement	
Load	Trial	Full	Light	Trial	Full	Light	Trial	Full	Light
Displ.	2,097	2,403	1,659	2,317	2,525	1,742	2,321	2,579	1,756
	2,068	2,388	1,623	2,452	2,660	1,875	2,429	2,630	1,863
d	3.31	3.62	2.80	3.56	3.78	2.93	3.55	3.76	2.94
	3.30	3.62	2.76	3.68	3.91	3.07	3.66	3.88	3.06
KG	4.29	4.11	4.54	4.24	4.14	4.53	4.22	4.12	4.51
	4.30	4.09	4.64	4.09	4.00	4.33	4.10	4.01	4.36
GM	0.88	0.81	0.83	0.77	0.76	0.83	0.73	0.74	0.80
	0.79	0.84	0.75	0.80	0.81	0.92	0.8	0.81	0.89
OG	0.96	0.48	1.74	0.68	0.35	1.60	0.67	0.36	1.57
	1.00	0.47	1.89	0.41	0.93	1.26	0.44	0.13	1.30
Range				75.0	80.4	63.6	76.7	81.5	64.3
				84.7	91.5	74.1	83.9	90.0	72.5
GZ				0.36	0.40	0.25	0.38	0.41	0.26
				0.44	0.47	0.38	0.44	0.47	0.35
A/Am				2.05	1.85	2.76	2.03	1.89	2.75
				1.87	1.69	2.48	1.90	1.71	2.48
Ballast				–	–	–	75	75	75
				60	60	60	110	110	110

Source: Fukuda, *op. cit.*, p.80

Notes:
1. Upper/lower data for *Hatsuyuki* and *Yugiri* are for before/after reinforcement. Note the major differences in the displacement conditions of *Fubuki/Akatsuki* as completed and *Hatsuyuki/Yugiri* before reinforcement
2. The mounting of ballast in *Yugiri* before reinforcement indicates stability improvement measures after *Tomozuru* Accident, but none of the sources the author was able to consult provides an explanation. It is generally stated that no stability improvements were made before the Fourth Fleet Incident, which is doubtful if Fukuda's data are correct. On the other hand, Fukuda does not explain the small difference in the displacements of *Hatsuyuki* and *Yugiri* if the latter mounted 75tons ballast

tions, remote control of the spindle type anchor chain compressors (from below the deck) was installed, and manholes were fitted at the uppermost part of the lateral bulkheads at the level of the after lower deck to be used as passageways in very rough weather. Other measures included fixed instructions for the order in which fuel tanks should be emptied in individual ships. The 1931 edition of the Regulations for the Construction and Repair of Warships (*Kansen Zoshu Kisoku*) was completely revised and improved as a consequence of the *Tomozuru* and Fourth Fleet Incidents. This voluminous book, comprising 12 chapters, regulated everything concerning warships, including the official testing of ships before commissioning.[24] New controls were introduced to monitor changes between the preliminary and detailed designs (the detailed design was to be executed according to the principles of the preliminary one,[25] etc.), and differences between the calculated (designed) weights and the actual weight in the shipyards.

A secret document entitled *The Current Progress of IJN Shipbuilding Technology* was issued by Vice-Adm. (naval architect) Tamazawa Akira, then Chief of the Fourth Division of the NTD, to the Chiefs of the Shipbuilding Divisions of the naval dockyards on 10 Jun 1937. Under the headline 'Destroyers' he referred to the new findings about sagging stress, but considered that longitudinal strength was now adequate in the wake of the measures undertaken following the 4th Fleet Incident. There is also a reference to the strength of the bulkheads which saved both destroyers after they lost their bows; this had been confirmed by experiments using a real-sized model of the *Hatsuharu* class.

Addendum: The Murakumo Case[26]

On 12 August 1935 destroyers of the 4th Destroyer Squadron made trial runs in Tateyama Bay (Chiba Prefecture) in an area about 20nm S of Nojimazaki. The trials commenced at 10.30 and the destroyer *Murakumo* ran at about 29kts (6/10 full speed) for one hour. After that, speed was reduced to about 20kts, but from 12.00 the destroyer made 8/10 full speed (about 32kts) for 40 minutes. When speed was again reduced, damage to the bow was discovered. At that time a 15m/sec wind blew from the NE, and the destroyer received it diagonally on the port side of the bow. The height of the waves was low, but they were exceptionally long and there were also occasional triangular waves. Green seas rolled over the forecastle and according to the report of *Murakumo*'s CO, Akiyama Taruo, the bridge was also sometimes awash, although not as noticeably as in a storm. The destroyer pitched heavily and when the bow plunged into the water, three-stepped shocks were recognised and described as 'fearsome' by the chief engineer of the 4th Destroyer Squadron, Nagamatsu. The ships had no uniform formation, but manoeuvred independently so that some destroyers had a following sea while others took the waves head-on.

Cdr. Akiyama judged the waves rolling over the forecastle of his and some other destroyers as too severe, and was inclined to call a halt to the trials, enabling speed to be reduced. He reported that the light cruiser *Naka* yawed less than his destroyer, which had to be taken into consideration because seaworthiness of the destroyers of the *Fubuki* class was normally better than that of the 5,500-ton cruisers. The CO of the torpedo forces, Ariji Jûgorô, was aboard the destroyer, and felt that the situation during constant high speed running was 'serious'. Pitching was generally about 5° and rolling in the range of 20°, but when the ship turned, the angle of heel sometimes increased to 30°.

When the damage was discovered, *Murakumo*'s displacement was 2,250 tonnes, draught about 3.55m, bow trim 0.34m. About 250 tonnes of heavy oil were in the tanks at the sides of the boiler rooms and in four bottom tanks. The fore trim tank contained about 7 tonnes of seawater. Stores and food amounted almost to full load condition.

The Chief of Staff of the Fourth Fleet, to which the squadron belonged, asked the NTD to despatch naval architects to investigate the damage. On the morning of 13 August, Lt.-Cdr. Makino Shigeru was ordered by the senior constructor, Murakami Yoshitsugu, to investigate the damage and to propose remedial measures.[27] Makino, the head of the Detailed Design Section of Yokosuka N.Y. (Shipbuilding Division) Yagasaki Moratsune, and the chief of hull work Yasuda Chiyoji, visited the Fourth Fleet at Tateyama on the morning of the 14th. After hearing the report of the chief engineer and senior staff officer of the 4th Destroyer Squadron, Nagamatsu, aboard the *Naka*, the team were received aboard *Murakumo* by her CO and began their investigation. After that Makino reported on the repairs required to the Chief of Staff of the Fourth Fleet, Niimi Masaichi,[28] aboard the cruiser *Ashigara*, and returned to *Naka* again to report to the CO of the destroyer squadron. Both officers agreed with his proposal that *Murakumo* should go to Yokosuka N.Y. for repair.

During the night Makino, Yasuda, and Yagasaki discussed the necessary remedial measures in Yokosuka's Draughtsmen's Shop, and the former returned to Tôkyô with repairs provisionally scheduled for two weeks hence. On 15 August he ordered staff of the Fourth Division of the NTD to calculate the longitudinal strength based on the planned measures and reported the outline of the investigation to Murakami and the head of the Fourth Division, Yamamoto Mikinosuke. Shortly afterwards, a meeting of the Fourth Division took place at which Makino delivered a lengthy and detailed report on the sea conditions, the condition of the ship, the estimated cause and extent of the damage, and the remedial measures prescribed to reinforce the hull – although at that time the calculations had not yet been completed and no definite measures had been decided. Ezaki and Murakami, Yagasaki from Yokosuka N.Y., CO Akiyama and senior staff member Nagamatsu met in the afternoon and conferred about the countermeasures (Makino did not take part).

The Damage
The forecastle deck plating and some side plates showed considerable deformations caused by buckling which was most marked at the crossing points of beams and girders. The key areas were on the centreline between Frames 42 and 45, outboard of the centreline between Frames 46 and

THE FOURTH FLEET INCIDENT AND THE FUBUKI CLASS

A starboard bow view of Murakumo, *which belonged also to the first group of the* Fubuki *class. On 12 August 1935, one and a half months before the loss of Hatsuyuki's and Yugiri's bows, this ship received significant damage in a heavy sea at Tateyama Bay. The damage was inspected by then Lt.-Cdr. Makino Shigeru, who proposed remedial measures and advised excluding the destroyers of the 'Special Type' from all the scheduled exercises until hull strength had been reinforced. His advice was rejected. The location of Murakumo's damage was identical to the position of the fracture of the bow in her sisters* Hatsuyuki *and* Yugiri.

47, and on the starboard side plating from Frame 41 to Frame 42. The plates in the latter position had wrinkled, indicating severe compression. The plates in this area of the forecastle were bent and deformed but not broken. The starboard no.1 girder was bent between Frames 44 and 45 and the face plate inclined; starboard no.2 girder was also deformed and rivets had sprung lose on several plates. In the CO's cabin on the upper deck some plates were also buckled; however, in the no.2 seamen's mess on the upper deck no bending of the pillars was found. The bulkhead at Frame 46 was bent just below no.2 deck girder in the paymaster's office. In the longitudinal partition of this room some deformations were visible just below the forecastle deck.

The upper deck steel plates to starboard had butt joints of 4mm to 8mm thickness between Frames 45 and 46 and were deformed, rising up about 10mm from the joints; the caulking was also damaged. The steel flanges on the starboard side of the upper deck connecting the deck to the sheer strake were deformed, but the rivets were undamaged. Between the no.2 deck girder and the fitting angles to the plating small gaps had appeared between Frames 45 and 46. Also one line of rivets was missing and those in the vicinity loosened. At Frame 45 gaps of 2-3mm appeared in the fixing of the beam to the upper deck plating above no.1 and no.2 deck girders. One section of riveting at the centreline of the latter girder at Frames 42, 43, and 44 had sprung loose and the girder was deformed by 2-10mm.

The outer plates of the starboard sheer strake of the forecastle had significant wrinkling of about 15mm between Frames 41 and 42. These wrinkles extended to the adjacent section of deck. The outer plating on the port side had no visible damage, but when the destroyer was docked for investigation abnormalities in the outer plates of the bottom to port were discovered, and also damage to the bilge at about Frame 46. The caulking in this area was also damaged. At the seam joints of the outer plates all the caulking was damaged and broken, because of the wrinkling from the forecastle deck to the lower no.4 outer strake.

The Nature of the Structural Problems

The thicknesses of the forecastle deck strakes were 3mm, 3mm, 3.5mm, 3.5mm and 4mm respectively from the centreline outwards, and each 4m width from the centreline had only two deck girders (see drawing). The resistance to buckling stress of the 3mm and 3.5mm thick plates was therefore very low.

The 5,500-ton cruiser experienced no exceptional yawing, but green seas frequently rolled over the forecastles of the *Fubuki* class destroyers. Judging from this situation the wave length was estimated to be in excess of 100m (probably about 120m, which corresponded roughly to the length of the destroyer) so that, applying the standard ratio of 1:20 for trochoidal waves used in the strength calculation, a height of 6m was unremarkable. The weight distribution was a little one-sided with the larger amount concentrated at the forward end. This condition reinforced the shock when the bow of the pitching ship plunged into the waves. In addition, it was supposed that the wave and ship speeds coincided (or nearly so) when the bow plunged into the waves and the triangular waves hit the bottom of the bow three times successively. In this case the force acting on the bow structure resulted in a much larger BM[29] at Frame 46 than expressed in the standard longitudinal strength calculation. However, the compression stress generated around Frame 46 already exceeded the buckling strength obtained by the Brian formula, and the thin deck plates buckled at Frames 45/46. The stress upon the undamaged plate strakes in the vicinity gradually increased, and finally the pressure upon the sheer strake and outer plating, and also on the deck girder, became so large that they collapsed at Frame 46.

This shows that the buckling and wrinkling of the forecastle deck was not limited to the temporary deformation of plates between beams, but resulted in permanent deformation resulting from excessive pressure. Starting from the centreline it stretched to the sides, particularly to starboard, and also embraced the sheer strake and lower outer hull strakes, which were likewise subject to deformation. Because of the significant damage to the deck and the sheer strake to starboard, the investigators supposed that *Murakumo* had been pushed up while heeling to port. Other circumstantial evidence was seen in the concentration of the damage to the port bilge strake at Frame 46.

The destroyers of the *Fubuki* class had occasionally sustained moderate damage, but this had generally been confined to local parts of the superstructure. In one incident part of the caulking in the outer hull bottom plating had been damaged (indicating high stress effects).. However, such damage had been ignored and no investigation and/or remedial measures were undertaken.[30] The damage to *Murakumo* was quite different from these cases. The severe deformation of the forecastle deck plates and the sheer strake indicated a large BM in the sagging condition. Damage of this nature could only occur because the structure of the hull was too weak when subjected to compression stress in the narrow area between Frames 42 and 46 on the forecastle deck, which was the upper strength deck.

Makino states that he recognised it as very serious damage. The first ships of the *Fubuki* class had been completed seven years previously, and during this period they had encountered several storms with more serious wave conditions, but they had never sustained damage of this nature. Now, suddenly and unexpectedly, this had happened to *Murakumo*. Makino imagined that most of the early ships of the *Fubuki* class had approached the same condition very closely, and if steaming under the same conditions as *Murakumo* would sooner or later have sustained similar damage. It was therefore natural that he should, following inspection and calculation, recognise the need for considerable reinforcement of the strength of the forecastle section.

The Structural Reinforcement Proposal
Makino proposed that the thickness of the forecastle strakes be increased from 3mm/3mm/3.5mm/3.5mm/4mm from the centreline to 4mm/4mm/4mm/4mm/4mm/5mm. Additional supporting girders should be fitted between the first and second deck girders and between the latter and the hull sides. The centreline and the second girders should be reinforced, as should the beam at Frame 45. The thickness of the sheer strake should be increased from 4mm to 5mm. (Double plating was out of the question because of the increase of weight.)

Alongside this proposal for the general reinforcement of the hull strength of all destroyers of the *Fubuki* class, urgent reinforcement measures for the damaged *Murakumo* and her companions, the destroyers *Amagiri* and *Akebono*, were proposed as follows:[31]

- All permanently buckled plates should be replaced.
- The replacement of the plating should be planned in accordance with the general reinforcement principle for the 'Special Type' destroyers in order to avoid the necessity to reinforce them again.
- The reinforcement of the plates just below the bridge was not possible in the time available[32] but should be done later. The butt joints of the entire forecastle except the part below the bridge should be reinforced.
- The sheer and bilge strakes should be replaced by thicker plates.

Because general reinforcement of the *Fubuki* class before the Great Manoeuvre of 1935 was not possible, Makino was ordered to work out urgent instructions for the destroyers scheduled to participate, and made the following recommendations (summarised):

> Given the severity of the damage recently sustained by the destroyer *Murakumo*, it is recommended that the Tokkei should not take part in the manoeuvre in their present condition. Their use should either be limited (ie speed restrictions imposed) or forbidden until the reinforcement measures have been executed. The latter is considered to be the most desirable option. Two reinforcement girders should be fitted to support the upper deck on either side of the forecastle as the minimum necessary remedial measure.

The recommendation was agreed by his immediate superiors but not by the head of the General Affairs Division (*Kampon Somobuchô* Rear-Admiral Toyoda Teijiro),[33] so no warnings were issued and the 'Special Type' destroyers participated in the Great Manoeuvre without any work being carried out. In the end, the damaged sections of *Murakumo* were repaired and the number of deck girders increased as recommended. In the case of the other destroyers it was decided to implement the reinforcement after the manoeuvre and further serious investigation.[34]

Footnotes:
1. It was received too late and there was a danger that the destroyers would capsize if they attempted to turn; it was also estimated that the typhoon would pass aft.
2. NE coast of Honshu as far as about Sendai.
3. See the addendum on the *Murakumo*. It should be noted that none of the ships of 4F had shown any sign of instability, thereby confirming the success of the remedial measures taken after the *Tomozuru* Incident.
4. Fujimoto died in Jan 1935, one day after returning to his former post as chief designer.
5. In the postwar US Report S-01-3 *Surface Warship Hull Design* it is stated: 'The use of both a transverse and longitudinal

system of framing appears to be a lavish use of hull weight' (p.21) and 'The use of riveting entirely for the construction of such members [longitudinals] forced the Japanese to a necessarily heavy system of angles to connect the longitudinals to the shell and inner plating and floors' (p.22), and 'The method used…to compensate for large openings cut in hull strength members [was] a conglomeration of doubling, and even tripling, of the plating around the uptake openings in conjunction with riveted coaming bars. It is questionable that so much material so disposed could properly have done the job that was asked of it' (p.23). There are other samples and the investigators often point out the lack of proper calculations for determining thicknesses and too much reference to previous, successful construction.
6. The torpedo forces (Destroyer Squadrons 3 & 4) were still between 80 to 100nm E of the Main Body.
7. The anemometers had already been destroyed.
8. CO Destroyer Div. 11: Secret Report no.10 (11 Ku Kimitsu Dai 10 gô; Dai 11 Kutai Shirei).
9. Watertight integrity measures had been conducted very strictly, and groups for bailing out water been formed. Even though not stated directly in the report, the flooding must have been via the ventilation ducts. The CO ordered an inspection of the watertight bulkheads.
10. Since 12.00 both turbines had been in operation; previously only the port turbine had been on line, and the destroyer had been at half speed (9 knots).
11. Since 13.20 the flagship and the other ships of the division had been separated.
12. The bow was discovered and observed by the light cruiser *Naka*. It was believed that about 20 men had survived (personnel losses were six petty officers and 19 ratings) but there was no way to rescue them. The drifting bow was sunk by gunfire the next morning in order to prevent the loss of the secret code book. It was claimed at the time that there were no survivors, but uncertainty remains.
13. To lower the centre of gravity of the ship.
14. At 00.05 on the 27th flooding of about 10 tonnes via the bilge pump of the refrigerator room and the sea water pump was reported, and after switching off both pumps flooding into BR1 ceased.
15. Data in parentheses show conditions at 00.00 on the 27th, otherwise conditions were the same.
16. The survey brought to light that the forecastle deck of several ships had been slightly buckled in heavy seas, and the '*Murakumo* Case' (see addendum), which dated from immediately before the Fourth Fleet Incident, was cited as evidence of insufficient longitudinal strength.
17. Almost the same can be said with regard to the differences between the old destroyers (*Kamikaze* and *Mutsuki* classes) and the new *Fubuki* class.
18. Supplemented by data from Hori, Makino, Fukuda, Niwada, *Shôwa Zôsen-shi*.
19. Data about waves may be found in Fukuda, *op. cit.*, p. 130-32. The theory of waves and the influence of the ship as known in Japan in 1934 are described popularly in a paper entitled *The Consideration of the Stability at the Design of Warships* read by Dr Hiraga Yuzuru to the Emperor on 31 May 1934 in reference to the *Tomozuru* Incident. It is printed in Naito Hatsuho's *Life of Dr. Hiraga Yuzuru*, p. 399-432.
20. It was 1936, the 'crisis year', and the report of the committee was delivered on 5 April.
21. It is unsurprising that these were the ships with hulls which had been electrically welded
22. After the adoption of the metric system in 1924 – although it took until 1926 before it was fully implemented – strength calculations were still made using the British system and this is reflected in the author's figures.
23. The single butt joints tended to develop cracks in the caulking, and there were small leaks not only in the *Fubuki* class but also other ships. For newly built ships lap joints would be used.
24. Vice-Admiral Niwada Shôzô, *op. cit.* p. 57, states: 'After these incidents, the specifications changed significantly, adding stability figures at the trial, full load, light load and other conditions. Displacements, draughts, KG, MG, maximum GZ, maximum stability angles, OG, weights of everything in every condition were to be written into the instructions and the trial protocols. Everything was to be inspected by the Central Committee.
25. Hori, *op. cit.*, p. 210, mentions differences such as the reduction of safety factors by the shipyards to save weight (without informing the central authorities) and the existence of doubt as to whether the detailed designers followed the principles of the designers in the NTD. On the other hand, it cannot be denied that some of the weight calculations in the preliminary design were unrealistic (as expressed in 11% excess), and the revision of the design and production process and their harmonisation would have been necessary even if these incidents had not occurred.
26. The principal source is Makino Shigeru, *Kansen Notes*, pp.244-255.
27. The Chief of the Second Design Team, the later Vice-Admiral Ezaki Iwakichi, was on an official tour and not present.
28. Later Vice-Admiral. In 1929, when still a Commander, he published a fine article about the IJN in *Brassey's Naval & Shipping Annual*.
29. The distance between the centre of buoyancy (B) and the metacentre (M).
30. This uniform argument is stated by Mori, Makino, Fukui etc. but the author has some doubts as expressed above, provided that Fukuda's data are correct. On the other hand, if these authors are referring to only strength reinforcement measures, the statement may be correct in the strictest sense.
31. Makino cites the Navy Ministry's annual report for FY1935 stating on p.537 that during the trials of the Fourth Squadron in Tateyama Bay 12 Aug 1935, *Murakumo* sustained buckling to part of her forecastle by wave action, and *Amagiri* and *Akebono* sustained damage in the vicinity of the first turret.
32. When Makino worked out this proposal, his superiors in the NTD had already decided that the 'Special Type' destroyers had to participate in the Great Manoeuvre, because their absence would have precluded its taking place – a pure face-saving argument! Therefore, only the urgent reinforcement of the sheer and bilge strakes by flanges was to be implemented before the ships sortied for the manoeuvre.
33. Makino believes that the head of the Fourth Division agreed with Toyoda.
34. According to Rear-Admiral Nijima Ryôji, who was the head of the Shipbuilding (Hull) Division of Yokosuka N.Y. at that time, the number of deck girders was also increased in *Shirakumo* and *Usugumo* which were with *Murakumo* (but did not sustain the same degree of damages), but Makino holds to his view that only *Murakumo* was reinforced.

THE 'SEMI-DREADNOUGHTS' OF THE *DANTON* CLASS

Widely considered obsolescent when they were completed in 1911, the six battleships of the *Danton* class formed the core of the French fleet in the Mediterranean when war broke out in August 1914. **John Jordan** looks at how the French came to build these ships and why their construction was so protracted.

The battleships of the *Danton* class have long been regarded as an anomaly. The construction of the all-big-gun HMS *Dreadnought* in 1906 was a revolutionary step which ushered in a naval arms race between Britain and Germany, with the Americans and the Japanese following close behind. Yet the French, still nominally the second naval power in the world when the *Dantons* were designed in 1905, opted initially not to take this particular fork in the road, and embarked upon a series of 'semi-dreadnoughts' with a powerful medium battery of twelve 240mm (9.4in) guns in twin turrets, supported by four heavier 305mm (12in) guns disposed in the customary fashion fore and aft.

The first of these ships was not laid down until June 1907, six months after *Dreadnought* nominally entered service, and the last of the six, *Vergniaud*, did not enter service until the end of 1911. By this time France had lost her position as second naval power to Germany. Between 1906 and 1911 Britain completed no fewer than 10 'dreadnought' battleships and four battlecruisers. The ambitious young German Navy had countered with eight dreadnought battleships and two battlecruisers. Even the United States had six dreadnought battleships in commission by the end of 1911. During this period only the fledgling Imperial Japanese Navy laid down similar ships to the *Dantons*, the 'semi-dreadnoughts' *Aki* and *Satsuma*, but

Danton *at her moorings in 1911, shortly after her completion.* (Philippe Caresse collection)

the dual battery of these ships (12in/10in) appears to have been due to a shortage of 12in guns rather than a shared belief in the military value of such ships.

When the Great War began in August 1914, the six battleships of the *Danton* class made up the *élite* 1st Battle Squadron of the *Armée navale*. France's first two dreadnoughts, *Courbet* and *Jean Bart*, had only recently joined the fleet and were barely worked up.

A Confused Design Process

The *Dantons* were to be the second instalment of a programme of fleet renewal drawn up in the face of German naval expansion. Their immediate predecessors, the six 15,000-tonne battleships of the *Patrie* class, had constituted a first attempt to build battleships in numbers to a common design after years of single-ship classes, each of which incorporated incremental improvements. Even the six *15,000-tonnes* did not constitute a uniform class, as after two ships had been laid down it was decided to increase the calibre of the medium battery from 16 – 164.7mm (6.5in) to 10 – 194mm (7.6in) in the remaining four ships,[1] in order to counter the heavier protective plating of the latest British battleships of the *King Edward VII* class. Given the comparatively lengthy construction times in the French naval dockyards and the rapid advances in technology which were taking place during this period, the Marine Nationale found it difficult to resist making constant improvements to its ships, even while they were on the stocks. The six *Dantons* would eventually be almost identical, but new plans issued in March 1907, and then again in June 1908 were to result in some 500 modifications to the original design, some of which had major structural implications. The builders were constantly having to dismantle parts of the hulls which had already been assembled, only to rebuild them to the new specifications. Not only was completion significantly delayed, but the overall cost of the programme increased by some 40% over the original estimate of 220m francs.

When the next stage of the programme was first discussed in May 1905, the *Conseil supérieur de la marine* (CSM) proposed the following characteristics for the new battleships:

- displacement: 16,500 tonnes;
- armament: 4 – 305mm; 12 – 194mm (or greater) plus an anti-torpedo boat battery of a calibre superior to 47mm;
- propulsion: three-shaft triple expansion; 18 knots (as *Patrie*);
- protection: as *Patrie*, but with superior underwater protection against torpedoes.

As usual the CSM was being unduly optimistic with regard to displacement – the size (and by extension cost) of battleships was always a major bone of contention when naval estimates were discussed in the French parliament. The director of naval construction of the day, Dudebout, regarded 17,000 tonnes as a minimum figure if the required underwater protection was to be provided.

On 20 June the head of the STCN, *Ingénieur de la génie*

DREADNOUGHT BATTLESHIPS AND BATTLECRUISERS COMPLETED 1906-1911

	Great Britain	Germany
1906	Dreadnought (12)	
1907		
1908	*Indomitable* (06)	
	Inflexible (10)	
1909	Bellerophon (02)	
	Invincible (03)	
	Superb (05)	
	Temeraire (05)	
	St Vincent (05)	
1910	Vanguard (02)	*Blücher* (03))
	Collingwood (04)	Nassau (05
		Westfalen (05)
		Rheinland (09)
		Posen (09)
1911	Neptune (01)	*Von der Tann* (02)
	Indefatigable (04)	Oldenburg (07)
	Colossus (07)	Ostfriesland (09)
	Hercules (08)	Thüringen (09)
		Helgoland (12)
Total	10 Battleships	8 Battleships
	4 Battlecruisers	2 Battlecruisers

Notes:
Month of completion in brackets after name.
Battleships in roman; battlecruisers in italics.
Completion dates from *Conway's All the World's Fighting Ships 1906-1921*.

maritime Lhomme, adressed a note to the DCN in which he offered the following solutions, depending on whether 194mm or 240mm was adopted as the secondary gun calibre:

- 10 – 240mm in four twin, two single turrets, disposed as in the British *Lord Nelson*; displacement 17,000 tonnes including torpedo protection;
- 12 – 240 in six twin turrets; displacement 17,000 tonnes but without torpedo protection;
- 16 – 194mm in six twin turrets + four casemates; displacement 17,000 tonnes including torpedo protection;
- 12 – 194mm in eight single turrets + four casemates; displacement 16,700 tonnes including torpedo protection.

At a subsequent conference between Dudebout, Lhomme, V-Ad. Touchard (Chief of the Naval Staff) and Col. Gossard (Head of the Gunnery Section) on 26 June it was decided that the increased range at which it was anticipated that future naval engagements would take place (5000-7000m) dictated a move to the 240mm gun. Gossard also proposed increasing the weight of the 240mm shell by approximately one third in order to secure penetration of armour of a similar thickness (240mm/9.4in) at ranges of 5900-8000m.

It is worth pausing here to note the naval engagement ranges proposed. The discussions make it clear that the French considered the 5000-7000m bracket to be the decisive range in a naval battle in which the fleets were

Condorcet: *Profile & Plan*

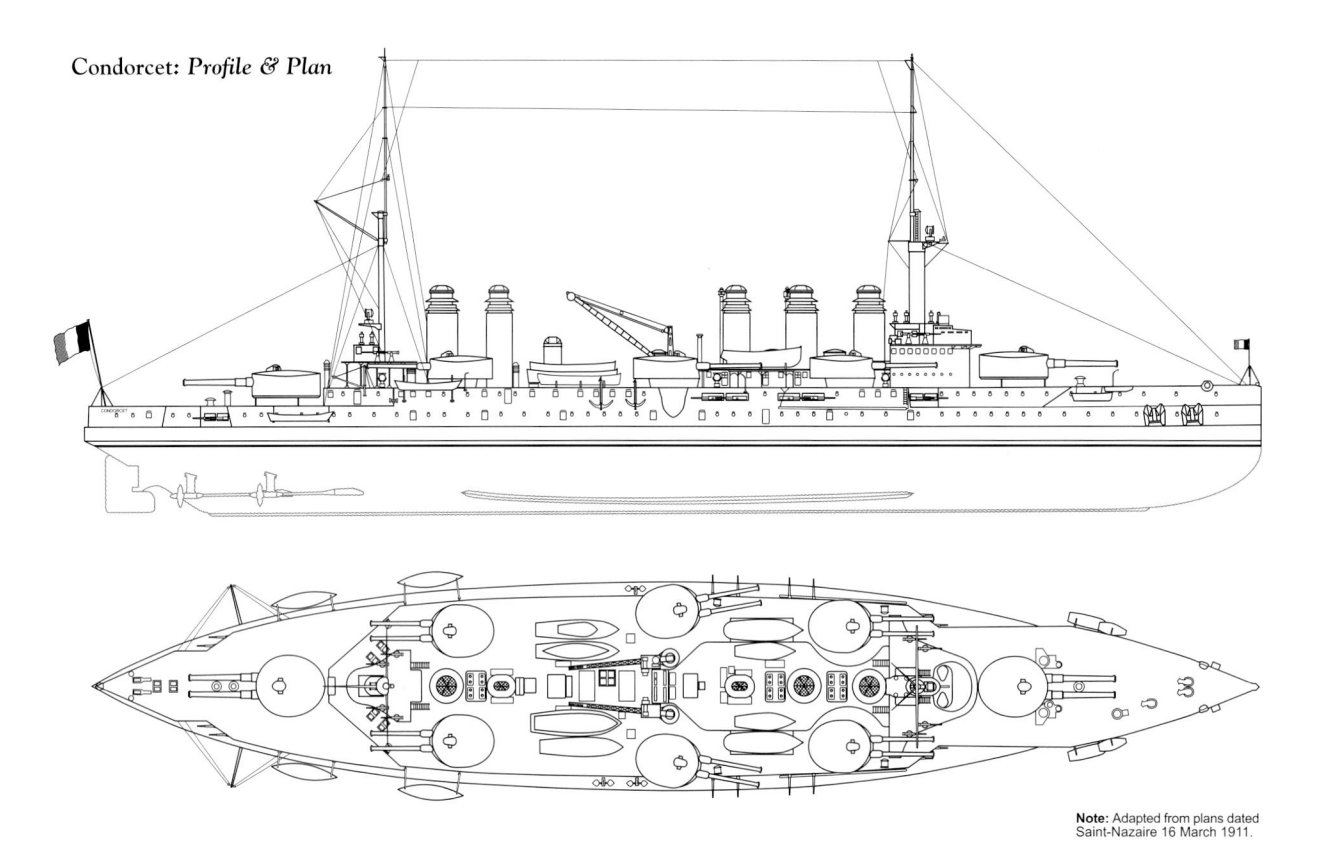

Note: Adapted from plans dated Saint-Nazaire 16 March 1911.

(© John Jordan, 2011)

engaged on broadly parallel courses. Beyond 7000m deficiencies in fire control would mean few (and comparatively 'lucky') hits, which might not favour the more powerful fleet; the latter would need to close to 'decisive' range in order to impose its superiority. Since the fleet with superior speed could effectively choose the range of engagement, these considerations dominated subsequent discussions regarding not only the armament but the propulsion system to be adopted for the ships.

The lessons of Tsushima were still being absorbed, and the French were convinced that the IJN had prevailed despite its disadvantage in major-calibre guns because of the superior speed and handling of its ships, and because the Russian battleships had been subjected a hail of fire (*la rafale*) from the Japanese medium-calibre and QF guns. The latter shells had caused violent explosions above decks and in the unarmoured (or lightly plated) parts of the ship, devastated superstructures, and caused multiple fires which were difficult to extinguish because damage control parties were exposed to constant shell bursts and toxic gases. The vessel's combat capability was effectively destroyed and its crew demoralised. Although it was hoped that the slow-firing heavy guns would deliver the occasional disabling 'lucky hit' (*le coup heureux*), the major value of such guns, whose effectiveness at longer ranges had been much-reduced by the advent of face-hardened armour, was seen to be the ability to finish off a ship already crippled by the hail of fire, much as torpedoes were used during the Second World War..

The proposals which emerged from the June conference were as follows:

A: 17,200 tonnes: 10 – 240mm (4 x II, 2 x I)
B: 18,000 tonnes: 12 – 240mm (6 x II)
C: 17,400 tonnes: 16 – 194mm (6 x II, 4 x I casemate)

All three were to have an identical main armament of four 305mm guns (2 x II), underwater protection, and an ATB armament of 16 x 75mm guns and 8 x 47mm semi-automatic weapons.

Design A was rejected because there were too few guns in the secondary battery. Design C was considered acceptable only if combat range could be kept to 5000m by manoeuvre – and given that the top speed currently proposed was slightly inferior to the ship's likely opponents this would be difficult to achieve. Design B, although the most expensive, was the only one which fully met the CSM's criteria. The Navy Minister, Gaston Thomson,[2] was inclined to accept this advice, but was insistent that the 18,000-tonne displacement proposed should be a maximum.

At this point the Budgetary Commission stated that the five ships proposed should be regarded as replacements for obsolescent units, which meant that the Navy now had to complete a further 16 (*vice* 11) battleships by its target date of 1919. The commission also expressed the view that the current design was too slow, and that the new ships should be capable of 20 knots to match those being built abroad. The *Service Technique* responded that it could increase speed to 19 knots, but only by reducing armour thicknesses. This proposal was therefore left in abeyance, but it would be revisited in the Spring of 1906, when the detailed characterstics of the new ships were discussed in Parliament.

Two competing designs, one by Lhomme, the other by the *Ingénieur général* Bahon of Brest Naval Dockyard, were drawn up and put before the *Comité Technique* for evaluation during March 1906, when the Lhomme design was accepted. However, further modifications were requested, and there were still concerns regarding the artillery and the speed of the ships, both of which were felt to lag behind developments abroad.

With regard to the artillery, the Naval Staff insisted on:

– a fire control system which provided for continuous aim;[3]
– a reloading system which would permit both guns in a twin turret to fire at the same rate as a gun in a single turret;
– complete independence of the two guns with regard to elevation, loading, etc. (but not, of course, for training);
– the installation of a replenishment system which would make possible a firing cycle of three rounds per minute for the 240mm guns and two rounds per minute for the 305mm guns for the first 25% of the ammunition, the demands made with respect to the 240mm guns (regarded as the main armament of the ship) being non-negotiable.

In the light of developments abroad there was brief consideration at this time of an 'all-big-gun' ship in which the twin 240mm beam turrets would be replaced by single 305mm turrets, for a total of ten 305mm guns (seven on the broadside). However, this would have raised displacement above the 18,000-tonne limit, and given that it would be easier using current technology to secure a firing cycle of 2-3rpm with continuous aim for the 240mm gun than one of 2rpm for the heavier 305mm gun, both the weight of broadside and the frequency of hitting would be significantly reduced. It was therefore decided that a true 'all-big-gun' ship would require a completely new design, rather than one derived from the twin-battery *Patrie*.[4]

The Propulsion Dilemma

Alarm at the increases in strength of the German, American and Japanese fleets, combined with the delay in implementing the new battleship programme, led Navy Minister Thomson, with the support of the Budgetary Commission, to increase the numbers to be ordered under the first *tranche* from five units to six. Ironically, the parliamentary debates, instead of rubber-stamping the *Danton* design as it currently stood, focused on concerns that France was being left behind in the technological race, and in particular by the adoption of steam turbines by the British Royal Navy in place of the traditional piston-driven reciprocating engines. At a time when the STCN was insisting that 19 knots was obtainable only with a reduction in protection, there were reports that HMS *Dreadnought* was capable of a sustained 20-21 knots.

Concerns were expressed in the naval establishment regarding: the loss of homogeneity in the battle fleet, with some ships powered by reciprocating engines and others by turbines; the absence of any technological base in

GENERAL CHARACTERISTICS

Displacement:
Legend	18,318 tonnes
As completed	18,754 tonnes

Dimensions:
Length pp	145.00m
Length wl	145.00m
Length oa	146.60m
Beam	25.80m
Draught	8.44m max.

Propulsion:
Boilers	26 Niclausse (C/Di/Ve) or Belleville (Da/Vo/M) boilers, 18kg/cm^2
Engines	four-shaft Parsons turbines
Horsepower	22,500ihp
Speed	19.25 knots (designed)
Coal	965/2027 tonnes
Endurance	3,500nm at 10kts

Armament:
Main guns	4 – 305mm/45 Mle 1906 in twin mountings
Secondary guns	12 – 240mm/50 Mle 1902 in twin mountings
ATB guns	16 – 75mm/62.5 Mle 1908 in single mountings
	8 – 47mm/50 Mle 1902 in single mountings
Torpedo tubes	2 submerged tubes for 450mm torpedoes (6 torpedoes Mle 1909R)

Ammunition:
305mm	65rpg (300 max.)
240mm	80rpg (1200 max.)
75mm	400rpg (6880 max.)
47mm	750rpg (10,000 max.)

Protection:
Main belt	250mm max.
Decks	48mm PBS + 45/70mm PBI
305 turrets	340-260mm
240 turrets	225-188mm
Conning tower	266-216mm

Complement:
flagship	40 officers + 875 men
private ship	28 officers + 824 men

Notes:

PBS (*Pont Blindé Supérieur*) — Upper Armoured Deck
PBI (*Pont Blindé Inférieur*) — Lower Armoured Deck
ATB — Anti-Torpedo Boat

France to build the turbines; and the inevitable further delays to the programme. However, the matter was considered sufficiently urgent for a naval mission to be detached to Britain, taking advantage both of improved Anglo-French relations following the *Entente cordiale* of 1904 and an offer from the Parsons company to inspect their turbine production facilities.

The technical mission was led by *Ingénieur* de Courtille; it left on 14 May and returned 1st June. There were visits to Parsons, Armstrong, Barr & Stroud, Vickers, and to the Swan Hunter shipyard, where the French delegation observed ships under construction for Japan. It studied not only the installation of turbines, but also main guns and

WARSHIP 2013

Danton: *Sections*

THE 'SEMI-DREADNOUGHTS' OF THE *DANTON* CLASS

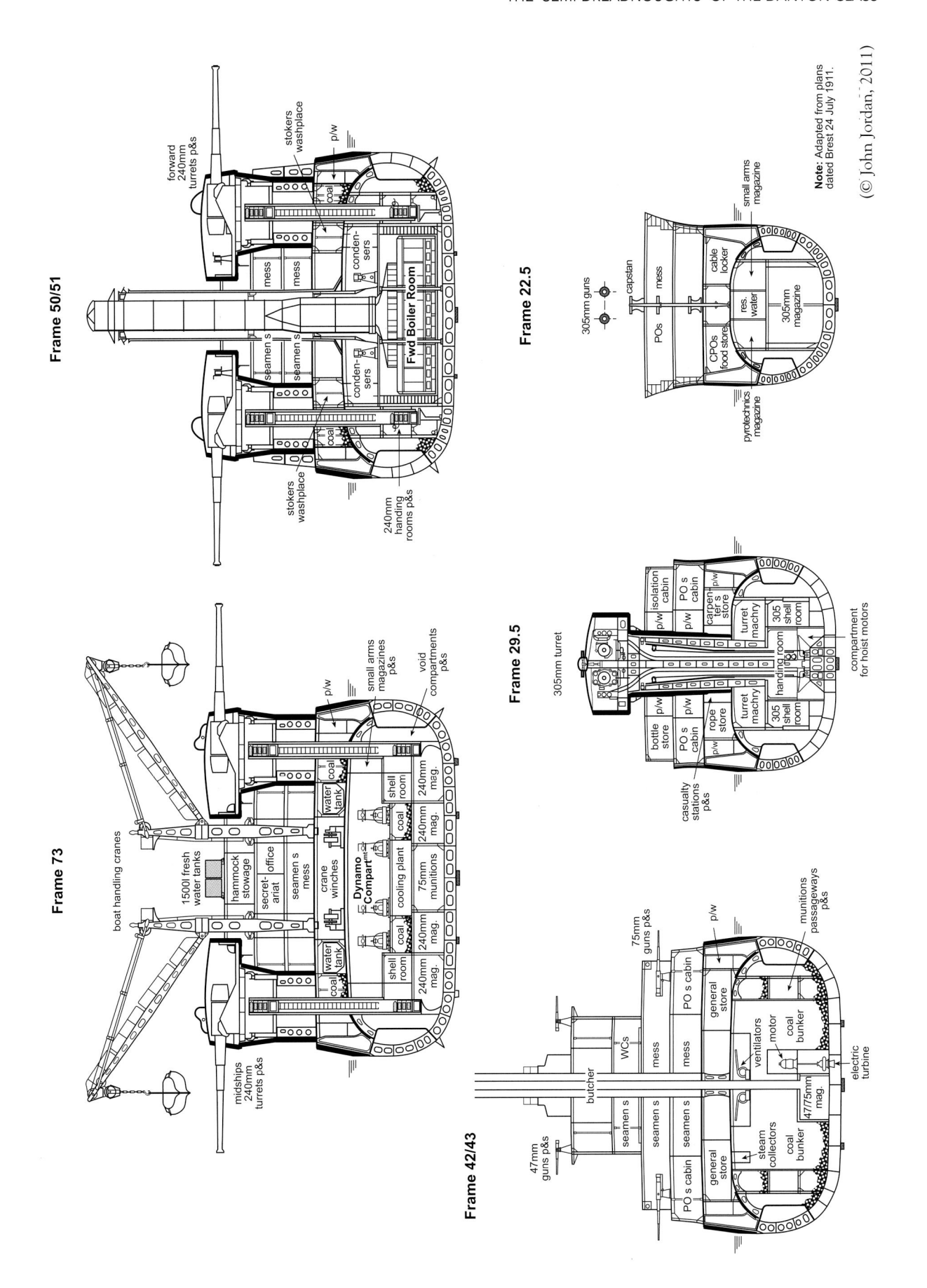

Frame 50/51

Frame 73

Frame 42/43

Frame 22.5

Frame 29.5

Note: Adapted from plans dated Brest 24 July 1911.

(© John Jordan, 2011)

WARSHIP 2013

Danton stalled on the Point-du-Jour slipway at her launch, which should have taken place on 22 May 1909 amid great fanfare. The tugs failed to pull her off the slipway, and she had to wait until the next high tide on 4 July for a further successful attempt. This was one more in a series of delays which plagued the construction of this class. (Philippe Caresse collection)

Vergniaud, still minus her guns, during the final stages of fitting out at AC Gironde, Bordeaux. (Philippe Caresse collection)

turrets, torpedo protection, submerged torpedo tube arrangements and windlass/capstan machinery. Its formal report, submitted 18 June 1906, enumerated the advantages and disadvantages of turbines as follows:

Advantages
– smaller: 20-30% less volume
– power/weight ratio superior by 30-40%
– no vibration, particularly at high speeds
– low wear on moving parts
– low fuel consumption at high speeds
– consumption of lubrication oil reduced by 50-66%
– ease of operation, surveillance and maintenance: manning requirement reduced by 50%

Disadvantages
– turbines mono-directional, so separate turbines required to go astern
– fuel consumption higher at lower speeds
– higher temperatures in engine rooms.

In the report it was estimated that by adopting turbines of the same mass there would be a 30-40% increase in power, a 5% increase in speed, and a 30% increase in endurance at maximum speed. (Alternatively, for the same speed and endurance machinery mass could be reduced by 33-50%.)

The major concerns of the mission were the reduction in efficiency at cruise speed, and in particular the difficulty of going astern, which was a potential problem for ships operating in close formations. However, the report concluded that the development of reciprocating turbines had reached its peak, whereas marine turbines were in their infancy and there would undoubtedly be improvements. These conclusions would prime the subsequent parliamentary debates on the characteristics to be adopted.

Further Indecision and Delay

On 11 July the *Service Technique* drew up a programme for the installation of Parsons turbines in the *Danton* class, and this was subsequently communicated to the builders. Orders for the first two ships had already been placed with the naval dockyards three months previously and a further four ships had been authorised, yet not only was there still considerable uncertainty regarding the propulsion machinery to be adopted, but on 3 August the Minister requested a study for a variant using the new 305mm Mle 1906 gun.

WHO WERE THEY?

The names allocated to the ships were not traditional, and reflected the personal preferences of the Navy Minister, Gaston Thomas. All were prominent 18th century rationalist philosophers and/or revolutionaries.

Danton: A leading figure in the early stages of the French Revolution of 1789 and the first President of the Committee of Public Safety.

Mirabeau: A leading figure in the French revolution, as well as a writer, diplomat, freemason, and journalist.

Vergniaud: A lawyer, statesman, and noted orator, he was a significant figure in the French Revolution.

Condorcet: A philosopher, mathematician and early political scientist; took a leading role in the French Revolution, and argued for a rationalist reconstruction of society

Diderot: A rationalist philosopher who founded the *encyclopédie*, which aimed to substitute knowledge and science for ignorance and was overtly anti-clerical.

Voltaire: A writer, philosopher and *encyplopédiste*; his novel *Candide* satirised national foibles and institutionalised religion.

On 6 October Dudebout advised the Minister that a decision on the machinery was urgently required. Only two of the ships' builders (FC Méditerranée and Penhoët) had proposed the adoption of turbines – a third had stated it had the technical capability to build them – and there would be an additional cost. A single set of turbines would cost an estimated 4.8m francs, as compared to only 1.5m francs for reciprocating engines; a three-shaft installation would therefore mean an additional cost of more than 9m francs per ship. The inevitable delays implicit in starting up new production lines threatened to push completion dates back even further.[5] Dudebout therefore proposed that the first three ships be completed with reciprocating machinery and the remaining three with turbines. This would deliver the first three ships on schedule, and would create two homogeneous three-ship divisions with competing machinery for evaluation.

The Minister was inclined to agree with Dudebout, but in parliamentary debates which took place in December there was overwhelming support both for the move to turbines and for homogeneity of propulsion machinery in the battle fleet. The Minister promptly reversed course, and on 26 December, the day after the debate in the Senate, contracts were signed with the private shipyards for the remaining four ships; all six would now be fitted with Parsons turbines.

BUILDING DATA

Name	Builder	Laid down	Launched	Completed*
Voltaire	FC Méditerranée (La Seyne)	08.06.07	16.01.09	05.08.11
Condorcet	AC Loire (St. Nazaire)	23.08.07	19.04.09	25.07.11
Diderot	Penhoët (St. Nazaire)	23.08.07	20.04.09	25.07.11
Danton	Arsenal de Brest	09.01.08	04.07.09	24.07.11
Mirabeau	Arsenal de Lorient	04.05.08	28.10.09	01.08.11
Vergniaud	AC Gironde (Bordeaux)	??.07.08	12.04.10	18.12.11

* *Armement définitif* = Commissioning date

Nor was this the only major modification to the design made at this time. Already on 8 December, the naval dockyards and private shipyards participating in the programme had been informed of the adoption of a new 45-calibre 305mm gun, the Mle 1906, in place of the 305/40 Mle 1993/1996M of the *Patrie* class. The gun itself would be 9 tonnes heavier (54t *vice* 45t), and it would fire a 440kg shell (*vice* 340kg) using a more powerful charge of 164kg (*vice* 129kg). This would mean a larger, heavier turret which had yet to be designed. There was also a decision to adopt a straight stem in place of the former ram bow and to change the lines of the hull aft to accommodate four shafts (*vice* three). Displacement was by now 18,318 tonnes, and it was estimated that the adoption of the new gun would take it above 18,400 tonnes.

New plans of the hull were ready on 28 March 2007, and although the first keel had yet to be laid, further modifications accompanied by new drawings would follow throughout this year and the next. Meanwhile, improvements in infrastructure to deliver the new construction programme and to maintain the ships once they entered service were proceeding concurrently. Quite apart from the enlargement of the graving docks at Toulon and Bizerte, these included:

- the building of a new covered slipway, to be named the *Point-du-Jour*, in the upper reaches of the River Penfeld at Brest;
- at Saint-Nazaire (where the private shipyards of AC Loire and Penhoët were located), the enlargement of Dock no.1 and of the lock gates between the two main basins, the cost of 2.2m francs being shared between the Navy and the Ministry of Works on a 25/75% basis);
- the construction of a floating dock 181m x 37m for fitting-out at Bordeaux;
- the construction of a large turbine assembly workshop at La Seyne.

The laying down of the two ships contracted to be built by the naval dockyards, *Danton* (Brest) and *Mirabeau* (Lorient), was delayed until 1908. The construction of the *Point-du-Jour* slipway at Brest was held up by water ingress under the lower end which was sealed off only in May 1908. In order to minimise construction delays, work on the bow of the ship proceeded on the dry, upper part of the slipway; work on the stern followed some four months later. In the case of Lorient the slipway on which the *Mirabeau* was to be laid down was occupied by the armoured cruiser *Waldeck Rousseau* until the latter ship was launched on 4 March 1908, and there was then a delay of some two months before the first elements of the battleship's hull could be assembled. In both the naval dockyards shortages of skilled labour were an issue; only a single major ship could be built at any one time, and Brest was still occupied with the fitting out of the *Rousseau*'s sister, the *Edgar Quinet*. There were also lengthy delays in delivering components due to the poor coordination of the different agencies, which meant that none of the six hulls was launched before 1909; fitting out, on the other hand, proceeded more smoothly and all except *Vergniaud* were in service by the summer of 1911.

The guns of the Mirabeau *are embarked at Brest, using the* Grande Grue, *the distinctive hammerhead crane on the fitting-out quay.* (Philippe Caresse collection)

Condorcet in the River Penfeld at Brest in 1911 following her gunnery trials. Note the swing bridge in the background. (Philippe Caresse collection)

Main Guns & Turrets

In the report of the naval commission to the UK headed by de Courtille the superiority of British turret arrangements (observed during a visit to a ship under construction for the IJN) was recognised:

- The firing chamber was broader, making it easier to service the guns.
- The guns were elevated hydraulically rather than electrically.
- Loading was theoretically possible at all angles.

However, as far as the *Dantons* were concerned, the adoption of a British-style turret would have required major redesign.

Current French turrets for major calibre gun mountings were of two types. Many used 'pivot' mountings in which a tapering trunk housing the ammunition hoists was suspended beneath the turret and seated on bearings in the depths of the ship, so that the whole assembly rotated. Ammunition was raised by dredger-type cage hoists

WEIGHT OF BROADSIDE

	Guns able to fire	Firing cycle	Weight of broadside
Danton	4 x 305mm (440kg)*	1.5rpm	2640kg
	6 x 240mm (220kg)	2rpm	2640kg = **5280kg**
Dreadnought	8 x 305mm (386kg)	1.5rpm	4632kg = **4632kg**

* using the new 'heavy' shell (*obus alourdi*)

Penetration of Harveyised Plate

		angle of incidence 0°		angle of incidence 20°	
	m/v	@ 6000m	@ 10,000m	@ 6000m	@ 10,000m
305/1906	780m/s	390mm	279mm	363mm	260mm
240/1902-06	800m/s	319mm	206mm	299mm	194mm

Note: Data from Dumas & Prévoteaux, *op. cit.*
The thickness of the main armour belt of the Danton's foreign contemporaries was:

Dreadnought 11in (280mm)
Deutschland 240mm
Nassau 300mm

Note that at 6000 metres the French 240mm gun could theoretically penetrate all these belts, but that at 10,000 metres it could penetrate none of them.

directly to the firing chamber, with shells and charges normally stowed at the rear of the turret so that fire could be sustained in the event of a breakdown in the hoists.

The other type of main gun turret was closer to the British model in that it had two-stage hoists, with transfer of shells and charges from the lower to the upper hoists in the working chamber. However, unlike the British model the cylindrical ammunition trunk connecting the magazines with the working chamber was fixed, only the working chamber being suspended from the turret. In the working chamber the shells and charges were transferred from the fixed part to the mobile part, which rotated with the turret. As with the pivot-style turret there was still an emphasis on the stowage of multiple ready-use rounds close to the guns, shells generally being stowed in the firing chamber while charges were stowed in the working chamber, where they were less exposed to enemy hits and flash-back.

The 305mm turrets in the *Dantons* were pivot mountings on the St. Chamond pattern. Eight shells were stowed on racks at the after end of the gunhouse, while stowage for their 32 quarter-charges was in cylindrical revolving chambers between the raised floor of the firing chamber and the floor of the turret. It took 28 seconds for the hoists to make the transit from the handing room below to the firing chamber. The complete charge was tipped manually onto waiting trays. The shell was moved electrically to the breech, and the quarter-charges, each of which weighed just over 36 kilos, were then placed by the loaders behind the open breech ready for ramming. Mechanical firing, using a spring-loaded firing pin, was retained – electrical firing had been trialled on the armoured cruiser *Edgar Quinet* but without success. The breech flushing mechanism used compressed air.

The turret was trained by an electric motor with manual back-up for use in emergency. Training by electric motor allowed for ten possible speeds up to 5 degrees per second. Manual training required ten men, and training speed was reduced to 1.5 degrees per second. Elevation of the guns was also via electric motors; there were 20 possible speeds up to 3 degrees per second. For emergency back-up, a single man could elevate the guns at a maximum speed of 0.5 degrees per second. All systems were designed to operate with a heel/list of 5 degrees.

There were three sights: two on the turret sides and a third, for training only, on the turret roof. A 1.37-metre (4ft 6in) Barr & Stroud rangefinder was incorporated into the latter sight for use by the turret commander (*chef de section*).

The 240mm turrets were of the second type, in which the working chamber was suspended beneath the firing chamber and rotated with it. It housed the winches and motors for the upper hoists, together with the mechanisms for the transfer of shells and charges from the fixed lower hoists to the upper hoists for the guns. The lower hoists had linked cages containing two complete rounds – a

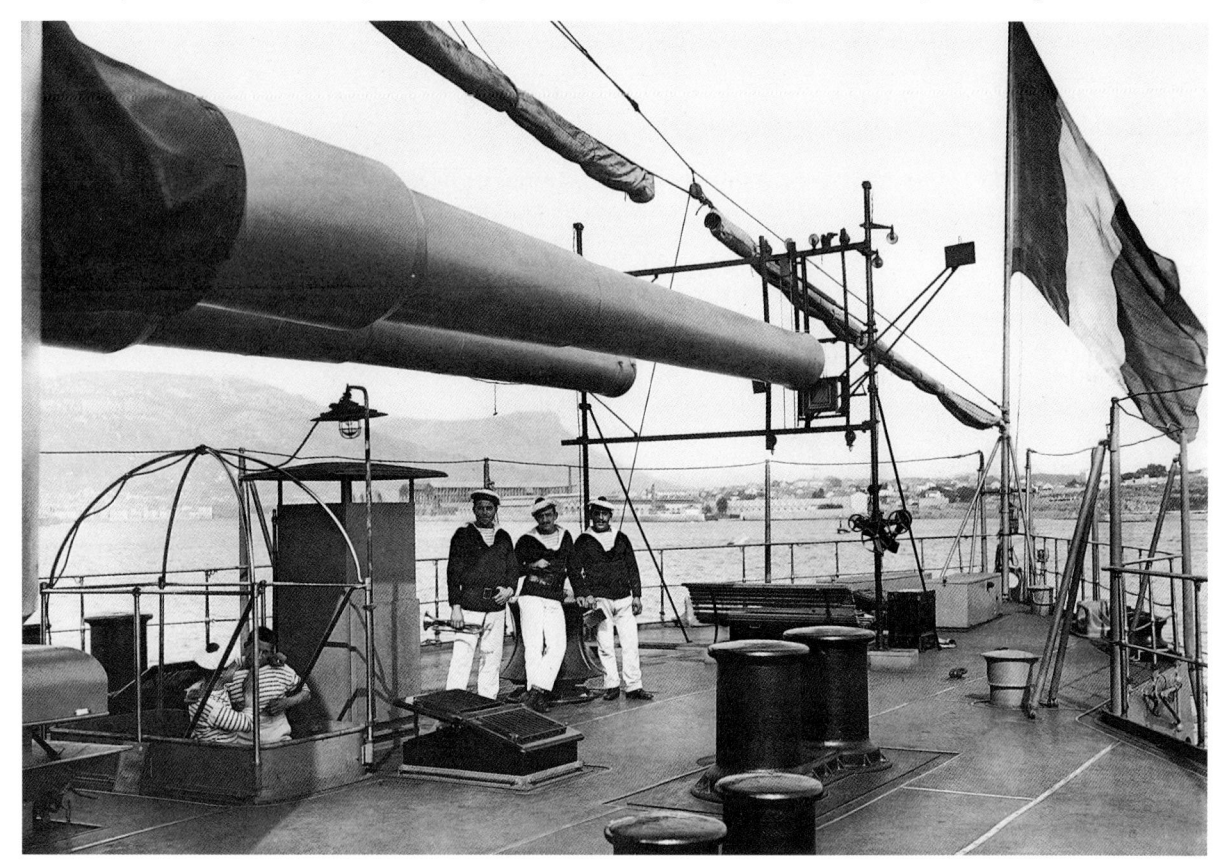

The quarterdeck of Vergniaud. *The frame structure is a collimator used to bore-sight the guns and to get all the mechanical components in the turrets and mountings to line up properly. In the Marine Nationale it was also used for gunnery instruction.* (Philippe Caresse collection)

MAIN GUNS: CHARACTERISTICS

	305/45 Mle 1906	240/50 Mle 1902-1906
construction	52 elements	46 elements
breech mechanism	Manz interrupted screw	Manz interrupted screw
weight of gun	54.65t	29.55t
length of barrel	12.775m	12.508m
grooves	90 helicoidal at 4°	72 helicoidal at 4°
firing mechanism	spring-loaded pin	spring-loaded pin
projectile	APC: 440kg	APC: 240kg
bursting charge	5% picric acid	5% picric acid
propellant	145kg BM17 (4/4)	75kg BM17 (3/3)
ammunition stowage	65rpg (75rpg max.)	80rpg (100rpg max.)
muzzle velocity	780m/s	800m/s
max. range	14,500m (12°)	14,000m (13°)

complete round was one shell plus three third-charges – and the loading cycle was designed to deliver 6rpm per turret. The guns could be loaded at elevations between –5° and +11° (maximum elevation was only 13°).

There was stowage for twelve shells on the walls of the turret, with lockers below for 36 charges. It took 20 seconds for shells and charges arriving via the hoists to be loaded ready for firing, and 25 seconds to load from the ready-use racks and lockers. The training mechanism for the turret and the elevation mechanisms for the guns were electrical, as in the 305mm turret. Training speeds of up to 6 degrees per second were possible using the electric motors, while in manual mode it took three men to train the turret at speeds of up to 2.5 degrees per second. Maximum speed of elevation was 3 degrees per second, and in back-up mode one man could elevate each gun one degree per second. As with the 305mm turret, all systems were designed to operate with a heel/list of 5 degrees. Firing mechanisms, breech flushing and sight arrangements were as for the 305mm turret. A new electro-mechanical firing system was fitted in both the 305mm and the 240mm guns from 1913.

This was the first generation of shells to have a burster of picric acid (*mélinite*). The older armour-piercing shell (*obus de rupture*) had a black powder filler which often failed to explode. The new shell, which was designated *obus alourdi* (heavyweight shell) also had a new dual base fuze (*à double bouchon de culot*) which theoretically made it equally effective against light plating and heavy armour. This proved less than satisfactory in service, but became the basis for more effective dual fuzes developed during the interwar period.

In the magazines, each quarter/third charge was kept in a case of soldered tin; the cases were stowed on shelving. The shells were stowed horizontally on wooden racks in the shell rooms.

Fire Control for Main Guns

The French naval mission to Britain had been particularly impressed by the rangefinders available from Barr & Stroud, which unlike the current French models were completely independent of any knowledge of the characteristics of the opposing ship.[6]

The *Dantons* would be fitted from the outset with two B&S 2-metre (6ft) FQ rangefinders, which were installed atop the conning tower behind a screen of special steel 50mm thick. Learning how to use these effectively and integrating them into the fire control system took a considerable time, and in the interim range data was provided by eight Ponthus & Therrode rangefinders, for which length and mast height of the enemy ship (provided in the *carnet de silhouettes*) was required.

Smaller B&S rangefinders with a 1.37-metre (4ft 6in) base were also purchased for the turret commander's roof sight in each of the eight turrets for the main guns. They were not ideally positioned – at ranges above 9000m the barrels of the guns obstructed the lenses – and vibration from the dynamos and the shock of the discharge of the guns tended to throw them out of alignment.

It took some time for the crews to adapt to the British-model rangefinders. There was sometimes a discrepancy of 400m in the ranges given by rangefinders only a few metres from one another. The solution was to use them in tandem, which led to the adoption of a triplex 4.57-metre (15ft) model in 1914-16. Other improvements included 2-metre (6ft) B&S rangefinders in the main turrets in place of the original 1.37-metre model. Eventually the rangefinders were effective up to 12,500m, which was close to the maximum range of the guns.

The ships continued to be fitted with the inexpensive but obsolescent Germain hydraulic order transmitters to provide gunnery data (see John Spencer, *Conduite du Tir* Part 1). Each turret was equipped with dials as follows:

– turret commander: firing command + elevation (*hausse*)[7] + deflection (*dérive*)
– gunlayers (on either side of the guns): elevation (*hausse*) + deflection (*dérive*)

As in all French battleships of the period, fire control was exercised from the conning tower, with raw data being processed in the *Poste Central Artillerie* below decks. The latter was enlarged during the Great War, with a plotting table (*conjugateur graphique*) being added and the fire control team being increased by three men.

For night firing there were eight 75cm searchlight projectors, each with a Breguet remote control system: two were in fixed positions on the masts; the remaining six (*de ligne basse*) could occupy one of three different positions:

– Night action position: two port & starboard forward of the first two 240mm turrets (II & III); two forward of the middle turrets (IV & V), and two abaft the after pair of 240mm turrets (VI & VII); in these positions the arcs covered were slightly greater than the firing arcs of the turrets.
– Sea position: the projectors were secured on the ship's axis, ready to be moved to their action positions on bronze rails.
– Daylight action position: the projectors were moved under armour.

ANTI-TORPEDO BOAT GUNS: CHARACTERISTICS

	75/62.5 Mle 1908 Sch	47/40 Mle 1902 Sch
construction	4 elements	3 elements
breech mechanism	Schneider screw	Hotchkiss sliding
weight of gun	1.61t	233kg
length of barrel	4.85m	2.05m
grooves	24 helicoidal at 6°	20 helicoidal at 6°
firing mechanism	mechanical	mechanical
projectile	6.4kg	
complete round	12.5kg	3.45kg
bursting charge	picric acid	-
propellant	0.09kg BM7	0.075kg BM2
ammunition stowage	400rpg (430rpg max.)	750rpg (800rpg max.)
muzzle velocity	950m/s	680m/s
max. range	8000m (25°)	6000m

UNDERWATER WEAPONS

450mm Torpedo Mle 1909R

Length:	5.25m
Weight:	716kg
Propulsion:	heater
Warhead:	114kg
Range:	2000nm @ 33kts (1min 58sec)
	3000nm @ 28kts (3min 28sec)

Harlé H3 Mine

Weight:	375kg
Depth of immersion:	9
Length of cable:	100m
Charge:	60kg guncotton

The remote power control mechanism proved to be fragile and unreliable, and was later discarded in favour of purely mechanical operation.

ATB Guns

The first two ships of the *Patrie* class had been armed exclusively with the Hotchkiss 47mm gun for anti-torpedo boat defence. The 24 guns were divided between the upper hull, the superstructures and the military foremast, and were intended to provide saturation fire at ranges up to 5-6000m As torpedo boats increased in size and were fitted with more capable, longer-range torpedoes, it became clear that the lightweight 47mm projectiles lacked the 'clout' to disable an attacking enemy craft before it could launch its torpedoes. *Patrie* and *République* had their sixteen hull guns replaced by thirteen 65mm guns, and the four modified ships of the *Liberté* sub-group were completed with the same armament. Even the 65mm calibre was subsequently judged too lightweight. It was pointed out that contemporary Royal Navy battleships were armed with 12-pounder (76mm) guns for this purpose, while the Imperial German Navy had opted for 88mm guns. It was therefore decided to increase the calibre to 75mm for the *Danton* class.

The First Deck amidships on Vergniaud, with the centre section of 75mm anti-torpedo boat guns. There was no armour protection for these guns; the gun ports were closed by hinged watertight doors. (Philippe Caresse collection)

The 75mm/62.5 Mle 1908 was a new long-barrelled model developed by Schneider; it fired a 6.4kg shell and had a firing cycle of around 6 seconds. Loading was semi-automatic, the spent cartridge being ejected when the breech was opened, and the breech closing automatically when the new round was rammed home. Twelve guns were located in embrasures in the upper hull on the First Deck: four abeam the bridge to cover forward arcs, and eight on the beam between the first two 240mm turrets on either side of the ship. The remaining four guns covered the after arcs, and were located on the Main Deck just abaft the after 305mm turret. Although these guns are often described as being in casemates, this is not strictly true; there was no protection beyond the thin plating of the upper hull and the deck above the guns, and the guns were in open mountings behind hinged watertight doors. The secondary (138.6mm) guns of the later dreadnoughts would be housed within armoured 'redoubts', but the ATB guns of the French pre-dreadnought battleships fired through open ports.

The fixed ammunition was stowed in cases of three rounds on shelves in magazines located directly beneath the superstructures fore and aft and between the machinery spaces amidships (see drawings). They were manhandled to the electrical bucket-type hoists and were raised three at a time at a rate of 1m/sec; manual back-up in the event of power failure or damage was possible, the rate declining to c.0.3m/sec. Because the ammunition cases were difficult to handle in the confined spaces of the magazines and the hoists were relatively slow, 432 ready-use rounds (27rpg) were stowed close to the mountings on the First Deck, and a further 144 rounds (36rpg) close to the after guns on the Main Deck, which were located some distance from their magazine. When opening fire using the ready-use ammunition, the guns were capable of firing 15 rounds per minute, but this slowed to 7rpm when the guns were replenished using the hoists.

The gun could be aimed using either a simple open sight (*cran de mire*) or a *collimateur Krauss* (see John Spencer), the latter being fixed to the chassis.

The 75mm guns were complemented by eight 47mm Hotchkiss guns. These were in open mountings atop the superstructures fore and aft. The rounds were stowed in wooden boxes and bronze cases. Electric hoists could lift two cases together, each containing six rounds. Ready-use lockers close to the guns could stow 36 rounds per gun. When opening fire using the ready-use ammunition the guns were capable of firing 15 rounds per minute, but this slowed to 6rpm when the guns were resupplied using the hoists. This was no better than for the 75mm guns, so the 47mm weapon was rightly considered of little practical value.

Underwater Weapons

The *Danton* class was equipped with two submerged torpedo tubes for 450mm torpedoes: one to port, the other to starboard. The submerged torpedo room was located on the 2nd Platform Deck between frames 33 and 42. The tubes, which were 5.85m long and 2.35m below the waterline, were angled at 10 degrees forward of the beam and were given a 3-degree downward angle. Six 450mm Mle 1909R torpedoes were carried (see table for characteristics), the reserve torpedoes being stowed in racks against the rear wall of the compartment.

Somewhat surprisingly the ships were also to have received 10 Harlé Mle 1906 mines (see table), which were stowed on the First Platform Deck along the boiler glacis. There was no provision for launching mines from the ships, which would have used pinnaces for this purpose. The mines could also be utilised to replenish minelayers present in the anchorages which would serve as bases in the central and eastern Mediterranean.

Hull & Protection

The hull and protection system of the *Danton* class was derived from that of the *Patrie*, with some adjustments to armour thicknesses to take account of the need for heavier armour on the 240mm turrets while keeping weights within acceptable limits. Construction was on the semi-longitudinal pattern, and the frame spacing was reduced from 1.5m in the *Patrie* to 1m in order to cope with the weight of the beam 240mm turrets. The only innovation was the anti-torpedo protection.

The protection system for French battleships against enemy gunfire was well established. It was based on certain fixed principles:

– The ship's vitals (magazines, machinery spaces, turrets and their ammunition trunking, and the conning tower) were protected by heavy, cemented armour plate. These plates were given reduced thickness towards the bow and stern.
– The main armour belt comprised two strakes: the plates of the upper strake were slightly tapered towards their upper edge, while the plates of the lower strake were at maximum thickness to around 0.5 metres below the waterline, and then tapered sharply towards their bottom edge. The belt, which extended up to the Main (upper protected) deck, was terminated short of the stern and was closed by a thick transverse bulkhead of cemented steel.
– A single strake of lighter plates of special steel (the

The midships section of Diderot, *seen here in the summer of 1911. (Philippe Caresse collection)*

WARSHIP 2013

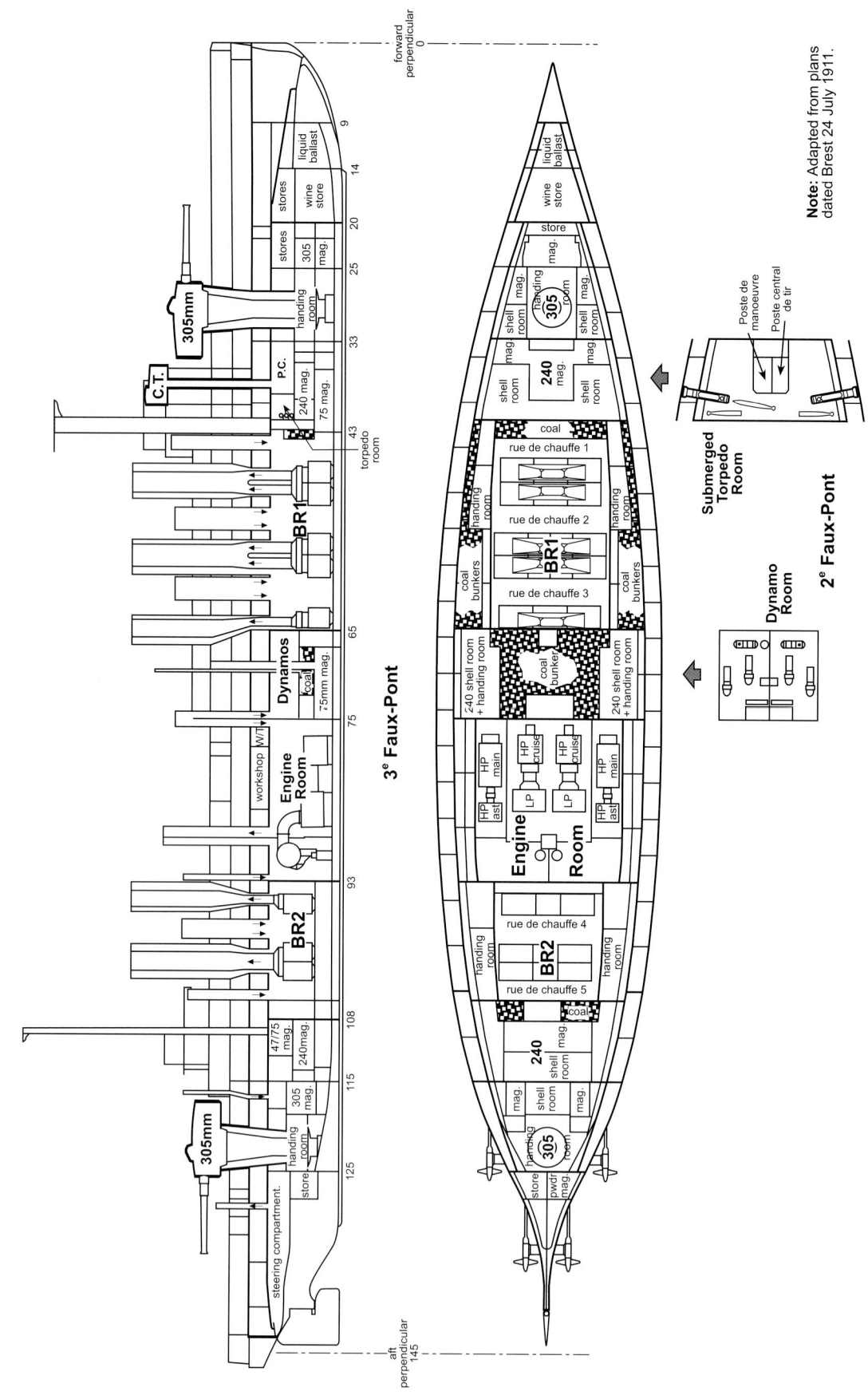

Danton: Inboard Profile

THE 'SEMI-DREADNOUGHTS' OF THE DANTON CLASS

DANTON: ARMOUR PLATE THICKNESS MAIN BELT

Danton: *Protection*

No.	Upper Strake upper/lower edge	Lower/Intermediate Strakes upper/lower edge
0	140/180	–
1	140/180	180/180
2	160/180	180/180
3	180/200	200/200
4	200/220	220/220
5	220/240	180/80
6	220/250	180/80
7	220/250	200/80
8	220/250	220/80
9	220/250	240/80
10	220/250	250/100
11	220/250	250/100
12	220/250	250/100
13	220/250	250/100
14	220/250	250/100
15	220/250	250/100
16	220/250	250/100
17	220/250	250/100
18	220/250	250/100
19	220/250	250/100
20	220/250	250/100
21	220/250	250/100
22	220/250	250/100
23	220/250	250/100
24	220/250	250/100
25	200/240	250/100
26	180/220	250/100
27	160/200	250/100
28	140/180	250/100
29	–	250/100
30	–	240/80
31	–	220/80
32	–	200/80
33	–	180/80

Total weight of armour belt: **1,953.29 tonnes**; all plates of cemented armour except Upper Strake 0, Lower/Intermediate 1 & 5; these three plates were of special steel. The seven plates (0–6) of the upper hull strake forward were of 64mm special steel.

(© John Jordan, 2011)

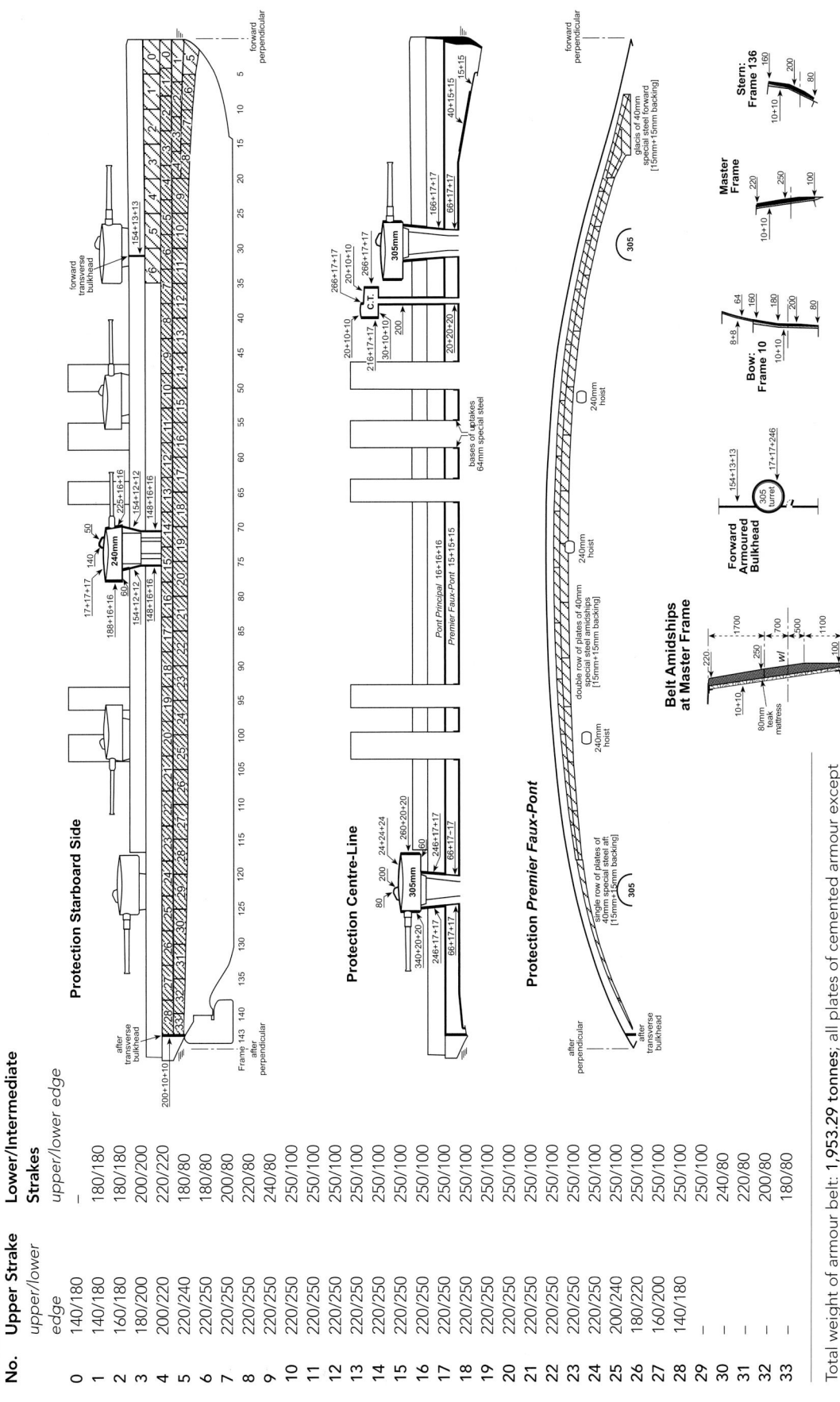

cuirasse mince) extended from the bow to just abaft the forward turret above the level of the main armour belt. Directly above its after end, and extending from the sides of the barbette for the turret, was a thick armoured bulkhead of special steel intended to keep shell fired from forward bearings from penetrating the working spaces on the First and Main Decks, where it might ricochet and cause devastation.

– There were two protected decks each constructed of three layers of standard construction (mild) steel generally 14-18mm thick for a total thickness of 42-54mm: the Main Deck (*pont blindé supérieur* or PBS), which was completely flat and extended from the bow to the after armoured transverse bulkhead; and the First Platform Deck (*pont blindé inférieur* or PBI), which was flat over the machinery spaces and the fore & after magazines but was inclined downwards at the sides to meet the bottom edge of the belt, and also at the bow to form a glacis. These inclines were reinforced, the upper layer of mild steel being replaced by armour plates of special steel 36-40mm thick.

– Between the two protected decks, in the space between the side incline of the Platform Deck and the Main Deck was a cellular structure termed the *entrepont cellulaire*, comprising small watertight compartments which were intended to limit any flooding which might result from penetration of the main belt at the waterline.

The complexity of the protection system for these ships defies description – at least in an article as brief as this – and the reader is referred to the drawings for the small detail. In principle the hull sides over the machinery spaces, the turrets (together with their barbettes and ammunition trunks), and the conning tower had armour sufficiently thick to prevent penetration from large-calibre shell. However, turrets were generally protected only against shell of similar calibre to their guns, and turret faces were more heavily protected than the turret sides, while turret roofs, except for the prominent sighting hoods, received only light layered protection similar to that of the decks. Armour plates for the turrets and conning tower were generally secured to a backing comprising a double layer of mild steel, while the belt was seated on a thick (normally 80mm) wooden mattress intended to absorb fragments, and secured to a double layer of steel plating with heavy bolts. Where barbettes and ammunition trunks passed through decks the thickness of the plates was progressively reduced to take account of the side plating a shell would need to pass through. This system of finely graduated all-over armour made sense while battle ranges remained close and the battleship was exposed to a hail of fire from medium-calibre and QF weaponry. It would become increasingly obsolescent with the adoption of the all-big-gun ship by the major navies.

The increase in displacement over the *Patrie* class was 3000 tonnes. However, the hull had to be significantly enlarged in order to accommodate the six twin 240mm turrets, and the proposed anti-torpedo protection system was costed by the STCN at around 1000 tonnes. There was also the issue of providing armour protection for the 240mm turrets, which were significantly larger than the single 194mm turrets of the later ships of the *Patrie* class, and required thicker plates commensurate with their 'status'. Thus in order to keep maximum designed displacement to 18,000 tonnes there was a considerable amount of 'salami slicing' to the thickness of armour accorded to the hull and the main turrets on the part of the designers. The maximum thickness of the belt was reduced from 280mm to 250mm and the armour protection of the main 305mm turrets from 360mm on the face and 280mm on the sides to 340mm and 260mm respectively. Each of the layers of the upper armoured deck was reduced from 18mm to 16mm, for a total thickness of 48mm, and each of the layers of the lower armoured deck from 17mm to 15mm, for a total thickness of 45mm. In part compensation the thickness of the special steel plates on the incline of the PBI was increased from 36mm to 40mm. And the twin 240mm turrets were protected by cemented armour with a thickness of 225mm on the faces and 188mm on the sides, as against 156mm for both on the 194mm single turrets of the later ships of the *Patrie* class.

The two-strake belt of the *Dantons* extended from the bow to Frame 143, where it was closed by a transverse bulkhead of 200mm cemented armour. It was approximately 4.5 metres high, the lowest 1.1m being below the waterline at normal loading, and was at its maximum thickness at the waterline. Each plate was approximately 5 metres long and extended over five frames; the plates were seated on a teak mattress 80mm thick and secured to a double layer of 10mm steel plating. The thickest plates were between Frames 28 and 123 with a steady reduction in thickness fore and aft (see drawing and accompanying data). All except the foremost three plates on either side of the bow were of cemented armour. Above the main belt forward of Frame 35 was the *cuirasse mince*, composed of plates of 64mm special steel on a 58mm wooden backing and secured to a double layer of 8mm mild steel. It was 5.15m high at the bow and 4.8m at Frame 35.

The underwater protection system adopted for these ships was essentially the same as that devised by Emile Bertin for the coast defence battleship *Henri VI*, and comprised an internal bulge subdivided into watertight

Condorcet: Master Frame

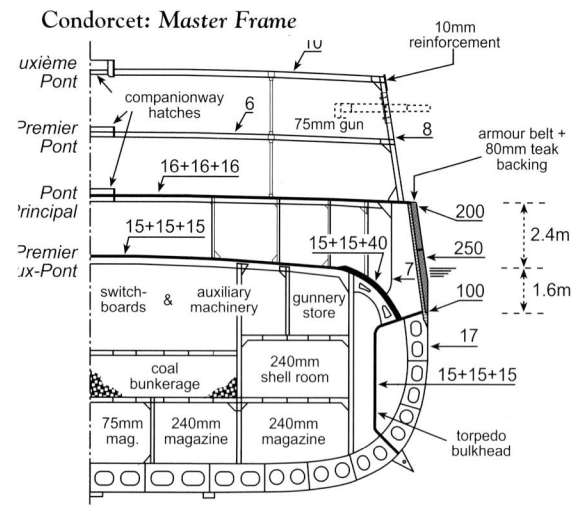

Note: Adapted from plans dated Saint-Nazaire 22 December 1910.

(© John Jordan, 2011)

THE 'SEMI-DREADNOUGHTS' OF THE *DANTON* CLASS

compartments. The same system had been a feature of the Russian battleship *Tsesarevich*, built in France at the La Seyne shipyard, and it had reportedly enabled the ship to survive the Japanese attack on Port Arthur in 1904.

The internal bulge fitted in the *Danton* class extended from Frame 20 to Frame 125 directly beneath the lower armoured deck (see master frame drawing). Its inner wall was 2 metres from the sides of the ship, and it was constructed of three layers of 15mm 60kg special steel. Between Frames 50 and 90 it was subdivided by bulkheads every 4 frames (ie 4m), while the bow and stern sections were subdivided every 5 frames, making for a total of 23 compartments each with a volume of around 30m³. Inboard of the bulge there 16 watertight compartments on each side of the ship, of which twelve were void and four were coal bunkers (located abeam the boiler rooms).

The effectiveness of this internal bulge against torpedoes armed with increasingly large warheads is questionable, although it did have the effect of moving the vulnerable magazines of the beam turrets away from the ship's sides. Unlike the later British and American systems, which utilised a combination of void spaces and hollow steel tubes (RN) or liquids (USN, then RN) to absorb the shock of the explosion, the French system provided only relatively large free-flooding spaces, which without an effective means of counter-flooding could quickly destabilise the ship. *Voltaire* would survive two torpedo hits by *UB-48* on 18 October 1918, but the previous year *Danton* had sustained two torpedo hits and capsized within 40 minutes.[8]

The total weight of protection in these ships was 6,725 tonnes (36% of designed displacement), of which the underwater protection system accounted for 612.5 tonnes. This was almost 1,200 tonnes greater than the corresponding figure for the *Patrie* class.

Machinery

The turbines for all six ships were ordered from the two companies which had initially expressed an interest. FC Méditerranée (La Seyne) built the turbines for *Danton*, *Voltaire* and *Diderot*; the Société de l'Atlantique de Saint-Nazaire those for *Diderot*, *Condorcet* and *Mirabeau*. The turbines were built to Parsons designs and were identical except for some of the auxiliary machinery, which was sub-contracted to other companies. Ideally there should have been a large degree of commonality in the latter, thereby facilitating maintenance and simplifying stocks of spare parts. In practice there was not: Dumas & Prévoteaux (*op. cit.*) cite five different types of ventilator alone.

Diderot on the slipway at Saint-Nazaire Penhoët. The hull is virtually complete up to the First Platform Deck, the Pont Blindé Inférieur. *Note the way the deck forms a carapace over the machinery and magazines, with the sides inclined downwards to meet the lower edge of the belt. In the* Dantons *these inclines would be reinforced by plates of 40mm special steel.* (Philippe Caresse collection)

Danton *in the Rade-Abri at Brest in 1911, shortly before her departure for Toulon.* (Philippe Caresse collection)

There were eight turbine bodies driving four shafts, which was a significant departure from previous practice. The *Patrie* class and the earlier battleships had three shafts, and their three reciprocating engines, which were directly coupled to the shafts, were housed abreast in a single large engine room separated by light partition bulkheads with their condensers in separate condenser rooms abaft them. For the *Dantons* a similar arrangement was

Voltaire *leads the 1st Battleship Division to sea; in her wake are* Condorcet *and* Diderot. *Note the Barr & Stroud 4ft 6in (1.37m) rangefinder in the turret hood of the midships port-side 240mm turret.* (Philippe Caresse collection)

THE 'SEMI-DREADNOUGHTS' OF THE *DANTON* CLASS

Stern quarter view of the Voltaire, *with a plume of black smoke emanating from her Belleville boilers.* (Philippe Caresse collection)

adopted, but the turbines for the inboard shafts were grouped together in a broader central compartment, while the condenser compartment was sub-divided into two (see inboard profile and hold plans). Each of the turbine sets for the wing shafts comprised one high-pressure (HP) ahead turbine and one HP astern turbine. The central turbines comprised low-pressure (LP) and medium-pressure (MP) turbines on the port shaft, and LP and HP turbines on the starboard shaft. The astern turbines for the centre shafts were housed in the casings for the LP turbines.

The contracts for the boilers were signed only on 3 June 1908; the delay was due to the competition process. Babcock & Wilcox (suppliers of boilers to HMS *Dreadnought*) wished to be considered, and following the decision to adopt Parsons turbines the Minister despatched a technical mission to Britain on 19 April 1907 to study these boilers. Its report was favourable but recognised that the B&W boilers were significantly larger and heavier than current French models. As the compartmentation of the ships had already been fixed this was a decisive factor. A mix of coal- and oil-fired boilers was also considered. In the end the Minister opted for boilers of the standard Belleville and Niclausse types, but this period of indecision was to result in a further 18-24 month delay in delivery. The contracts were duly awarded to Belleville of St. Denis, and to Niclausse of Paris; Belleville supplied the boilers for *Danton*, *Mirabeau* and *Voltaire*, Niclausse the boilers for *Diderot*, *Vergniaud* and *Condorcet*.

There no fewer than 26 boilers, which were housed in two large boiler rooms separated by the Dynamo Room and the Engine Room. Seventeen were located in the forward boiler room, nine in the after boiler room. The floor of the after boiler room was one deck higher than that of the forward room, at the level of the 3rd Platform Deck, in order to clear the four propeller shafts which ran beneath it. The boilers were in five groups, each served by one of the five funnels. They were arranged as follows:

– BR1 Group 1: six boilers in two rows of three (served by *rues de chauffe* 1 & 2)
– BR1 Group 2: eight boilers in two rows of four (served by *rues de chauffe* 2 & 3)
– BR1 Group 3: three boilers in a single row (served by *rue de chauffe* 3)
– BR1 Group 4: three boilers in a single row (served by *rue de chauffe* 4)
– BR1 Group 5: six boilers in two rows of three (served by *rues de chauffe* 4 & 5)

The two groups with only a single row of boilers had their exhaust uptakes run up into the two slimmer funnels (see drawing). The coal bunkers were generally adjacent to the two boiler rooms.

To supply electrical power to the ship there were four turbo-dynamos, which were located in a separate compartment on the 2nd Platform Deck just abaft the forward boiler room. The turbo-dynamos were supplied by SACM for *Danton*, *Mirabeau* and *Condorcet*, and by Breguet for the remaining three. The Dynamo Room was divided into port and starboard compartments by a light partition bulkhead, and the turbo-dynamos were in pairs each of which had its own switchboard.

The new turbines experienced numerous teething problems. Parsons had hoped to win a contract to supply the machinery rather than grant a licence for the turbines to be built in France, and was less than forthcoming with its advice on the potential pitfalls Although the French turbines were all built to Parsons designs, measurements had to be converted to the metric system, and different steels were undoubtedly used in the manufacture of components. The turbines gave no problems when tested in the factories, but when installed aboard ship and operated at full speed and high temperature/pressure there was found to be insufficient clearance between rotors and stators and many turbines stripped their blades. This problem had, however, largely been resolved before the Great War, although *Condorcet* had to have no fewer than 60,000 blades replaced during the period 1913-15.

The Belleville boilers performed reasonably well, but the Niclausse boiler was found to have insufficient flexibility and power to work well with turbines. It also had poor combustion and burnt more coal; copious quantities of black smoke were generated, and showers of sparks and even flames regularly emanated from the funnels.

The fastest ship on trials was *Voltaire*, with 20.66 knots, followed by *Danton* with 20.17 knots; the maximum speed attained by the other four ships was between 19.7 and 19.9 knots.

Once the turbine machinery had been worked in, the main issue was its high fuel consumption, which reduced endurance compared with the five *Patries* with which these ships generally operated. The most economical speed was 12.3 knots using only the HP turbines with 16 boilers lit. Range was estimated at 3120-4866nm at 12 knots, as compared with 8400nm at 10 knots for the *Patries*. The nature of the ships' employment in the Mediterranean, which involved lengthy periods of patrolling and virtually no action, meant frequent coaling for the crews and put a strain on French logistics in the central Mediterranean.

Conclusion

Despite the obsolescent features and the dated concepts embodied in their design, the *Dantons* formed the core of the French fleet during the first two years of the war, and gave good service during the postwar period. *Condorcet*, *Diderot* and *Voltaire* were counted in France's battleship allocation under the Washington Treaty of 1922; they were subsequently modernised and remained in active service until 1927, when they became training ships.

The *Dantons* were the first French battleships to be propelled by turbines, and they incorporated a number of measures designed to meet the increasing threat from torpedo boats and submarines. They need to be judged on their own terms, and in the context of a technological revolution in which established concepts were being regularly questioned and overturned, rather than with the benefit of hindsight, in order to place their design in its proper perspective.

Sources:
Robert Dumas & Gérard Prévoteaux, *Les Cuirassés de 18 000t*, Lela Presse (Outreau, 2011).
Official Plans of *Danton* and *Condorcet* published on the website of the Service Historique de la Marine.

Acknowledgements:
The author acknowledges a profound debt to Robert Dumas and Gérard Prévoteaux, on whose recent book (see Sources) the data published in this article are largely based. Sincere thanks are also due to Philipped Caresse, who allowed me to mine his extensive personal collection of photographs.

Footnotes:

[1.] *Patrie* and *République* had their 164.7mm guns in six beam-mounted twin turrets and four casemate mountings; the 194mm guns of the *Liberté* sub-group were in six beam-mounted single turrets and four casemate mountings.

[2.] Thomson was Navy Minister from 24 January 1905 to 25 October 1908, and therefore oversaw the design, the authorisation process and the laying down of the *Danton* class. He was also responsible for the unusual choice of names for the ships, which were named after prominent *encyclopédistes* and French revolutionary figures.

[3.] Before the advent of continuous aim, the gunners of larger guns waited for the ship to roll through the horizontal, see the target pass through the cross hairs and pull the trigger. The advent of torpedo boats demanded rapid fire, so the pointers kept moving the gun up and down in order to keep the target in the crosshairs; as soon as the weapon was loaded it was fired. This concept was then employed on even major-calibre guns, which brought with it a requirement for rapid loading and easy pointing. The latter required fast elevation and train rates combined with a system that was supple to use; this was easier to achieve with smaller weapons than with the major-calibre guns, which also had a longer firing cycle.

[4.] The official displacement of France's first dreadnoughts of the *Courbet* class would be 22,475 tonnes (normal). Dimensions would be 165m pp x 28.2m, as compared with only 145m x 25.8m for the *Dantons*.

[5.] FC Méditerranée and Penhoët were estimating 36 months for delivery of a second complete turbine installation, 45 months for a third, to which would have to be added three months for installation of the main artillery plus a further 12 months for fitting-out and trials. This implied a construction period of at least five years for the fifth and sixth ships.

[6.] For a full account of fire control equipment of French design and manufacture, and of the techniques employed to determine the range and bearing of the target, see John Spencer, *Conduite du Tir* Parts 1 & 2, *Warship* 2010 and *Warship* 2012.

[7.] *Hausse* was 'tangent elevation': the angle between the pointing of the gun in elevation and the line of aim (normally the gun sight); in practice it was the gun range. This angle was chosen to ensure that, when the target lay under the cross-wires, the gun was correctly elevated to hit the target. Tangent elevation varied with range but did not depend on pitch and roll. The transmitters would transmit range, and devices on the gun sighting gear would convert that into an angle (which in more sophisticated versions, took into account gun wear).

[8.] See the Warship Note by Gérard Prévoteaux, *Warship* 2010, pp.177-179.

THE BATTLE CRUISERS *LION* AND *TIGER* AT DOGGER BANK:
The View of the Ships' Medical Officers

The poor performance of the newly-completed battle cruiser HMS *Tiger* at the Battle of Dogger Bank was noted at the time, and various theories were advanced to explain this. While undertaking research in the Admiralty Library, **Matthew Seligmann** happened upon the Medical Officers' Journals of *Lion* and *Tiger* for 1915, which opened up a new perspective both on *Tiger*'s performance and on the treatment of casualties during the period in question.

On 24 January 1915, an engagement took place between the German First Scouting Group, led by Rear-Admiral Franz Hipper, and the British Battle Cruiser Squadron, under the command of acting Vice-Admiral Sir David Beatty. A great deal is already known about this encounter, generally known as the Battle of Dogger Bank, and many excellent analyses of it have been written.[1] However, as with any major historical event, new sources, especially ones which can offer a different perspective, are always welcome. The purpose of this article is to suggest that for the battle of Dogger Bank new insights can be provided by the formal accounts written by the Medical Officers of the Battle Cruisers HMS *Lion* and HMS *Tiger*.

It was customary in this period for the Royal Navy to allocate a specially trained medical officer to all large warships as well as to any smaller man-of-war that had to operate independently on distant stations far from any medical facilities. These officers were there for two

HMS Lion *had completed in 1912. By the outbreak of war she was fully worked up and serving as the flagship of (Acting) Vice-Admiral Sir David Beatty. Although* Lion *was hit by 16 shells at Dogger Bank as compared with only six for* Tiger *and in consequence had to pull out of the line, she sustained fewer casualties and many fewer fatalities due to the nature of the hits. (Courtesy of John Roberts)*

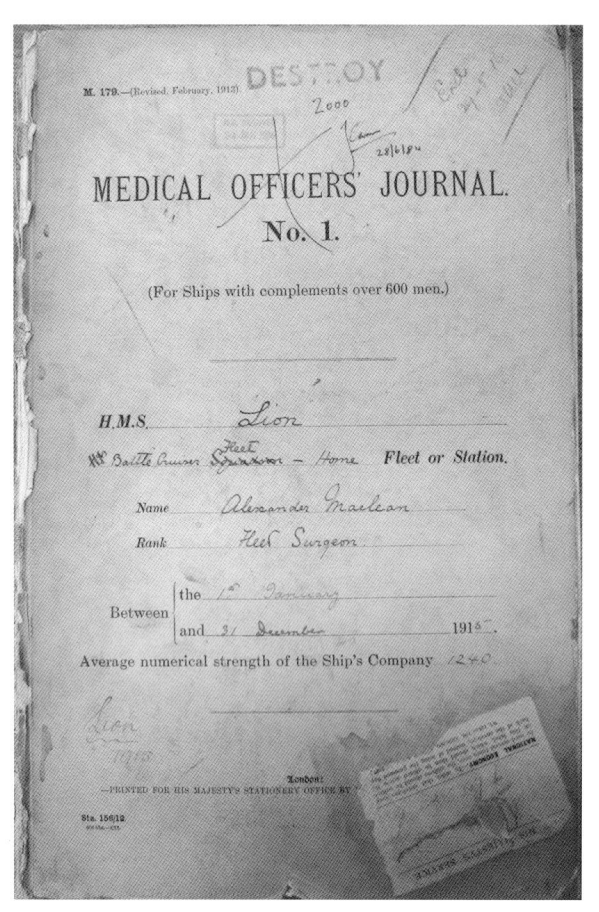

The cover of the Medical Officer's Journal (MOJ) for HMS Lion for the period 1st January to 31 December 1915. (Matthew Seligmann)

purposes: to monitor and maintain the general health of the crew when the ship was undertaking its routine business; and to provide emergency medical care for any casualties should the ship go into battle. For the better undertaking of these tasks, as well as for ensuring continuity of care should a ship's surgeon ever need to be replaced by another officer, it was necessary to keep a record of all treatments provided, and accordingly medical officers were required to produce a detailed log – officially known as the Medical Officer's Journal (MOJ) – in which were written down the names of all patients, their conditions and the treatments afforded, as well as particulars of any incident or occurrence that could affect the general health and well-being of the crew. Damage sustained in battle, being an event more likely than most to impact adversely upon the health of the ship's company, was just such a factor. Accordingly, medical officers attached to ships that both took part in an engagement and were damaged in the process not only recorded the details of the casualties they treated, they also produced an account of the battle itself as seen from their particular point of view. On this basis, one would expect the Medical Officers' Journals from HMS *Princess Royal*, *New Zealand* and *Indomitable*, all of which were unscathed at Dogger Bank, to offer little about the battle; and, indeed, they say little about it. However, HMS *Lion* and *Tiger* were repeatedly hit by enemy gunfire and, consequently, it would have been the norm for the medical officers' journals of these vessels to incorporate a mass of data about the battle, which they do. Much of this data would not be recorded anywhere else.[2]

The Medical Officer's Journals for the battle cruisers *Lion* and *Tiger* have not been extensively used before.[3] This is perhaps surprising, and is closely related to the manner of their preservation. A small sample of MOJs from this period is kept in the National Archives in Kew, West London, in the record group ADM 101. However, those from *Lion* and *Tiger* for 1915 were not chosen for inclusion in this sample when the selection process was undertaken. Instead, they were piled among the residue of unwanted examples that were then cleared for destruction. Fortunately, the value of these documents was recognised by the Royal Navy Medical Service, which declined to destroy them and, instead, deposited them at the Admiralty Library where, known to very few, they remain to this day. As a result the MOJs for *Lion* and *Tiger*, the two British battle cruisers that were most heavily engaged at Dogger Bank, still exist and can be analysed for insights into the action.[4]

Early Problems with HMS *Tiger*

One of the first matters on which these documents cast a new light is on the correlation between the health of a ship's company and the performance of that ship in combat. It has long been recognised that for HMS *Tiger* the Battle of Dogger Bank was a very unsatisfactory affair, with poor seamanship and inadequate gunnery being the principal faults exposed by that most unforgiving of examinations, the test of battle. In the post-engagement analyses conducted at the time such inefficiencies were put down to two factors. First, she was a new ship manned by sailors all of whom were unfamiliar with her and many of whom were untrained in the working of so large and complex a vessel. Secondly, the crew was, in Beatty's words, 'very mixed', with a large number of recovered deserters and other miscreants and malcontents among their number.[5]

Historians have tended to accept this judgement.[6] However, the 'Review of Health' for the year 1915 produced by *Tiger's* senior medical officer, Staff Surgeon John Reid Muir, suggests that other factors, related more to fitness and well-being, may have been at play.[7] As he explained, in the weeks and months leading up to the action with Hipper's squadron, 'the general health of the ship's company [was] in very poor condition.' In his view, the cause of this unsatisfactory state of affairs was to be found in the unfortunate circumstances surrounding her commissioning. Most new ships accepted into the Royal Navy enjoyed a protracted period in which they were both brought to martial readiness and transformed from naked steel into hospitable habitations for the crew that would live in them. However, as *Tiger* came into service at the very start of a major war, the usual opportunities did not exist to turn the vessel into a clean and comfortable living environment. Instead, the natural priority was to ready the ship for battle on the not unreasonable grounds that such an action was imminent, and all other considerations, including such an 'important point as the health of the crew', had to give way to this urgent consideration. The result, according to Muir, was that the ship's company experienced three months of 'overcrowding, overwork, damp, dirt and poor ventilation'. This produced an epidemic of tonsillitis that was 'in full swing' by the time of Dogger Bank. There were numerous other complaints, with the result that a staggering 334 men were added to the sick list in the last quarter of 1914, producing an aggregate total of 1646 crew days lost to sickness. By way of illustration, the comparable figures for the last quarter of 1915 – by which time the battle cruiser had been thoroughly cleaned, disinfected, repainted and aired – were 90 and 332 respectively. The dire state of health of the ship's company which had resulted from the need to focus immediately after commissioning first and foremost on the fighting elements of the ship to the exclusion of all else was starkly revealed in these statistics. Yet, for Muir, the official health returns for *Tiger* did not do justice to the problem. In addition to the many men 'actually incapacitated from duty by sickness,' he wrote, there were 'enormous numbers whose efficiency was materially impaired by the state of health known as being "below par"...' Indeed, in Muir's assessment, 'there seemed scarcely to be a man on board who was really fit.' What was needed was an extended period of rest and leisure, games, exercises and physical training. Unfortunately, the opportunity for this would only arise after 24 January 1915.

The Battle of Dogger Bank

Another feature that comes out clearly from the MOJs is the human costs of the battle. When discussing the physical effects of the engagement, most existing accounts of Dogger Bank tend to focus on the nature and extent of the damage inflicted on the ships. Very full descriptions are readily available of the destruction caused to participating vessels by individual and particular shell hits. These are so detailed that they often include particulars of the name and number of the compartments affected, the extent of the flooding (if any), the dimensions of those areas holed or dented, and the collateral effect of this damage on the

A fine view of HMS Tiger *fitting out at the John Brown shipyard in early October 1914. The war was already two months old.* (National Records of Scotland, courtesy of Ian Johnston)

HMS Lion Hit no.3:
Engineers' Workshop

Two 6pdr sub-calibre guns damaged, and one fell into Engineers' Workshop. The piece of armour punched out pierced the after L.P. Board. Engineers' Workshop, trunk to 'X' turret and L.P. Board flooded.

HMS Lion Hit no.5:
Torpedo Body Room

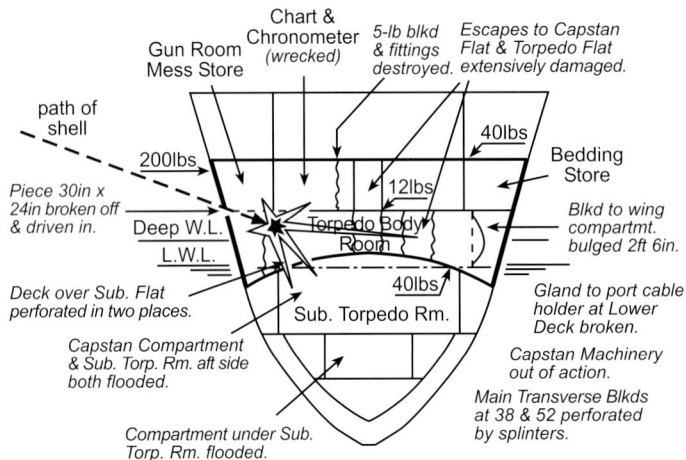

(Drawings © John Jordan 2011)

DOGGER BANK: HITS ON *LION*

Hit No.3

Position	Approximate angle of Descent	Impact	Plating at point of impact	Plates passed through	Distance of burst from point of impact	Whether deflected before bursting
Engineers' Workshop about Station 257	–	–	200-lb side armour	10-lb Main Deck below up through	Blind	Deflected downwards from 40-lb Upper Deck

Remarks: This was evidently a ricochet hit which struck the water about 15ft from the side, and punched out or destroyed a large piece of 5-inch armour plate, and did a good deal of damage along its path. It was recovered nearly whole on the main deck.

Hit No.5

Position	Approximate angle of Descent	Impact	Plating at point of impact	Plates passed through	Distance of burst from point of impact	Whether deflected before bursting
Station 40	10-15°	Unknown	200-lb side armour	Nil	6ft	No

Remarks: Burst in wing compartment abreast of Torpedo Body Room. 40-lb (protective) deck over submerged flat perforated in two places by fragments. Severe damage in Body Room, all light structure wrecked in neighbourhood of burst, and opposite side bulkhead of wing compartment bulged deeply by blast. Leaks caused in armoured structure and submerged flat, and adjacent compartment flooded.

Hits No.6 & 7

Position	Approximate angle of Descent	Impact	Plating at point of impact	Plates passed through	Distance of burst from point of impact	Whether deflected before bursting
Station 142	20°	Unknown	(1) 240-lb side armour (2) junction of 240-lb & 360-lb plates	Nil Nil	(1) 8ft (2) 2ft	No

Remarks: Much damage to light structure by both shells. Leaks caused through armoured structure and bunkers flooded. Many fragments swept across main deck; caused severe damage to this deck near ship's side.

HMS Lion Hits nos. 6 & 7: ERAs' Bathroom

Diagram annotations:
- A large portion of shell entered CPOs' Bathroom abaft ERAs', partially destroying blkd, & also Stoker POs' Bathroom (after side).
- Holes in side armour 14in (outer surface) & 42in (inner surface).
- paths of shells
- ERAs' Bathroom
- 5-lb blkd pierced.
- Indented & grooved.
- Forecastle Deck
- 40lbs
- 240lbs
- Funnel Casing
- A portion of shell passed thro' longitudinal blkd to Bathroom & perforated Funnel Casings.
- 14lbs
- 12ft of plating & framing behind armour and Main Stringer destroyed. Bath Room wrecked. Bunkers flooded in vicinity.
- Deep W.L.
- 14lbs 40lbs
- Main Deck
- L.W.L.
- Lower Deck
- 360lbs
- Hole 5ft x 4ft.
- [LOOKING FWD]

(Drawing © John Jordan 2011)

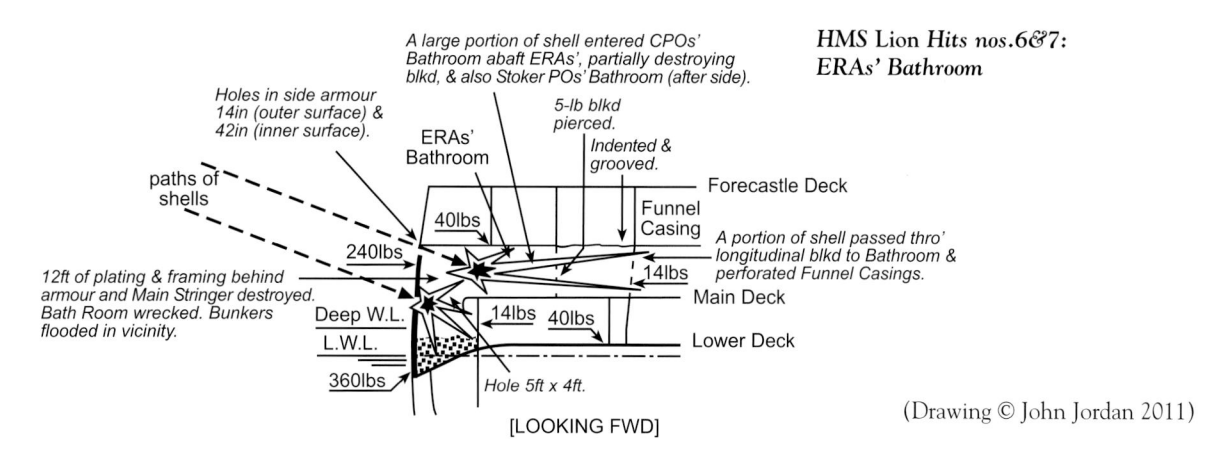

functioning of the ship.[8] Yet, no comparable assessment is made about how the people who manned these vessels were affected by these very same events. Their story, if covered at all, is generally relayed only through final casualty and fatality statistics, impersonal data that often reveals little beyond the butcher's tally, itself a number of very limited utility to naval warfare. By contrast, the information available in the MOJs allows the historian a glimpse behind the simple numbers of dead and wounded to the terrible experience that is modern naval warfare.

It is clear from the MOJs that Dogger Bank was as destructive to people as it was to ships. However, there was surprisingly little correlation between the seriousness of the damage wrought on the ships and the number of casualties inflicted on the men. As is well known, HMS *Lion* was struck by 16 heavy calibre shells and was effectively put out of action by the damage thus caused. Nevertheless, she experienced fewer casualties (and many fewer fatalities) than HMS *Tiger*, which was hit less frequently – six times by heavy shells and once by a medium calibre shell – and was never in danger of having to pull out of the battle. The reason for this discrepancy appears to be that the hits that were most destructive of human life were in general of marginal significance to the fighting efficiency of the ship; while the hits that most seriously impaired the operation of the ship were the least lethal to their respective crews. In the case of the *Lion*, the greatest concentration of casualties occurred when a shell penetrated what was referred to as 'the mess deck'. According to Fleet Surgeon Maclean, nine of his 21 patients sustained their injuries there. Yet this hit had no appreciable impact on the operation of the ship. By contrast, a subsequent hit on the torpedo body room, which punctured some piping and effectively disabled the vessel – it allowed sea water to enter the auxiliary condenser, thereby salting the boilers and making it necessary to stop the starboard engine – resulted in only two minor casualties. This very same inverse ratio of significance to death is evident in *Tiger*. Ten men died in this battle cruiser, most of them while serving in the gun-control tower or Q turret, but the ship itself was never in serious danger.

The cause and nature of the injuries sustained at Dogger Bank were varied. The least significant factor, both in terms of the severity of the wounds and the number of cases, was misadventure. Of the 22 men of HMS *Tiger* who were hurt in the engagement, most could ascribe the blame to enemy action. There were two exceptions. One was a sailor who was knocked down on the upper deck when he strayed into the path of a 13.5-inch gun that was training on its target. The impact of 76 tons of heavy ordnance and the subsequent fall fractured his shoulder.[9] The other victim of carelessness was a man who fell through an escape hatch.[10] He, too, sustained a fracture, this time of the femur. The crew of HMS *Lion* seem to have been less prone to accidents than their counterparts on the *Tiger*, but even on board this vessel there was one injury that could only partly be ascribed to direct action by the Germans. Early in the battle an 11-inch shell from the German battle cruiser *Seydlitz* struck *Lion* near the waterline and put a large hole in the side of the ship next to the engineers' workshop. Although no one was hurt by the hit, the attempt to plug the gap and so prevent the compartment from flooding would be a source of injury. As the MOJ records, one of the men involved in this attempted sealing was knocked down by the torrent of water entering the ship, sustaining contusions of the lumbar region in the process.[11]

Of course, these injuries were the exception. The vast majority of wounds were inflicted as a result of exposure to the detonation of heavy calibre ammunition. In an enclosed space a bursting shell could have a number of adverse effects, attributable for the most part either to gas

SMS *Seydlitz*, *the flagship of Vice-Admiral Franz Hipper, commanding the 1st Scouting Force. Seydlitz was responsible for many of the early hits on the British flagship before her own after turrets were disabled by a devastating cordite fire.* (Drüppel)

DOGGER BANK: HITS ON *TIGER*

Hit No.1

Position	Approximate angle of Descent	Impact	Plating at point of impact	Plates passed through	Distance of burst from point of impact	Whether deflected before bursting
'Q' turret	10-15°	60-65° to normal	130-lb turret roof plate	Nil	In plate	Greater part of shell deflected overboard after bursting

Remarks: Turret roof holed (scooped). Greater part of burst kept out, but fragments entered Turret, causing casualties and putting Turret out of action.

Hit No.2

Position	Approximate angle of Descent	Impact	Plating at point of impact	Plates passed through	Distance of burst from point of impact	Whether deflected before bursting
Station 132	Not known	Not known	360-lb side armour	Nil	On impact	No

Remarks: Probably a glancing hit on a butt joint between two 360-lb plates. Surface damage only to plates.

Hit No.3

Position	Approximate angle of Descent	Impact	Plating at point of impact	Plates passed through	Distance of burst from point of impact	Whether deflected before bursting
Station 100	10-15°	25-30° to normal	80-lb (vertical)	20-lb (deck)	9ft	No

Remarks: An important hit. Burst in Intelligence Office, causing very severe damage to light structure in neighbourhood of burst and many casualties; the position of the burst being directly under Signal Distributing Station, Conning Tower and Control Towers, and the blast killed people in the Control Towers. 60-lb deck under perforated in many places by fragments, damaging bakery, etc. 20-lb deck (over) blown upwards over wide area. Communication between Control Tower and Control Top destroyed.

Hit No.4

Position	Approximate angle of Descent	Impact	Plating at point of impact	Plates passed through	Distance of burst from point of impact	Whether deflected before bursting
Station 183	10-15°	75-80° to normal	60-lb (deckl)	Nil	4ft	No

Remarks: This shell burst after detonating, and just under 60-lb deck, tearing a large hole in this deck and causing severe damage to light structure in the neighbourhood. 20-lb deck under, perforated in many places by fragments. Side armour 240-lb not damaged.

Hit No.5

Position	Approximate angle of Descent	Impact	Plating at point of impact	Plates passed through	Distance of burst from point of impact	Whether deflected before bursting
Station 132	Not known	Not less than 15°	360-lb side armour	Nil	On impact	No

Remarks: This may have been an 11-inch **APC** shell, which could not be expected to perforate this thickness of armour at angle attack.

---

fumes, flash or blast.

The least serious of these three, at least at Dogger Bank, was smoke. Theoretically, the combustion of the bursting charge of an armoured piercing shell could suck the oxygen out of a compartment and replace it with a number of asphyxiating gases. Suffocation from the fumes and poisonous inhalation were, therefore, health threats genuinely to be reckoned with. However, although the spread of gas and fumes was not something that could be prevented in battle, the danger it posed was easily mitigated, by placing smoke pads and water to dampen them throughout the ship. As the medical officer of the *Lion* reported, these 'were found very useful and efficient when smoke and fumes became troublesome between decks' and possibly for this reason no cases of gassing were recorded on *Tiger*, and only one of the 21 patients on board *Lion* was diagnosed with respiratory problems derived from this cause and it was a very minor affliction.[12] It was, thus, the least significant cause of injury in the battle.

Burns from the flash of the explosion were a more common and obvious danger, but it was a danger that was very unevenly distributed between the two leading battle cruisers. On *Lion*, it was a surprisingly minor form of injury, with only three of the casualties suffering from any form of burns, none of which were extensive. By contrast eight of the 12 casualties on *Tiger* received burns, many of them severe. The reason for this discrepancy appears to relate to the location on board ship where the injuries were sustained. At least nine of those injured on *Lion* were hit while on what was described as the 'mess deck', by which it is presumably meant one of the many messing spaces on the upper, main or lower decks. These were larger than many of the other compartments aboard the ship and were less heavily subdivided, and, as a result, this was an area where the flash and heat from the explosion could dissipate more freely and in all directions. By contrast, those exposed on *Tiger* were mostly in smaller enclosed spaces, where the flames could not easily vent and so were hotter and more intense when they reached their victims.

Blast was the source of most of the traumas caused by

THE BATTLE CRUISERS *LION* AND *TIGER* AT DOGGER BANK: THE VIEW OF THE SHIPS' MEDICAL OFFICERS

HMS Tiger Hit no.1: 'Q' Turret

- path of shell
- Shell hit top of turret at joint of front & second plates, about 2ft from left side.
- Greater part of shell went overboard.
- Centre sight hood lifted.
- 130lbs
- Fittings damaged in gunhouse & four men injured
- Forecastle Deck
- Upper Deck
- Deep W.L.
- L.W.L.

HMS Tiger Hit no.2: 9in Belt Below Waterline

[LOOKING AFT]

- 40lbs / 60lbs / 240lbs / 240lbs / 360lbs / 14lbs / 40lbs / 60lbs
- Gun Room Galley / Seamen's Mess / p/w / coal / coal
- Plate 91 / Plate 58
- Deep W.L. / L.W.L.

Lower edge of plate 91 forced back 5/8in and a piece broken off 14in x 9in x 2¾in, and surface of plate cracked and liable to flake.
Upper edge of plate 58: a piece broken off 14in x 4in x 2¾in, and surface of plate liable to flake.

HMS Tiger Hit no.3: Distributing Office

- Gun Control Tower
- Conning Tower
- holes for access
- Signal Distribution Office
- 6in
- path of shell
- 160lbs / 80lbs / 20lbs
- Intelligence Office
- Shelter Deck
- 60lbs
- Bakery (fittings damaged)
- 20lbs
- Forecastle Deck
- Upper Deck
- Deep W.L.
- L.W.L.

HMS Tiger Hit no.4: Forecastle Deck Amidships

[LOOKING AFT]

- Deck torn for 11ft athwartships, carrying away fittings, girder shattered.
- Coal shoot wrecked.
- Boats damaged by fire, fittings in vicinity broken.
- path of shell
- Shelter Deck
- 10lbs / 60lbs
- Marines' Mess (wrecked)
- 240lbs
- Ward Room Galley / 20lbs / Gun Room Pantry
- Provision Room / 30lbs / 14lbs
- Forecastle Deck
- Upper Deck
- coal / coal
- Main Deck
- Deep W.L. / 14lbs / L.W.L.

HMS Tiger Hit no.5: Side Armour Forward

[LOOKING FWD]

- 240lbs
- 14lbs / coal / coal
- 40lbs / coal / coal (full)
- Boiler Room / coal / 360lbs
- Deep W.L. / L.W.L.

132 bulkhead plating and boundary angle buckled. 25-lb side plating forced in. Frames in vicinity deformed & rivets sheared.

Small amount of water entered abaft 132 transverse bulkhead.

shell fire. The impact from the explosion could lift a man off his feet and throw him some distance causing considerable concussion, not to say shock, disorientation and nausea. In *Lion*, ten of the wounded, including many of those caught by the hit on the mess deck, were injured in this way, suffering contusions, abrasions, bruising and dislocations of various kinds as a result. In addition, the blast waves from the explosion were often accompanied by shell fragments and/or pieces of the ship – rivets, bolts, bits of wire – that had been loosened by the detonation. In *Lion*, 11 of the casualties had wounds caused by such means, including one able seaman who was unlucky enough to be struck by a torpedo that had been dislodged

(Drawings © John Jordan 2011)

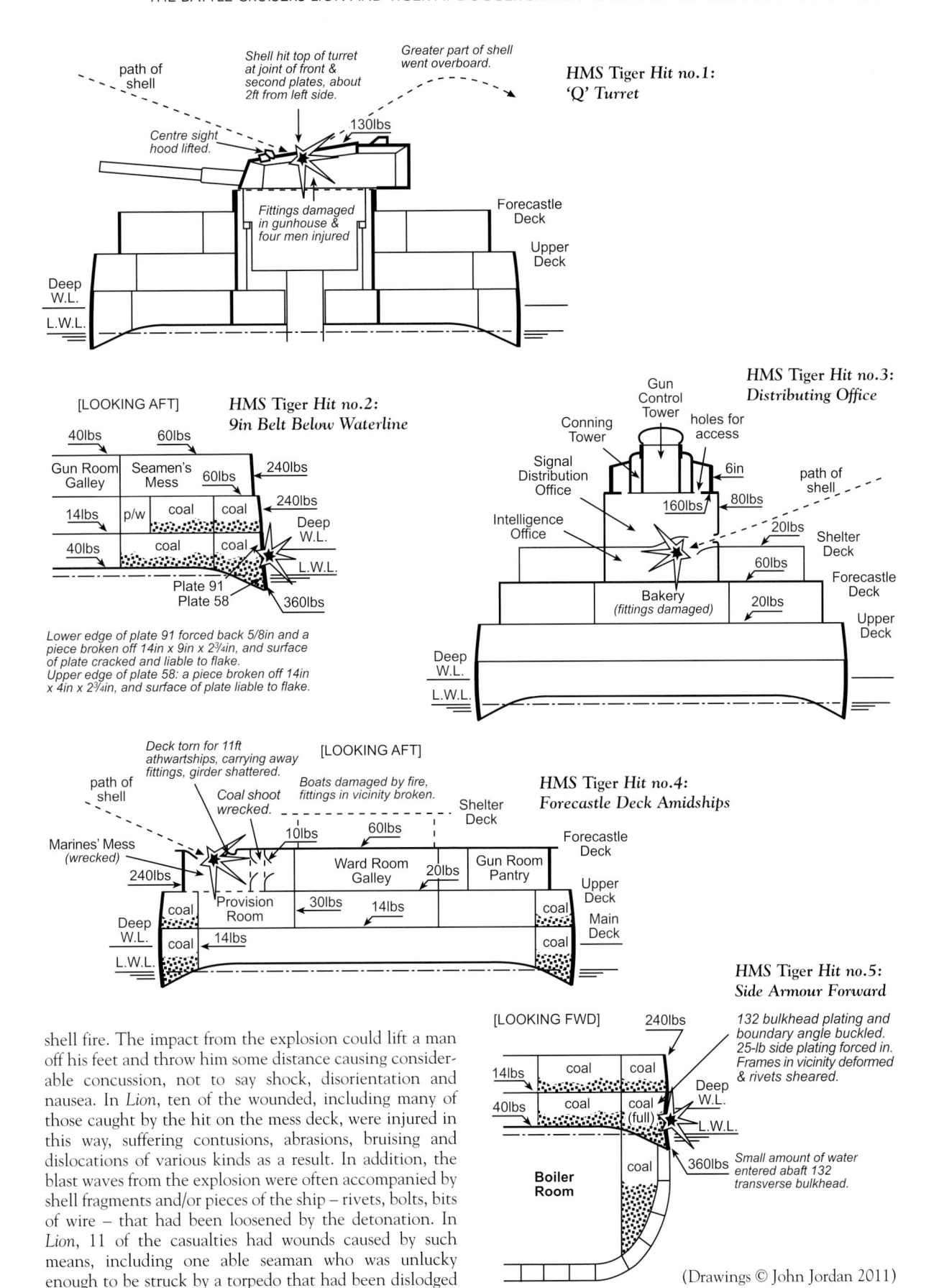

Close-up of the conning tower and 'B' turret of HMS Tiger. *One of the major hits on the ship at Dogger Bank penetrated the Signal Distributing Office, which was located directly beneath the conning tower.* (National Records of Scotland, courtesy of Ian Johnston)

from its storage slips and then fell upon him.[13] In *Tiger*, where the shells often exploded in confined spaces, blast was the source of many of the severest injuries. To give one example, a young midshipman in the gun control tower was thrown by the force of the detonation against a Dumaresq – one of his principal fire control instruments – the metal point of which was forced into his abdominal wall causing a severe lacerated wound and a fracture of the lower end of the sternum.[14] Blast was also the principal cause of all ten of the *Tiger*'s fatalities. Many of those killed were 'literally blown to bits' by the force of the explosion.[15] One officer, who was directly exposed to the blast and took the full force of the sudden expansion of air pressure, had his entire body below the waist incinerated;[16] others were so mangled as to be unrecognisable. Death in such cases was normally instantaneous, although one unfortunate rating, who had his right foot blown away and his right leg incinerated, lived long enough to be brought to the distributing station for treatment. Unsurprisingly, and possibly mercifully, he died a few minutes thereafter.[17] Where the blast was accompanied by fragments, the results could be especially horrific. One stoker, who was probably killed outright by close exposure to a bursting shell, had, in addition, a piece of shell pass through his skull. As his head was split in two, there is little doubt that if the blast had not killed him, the flying debris would certainly have done so.[18]

The Treatment of Battle Casualties

The dreadful nature of the wounds was exacerbated by the difficulties of applying treatment in battle. In theory, those injured were supposed, if able, to head for a designated dressing station to receive succour. If unable, they were meant to be stretchered there. In practice, it was not always possible to do this. Many doors and hatches were closed during combat, leaving several parts of the ship, especially sensitive areas, difficult to reach; this could restrict access to treatment. Two men, for example, were injured when a shell struck *Lion*'s forward turret. One of these was not badly hurt, experiencing only a gashed cheek and some bruising. None of these injuries impaired his mobility and so he was able to leave his post to seek help.[19] However, because the turret was sealed, the most direct route out was barred to him, and to reach a distributing station he faced the difficult task of climbing down the shell hoist in order to gain access to a suitable passageway. Although he was fit enough to do this, such a journey was quite beyond his more severely wounded shipmate. He had been struck on the skull by a piece of shell that had caused a depressed compound fracture and rendered him unconscious. As he could not be reached by a stretcher party – which could hardly ascend a hoist – or move by himself, he had to remain where he had fallen until after the battle and, therefore, effectively received no treatment until then.[20]

Even if a man could be moved, given the large size of a battle cruiser, the small number of medical personnel, and the difficulties, if communications were disrupted, of calling for help, it was not always clear how quickly the stretcher bearers would arrive to undertake this task. For this reason, those that could make it on their own to one of the two distributing stations, the designated treatment areas, invariably chose to do so, even if they were badly enough wounded to be seen less as a 'walking case' than a 'stretcher case'. One sub-lieutenant on the *Tiger* caused some surprise by walking into a dressing station unassisted despite having a deep scalp wound some 2 inches long, blood coming from the right ear, a severely cut lip, several broken teeth, a fractured lower jaw, a large flap of skin and tissue hanging off his left knee, second degree burns of his right thigh, and several puncture wounds on both legs and forearms, many of which had dirt and fabric blown into them.[21] Another man arrived on his own with a severe compound communicated fracture of the right second metacarpal, a communicated fracture of the fibula, some 40 puncture wounds over the face, upper body, arms, hands and legs, and extensive burns of the face and hands.[22] Given the mobility impairment consequent upon the leg wound, this was no mean feat.

However, whether the injured arrived at a distributing station on stretcher or under their own power, for as long as the battle was raging, the chances were that they would receive little more than first aid. For the most part, this consisted of the cleaning and disinfecting of wounds, the stopping of haemorrhaging, the application of gauze dressings and, where needed, sutures, splints and tourniquets, and the liberal administration of morphine by syringe.

Once the fighting had ceased, it was possible to consider more complex treatment, but only if the state of the warship made this possible. In *Tiger*, which was not seriously damaged, this was possible, but largely unnecessary, as all the most seriously wounded patients had already died. Additional measures consisted, therefore, mostly of injections of antistreptococcus serum and the occasional changing of splints and dressings.

On *Lion*, there were several patients in need of further treatment. The question was where to carry it out. The distributing stations, where all the injured were to be found at the close of battle, were not especially suitable locations

Lion: Medical Treatment Facilities

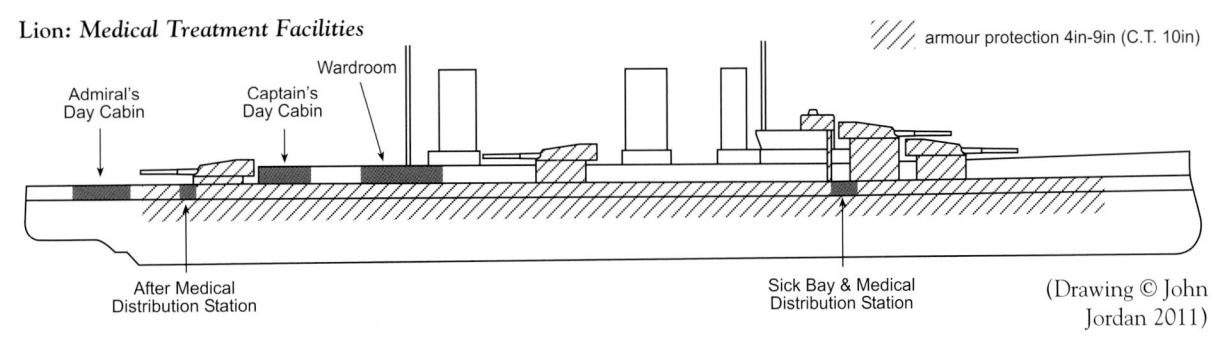

Diagram labels: Admiral's Day Cabin; Captain's Day Cabin; Wardroom; After Medical Distribution Station; Sick Bay & Medical Distribution Station; armour protection 4in-9in (C.T. 10in)

(Drawing © John Jordan 2011)

for this. They had been selected purely as places to receive the wounded, being parts of the ship that were not needed for fighting, but which were under armour protection and large enough to accommodate multiple casualties and the sick berth staff needed to tend to them. They served this purpose admirably during the battle, but one of them was now beginning to flood, rendering a move imperative and, in any case, it had never been intended that they would be the sites for any after-battle-care. This was supposed to take place in a number of pre-selected sites: large, airy venues such as the wardroom, the Captain's cabin and the Admiral's cabin. German gunnery had, however, put paid to any such ideas. All the pre-selected areas had been splintered by shellfire and had water seeping in. In the end, the site selected was the sick bay.

The sick bay, despite any impression given by its name, was not an especially suitable area for after-battle treatment. Designed as a venue for seeing and dealing with a regular flow of a few daily patients in peace-time, it was much smaller than was desirable for holding and treating multiple casualties all at the same time. If used for this purpose, patients would have to be very close together, so close, in fact, that they would be able to witness the procedures carried out on their shipmates. On the other hand, it was undamaged, relatively free of seawater, and well supplied with medical stores. In the absence of any other obvious choice, it became the hub of medical treatment in *Lion* after Dogger Bank.

Finding a site for treatment would be just the first problem for *Lion*'s medical staff. The shellfire that damaged the pre-selected sites was also responsible for putting the ship's dynamos out of action. This led to a total loss of power that, among other things, caused the failure of electric lighting throughout the ship. As concussion had also blown out many of the oil lamps, this plunged much of the area between decks into darkness. As a result, until electric power could be restored, medical operations on the stricken battle cruiser had to be conducted first by candle light and then, when they became available, through the illumination of portable electric lamps. This was hardly ideal.

Equally unhelpful, enemy action had damaged the pipes

Wounded from HMS Tiger *on board HMHS* Plassey *following the later Battle of Jutland; note the number of 'flash' casualties.* (National Museum of the Royal Navy)

that distributed fresh water around the ship, cutting off the flow to the sick bay entirely. The water needed for the patients had to brought in kettles to the sick bay from some considerable distance, a process that was time consuming and led, in Fleet Surgeon Maclean's words, to a situation where water 'was so scarce on board that one had to be as economical as possible.' Hot water, it may be noted, was even harder to obtain, as it had to be boiled in the galley and carried to the sick bay. This, too, rendered the treatment of the wounded very difficult. Labouring under these adverse conditions, it was probably as much a relief to the physicians as it was to the patients when the ship reached port and the wounded could be discharged ashore to naval hospitals.

If the medical officers of the *Lion* had difficulties in arranging treatment, a different problem occupied their counterparts on *Tiger*, namely identifying the dead. Because the German shells that struck this vessel had often detonated in small fully enclosed spaces, there had been nowhere for the blast to vent and, thus, those in the vicinity of these hits had generally been struck by the full force of the explosion. In such circumstances, bodies were often mangled beyond recognition. In such cases, the ship's medical staff were sometimes able to identify a body only via 'a process of exclusion'.[23] In other cases, they looked for personal effects for a clue to exactly who had been killed. This could prove misleading. The body of one unfortunate stoker was identified through a name stamp on an article of clothing he had been wearing. However, Staff Surgeon Muir evidently had doubts about the reliability of such a method of identification and asked the Senior Engineer to muster his men. This revealed that the owner of the said clothing had lent it to a comrade and that it was the borrower not the owner who was lying in unrecognisable pieces in the temporary mortuary. Fortunately this error was discovered before the names of the dead were telegraphed ashore, ensuring that the Navy did not notify the wrong family of the loss.[24]

Conclusion

In his summary of the Battle of Dogger Bank, Rear-Admiral Chalmers, one of Beatty's early biographers, notes that 'total British casualties were fifteen killed and thirty-two wounded'.[25] This statistic compared favourably to the German losses of over 1,000 souls, most of whom were lost either on the ill-fated *Blücher* or in the cordite fire that destroyed the after turrets of the *Seydlitz*, and is, therefore, not entirely without utility in understanding the outcome of the engagement. However, for all that, it is remarkably bland. It says nothing at all about the fearsome experience of naval warfare. Nor does it convey what it meant to be one of those numbers. The Medical Officers' Journals for *Lion* and *Tiger* give some depth to such raw data. They allow a battle that is normally interpreted through its impact on armour plate and machinery to be understood in terms of its effect on flesh, blood and bone.

Acknowledgements:
The author would like to thank John Roberts for his help in matching up the shell hits as described in the after-battle reports and various other more contemporary sources with the diagrams contained in the 'Final Report of the President, Projectile

Tiger *on the Tyne, 6 February 1915, where she was sent for repairs after the battle. Note the three-tone paint scheme.* Tiger *had arrived early on Monday 1 February, being towed stern-first up the river, to secure alongside Armstrong's yard, at Bill Quay. The wounded were discharged to hospital and 48 hours' leave was given to all men who lived within 4 hours journey time of Newcastle, the remainder of the crew then being engaged in refitting the ship. Divers spent much of the next few days working on the propellers, and examining the ship's bottom and underwater fittings. A launch was borrowed from HMS Victorious, which had recently paid off, presumably to replace one lost in the battle.* Tiger *departed at 20.00 on 8 February, arriving at Scapa the following day, where she immediately embarked on an intensive programme of training and exercises, before returning to Rosyth on 19 February.* (Photograph courtesy of Conrad Waters)

Lion *returns to Invergordon, March 1915, after repairs. Note the new three-tone paint scheme, similar to that on* Tiger *(opposite). She had also acquired a director for her main armament.* (Imperial War Museum, SP510)

Committee, 1917' (TNA: ADM 186/166). Dr John Brooks and Stephen McLaughlin were kind enough to read an earlier draft of the manuscript and make some very helpful suggestions. The Editor would like to thank Byron Angel for making available the drawings of the shell hits from the Projectile Committee's report, which have been adapted to illustrate this article.

Footnotes:

1. Among their number are: Brian Schofield, 'Jacky Fisher, HMS *Indomitable* and the Dogger bank Action: A Personal Memoir', in Gerald Jordan (ed.), *Naval Warfare in the Twentieth century* (London, 1977); Geoffrey Bennett, *Naval Battles of the First World War* (London, 1974), pp.141-50; Andrew Gordon, *The Rules of the Game: Jutland and the Naval Command* (London, 2000), pp.94-5; Paul G. Halpern, *A Naval History of World War I* (London, 1994), pp.44-7; James Goldrick, *The King's Ships were at Sea: The War in the North Sea, August 1914-February 1915* (Annapolis, MD, 1984).

2. Short medical reports were appended to the after-action summaries produced by the captains of these vessels, but these are brief and lacking in detail. The Medical Report for *Lion* by Fleet Surgeon Alexander Mclean has been reproduced in Brian Ranft (ed.), *The Beatty Papers: Selections from the Private and Official Correspondence of Admiral of the Fleet Earl Beatty*, (two Volumes, Navy Records Society, 1989-93), I, pp.239-40.

3. They do not, for example, appear in David McLean's vivid new study of naval medical officers, a study which does not touch on the issues surrounding naval medicine at Dogger Bank. See, David McLean, *Surgeon's of the Fleet: The Royal Navy and its Medics from Trafalgar to Jutland* (London, 2010).

4. Except where otherwise noted, all the information about the battle comes from the Medical Officers' Journals for 1915 of the battle cruisers *Lion* and *Tiger*, which were viewed at The Admiralty Library, Portsmouth. Before being provided with access to these documents the author was required to sign a data protection form. As a result, the personal details of individual patients will not be revealed in what follows. However, the case numbers used by the Medical Officers in the journals will be cited in the footnotes to this article to enable other scholars to check the information, should they so wish.

5. Beatty to Hamilton, 17 and 21 February 1915. Ranft, *Beatty Papers*, I, pp.249 and 260-1.

6. Marder, FGDN, II, pp.170-1.

7. Although he did discuss the battle, Muir did not develop this point in his autobiography. J.R. Muir, *Years of Endurance* (London, 1936).

8. See, for example, N.J.M. Campbell, *Battlecruisers: The Design and Development of British and German Battlecruisers of the First World War Era* (London, 1978). This excellent volume includes detailed and extremely useful descriptions of the damage to the ships that fought at Dogger Bank but, justifiably given the title, tends to ignore the human dimension.

9. *Tiger*, Case No. 33.
10. *Tiger*, Case No. 15.
11. *Lion*, Case No. 21.
12. *Lion*, Case No.9.
13. *Lion*, Case No. 12.
14. *Tiger*, Case No.16.
15. *Tiger*, Case No.27.
16. *Tiger*, Case No.18.
17. *Tiger*, Case No. 23.
18. *Tiger*, case No. 20.
19. *Lion*, Case No.15.
20. *Lion*, Case No.8.
21. *Tiger*, Case No.32.
22. *Tiger*, Case No.34.
23. *Tiger*, Case No.27.
24. *Tiger*, Case No.22.
25. Rear-Admiral W. S. Chalmers, *The Life and Letters of David, Earl Beatty* (London, 1951), p.192.

MODERN EUROPEAN OFFSHORE PATROL VESSELS

Faced with the increasing cost of regular warships, many navies are investing in Offshore Patrol Vessels built to commercial standards for low-level security missions. **Conrad Waters** looks at four key designs which have entered service in the last few years.

One of the most significant trends in naval procurement in recent years has been the growth in importance of the purpose-built offshore patrol vessel (OPV). Although enjoying a much lower profile than, for example, modern air-independent propulsion equipped submarines or front-line surface escorts, these relatively inexpensive but hugely important warships occupy one of the fastest expanding segments of the world market for naval vessels. Whilst this trend is apparent across the world, it is particularly notable in Europe. Here, programmes for new offshore patrol vessels have largely survived the curtailment in construction that has accompanied the recent financial crisis. This short review aims to explain the factors behind this procurement phenomenon and assess how they have impacted on designs recently completed by four of the region's major navies.

Factors Influencing OPV Procurement

The term 'offshore patrol vessel' has been used to describe a range of warships, including sophisticated corvette-type war-fighting vessels with advanced combat management capabilities and an extensive range of weapons and sensors. However, the true OPV – accounting for the majority of ships currently under construction – is probably best categorised as a more basic warship primarily intended for lower-intensity policing operations. The capability of the ship's weapons systems is therefore often secondary to other qualities, such as economy of operation and endurance. Equally, commercial building practices are often adopted for cost-effectiveness. Across the world many of these ships are operated by paramilitary coast guard forces, most notably in the United States, Japan, India and South Korea. European practice has more frequently seen these ships integrated into the regular naval service, often forming the low end of a spectrum of naval capabilities.

Whilst there are many reasons for the increase in the OPV's popularity, a key driving force has been the considerable expansion in national maritime rights and responsibilities that have accompanied the present United

A computer-generated image of the new German F-125 type frigate of the Baden-Württemberg class, which has been specifically designed to support prolonged medium-intensity operations. Whilst few nations can afford specialised ships of this nature, many European fleets have designed their new offshore patrol vessels with an eye to international stabilisation missions. (German Navy)

Nations Convention on the Law of the Sea (UNCLOS). Concluded in 1982 but not taking effect until November 1994, the current UNCLOS III regime formally adopted the concept of a national Exclusive Economic Zone (EEZ). This essentially gives states sole rights to marine resources up to 200 nautical miles from their coasts.[1] The extension of sovereign rights beyond previous maritime boundaries – frequently limited to 12nm territorial waters – has been accompanied by a need to acquire assets to monitor and protect resources such as fisheries, oil, gas and other minerals contained within this enlarged area of national interest. The requirement was often initially met by extending the duties of coastal patrol vessels or revising the roles of existing ships such as light frigates to provide a longer-range patrol capability. However, neither solution is altogether desirable in terms of either economy or efficiency. This has given rise to more bespoke approaches.

MODERN EUROPEAN OFFSHORE PATROL VESSELS

The British 'River' class offshore patrol vessel Tyne *leads her two sisters on exercise early in 2012. The 'River' class design provides a relatively simple, seaworthy ship with high levels of operational availability for EEZ patrols.* (UK/MOD Crown Copyright 2012)

Broader issues relating to cost and force structure are also playing a part in new OPV construction, particularly within Europe. The end of the Cold War and the more recent economic crisis has meant that it has been impossible to replace the large number of surface escorts maintained by many European fleets on a like-for-like basis. This has made the acquisition of cheaper ships with lower ongoing running costs more attractive for secondary missions: a situation which is likely to persist for some time to come. Equally, the increased importance of asymmetrical threats such as those posed by terrorists or pirates in the new post-'9/11' global environment, as well as the absence of a direct maritime threat in home waters, has resulted in a number of European fleets rebalancing their structures to place greater emphasis on so-called 'stabilisation' missions. An extreme example of this process is being seen in Germany. Here Cold War-era escorts are being replaced by the new, 7,000-ton F-125 frigates of the *Baden-Württemberg* class that give priority to the requirements of extended deployment on medium-intensity operations for up to two years away from home.[2] With few European fleets able to justify the substantial investment needed for such large and sophisticated ships, the offshore patrol vessel is a practical solution to this emerging operational requirement.

The OPV designs that have emerged as a result of these broad influences have also inevitably been impacted by specific national requirements, even within the confines of Europe. For example, the Irish Naval Service's PV80 (*Róisín*) and modified PV90 patrol vessels reflect the fact that the country's substantial EEZ extends far into the harsh waters of the North Atlantic. The need to maintain a continuous naval presence in this challenging maritime environment has placed a premium on seaworthiness in adverse weather conditions, along with adequate range, over other capabilities. The ice-strengthened Danish offshore patrol vessels of the *Knud Rasmussen* class, which are largely assigned to sovereignty patrols around Greenland, have arguably been built for an even more specialised role. However, Denmark's 'Stanflex' system of modularised mission payloads gives them much more operational flexibility than this primary function might suggest. A wider trend has been the development of basic OPV designs that can be modified for a range of uses. An example is Portugal's NPO2000 *Viana do Castelo* class. This can be ordered as a specialised anti-pollution (NPC) variant in addition to the standard OPV specification.

In short, whilst a number of common themes have been driving OPV acquisition, varying priorities – and philosophies – have meant that the resultant ships have been built to widely different specifications. This is the case

79

even for European navies with broadly similar overall mission profiles and fleet structures. Some of the different design solutions arrived at, and the reasons behind them, are demonstrated by the four specific classes selected in this article for more detailed consideration.

United Kingdom: 'River' Class

Three 'River' class offshore patrol vessels were ordered from the then Vosper Thornycroft in May 2001.[3] The contract was placed as part of the British Royal Navy's Future Offshore Patrol Vessel (FOPV) programme and followed an unsolicited Vosper Thornycroft bid to replace five remaining 'Island' class OPVs with more economic and reliable units. The first vessel of the class, *Tyne*, was laid down at the Woolston yard in Southampton in September 2001 and she was delivered in January 2003. The two other ships, *Severn* and *Mersey*, followed at roughly six-monthly intervals.

The design of the 'River' class was based on Vosper Thornycroft's EEZ Management Vessel concept. The intention was to produce a simple, seaworthy ship capable of providing high levels of operational availability for low intensity policing duties, principally fishery protection, at a cost-effective price. The result has been a relatively large, seaworthy vessel displacing 1,800 tonnes at full load and 80m in length that has been built largely to commercial shipbuilding standards.[4] It features a double chine hull form for simplified construction, with a fine ram bow to assist good sea-keeping. This basic simplicity extends to a propulsion system that pairs two MAN 12RK 270 diesel engines to two controllable pitch propellers. They provide a modest sustained sea speed of c.16.5 knots but an excellent range: more than 7,800 nautical miles (14,400km) at 12 knots. The relatively low speed is counterbalanced by the provision of two rigid inflatable boats (RIBs) for rapid interception and associated boarding operations, with installation of a semi-active stabiliser tank assisting their deployment. The class is also equipped with a bow thruster to improve manoeuvrability. There is sufficient storage capacity to support deployments of up to twenty-one days' duration.

The 'River' class's basic commercial design has only a minimal overlay of military specifications – for example in the area of damage control. Armament is similarly modest, consisting of a single 20mm gun forward of the bridge and additional light machine guns. There is no combat management suite, only a limited outfit of navigation radars and no helicopter landing or maintenance facilities. To some extent, this approach is a reflection of the Royal Navy's longstanding determination to resist any blurring of the distinction between its front-line surface combatants – capable of undertaking a full spectrum of naval missions – and secondary vessels intended for specialised or auxiliary, non war-fighting roles.

Tyne leads one of her 'River' class sisters in coastal waters during 2011. The class is built to commercial standards with a modest overlay of military equipment, including an armament comprising one 20mm canon and light machine guns. (UK/MOD Crown Copyright 2011)

MODERN EUROPEAN OFFSHORE PATROL VESSELS

River Class – Batch 2: Clyde (UK)

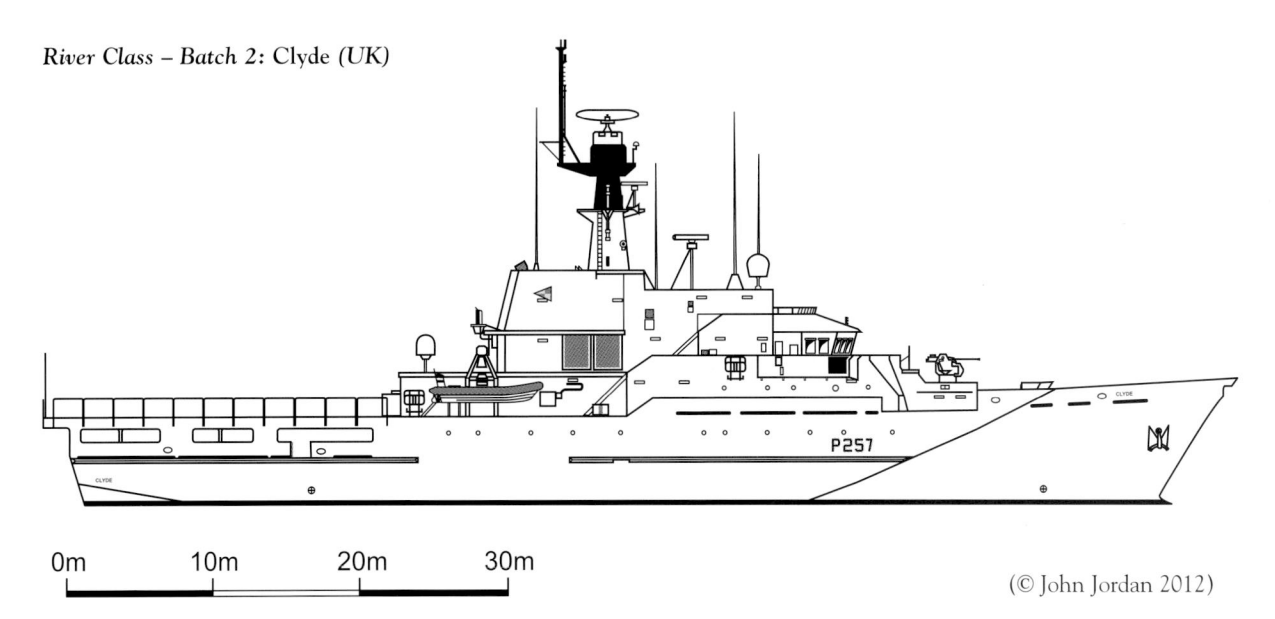

(© John Jordan 2012)

Investment has, however, been channelled towards those areas directly relevant to the policing role, notably an extensive communications outfit encompassing comprehensive radio and satellite links. Operational flexibility is provided by provision of a large working deck and heavy crane at the aft end of the ship, which can handle and accommodate up to seven containers with various equipment outfits. These could be used, for example, to provide medical facilities in response to a civil emergency or to support diving or mine-countermeasures operations in a peacekeeping or conflict scenario.[5]

Whilst the 'River' class are clearly well-designed ships that are well-suited for their intended policing role, it is probably the support arrangements that underpin their operation that have been most influential. Vosper Thornycroft's original bid for the FOPV programme

A profile view of Tyne *in the summer of 2011. Key design features include a ram bow to facilitate good sea-keeping, an excellent communications outfit and a large working deck aft where containers with specialised mission equipment can be stowed.* (Conrad Waters)

The sole 'Modified River' class OPV Clyde is an upgraded variant of the basic 'River' design ordered for Falkland Island patrol duties. Improvements include a surveillance radar and a basic combat management system, a larger gun and a landing platform to support helicopter operations. (Conrad Waters)

comprised an arrangement under which it would finance the design and construction of the new ships, chartering them to the UK Ministry of Defence (MOD) for an initial period of five years. Additionally, a linked contractor logistic support (CLS) agreement committed the company to ensuring a minimum level of operational availability – 320 days per annum – that was essentially double that of the ships being replaced. This proposal, reportedly valued at c.£60m (US$95m), essentially allowed the MOD to maintain an equivalent level of patrol cover with three new ships compared with five older vessels. At the same time it avoided the immediate capital outlay involved in investing in new equipment.

Although there has been considerable debate about the comparative benefits of purchasing and leasing military equipment, it seems that the main driver behind the original charter component of the deal was the short-term cash saving achieved by the MOD rather than any longer term economic gain. This contention has been given additional weight by a decision first announced in May 2012 and confirmed in September of the same year to purchase the three ships outright for £39m (US$60m) to save annual lease payments of £7m (US$11m). By way of contrast, the CLS agreement has been an undoubted success. The contractual, fixed price nature of the obligation undertaken has provided the contractor with a strong incentive to achieve support efficiencies whilst ensuring the level of operational availability guaranteed by the arrangement has been achieved in practice. At the same time, the Royal Navy has developed more flexible operating concepts to ensure the vessels are deployed to best effect. This has included a three-watch manning system under which each OPV's thirty-strong crew is drawn from a pool of forty-five personnel allocated to each ship to maximise time at sea. Most significantly, the CLS availability arrangements pioneered with the 'River' class have been steadily extended, in modified format, to maintenance of front-line Royal Navy major surface ships under the Class Output Management (COM) concept. This is providing the fleet with much greater certainty with respect to future support costs while reportedly producing savings of between 10-15 per cent compared with the previous maintenance regime.

Although clearly intended for the lowest intensity policing missions, the 'River' class is also indicative of the increased scope for adaptability that is an increasingly important feature of recent OPV designs. This is demonstrated by development of the basic 'River' class to meet a requirement for a new Falkland Islands patrol vessel with upgraded surveillance and war-fighting potential. The resultant modified 'River' class OPV *Clyde* was ordered in February 2005 and delivered from Vosper Thornycroft's new facility at Portsmouth in January 2007. She departed for her assigned operating area in August 2007 after a period of further trials and training. Whilst built to the original class's largely commercial specifications, she features a Danish Terma Scanter 4100 air and surface surveillance radar and a downscaled variant of the CMS-1 combat management system also found in the high-end Type 45 air defence destroyers. Other enhancements comprise a more potent 30mm gun and a landing platform to support helicopter operations, along with associated fin stabilisers. The 'River' class has also been used as the basis of the larger, 90m *Port of Spain* class design that has been exported to Brazil and Thailand.

France – 'Gowind' Type L'Adroit

A somewhat higher level of capability than that provided by the British 'River' class is represented by France's *L'Adroit*, which forms the lower end of a new family of 'Gowind' vessels encompassing the offshore patrol vessel, corvette and light frigate categories.[6] The 'Gowind' concept was created to re-establish the presence of French shipbuilder DCNS in this important segment of the market following a previous focus on more sophisticated warships and submarines. As part of this initiative, DCNS decided to construct a prototype vessel with its own funds that would be loaned to the French Navy for three years to publicise the new design concept. Work on the resultant *L'Adroit* started at Lorient in Brittany in May 2010, and launch followed just over a year later. Sea trials commenced in July 2011 and the ship was handed over to the *Marine Nationale* on 21 October of the same year.

L'Adroit is very much a product of the new, post-'9/11' security environment. As such, her intended mission profile encompasses a broader range of maritime operations – such as anti-piracy and anti-terrorist deployments – than that envisaged for the 'River' class, which are deployed to police a maritime zone that is essentially free from any significant threat. At the same time, the cost constraints that were a key determinant of the British ships' design remain a very significant factor. The result has been the adoption of design and construction practices that have been heavily influenced by those used in commercial shipbuilding. However, these have been supplemented by recourse to a range of technology, much of it quite innovative, that places a much greater emphasis on the maintenance of maritime security in an unstable environment, particularly in littoral waters.

The result is a distinctive, flush decked design with a length of 87m and a full load displacement of c.1,500 tonnes that is dominated by a tall, central island structure providing 360 degree vision by virtue of a single, integrated mast and panoramic bridge. This also provides accommodation for a light helicopter or for unmanned aerial vehicles (UAVs) that can be operated from a large flight deck immediately abaft the bridge structure. Twin ramps in the stern, modified from commercial shipping practice, permit the safe and speedy launch of RIBs in adverse weather conditions. In the words of DCNS, the 'Gowind' type OPV provides, '…a compromise between aesthetics, performance and costs.'

Although *L'Adroit* is as lightly armed as her British counterparts – her main armament is a 20mm gun, supplemented by 12.7mm heavy machine guns – this disguises the sophistication of the ship's overall capabilities. At the heart of these is the new POLARIS combat management system. This has been specifically developed by DCNS to integrate the radar, communications equipment and weapons systems of OPV-sized vessels. In essence, *L'Adroit* can use POLARIS to collect and coordinate information gathered from the sensors located on

France's L'Adroit *represents a somewhat higher level of OPV capability than that provided by Britain's 'River class'. A distinctive feature is her panoramic bridge and integrated mast, which provides excellent surveillance characteristics.* (DCNS)

and within the integrated mast, from remotely deployed assets such as unmanned vehicles or Special Forces operating from the ship's RIBs, and from external sources communicated by data links. This provides a clear picture of the ship's operating environment by means of multi-function console displays. This clarity of information is particularly important for minimally-manned warships such as OPVs – *L'Adroit* has a core crew of just thirty-two personnel. POLARIS can also be integrated with DCNS' MATRICS maritime traffic intelligence system, which detects suspicious course profiles automatically, whilst a further 'add on' allows the control of guns and surface-to-surface missiles.

L'Adroit's principal radar systems are supplied by Danish company Terma. They comprise a Scanter 4102 medium range air/surface surveillance radar similar to that fitted on *Clyde* and a shorter range Scanter 6002 system. The two radars share a single 10ft antenna, which is located within the composite cone of the integrated mast. In addition to providing search and surveillance capabilities out to around 100 nautical miles, they can also be used for helicopter and UAV guidance. Radar surveillance is supplemented by a Thales electronic support measures suite encompassing the Vigile system for detecting radar emissions (R-ESM) and the ALTESSE system for commu-

Gowind Control Type: L'Adroit (France)

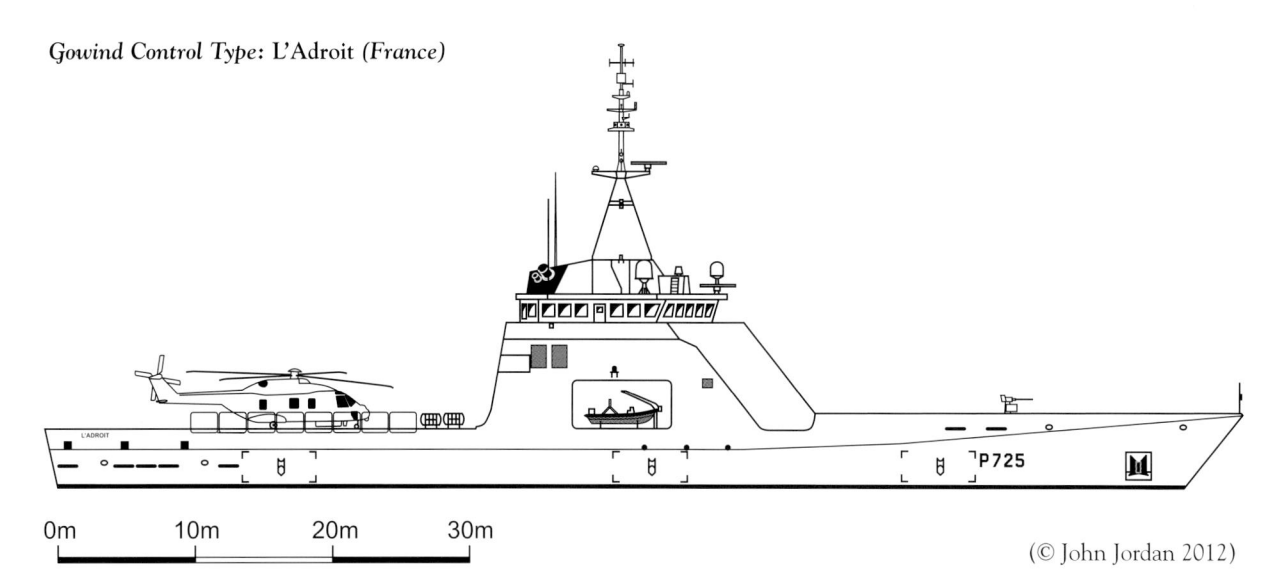

(© John Jordan 2012)

nications intercepts (C-ESM). Thales also supplies the integrated communications suite, encompassing comprehensive radio and satellite links. Other key sensors include a Sagem EOMS multi-function optronic unit, which combines infrared tracking with electro-optical gunfire control, and the FLIR Talon thermal imaging system. Lacroix SYLENA lightweight decoy launchers are installed to combat surface-to-surface missiles with radar or infrared guidance. The overall intention appears to be to provide a similar range of capabilities to those found on

A stern view of L'Adroit showing the twin ramps used for launching small boats, which have been modified from commercial practice. A strong focus on cost reduction means that most modern OPV classes are heavily reliant on techniques used in merchant shipbuilding. (DCNS)

L'Adroit pictured launching a RIB type interceptor from one of her stern ramps. Fast interceptors, helicopters and, increasingly, UAVs are becoming an increasingly important part of modern OPV capabilities. (DCNS)

front-line surface combatants such as the new FREMM type multi-mission frigates: however, many of the systems are scaled down or otherwise have more limited effectiveness in recognition both of economy and of the lower threat environment in which an OPV such as *L'Adroit* will typically operate.

This need to balance performance and cost is also reflected in allowing a considerable degree of flexibility in determining precise equipment fit depending on the requirements – and depth of pocket – of a particular customer. For example, *L'Adroit* is equipped with an adequate but relatively simple twin diesel engine power plant based on the Anglo Belgian Corporation's DZC series which provides a maximum speed of over 20 knots and range of around 8,000 miles at 12 knots. However, this can be replaced by a more powerful propulsion system for greater speed or a combined diesel or electric (CODOE) installation to give greater operational flexibility. It is also possible to provide the ship with greater war-fighting capability through installation of a larger-calibre gun, whilst there is also scope for installing surface-to-surface missiles forward of the bridge. Provision of a total of fifty-nine berths – nearly double those required by the core crew – ensures that it is relatively easy to support additional systems in addition to facilitating disaster recovery or Special Forces operations. Interestingly, the *Marine Nationale* has decided to build on the Royal Navy's practice with the 'River' class by assigning two crews to the vessel. They will rotate every four months with the objective of ensuring at sea availability of 220 days per annum.

L'Adroit is essentially a demonstrator for the potential of the broader 'Gowind' family, as well as for the technologies supplied by DCNS' various partners in the project. The main hope for the design appears to compensate for limited prospects for further immediate orders in the French domestic market by tapping the growing market that exists for OPV-type vessels around the world.[7] Nevertheless, the ongoing withdrawal of French P400-type colonial patrol vessels and increasing age of the larger A69 corvettes suggests that the *Marine Nationale* will also eventually have a need for ships of this type to supplement the more sophisticated FREMM multi-mission frigates if the money can be found. In both cases, however, it seems likely that any ships that are eventually ordered will feature significant differences from the prototype vessel to meet specific national role requirements. As such, *L'Adroit* may well represent a unique, 'one off'.

Spain – Buque de Acción Marítima (BAM) Type

Broadly similar in concept to *L'Adroit* – but arguably representing a further uplift in capability – is the Spanish Navy's *Buque de Acción Marítima* or BAM. Designed to deploy on operations against asymmetric threats in low-intensity scenarios as well as carrying out surveillance and

The lead Spanish Buque de Acción Marítima (BAM) *type OPV* Meteoro *was commissioned in 2011. The type falls somewhere between the traditional OPV and light frigate categories, being capable of global deployment in support of low-intensity operations.* (Navantia)

A September 2011 image of the Spanish BAM Rayo. The class has only modest offensive weaponry but features a good range of sensors and communications systems, controlled by the Spanish Navy's generic SCOMBA combat management system. A large flight deck and hangar allows operation of a large variety of helicopters and UAVs. (Navantia)

policing duties, the class was intended to replace a wide range of vessels ranging from light frigates to coastal patrol vessels. As for Portugal's NPO2000 *Viana do Castelo* class, the basic design was given sufficient flexibility to be adaptable to other tasks. More specifically, hydrographic, intelligence gathering and submarine support variants were initially envisaged. The original programme encompassed between twelve and fourteen units of the class, of which four would be specialist types. However, it seems that this total will be significantly curtailed as a result of Spain's current financial problems. An initial batch of four ships was authorised in 2005. These were ordered from builder Navantia's yards in the Bay of Cadiz in July 2006 under a contract reportedly valued at c.€350m (c.US$450m). The first ship, *Meteoro*, was launched in October 2009 and commissioned on 28 July 2011. The other three vessels followed her into service over the succeeding twelve months. Although a further batch of five vessels, including a hydrographic ship and a submarine rescue ship, was authorised at a reported cost of c.€740m in 2011, these have yet to be contracted.[8]

With a length of 94m and a full load displacement in the region of 2,600 tonnes, *Meteoro* is a significantly larger ship than her French counterpart. This may be a reflection of a greater emphasis on oceanic patrol duties than for *L'Adroit*: Spanish interests extend to the Balearics and the Canaries and it is planned to base the initial vessels in the latter islands. The size of the hull – together with its basic modular design – also makes adaption to alternative missions somewhat easier than would otherwise be the case. Another key design difference with the French ship is the adoption of a CODOE propulsion arrangement in all vessels of the class. The plant comprises two MTU 16V 1163 diesel engines with a total power output of c.10MW and two 750kW Siemens electric motors linked to an electrical network powered by four MTU 12V 2000 generators. The diesel engines are used for medium and high speed transit, whilst the electric motors allow low speed operation whilst loitering in a patrol area. Although the maximum range of 8,000 nautical miles at 15 knots is similar to other classes, the electric propulsion permits extended economical endurance whilst on patrol.

Other aspects of the BAM design show a marked similarity to *L'Adroit*. These include the adoption of commercial construction practices to reduce capital outlay, a focus on automation to minimise crew size and other through-life costs, and the incorporation of a range of military technologies designed largely to ensure effective operation during low-intensity missions. The basic hull design has been built to Bureau Veritas standards and has a largely longitudinal structure for ease of construction. There has been a particular focus on safety and ship survivability which extends to the propulsion system and auxiliary services. An integrated platform management system reduces manning requirements, with the core crew comprising around thirty-five personnel.[9] This compares with the crew of almost 120 needed to operate one of the *Descubierta* class light frigates of the previous generation.

Buque de Acción Maritima (BAM): Meteoro (Spain)

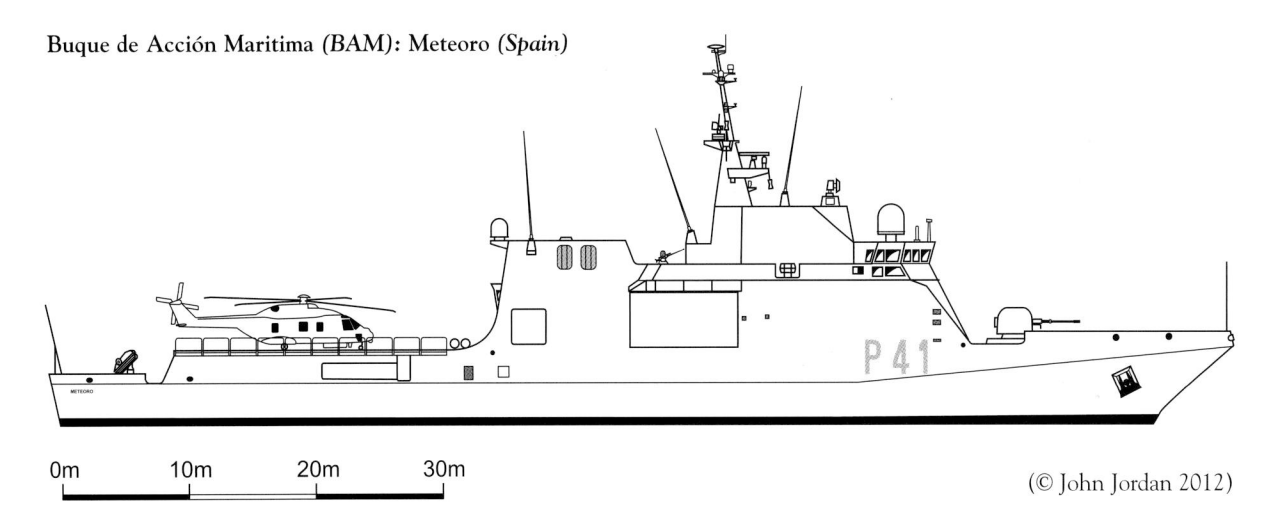

(© John Jordan 2012)

There is, however, capacity to accommodate a further thirty five personnel, and this can be increased to eighty in a disaster relief situation.

The weapons and sensors are controlled by the indigenously-developed SCOMBA (*Sistema de Combate de los Buques de la Armada*) combat management system. Based on a common core, this is being rolled out in different variants according to the level of capability required across the majority of the Spanish fleet. This solution contrasts with the French twin-track approach of specifying POLARIS for ships involved in low intensity operations whilst installing the more capable SETIS in frontline surface escorts such as the FREMM type frigates and would suggest a greater level of integration across the entire fleet. SCOMBA is linked to a range of technology that also reflects strong support for Iberian industry, including an Indra ARIES 2 medium-range surveillance radar that can also be used for helicopter and UAV control, as well as a DORNA 2 fire control director. The integrated communications suite includes Link 11 capability for secure data exchange with other NATO forces.

BAM weaponry reflects the limited war-fighting capability seen in all OPV types. However, the standard outfit of a 76mm Oto Melara Compact and two lighter Mk 38

A picture of the Spanish BAM Tornado in the spring of 2012. The design is large enough for oceanic operation and can be easily converted for other roles, such as hydrographic operations or submarine support. (Navantia)

Mod 2 25mm canon, typically supplemented by heavy machine guns, provides excellent protection against asymmetric threats and a reasonable level of capability against more sophisticated opposition. Of equal importance is a suite of electronic and physical countermeasures that includes Indra's RIGEL electronic countermeasures (jamming) and support system as well as Mk 36 SRBOC decoy launchers. Helicopter support arrangements cater for a wide range of rotorcraft in service with the Spanish armed forces and UAVs can also be operated. Two RIBs are carried to facilitate high speed interception and boarding requirements. As for the 'River' class, provision has also been made for the handling and storage of a number of containers in the after area of the ship to provide additional flexibility in mission profiles.

It is undoubtedly flexibility that is the BAM's greatest attribute. The design is of sufficient size to be suitable for both oceanic and littoral operations, whilst the focus on a modular structure allows the basic patrol variant to be reconfigured for a wide range of roles. The combat system is sufficiently capable to support a wide range of military operations short of a high intensity, war-fighting scenario. At the same time, the provision of medical facilities, spare accommodation and rescue equipment makes them equally useful for non-combat missions. As such, the class is suitable for both EEZ patrol and 'out of area' stabilisation duties. Third of class *Relámpago* has already demonstrated the class's potential with respect to the latter mission profile, departing Spain during August 2012 to disrupt piracy in the Indian Ocean as part of the European Union's Operation 'Atalanta'. The six-month voyage encompassed calls at a number of African ports, demonstrating the attractions of the BAM to regional navies looking to bolster their own maritime patrol capabilities.

The Netherlands – Holland Class

The Royal Netherlands Navy's *Holland* class is arguably the 'Rolls Royce' of current European OPV designs. Four of these oceanic patrol vessels were ordered from the Dutch Damen group in December 2007 as part of a programme designed to reconfigure a fleet dominated by 'high-end' Cold War-era frigates towards a more balanced structure with a greater emphasis on maritime security and stabilisation operations. As for many naval projects, an important secondary consideration was to support domestic naval industries at a time when existing construction was winding down. The first two vessels were built at Schelde Naval Shipbuilding at Vlissingen, where *Holland* was laid down in December 2008. However, the second pair was allocated to Damen's yard at Galati in Romania, with only final fitting out being completed in the Netherlands. *Holland* was commissioned in July 2012 after an extensive series of trials. All four ships should be in service by the end of 2014.

With a full load displacement approaching 3,800 tonnes – larger than the frigates that the new class replaces – *Holland* and her sisters set new parameters for OPV design. The size of the new ships was driven by a range of factors,

The current 'Rolls Royce' of European OPV capabilities is represented by the Dutch Holland *design, which is larger than many traditional frigates. It has very sophisticated sensors and communications systems but a relatively light armament.* (Thales Nederland)

MODERN EUROPEAN OFFSHORE PATROL VESSELS

The Holland *class OPV Zeeland is pictured in November 2011, shortly after delivery. Ships of the class are delivered without the integrated mast that houses key radar and communications systems: this is installed separately at a later date.* (Leo van Ginderen collection)

most notably the intention to deploy the class on global operations, a requirement to ensure helicopter and boat operations in adverse weather conditions, and the desirability of ensuring good sea-keeping for reasons of operational efficiency and crew comfort. Another influence has been the need to maintain a presence in the waters of the Dutch possessions in the Caribbean. As for the other designs considered in this chapter, the ships' basic structure was designed to Det Norske Veritas commercial standards with an overlay of Dutch naval requirements in areas such as stability, ballistic protection and blast-resistant bulkheads. Attention to survivability is also evident in a level of decentralisation/redundancy and the provision of a gas-protected citadel.

The use of a hybrid CODOE propulsion plant reflects the same considerations of efficiency and economy influencing Spain's selection of this system in the BAM, although the equipment suppliers are different. The Dutch ships have a maximum range which is lower than many other recent OPV designs, reflecting an emphasis on endurance whilst 'on station'. Maximum speed of c.21.5 knots is similar to their foreign counterparts, with the availability of RIBs and helicopters for interception duties being regarded as an acceptable trade-off. The high level of situational awareness provided by a sophisticated suite of sensors is another mitigating factor.

In addition to their comparatively large displacement, the most notable feature of the *Holland* class is their utilisation of Thales' new integrated mast concept. This consists of a discrete housing that incorporates all major radars, other sensors and communications equipment in a single structure. Thales claims that this approach has a number of advantages over traditional sensor layouts. These include avoidance of interference between different sensors, more efficient and economic installation (an I-Mast is completed and tested away from the shipyard before simply being bolted onto the receiving ship and connected to power supplies and transmission links) and subsequent ease of maintenance. The IM-400 variant of the system fitted to *Holland* incorporates a range of sophisticated equipment, most notably:

– Sea Master Surveillance Radar: Also known as SMILE, this is a non-rotating, four-faced, phased array developed from Thales' SMART series of radars. Using multiple beams generated by computer software, it provides air and surface surveillance at medium ranges. It can also provide target tracking and will be used to control the ship's main gun.
– Sea Watcher Tracking & Detection Radar: Another four-faced phased array, Sea Watcher complements Sea Master's capabilities by providing detection and tracking of small surface targets, including floating mines, swimmers and periscopes.
– Gatekeeper Passive Surveillance System: An electro-optical surveillance system, Gatekeeper combines TV and infra-red images to provide panoramic surveillance at shorter ranges.

WARSHIP 2013

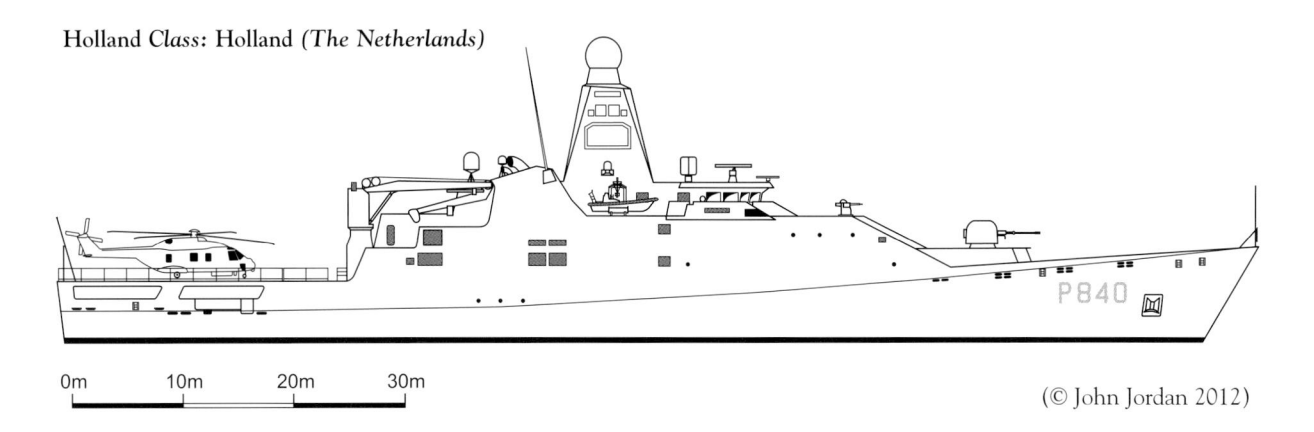

Holland Class: *Holland (The Netherlands)*

0m 10m 20m 30m

(© John Jordan 2012)

A view of Holland's IM-400 integrated mast being installed in November 2011. The mast provides the class with excellent maritime surveillance capabilities, but the design has only limited war-fighting potential. (Thales Nederland)

- Non-Rotating IFF: This uses a cylindrical array at the top of the integrated mast structure. It is optimised for operation in conjunction with the non-rotating primary radar.
- ICAS Integrated Communications System: The Integrated Communications Antenna System (ICAS) is fitted flush with the I-Mast's structure and, together with satellite antennae, supports a wide range of communications and associated C-ESM. The main NATO Link 11 and Link 16 channels are supported to assist with the compilation of a comprehensive tactical picture.

The various sensors in the I-Mast are linked to a SEWACO (sensor weapon and command system) series combat management system. This combines Thales multi-function consoles with software from Cams Force Vision, the Dutch Ministry of Defence's 'in house' systems group, which has been tailored to the class's low intensity mission profile. This profile is also reflected in a light armament for the ship's size, which is focused on Oto Melara 76mm and 30mm guns, supported by lighter weapons. The hangar and flight deck allow operation and support of the NFH variant of the medium-sized NH90 helicopter, which has replaced the older Lynx in Royal Netherlands Navy service. Space is provided under the flight deck for containers and pallets, which are handled by a crane located to the starboard side of the hangar. There is a slipway at the stern to supplement more traditional launch and recovery of fast interceptors.

As for all modern OPVs, a key driver behind *Holland's* design specification was the achievement of ongoing economies in operation, maintenance and manning. This was one of the factors that resulted in the specification of the CODOE propulsion system. It can also be seen in the high level of platform automation that facilitates manning by a core crew of around fifty personnel. All principal operations are controlled from linked bridge and operations areas on the bridge deck, whilst the integrated bridge and platform management systems supplied by Dutch company Imtech Marine encompass one-man bridge operation and an unmanned machinery control room. There is considerable use of handheld personal digital assistants (PDAs) for internal communication. Operating costs have been estimated at around €5m (US$6m) per annum, which is considerably less than for a fully-fledged frigate.

The *Holland* design pushes the OPV concept to its logical limits in terms of size and sophistication. The ships' comprehensive range of powerful sensors means that they are superbly well-equipped to carry out maritime surveillance operations. Moreover, their advanced propulsion system – particularly the benefits of low-speed electric operation – will permit lengthy deployment in a designated operating area. Provision for helicopter and fast boat operations provide interception and blockade capabilities, whilst the comparatively large internal volume facilitates participation in humanitarian missions: up to 100 evacuees can be transported in an emergency. Nevertheless, there has been considerable criticism of the ships' limited armament and the restrictions that this would place on their utilisation in a combat scenario.[11]

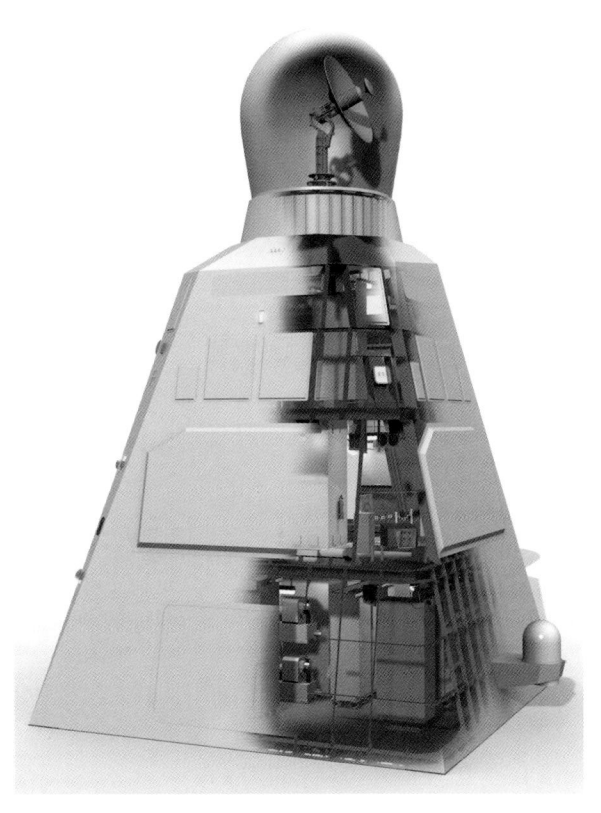

A graphic of the Thales IM-400 integrated mast installed in the Dutch Holland *class. This contains all major radars, sensors and communications equipment in a discrete housing that avoids mutual interference and facilitates installation and subsequent maintenance.* (Thales Nederland)

Acquisition costs are also inevitably high: programme cost was being quoted as c.€470m (c. US$610m), for a unit price of around €120m (c.US$155m), at the time the ships were ordered in 2007. Around a quarter of this figure is accounted for by the Integrated Mast.

Conclusion

It is evident from this brief review that a number of common design themes are present across the range of recent European OPV construction. All four classes considered have been built in accordance with commercial design practices to minimise initial capital costs. Equally, considerable attention has been paid to minimising crew size and achieving other efficiencies to minimise the ongoing cost of operation. Other similarities include an emphasis on high-grade communication systems to ensure coordinated surveillance operations, as well as the ability to deploy fast boats – and in some cases airborne vehicles – to compensate for the limitations of propulsion systems that prioritise range and economy over absolute speed. All the designs benefit from a degree of inherent flexibility that allows the ships to be modified to carry out a wide range of secondary naval activities.

At the same time, consideration of the strengths and weaknesses of the four designs is also instructive. The

THE UNLUCKY DESTROYER *ESPINGOLE*

Philippe Caresse tells the story of one of France's first destroyers.

First Contact

On a fine Spring morning, Cavalaire Bay was looking its best. The air bottles and the diving bags were secured and we were able to head for Andati Point. After a short trip the buoys were quickly located and we were securely moored. The GPS read 43°09'80N, 06°36'30'E. The depth of the sea at this point is 38 metres. The friend who had offered us his small boat had guaranteed we would have a pleasant dive on an interesting wreck. It remained only for us to ease ourselves into the water and to begin our descent to the depths.

There was no current and the visibility was excellent. At a depth of 15 metres we could already see a white, sandy bottom against which a large dark shape stood out. It is true that the exploration of a ship in its final resting place is always impressive and can prove to be dangerous. The destroyer *Espingole*, which sank here, had a reassuring air. The anchor was close to the stern on the port side. From the state of the wreck, it was immediately apparent that the vessel had been beneath these waters for a very long time. The after deck had been completely eaten away, so that on looking in you could see the bronze propellers sticking out of the sand. Moving to the left, we found what appeared to be the general store room, as there was a large quantity of broken bottles and crockery. Many interesting discoveries have been made in these waters. Despite all the objects which presented themselves to our gaze, at a depth of 40 metres the time available to us was limited by our air supply. The wreck of the *Espingole* is unusual in that all the side plating had become detached from the frames, giving the impression that we were in the presence of a sea monster. We could therefore dive on either side of the ship and see into the hull without needing to penetrate into the wreck itself. Scattered around the wreck were huge quantities of coal,

Divers reconnoitre the hull of the Espingole, *the side plating of which has become detached over the years. To the right chunks of coal can be seen lying on the sea bed.* (P. Strazzera)

some of which were stamped with the letters R and B. Moving further on, we found large quantities of 65mm and 47mm ammunition. Towards the forward part of the ship, the bow had separated from the remainder of the wreck and listed to starboard. It is true that this part of the wreck is of less interest than the centre part and the stern, which are nearly upright on the bottom. No point in lingering any longer, so we made a half turn, passing over the superstructures. As we swam over the destroyer, we saw that the deck was far better preserved than the ship's sides. From our position above the ship we could see the 65mm gun mounting which had fallen away to starboard. The ship had lost all her guns. We didn't see evidence of any of the 47mm guns, nor of the torpedo tubes. The bridge had disappeared and the masts were resting on the bottom. The machinery rooms were particularly interesting. There was pipework everywhere, and the two boilers remained impressive. When you scraped at the growth with a knife yellow, shiny metal appeared. It was as if the *Espingole* had been built entirely of copper and bronze, as these metals were everywhere.

Clearly it would take a number of dives in order to really get to know this vessel. To dive on this wreck, which has a particular 'feel' to it, is truly a return to the past. So, as we returned to the surface, one question sprang immediately to mind: How did the destroyer *Espingole* come to end her days in Cavalaire Bay?

M3 Espingole

The name *Espingole* comes from the old French 'espringuer'. This was a fat, short musket with a flared barrel, used first in Spain and Italy, and eventually in 16th century France. The word 'espingole' was also employed to denote a small firearm, used during boardings in the sail navy and placed in the tops.

Following the disastrous Franco-Prussian war of 1871, it was obvious that France needed to rebuild its Army, and to invest in fortifications on the new frontiers and the refurbishment of the railways in the east of the country. Reparations and war debts were considerable. The Navy was hit hard by budgetary cuts, particularly during 1872/1873. There were certain commentators who described naval forces as 'luxury items'. Thus it was only natural that the politicians would incline towards the ideas of the *Jeune Ecole*, which favoured an emphasis on cruisers and, in particular, torpedo-boats as the core of the fleet. This new type of ship, easy to build and to maintain, threatened to dethrone the battleship, each of which took years to plan and complete. Armed with torpedoes,[1] it was able to make a hit-and run attack on these leviathans before making a speedy escape. By the end of the 19th century more than 200 torpedo-boats, designated by numbers rather than names, constituted a 'mobile defence' force along the French coasts. The shipyard of Jacques-Augustin Normand was particularly prominent in the design and construction of these small combatants. To counter their construction the British devised the torpedo-boat destroyer (later 'destroyer'), which had greater displacement, was armed with quick-firing guns and torpedoes, and which had superior sea-going capabilities and endurance.

From 1895 the French Navy had followed with interest the development of the first British destroyers, and acknowledged the necessity of building similar units which could compete. Augustin Normand proposed a ship of 300 tonnes which serve as either a fleet torpedo boat

The destroyer M3 on the building way at Le Havre ; she would be launched the following day. (Author's collection)

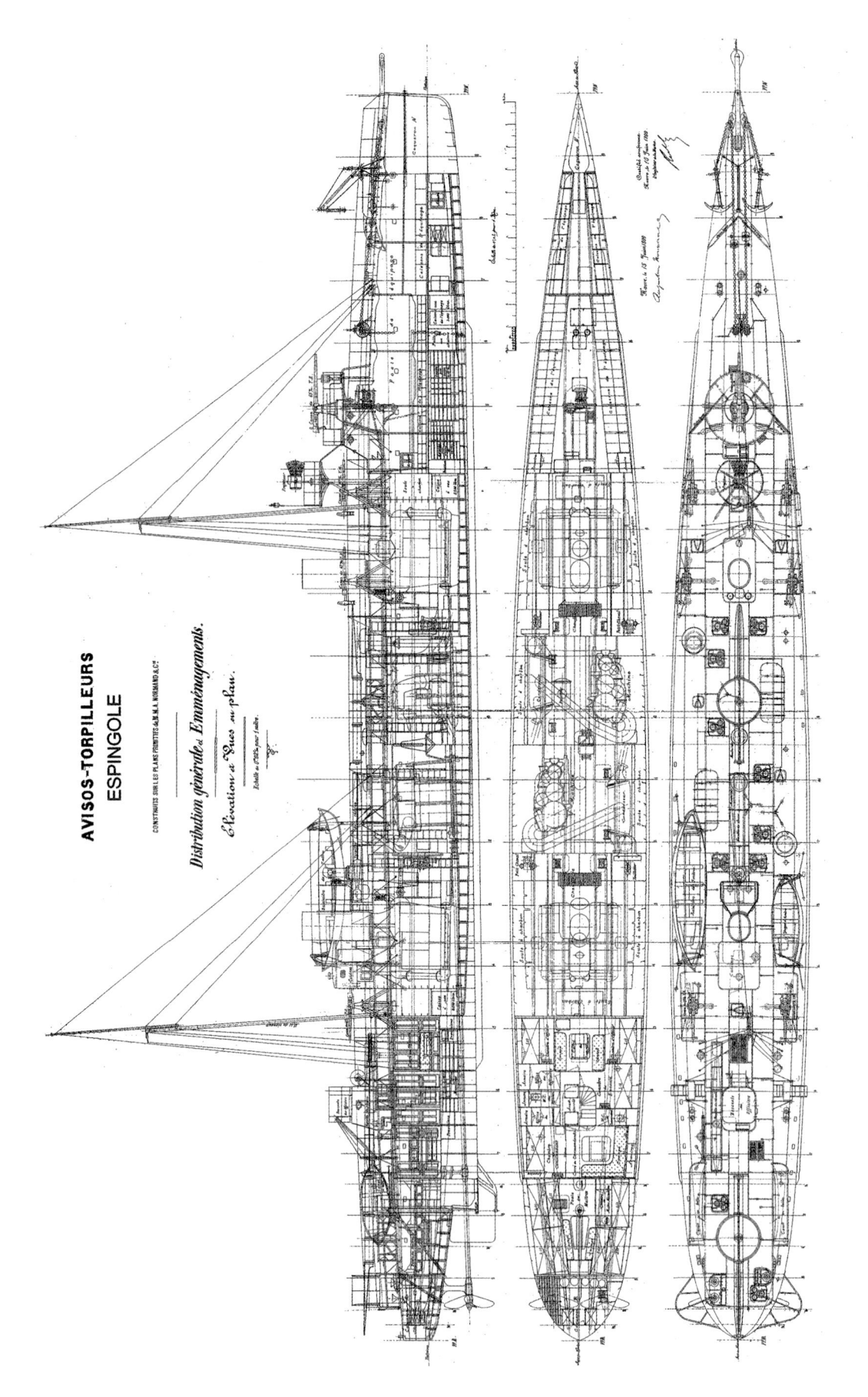

Official plans of the destroyer Espingole. Note the designation aviso-torpilleur (torpedo sloop) in usage at the time. (Centre d'Archives de l'Armement, Châtellerault)

(*torpilleur d'escadre*) or as a torpedo-armed sloop (*aviso torpilleur*). Speed was to be 25 knots, and the ship was to have sufficient endurance to accompany the battle fleet, which it was designed to protect. A relatively heavy armament and a high rate of fire were essential. The plans for the first 'prototype' 300-tonne destroyers were submitted to the Council of Works on 14 April 1896. They constituted the first draft for the M0 *Durandal*, M1 *Hallebarde*, M2 *Fauconneau* and the M3 *Espingole*.

The *Espingole* was launched in June 1900 at the Le Havre shipyard of Normand. The hull had a waterline length of 56 metres, and a length overall of 57.64 metres. The original design featured a ram bow, which was constructed but never fitted.[2] Maximum beam was 6.30m, and beam at the waterline 5.95m. Depth was 4.10m, and draught at the stern was 3.20m. Displacement at full load was 311.10 tonnes. There was a centre-line keel 0.30m high over a length of 32 metres. Despite this feature the turning radius of *Espingole* was 450m at 17 knots, which was considered to be on the high side.

Two Normand watertube boilers, operating at a pressure of 16kg/cm^2, provided the steam for two triple-expansion engines driving twin shafts which turned at 300rpm. The engines were located between the boilers amidships in two separate compartments; each was provided with its own condenser. The total weight of the machinery was 112 tonnes. It proved very satisfactory in service, consuming 0.8kg of fuel per CV/hour at its full power rating of 5200CV. The tops of the propeller blades were 0.9m beneath the surface, which was a significant figure for this type of vessel. The single rudder was located well forward of the propellers and was fully 5.5 metres forward of the after perpendicular; its upper edge was 1 metre below the waterline. The designed speed was 26 knots; this was exceeded by more than one knot on trials.

The fuel bunkers held 37.6 tonnes of coal in peacetime. They were located around the boiler rooms; some were transverse, others longitudinal. This arrangement facilitated the maintenance of the vessel's trim whatever the loading of the bunkers. The operating radius was 2300nm at 10 knots, equivalent to nine days at sea at 13 knots.

No fewer than 75 destroyers of the 300-tonne type would be built by the French, of which 20 were destined for two foreign navies.

Armament

Espingole was armed with a single 65mm/50-cal. gun Mle 1891, which was installed on a small circular platform just forward of the bridge. A total of 375 rounds were provided. The theoretical firing cycle in accelerated-fire mode was five rounds per minute. The angle of elevation was +20° to –10°, and maximum range was 9000 metres. The gun fired a shell weighing 4kg.

Six 47mm/40-cal. guns Mle 1885 were disposed three per side as follows: four were between the bridge and the fore-funnel; the after pair were abreast the mainmast. The 47mm gun fired a 1.49kg shell to a range of 4000 metres. The firing cycle in accelerated-fire mode was 15 rounds per minute; in sustained-fire mode it was 7rpm. A total of 2850 47mm rounds were provided. All the main guns were on open pivot mountings; there were no gun shields.

Finally, there were two single torpedo tubes: the first was located between the two funnels, the second above the stern. The tubes could be trained on forward bearings at 40 degrees and 55 degrees to the ship's axis respectively. Two reserve torpedoes were stowed in lockers. The latter were not available immediately, as it took some three hours to charge them with compressed air. The 381mm torpedo Mle 1887 had a length of 5.62m and an all-up weight of 1688kg, which included a 42kg warhead.

General Arrangement and Equipment

The hull was divided by nine watertight bulkheads. The compartments thereby created were as follows: a void compartment in the bow, referred to as the *compartiment de choc*, 3.6m long; a seamen's mess 13.2m long divided into two compartments, with stores, provisions, magazines and the cable locker beneath; the forward boiler room, 6m long and separated from the seamen's mess by a transverse coal bunker with a depth of 1.2m; the two engine rooms, each 4.8m, then the after boiler room and a similar transverse coal bunker; the officers' accommodation (for three officers plus the CO), 7.2m long; and finally, the POs' mess, 4.2m long, and the after storeroom.

A distinctive feature of the design was the 'flying deck' (*pont volant*) which extended from the stern to the 65mm gun platform 7.5m from the bow. It was raised 0.8m above the upper deck and weighed 7 tonnes. It allowed the seas to pass between the deck and the hull, thereby preventing the equipment located on it from being washed out.

The outfit of boats comprised a 7-metre service cutter and a light 4-metre dinghy on davits abeam the second funnel, and a Berthon secured to the port quarter. There was a small 40cm searchlight projector to assist navigation atop the bridge.

The mooring lines comprised two 780-tonne stock anchors located on either side of the bow which were hoisted into the 'sea' position on deck using a small crane. There was also a spare anchor weighing 192kg. These installations were separated from the capstan by a breakwater located just forward of the 65mm gun.

The original complement of the *Espingole* comprised four officers and 48 petty officers and ratings. From 1899 the number of POs and seamen was increased to 60, the number of officers remaining the same.

Their commanding officers were unanimous in their praise for the qualities of these ships, the only reservation being the excessive topweight. In the first *devis de campagne* of the *Espingole*, LV Langier reported:

> Although the turning circle is excessive, it has to be said that the ship is solid, the machinery robust, that speed is relatively unaffected by the state of the sea, and that on the occasion of a voyage to Mytilene [Lesbos, Greece] in November 1901 she coped well with very heavy seas, and never gave the slightest cause for concern.

In another report the C-in-C of the Mediterranean Squadron, Vice-admiral Fournier, stated:

Espingole *on the building way at Le Havre on 27 June 1900.* (Author's collection)

Espingole *departs Toulon shortly after her entry into service.* (Marius Bar)

Espingole at anchor. The original photo is in poor condition and has been heavily retouched – testimony to the shortage of photos of the ship in service. (Author's collection)

In summary, the destroyers of the *Hallebarde* class are excellent sea-boats for their size, and would be a valuable resource in combat. They have performed particularly well on liaison duties with the fleet. The construction of this type of ship reflects great credit on M. Normand.

The cost to the French state of the *Espingole* was 1,690,994 francs.

Launch & Service

Espingole was launched at Le Havre on 28 June 1900. Present at the ceremony were Prince Wilhelm Duke of Södermanland (Sweden) and the officers and cadets of the sail training ship *Saga* as well as representatives of the civil and military authorities of the town. As soon as the hull had been launched, it was towed to the fitting-out quay. Following completion *Espingole* went to Cherbourg for her sea trials.

The first official sortie took place on 13 August 1900 for tests of fuel consumption at 14 knots. During trials which lasted eight hours the ship gave complete satisfaction, endurance being subsequently calculated to be 1729nm with 37.63 tonnes of coal embarked. The three speed trials took place on 25 August and 5/24 September; maximum recorded speed was 27.41 knots. The report of the ship's first CO, *Lieutenant de vaisseau* (LV) Langier, makes it clear that he was completely satisfied with the ship's sea-going qualities :

> The ship steers well at all speeds and holds her course exceptionally well. She was always steered using the servo motor, but switching from steam power to manual steering is very straightforward and very quick. One small criticism is the excessive turning circle (c.400m). It is true that one can always reverse one of the engines, and if this is done the ship can be made to turn virtually on the spot. The ship holds her course even with only a single propeller.

She has a gentle roll of about 5.5 seconds. Rolling is accentuated with the sea on the beam but it was not possible to measure this.

In December, *Espingole* joined the Mediterranean Squadron. The destroyer left Toulon on 22 January 1901 for a visit to Les Salins, followed by Nice on the morning of the 24th, Golfe Juan in the evening and Antibes from 26 January to 8 February. This was followed by a succession of port visits throughout the year which included Ajaccio, Bonifacio (both in Corsica), Villefranche, Port de Bouc, Porto Veccio, Algiers, Palma, Mers el-Kebir and Oran. From 3 to 27 September *Espingole* was docked for repairs to her rudder which had scraped the bottom in the shallows of Golfe Juan.

At the end of 1901 there were numerous unresolved legal disputes between France and Turkey. One particular issue was the non-repayment of 750,000 Turkish pounds loaned in 1876 to finance the plot aiming to depose Sultan Abdülaziz. Diplomatic negotiations having led

The squadron of Rear-admiral Caillard, during the intervention in the Aegean October to December 1901. (Author's collection)

M0 Durandal, the prototype of the series, is seen here at Boulogne in northern France. (Author's collection)

nowhere, the two countries broke off relations. Each of the respective ambassadors was recalled, and the French government resolved to despatch a large naval force to Constantinople to exert pressure on the Turks. On 1st October 1901 a division of the Mediterranean Squadron, under the command of Rear-admiral Caillard, was deployed off the coasts of the Isle of Lesbos. This formation comprised the battleships *Gaulois* and *Charlemagne*, the armoured cruisers *Pothuau* (flag of R-Ad Caillard) and *Chanzy*, the cruiser *Linois* and the destroyers *Espingole* and *Epée*. The squadron called in at Vatika Bay on 3 November, Milos on the 4th, Smyrna on the 6th/7th, Mytelene on the 7th, Syros from the 13th to the 25th, Tinos on the 25th, Syros (again) from the 25th to the 29th, Pyraeus on the 29th. then Syros again from 29 November to 7 December. After disembarking troops at Mytilene on 5 November, all the ships returned to Toulon on 12 December without having had recourse to force.

The destroyer was docked from 3 to 17 April, then sailed for the usual visits to the coasts of Provence and North Africa.

In June 1902, LV Marcotte de Sainte-Marie became the ship's new commanding officer ('*pacha*') The ship conducted numerous sorties and then stayed in the dockyard at Toulon from 13 November to 2 December. Following a visit to Port Cros, *Espingole* returned to Toulon on 18 December and remained there until 1903. The ship made a brief appearance at Rochefort on the west coast, then returned to the Mediterranean for further work-up which culminated in the unfortunate incident of 4 February 1903. At that time the general staff of the ship comprised LV Marcotte de Sainte Marie (CO), *Enseigne de vaisseau* (EV) Blanchet (First Officer) and *Mécanicien de 2e classe* Blanc (Engineering Officer).

The Sinking

One of the crew members gave the following account of the destroyer's last sortie:

Lieutenant de vaisseau Marcotte de Sainte-Marie, the ship's commanding officer throughout her brief career. (Author's collection)

THE UNLUCKY DESTROYER ESPINGOLE

Espingole *at sea*. (Marius Bar)

We had left port at 06.40 with the other destroyers which made up the Salins squadron for Cannes. When we arrived at Cape Lardier, the *Espingole* ran aground and remained in that position from 09.40 to 13.00 in the dangerous waters of Cavalaire Bay. The pilot, seeing that she had strayed outside the channel, had expressed his concerns to the captain. The command '15 degrees to starboard' was given, but the pilot, who considered this was not sufficient to avoid the rock which had just been passed by the *Pique*, ordered 'full rudder starboard' – in effect 25 degrees. Hardly had he ordered the change of course than the *Espingole* struck the reef, which tore a hole 2.5-3 metres long in the hull. Immediately the order was given to go astern to refloat the ship, but to no avail. The CO and the First Officer inspected the compartment in question and confirmed that water was pouring into the ship. An attempt was made to stem the flow with Makaroff mats[3] but these could not be secured. The *Pertuisane*, which was close by, attempted to refloat the ship, but in vain. From 09.40 to 12.00 coal, ammunition, two 47mm guns and some of the personal effects of the crew were jettisoned. By 13.00 this operation was complete but the captain, despite

M2 Fauconnau, *another of* Espingole's *sisterships*. (Author's collection)

Espingole *comes alongside in the old port of Marseille*. (Private collection)

the danger he was exposed to, remained on board to give the final orders. At about 13.30 the ship had slightly lifted clear and the captain signalled to the CO of the *Hallebarde* that he was going to attempt to go astern, and if the other destroyer could get a line aboard he was hopeful of freeing *Espingole*. *Hallebarde* managed to tow her sister some 5-6 metres before the hawser broke, injuring two of her crew, and almost at once the *Espingole* began to sink. Her captain left the ship only at the last moment after ascertaining that all the crew had got off safely.

Marcotte de Sainte-Marie stated in his report to the Navy Ministry that his ship was manoeuvring in waters with a depth of 4.5m while she was drawing 3.5m. This was a very small margin given that the ship's speed was 15 knots! On 4 February the *Hallebarde* (LV Grand Clément) brought the CO of the unlucky ship back to Toulon. Elsewhere it was stated that on 27 February the petty officers and seamen were accommodated on the *Chanzy* and that the CO and his staff were on the *Bouvet*.

Returning to the incident, the magazine *Illustration*, in

The destroyers Espingole *and* Pique *moored in the historic basin of Villefranche.* (Author's collection)

Espingole off the coast of southern France. For her size she was a remarkably well-armed ship. (Marius Bar)

its 14 February 1903 edition, gave its own report of the facts:

> On the morning of 4 February, the destroyer flotilla of the Mediterranean, comprising the *Espingole*, the *Pique*, the *Hallebarde*, the *Pertuisane* and the *Epée*, had sailed from Salins d'Hyères for a navigation of the coasts of Provence, in waters littered with reefs. Near Cape Lardier the five destroyers were steaming in line ahead led by the *Pique*; the latter passed safely through the channel between the land and a rock (marked B on the accompanying map), which was covered with only a metre of water, but the *Espingole* following her, under the command of LV Marcotte de Sainte-Marie, realised that she had made insufficient turns to pass safely through (track CA) and turned hard to starboard to clear the reef (direction track CB). Unfortunately, this manœuvre was executed too

M1 Hallebarde, *which attempted to tow the* Espingole *to a beach in Cavalaire Bay.* (Author's collection)

Artist's impression of the destroyer grounded on a rock off Cape Lardier. In the centre-frame, a boat is starting to evacuate the official documents. (L'Illustration)

late: the vessel struck the rock and became impaled on it. The *Hallebarde*, which had hurried to her assistance, managed to save the crew of 62 men, their kitbags, the accounts and the important documents; at the same time as much of the matériel and coal as possible was removed.

The swell freed the lightened hull of the destroyer and the *Hallebarde*, towing her by the stern, attempted to beach her on the coast on a bed of sand and in shallow waters. However, when she arrived at point D, the *Espingole* was sinking by the bows with 37 metres of water beneath her keel, roughly 500 metres from land and at about 700 metres to the northwest of the tip of Cape Lardier.

Measures were taken to try to refloat her, an operation whose success was always in doubt given the difficulties presented by such circumstances.

The attempts to salvage the ship would be lengthy and labour-intensive. For the moment, the wreck was marked by only a single buoy. Following the accident the four surviving destroyers put into Antibes.

Soon, ships with special equipment to carry out underwater work arrived in Toulon : the *Dromadaire* (*Premier maître* Josselin), *Polyphème* (PM Festa), *Filtre* (PM Blachon) and *Arrosoir* (PM Alzeari). Stacked on their decks were divers' helmets, lead-weighted boots, and pumps – equipment indispensable to any diver of the period. The first underwater inspection revealed that the

The Espingole *sinking by the bows, directly opposite Andati Point. (Author's collection)*

ship was resting on her port side, and a fissure in the hull plating measuring 1.6m by 0.2m was visible to starboard some 10 metres from the bow. During the first stage of the recovery process a hawser was secured to the prow of the *Espingole*, but it was quickly realised that this would not be capable of withstanding efforts to tow the ship. LV Faure, seconded by PM Josselin and PM Festa, was in charge of the recovery. It was decided to use chains, but the unfavourable weather conditions forced a suspension of diving operations and the ships anchored off Cavalaire. As soon as weather permitted, the diving ships returned to the site of the wreck, and the regional *Préfet maritime*, Admiral Bienaimé, came in person to witness the difficulties met with by the divers.

The refloating operation promised to be difficult and time-consuming, as it had been planned to lower two cylinders and secure them to the wreck. Once the barges had raised the ship from the bottom, the entire assembly was to have been towed to shallower waters. The cylinders would then need to be immersed again and the collars tightened in order to tow the assembly into ever shallower waters. It was hoped to gain 5 metres per day. There were five divers[4] tasked with bringing this delicate enterprise to fruition. Despite their efforts, it quickly became apparent that with the means available from the port managers it would be impossible to secure the desired results, and Admiral Bienaimé drafted a report explaining this. The latter was submitted to the Navy Ministry, which decided to abandon the salvage work and to subcontract it to a private company.

In the meantime, the *Espingole* was removed from the fleet listings on 16 September 1903 and her wreck sold at auction in December 1909. With the court martial hovering over his head for seven years, LV Marcotte de Sainte Marie was tried and acquitted. However, in certain naval circles there were those who questioned this judgement, given that *Espingole* was following in the wake of another ship in clear visibility, and she was manoeuvring in waters unaffected by the current or by the tides. Despite this, Marcotte de Sainte Marie would again be given command of a ship, being appointed to the armoured cruiser *Latouche-Tréville* in 1914 with the rank of *Capitaine de frégate* (RN: Commander), before disappearing in the course of the Great War.

Off Andati Point, the port management at Toulon had placed at the disposition of M. Lanthiome, who had won the contract with a deposit of 4000 francs, the barge *Polyphème*, four 100-ton *bugalets* (two-masted coastal sailing boats used to transport goods and personnel within harbours and anchorages), a 300-tonne pontoon and 250 tonnes of chains. The contract allowed him two months to complete the job. Should he succeed in refloating the ship he would receive 60,000 francs; bringing the wreck into a dry dock would merit a bonus of 10,000 francs. He would receive a further 20,000 francs from the Navy if the boilers, guns and accessories were in a fit condition to be reused, plus 30,000 francs if the hull proved to be worth repairing.

The foundering of the Espingole *seen from the* Hallebarde. *On the stern of the latter ship can be seen a seaman injured by the rupture of the hawser used for the tow. (Author's collection)*

This diver is going to work in the significant depth of 38 metres. Diving at these depths was even more dangerous during the period in question because regulations regarding ascent speeds and the regulatory decompression stages were often ignored. (J P Paszula collection)

The attempted recovery took five months, and Lanthiome was no more successful than the Navy in salvaging the vessel. To make matters worse the barge was damaged by the floating pontoon and the condition of the *Espingole*, which remained firmly embedded in the white sandy bottom, deteriorated further. Lanthiome accused the Navy of having 'disturbed' the wreck and demanded that this be rectified, before submitting a claim for damages (+ interest) of 60,000 francs. A legal dispute was declared between the Navy and the contractor which was settled only on 3 March 1926! Throughout this time, and for always, the destroyer remained on the bottom of Cavalaire Bay.

As if to twist the knife in the wound, the maritime magazine *Le Yacht* wrote in its issue of 20 October 1903 :

> We have spoken on a number of occasions of the failed salvage attempt on the destroyer *Espingole*, which remains on the bottom 37 metres below the surface. A local newspaper sought out the exact figures for the expenses incurred by the Navy Department as a result of these poorly-conducted operations. According to the official tariff of hire relating to the boats and equipment serving the port, a tariff which varies according to the number of tugs employed, the report estimated a total cost of 58,028 francs simply for the boats employed. The 4335 days of the trained seamen, at 5 francs per day, come to 21,675 francs. The quantity of coal burned by the tugs was 537,461kg which, at 34 francs per tonne, comes to 18,273 francs.
>
> The expenses relating to the sheer-hulks and *bugalets* employed in the recovery total 77,398 francs. The damage to armed pontoon no.4 is estimated at 1800 francs, which gives us a grand total of 177,175 francs. To this needs to be added the cost of lost chains and anchors, the dislocation costs of engineers, officers and delegates, some of whom were despatched from Paris, the cost of provisions provided to the salvage company, etc. It is difficult too give a precise estimate of all of this, but the foregoing is sufficient to demonstrate that these huge sums were expended without any tangible result and as a result of poor organisation. At a time when savings in naval expenditure are being actively discussed, the facts suggest that serious consideration needs to be given to these failings by the Budgetary Commission.

As the author stated earlier in this article, *Espingole* began her first trials in August 1900 and foundered on 4 February 1903. Her service career was barely 30 months, which seems unduly short for this well-regarded ship.

Sources :.
- Henri Le Masson: *Histoire du torpilleur en France*.
- *L'Illustration* n°3129, 14 February 1903.
- *Armée et Marine*.
- *Le Yacht*.
- *Le moniteur de la flotte*.

Footnotes:
1. Conceived in 1865 by the Austrian Captain Luppis and developed by the Englishman Whitehead.
2. It was sold to the Imperial Russian Navy, and was subsequently fitted to one of their own 300-tonne destroyers.
3. Squares of strong canvas impregnated with tallow, which were used to stem water leaks.
4. The divers who stood out for the high quality of their work were Le Marchand, Raffaëli et Salducci.

The last known photograph of the Espingole, *taken in the port of Marseille. The wreck of the ship is all that remains of the famous destroyers of the 300-tonnes series.* (Private collection)

THE SOVIET AIRCRAFT CARRIER:
The Interwar Projects

Despite infrastructure problems, the aircraft carrier was the subject of serious study in the Soviet Union during the period 1918-1944. **Richard Worth** *and* **Vladimir Yakubov** *look in detail at the various projects proposed, which included both conversions of existing ships and new-build carriers.*

As the Soviets failed to develop any aircraft carriers between the World Wars, the subject of Stalin's flattops may seem an unpromising vein to mine. However, a survey of the factors that stymied carrier development also casts a revealing light on Soviet naval policy and construction, a context for all design histories. Only powerful forces could negate the promising foundation that Russia's imperial navy had created for its aviation arm.

As early as the Russo-Japanese War, the Russian fleet developed a practical system for using air assets (balloons) for reconnaissance, and the following decade saw a series of cutting-edge developments by Russian heavier-than-air craft. Aircraft showed that they could detect submerged submarines, could carry radio equipment, and could attack battleships. (Seaplanes enlivened one fleet exercise by 'bombing' *Rostislav* and *Ioann Zlatoust* with oranges.) After the outbreak of the First World War, the Russians formed the first carrier-battleship task force for operations in the Black Sea, as Russian seaplane tenders executed effective air raids on coastal targets, demonstrating a shipborne aviation capability second only to that of Britain.

This fledgling naval aviation capability became a casualty of the Russian Civil War. Even more than the battleship, a nascent system like the aircraft carrier was vulnerable to the industrial, political, and doctrinal upheaval which ensued. Worthwhile proposals in the 1920's failed to gain support, and the embryonic projects of the 1930s foundered in the face of a lack of enthusiasm on the part of Joseph Stalin and were effectively brought to a halt by the Second World War

The Reorganisation of Aviation

An early blow to Soviet naval aviation came in March 1920 when the Revolutionary War Council directed that all planes transfer to an independent Aviation Ministry. The order had little immediate impact during a period when the armed services were all withering for lack of funds. If enforced, though, it would create a disconnect between the Navy and the aircraft it relied on, similar to the loss suffered by Britain's Royal Navy, whose prestige could not save it from a twenty-year path of stunted carrier development. The Red Fleet, in contrast, had no prestige; it had only the stain of the Kronshtadt revolt. The next year, the Army seized command of the coastal artillery, and a writer for *Morskoi sbornik*, the navy's professional journal, bemoaned that 'the term "Red Army" has come to include the "Red Navy" as well.'[1] With the Revolutionary War Council dominated by army personnel, the fleet had reason for worry.

Administrative issues were heaped on top of more fundamental problems – the warship industry would pass through the 1920's without completing any new units as large as 500 tons – but the Admiralty tried to ignore its handicaps and approached aircraft carriers with great enthusiasm, arguably greater than in countries like Britain, America, and Japan that were actually building carriers in 1920. An article in the November 1922 issue of *Morskoi sbornik* declared, 'Aviation must exist in the fleet itself.' Aircraft carriers had a 'special purpose' to support surface units in fleet operations. The Revolutionary War Council, coincidentally or not, chose that same month to issue a directive confirming the monopoly of the Red Air Force.

The Navy itself suffered heated divisions. Many veterans from the tsarist officer corps advocated large battle fleets and a Mahanian view of naval combat. One of these 'Old School' leaders headed the Soviet delegation at the Rome naval conference in February 1924 where he argued that the international powers should recognise the Soviet Union's right to a tonnage of battleships nearly equal to Britain's and America's – effectively a claim to the third largest fleet in the world. But rather than implying a snub of naval aviation, this love of battleships led the Old School to prize the aircraft carrier as a vital auxiliary for the dreadnoughts. This meshed well with the call from the Revolutionary War Council for a high-seas fleet to defend 'world revolution.' However, the mid-1920's saw an ongoing campaign – a relatively benign purge – against holdovers from the tsarist days. This bolstered the position of the more politically reliable 'Young School,' which denounced battleships as an expensive expression of fraudulent naval theory, draping them with ideological invective and proposing coast defence and submarines as an alternative. For the Young School, aviation represented a cheap counter to blundering dreadnoughts, a trendy concept making air power the darling of war planners around the globe. Such was the giddiness regarding aircraft that even the Red Army journal *Voennyi vestnik* in March 1924 published a review article affirming the importance of aircraft carriers – not a lapse in inter-service rivalry, but a ploy to quash battleships.

The Conversions Projects

The Navy got a boost in 1925. In January, Stalin's machinations installed M. V. Frunze atop the Revolutionary War Council. Frunze reinstated the fleet's command over coastal artillery, and he expressed support for naval development. He personally observed fleet manoeuvres designed to illuminate the Navy's capabilities and needs, thus aiding in the formulation of shipbuilding proposals. The Admiralty discussed a variety of plans, the most ambitious of which called for three carriers: one in the Black Sea and two in the Baltic. Attention focused on the battle-cruiser *Izmail*, whose incomplete hull offered a shortcut to completing a carrier. By June, consideration was also given to converting the damaged battleship *Frunze* with a flushdeck configuration; she could serve in the Black Sea while *Izmail* stayed in the Baltic. (See Table 1.)

In July, the Council of Labour and Defence approved a carrier conversion, and the Navy's Scientific Technical Committee got the order to study the *Izmail* project. The tsarist past actually provided a precedent for this work: in 1910 pioneering airman Colonel M. M. Konokotin had suggested rebuilding the elderly turret ship *Admiral*

TABLE 1: PROPOSED CAPITAL SHIP CONVERSIONS

Izmail proposal, 1925

Displacement:	20,000-22,000 tons normal load
Dimensions:	223.9m oa x 30.5m x 7.6-7.9m
Machinery:	twenty-five Yarrow boilers (sixteen mixed, nine oil), 4-shaft geared turbines; 66,000shp = 27-30 knots
Range:	1000nm at full speed, 3000nm at cruising speed
Guns:	eight 183mm (8 x I), eight 102-127mm DP (8 x I), twenty 20-40mm (4 x V)
Aircraft:	twelve torpedo bombers, twenty-seven fighters, six reconnaissance, five artillery spotters, plus broken down aircraft stored in the 14-inch magazines; two catapults
Protection:	two versions, one retaining original 237mm belt and another replacing it with 75mm belt; flight deck 50-64mm

Poltava proposal

Speed:	30 knots
Range:	1800nm at 30 knots, 3800nm at cruising speed
Armament:	two 76mm guns, ten 'AA and anti-torpedo guns', four torpedo tubes
Aircraft:	50
Protection:	belt 250mm, deck 100mm

Kinburn of the Izmail *class. The availability of a complete hull was not enough to secure a carrier project.* (Courtesy of the Lemachko Collection)

THE SOVIET AIRCRAFT CARRIER: THE INTERWAR PROJECTS

Limited as she was, Komsomolets *nevertheless offered the Soviets an opportunity to near the major powers in carrier development.* (Courtesy of the Lemachko Collection)

Lazarev with a full-length flight deck and an internal hangar. Though *Izmail* far exceeded *Admiral Lazarev* as a potential aviation platform, both ships came to the same end: scrapping.

The fleet's fortunes reversed abruptly. Probably with Stalin's help, Frunze died in late 1925, and an army-minded K. E. Voroshilov assumed his office. Army lip-service for carriers vanished as the services squabbled over the meagre funds available. In January 1926, the Navy presented its construction plan aimed at creating a substantial battle fleet. The Army objected at once, informing the Navy that it had no business with battle fleets since its proper job was supporting the Army. A committee headed by Voroshilov's deputy took the issue under consideration, and the Army's version of the naval plan won out. The committee advised cancelling the conversion of *Izmail*; *Frunze*, not merely excluded from conversion, would not receive any rehabilitation at all. The carrier conversions were officially rejected by March 1926, and the fleet's situation only worsened. The Army suggested a thorough reorganisation of naval operational and construction planning. It became official in July: the Navy itself was demoted, and subordinated to the Army.

Carrier advocacy petered out, although 'certain circles' within the Admiralty remained sympathetic. The movement's last gasp came in 1927 when the Scientific Technical Committee sketched a final conversion plan. With the qualification that it 'should be viewed only as a first approach to the questions of outfitting an aircraft carrier,' the plan depicted the training ship *Komsomolets*

TABLE 2: PROPOSED TRAINING SHIP CONVERSION

Komsomolets proposal, 1927

Displacement:	12,000 tons full load
Dimensions:	149.4m oa x 17.4m x 7.62m (full)
Machinery:	twelve Yarrow boilers, 11,000shp = 15 knots
Guns:	sixteen 102mm DP (8 x II), ten 40mm (2 x V)
Aircraft:	sixteen torpedo bombers, twenty-six fighters
Complement:	530

(ex-*Okean*). Other than having its island and funnels on the port side, the design looked conventional enough. Modifications included new bulges and the replacement of the original variety of boilers by a set lifted from the doomed *Izmail*. Although critics rightly pointed to the ship's limited speed, the fundamentals of the design show a resemblance to America's *Langley* carrier conversion, which proved indispensable as a training and experimentation platform despite its 15.5-knot maximum speed. The *Komsomolets* plan actually surpassed *Langley* in having a sheltered hangar deck. (See Table 2.) If the Soviets had been able to muster their resources and make the conversion a reality, they might have placed themselves near the forefront of developing carrier aviation. Instead, the shipbuilding component of the First Five-Year Plan (formulated for 1928-1932) provided for no new warships larger than a destroyer leader.

The Admiralty was riven by increasingly bitter contro-

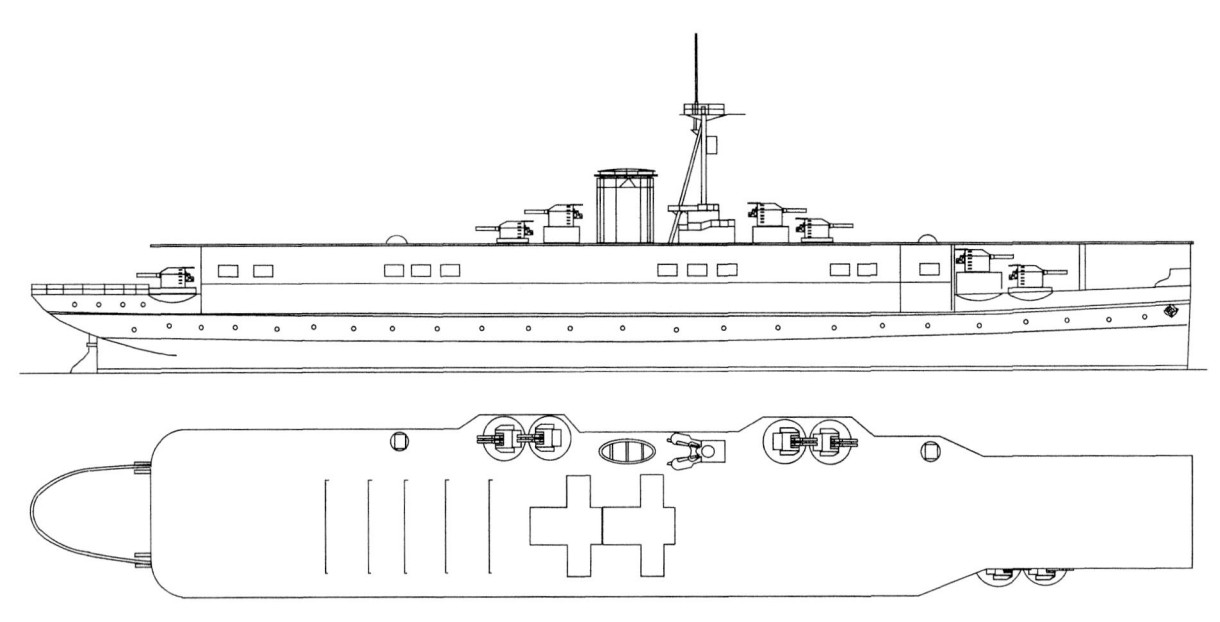

Estimated appearance for the proposed Komsomolets *conversion.* (Drawing by Rob Lundgren)

versy and division as the decade closed and the party leadership indulged its distaste for the Old School. The Young School had its victory, though few foresaw how short-lived the victory would be. Largely overlooked were hints such as Stalin's comment in July 1931 that he '…did not exclude that in five years we will build battleships.' More obvious was the fact that, for the time being, strategies featuring large warships had gone forcibly out of style. The aircraft carrier virtually disappeared from naval dialogue except as a player in enemy aggression.

At the time of this setback for wheeled aircraft, the other side of naval aviation made important advances. The NIVK considered seaplanes important enough in 1931 to study possible wartime conversion of two new motor ships: a 'light' tender conversion of the passenger ship *Krym* and a 'heavy' conversion for her sister *Gruziya*. Though the light tender could carry more aircraft, the heavy tender could accommodate attack planes. In either case, the ship would act as a ferry or, if the situation demanded, remain in an active sector to perform combat duty as a tender. (See Table 3.)

As a 'mobilisation project,' the conversion involved minimal alterations: removal of some superstructure, installation of a bow catapult, arrangements for aviation supply stowage, and so forth. Upon finalisation, the plan sat on a shelf to await a suitable emergency. When war actually arrived, the crisis allowed no time for such things, and the plan was not implemented, perhaps forgotten. However, seaplanes for use aboard warships had become an ongoing project.

In 1928, the battleship *Marat* began a modernisation which included facilities for a seaplane – an acknowledgment of Great War experience showing the value of aerial spotting. Though the war had stunted a plan to equip cruisers with seaplanes to enhance their scouting ability, the cruisers *Chervona Ukraina* and *Profintern* entered service in 1927-28, each carrying a pair of brand-new German-designed floatplanes. The 1932 commissioning of the cruiser *Krasnyi Kavkaz* underscored the situation;

When the emergency finally arrived, no one gave thought to Gruziya's *emergency conversion plans.* (Courtesy of the Lemachko Collection)

TABLE 3: AUXILIARY TENDER PLANS, 1931

Krym conversion, operational light transport

Displacement:	4090 tons standard, 4743 tons normal
Dimensions:	112m oa x 15.5m x 4.75m
Machinery:	2-shaft 7-cylinder M.A.N. diesels, 4000bhp = 14.5 knots
Range:	5400nm
Guns:	four 75mm AA (4 x I), ten 7.62mm mg (10 x I)
Aircraft:	four reconnaissance aircraft, twelve fighters

Gruziya conversion, auxiliary heavy transport

Displacement:	4280 tons standard, 4933 tons normal
Dimensions:	112m oa x 15.5m x 4.75m
Machinery:	2-shaft 7-cylinder M.A.N. diesels, 4000bhp = 14.5 knots
Range:	5400nm
Guns:	six 45mm AA (6 x I), ten 7.62mm mg (10 x I)
Aircraft:	three reconnaissance aircraft, nine torpedo bombers

THE SOVIET AIRCRAFT CARRIER: THE INTERWAR PROJECTS

A Heinkel HD-55, known in the Soviet Navy as a KR-1, being raised aboard the battleship Oktyabr'skaya Revolyutsiya. *Most of the large warships in the Soviet Navy were equipped with floatplanes.* (Courtesy of the Lemachko Collection)

here was a cruiser needing not only scoutplanes but also aerial spotters for her modern, extreme-range weaponry. Nevertheless, the cruiser seaplane programme slipped into decline as domestic industry struggled to produce capable aircraft.

Another line of development made headway during the warm naval interchange with Italy. Among the items purchased by the Soviets was a 1932 Ansaldo design for a flying-boat tender with a superficial resemblance to the Japanese *Oyodo* design: good speed and an all-forward armament. To test the concept, the elderly *Komintern* underwent modification in 1936. Plans went ahead for a pair of ships intended for reconnaissance duty in the Far East, but construction was cancelled in 1939. With war underway in 1943, the fleet made a final stab at a seaplane tender, requesting a study for converting *Krasnyi Krym*. Initial design work accommodated two fully assembled aircraft with ten others broken down. In theory this

Komintern *shortly before she underwent conversion as a testbed for seaplane carrier operations.* (Courtesy of the Lemachko Collection)

allowed the launch of all planes within an hour or two, until naval technicians pointed out that affixing the wings was merely the first step in readying a plane for launch. A practical assessment of recovery procedures indicated a duration of four hours or more. The Navy offered this final decision: 'Because operating fighters of types Yak-7 and LaGG-5 – far more capable than the Be-4 (KOR-2) as the fleet's air defence – from this ship is impossible, the design is hereby rejected.'

Carriers Return to the Agenda

Flattops capable of operating modern fighters returned to the Soviet naval dialogue in 1932 after a five-year exile. A luminary of the Young School, A. P. Aleksandrov, wrote a review in *Morskoi sbornik* rebuking any underestimation of carrier capabilities and affirming the value of the type, a direct channeling of the Young School's love of aircraft. By the end of the same year, Deputy Defence Minister M. N. Tukhachevskiy assessed the recent Baltic Fleet manoeuvres as confirming the need for a ship to 'carry planes capable of climbing into the air at any moment for the defence of the capital ships against air attack.' In such statements the Young School could find vindication of its stance on aviation, but also a cause for alarm: aircraft carriers had been linked to the hated battleship.

The naval programme under the Second Five-Year Plan received approval in July 1933; it was completely free of new battleships and carriers – not a reflection of Young School theory but of reality. The cruisers it included, at 8000 tons, represented challenge enough for Soviet industry. The following autumn, the new book *Anglo-amerikanskoe morskoe sopernichestvo* (Anglo-American Naval Rivalry) examined the nature of sea power and offered conclusions with a distinctly Old School bent. Virulent critique from the Admiralty failed to anticipate that Stalin himself would approve the book. At the same time, a professor at the Naval War College, V. A. Belli, published an unusually accommodating treatment of Old School concepts. The clearest indication of a policy shift came in January 1934 when Voroshilov announced that Stalin himself, the man who had hinted at ocean-going ships in 1931, would oversee the naval expansion programme.

Little overt change ensued. In each of the three months following Voroshilov's announcement, *Morskoi sbornik* published an article explicit on the value of aircraft. Treatments ranged from the docile adherence to Young School coast defence doctrine to enthusiastic endorsement of the carrier as an offensive weapon. The frequency of significant essays then slumped, but international events stepped in to drive the pace of change. Hitler's rise to power was attended by reborn German militarism. A German-Polish friendship pact in January 1934 changed the Baltic strategic scene. On 9 March 1935 Hitler announced the existence of a German air force, and the Soviet Baltic Fleet officially reclassified Germany as the primary threat. At the same time, Japanese expansionism presented an active menace in the Far East, where the conquest of Manchuria led Japan to create the Manchukuo puppet state.[2] Eastern and western threats came together in 1936 when Germany and Japan signed the Anti-Comintern Pact, uniting them in opposition to the Soviet Union. However, while Japan possessed the third largest fleet in the world and Hitler spoke of explosive growth of his navy to 400,000 tons, Stalin had other concerns besides the naval threats posed by continental powers.

Japan delivered its denunciation of the Washington Treaty on 29 December 1934, setting the stage for increased demands in subsequent negotiations. On 18 June 1935 Germany signed the Anglo-German naval agreement, which legitimised Hitler's rejection of Versailles restrictions and authorised a German fleet larger than the one Hitler had forecast just months before. These events had a common theme: the interaction of naval construction and diplomacy, giving clear illustration of the non-military value of an ocean-going fleet.

The Soviet Navy began a renaissance in 1935. Administrative reform provided the Admiralty with new powers, even restoring naval command over naval aircraft. The design bureaux received instructions to initiate a new line of study into large warships, to include battleships. On 24 December 1935, the Party's newspaper *Pravda* announced that the Soviet Union's days as a naval doormat were coming to a close.

Aviation had its place in the new design campaign. With aircraft carriers now doctrinally linked to capital ships, the Soviets considered linking the two types architecturally as well, a hybrid of the sort that enjoyed international enthusiasm at the time. The 1930 London Treaty included a loophole allowing unrestricted building of hybrid designs under 10,000 tons, yet no navy attempted to take advantage. Having no treaty obligations, TsKBS-1 studied four variants ranging from 21,500 to 28,500 tons, with forty-nine to sixty aircraft, and high speed – 35 to 39.5 knots. Designers forwarded the primary variant to the naval staff. (See Table 4.)

The horsepower figure indicates a three-shaft layout of Brown-Boveri turbines, which figured in many projects during this period. The 130mm DP battery was an attractive feature, and its further development would have benefited other types of warship. However, the specifications attempted far too much on the displacement. The American cruiser *Alaska* of 1943 makes a revealing point of comparison: 27,000 tons, nine 12-inch guns, 33 knots, four catapult seaplanes.

Balking at a complex project of unproven merit, designers decided against the cruiser-carrier in 1936, though interest in hybrids survived in subdued form. An

TABLE 4: HYBRID PROPOSAL

1935 Cruiser-Carrier

Displacement:	27,000 tons standard, 29,800 tons normal
Dimensions:	256m oa x 31m x 7.2m
Machinery:	steam turbines, 210,000shp = 36.1 knots
Range:	5000nm
Guns:	nine 305mm (3 x III), sixteen 130mm DP (8 x II), eighteen 45mm (9 x II)
Aircraft:	sixty
Protection:	belt 200mm, deck 125mm

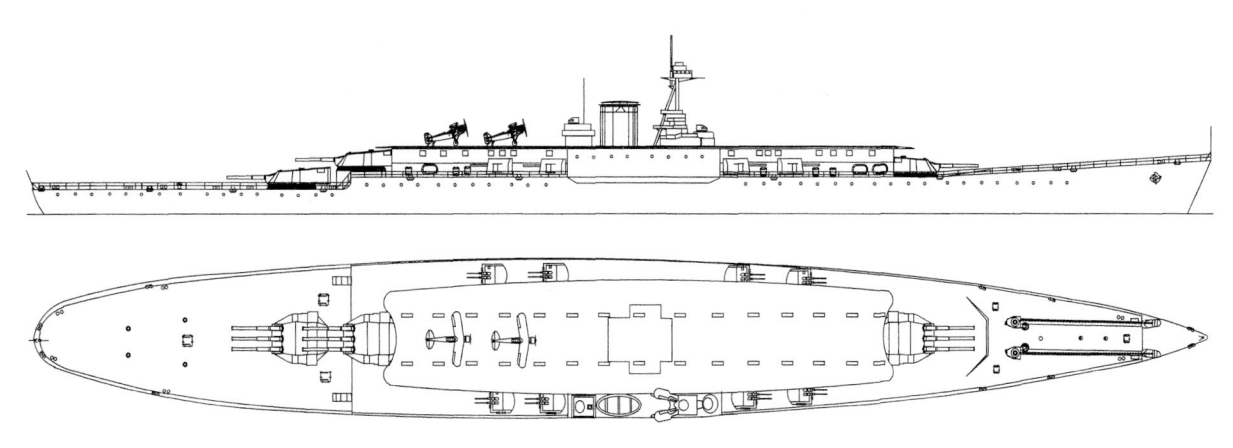

THE SOVIET AIRCRAFT CARRIER: THE INTERWAR PROJECTS

Proposed hybrid with 12-inch guns. (Drawing by Rob Lundgren)

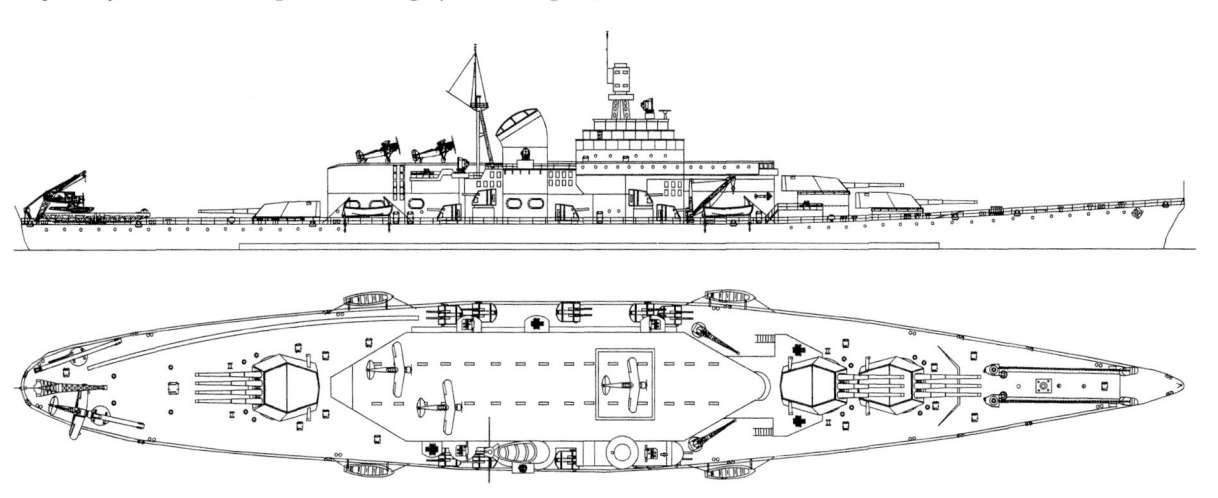

One variant of the design prepared by Gibbs and Cox with a quad turret aft. (Drawing by Rob Lundgren)

article appeared August, not in *Morskoi sbornik* but *Teknika i vooruzheniye*, with the title '*Kreisora-avionostsy*' ('Cruiser-Carrier'). There was a final dalliance with the concept at the end of the year when talks took place in America regarding the purchase of battleship armour, naval vessels including battleships and submarines (either in completed form or for assembly in the Soviet Union), and plans of American warships including the carrier *Lexington* (with some tentative feelers in Britain as well). The Roosevelt government rejected the request for plans but permitted discussion on the purchase of ships from private yards. Dealings with the marine architect firm Gibbs & Cox resulted in a battleship-carrier design – remarkable for its size, impracticality, and ugliness – but not in any construction. The experience snuffed out any lingering interest in hybrids.

In any case, the vast size of anticipated Soviet programmes obviated the need for ships combining two roles. With the floodgates open, various planning bodies dreamed their own versions of the coming Soviet superfleet. By April 1936 the head of the Navy, V. M. Orlov, proposed a plan for a fleet totalling 1,727,000 tons by 1947; even more generous, A. I. Yegorov and his army general staff suggested a fleet totalling 1,868,000 tons. The Council on Labour and Defence made its decision and presented its ten-year projection to the Politburo on 26 June 1936, detailing a navy of 1,360,000 tons. At that time, the entire British Navy totalled 1,250,000 tons, the American Navy 1,100,000 tons, and the Japanese Navy 800,000 tons.

In November, official announcement of the plan with its twenty-four battleships—Japan had nine battleships in 1936, Britain and America had fifteen each—dealt the Young School a mortal blow, but the reorientation of views became complete only two years later, and in typical Stalinist fashion. In the meantime, the about-face stripped carrier policy of any clear direction, resulting in meagre representation for flattops in the massive fleet projections. Yegorov's plan included four flattops to operate in the Pacific and two in the Arctic, while Orlov was happy with just a pair of 8000-ton Pacific units.

Issued in 1937, the 'Naval Forces Combat Regulations (BUMS-37)' had nothing to say on the subject of carriers. However, the carrier dialogue was renewed with a flurry of publications early in the year. A Naval War College handbook, newly revised, noted the carrier's ability to provide air support on distant operations. A high-profile convert from the Young School, I. M. Ludri, published an article trumpeting the capabilities of battleships and affirming the value of carriers, especially in open-sea settings. *Morskoi sbornik* started the year with an excerpt from a British study into the vulnerability of battleships to air attack, which it followed in 1938 with a set of articles scrutinising the carrier from a wide range of angles. Naval War College professor V. F. Chernyshev produced the most revealing essay. He expressed concern about carrier vulnerability within range of land bases, then stated outright that carriers were the one ship type that the Soviet Navy did not need. Yet he ranked modern aviation as a greater ship-killer than the submarine, noting that aircraft also provided the versatility to target the enemy on land. He foresaw that a future war might reveal the aircraft carrier as a genuine capital ship. Well beyond ideological cat-fighting, the subject of aircraft carriers underwent conscientious investigation from serious professionals.

The Great Purge of 1937-38

These discussions took place precisely at the time when the Admiralty fell into its greatest crisis. The Great Purge hit the Navy in May 1937 and continued until November 1938. Not a measure specifically targeted against the Young School – it extended beyond the Navy to all segments of Soviet society – the campaign was often cloaked in ideology but showed no rational direction. (Repentant Young Schooler Ludri was shot while former Young School spokesman Aleksandrov survived, though not without some controversy). The number of naval officers who lost their posts, with varying degrees of finality, reached 3000, a number almost half as large as the number of commanders and specialists who had graduated into the service since 1922.

It was amid these traumatic events horror that the Navy grasped its most coveted prizes. On 17 July 1937, the Soviet Union and Great Britain signed a naval agreement that introduced the Soviets into the treaty system, granting a Baltic fleet to match Germany's along with the freedom to counter Japan in the East. The mere prospect that his super-fleet might someday exist had made Stalin a key player in the international naval scene. The Navy was rewarded for this service; in November, it officially stepped out from under the command of the army and reclaimed its independence.

Out of the tumult arose a new strain of naval thought, embracing many concepts of the Old School and its battleships, in combination with the Young School's defensive assets such as coastal craft, submarines, and aviation. This 'Soviet School' featured many Young School alumni but showed no sentimentality toward former comrades, described in an August 1938 article as 'enemies of the people,' 'false leaders,' and 'the head of the snake' – unwelcome attention when the purges were ongoing. Thus the new doctrine comprehensively displaced all others and accommodated the most ambitious and varied shipbuilding plans.

The Navy's vast programme would begin under the Third Five-Year Plan, but the specifics never reached a final form. Projections became increasingly fantastical, inflating past 3,000,000 tons by the time war broke out. (See Table 5.) Amid the frenzy of planning, though, the aircraft carrier got left behind. While the number of new dreadnoughts went from twenty-four in the original draft to thirty-one in 1939, and cruisers went from twenty to twenty-eight, the number of carriers ended up at a lonely two (one Pacific and one Northern), postponed until the start of the Fourth Five-Year Plan. One would start building in 1941, the other in 1942. The aircraft carrier never won a place in Stalin's heart, and in the end, that would determine its fate.

Nevertheless, carriers had passed from the hypothetical. A commission on warship construction headed by Yegorov delivered its findings to the Defence Committee of People's Commissars Council. This led to a document on 15 August 1937 detailing the Navy's needs, and to a set of basic requirements for carrier design. (See Table 6.) At first glance, the numbers appear realistic apart from the heavy gun armament. However, the design relied on theory in the absence of experience. The meagre tonnage implied a narrow-seas scenario and a fleet defence role. However, the document dictated a genuine high-seas capability, for which the range was inadequate, and the air group included torpedo and reconnaissance planes as well as fighters.

The Tactical-Technical Requirements, approved in February, called for thirty reconnaissance bombers with fifteen fighters; a main battery of 130mm guns and AA outfits of 100mm guns, 37mm cannon, and heavy machine guns; together with armour for the vitals

TABLE 5: PLANNED TONNAGE BY FLEET (NOT INCLUDING RIVER AND LAKE FLOTILLAS)

date	Pacific Fleet	Baltic Fleet	Black Sea Fleet	Northern Fleet
27 May 36	450,000	400,000	300,000	150,000
7 Sep 37	796,000	514,000	342,000	338,000
28 Feb 38	910,692	581,787	396,393	343,629
10 Aug 39	1,154,078	797,113	558,082	518,628

Note: the 400,000-ton figure for the Baltic Fleet exactly equalled the tonnage cited for the German Navy by Hitler in 1935.

TABLE 6: INITIAL CARRIER SPECIFICATIONS

Displacement:	10,000-11,000 tons
Speed:	about 30 knots
Range:	4000nm
Guns:	six to eight 130mm, four to six 100mm DP, eight 37mm
Aircraft:	40-50

TABLE 7: 1938 CARRIER SPECIFICATIONS

Displacement:	13,000 tons
Machinery:	turbines or diesels, 34 knots
Armament:	six 130mm guns (3 x II), eight 100mm AA guns (8 x I), sixteen 37mm guns (4 x IV), twelve heavy machine guns, elaborate fire control comparable to that of the *Kirov*-class cruisers

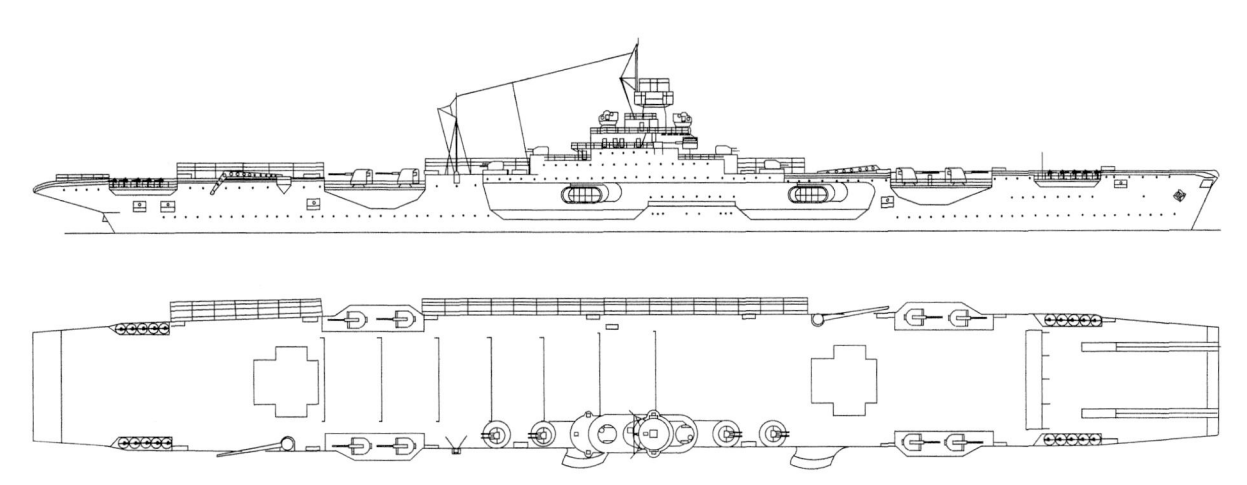

Estimated appearance for Project 71. (Drawing by Rob Lundgren)

corresponding to that of the Project 68 light cruisers. The ship would operate on the high seas, even against enemy shores, yet without a higher tonnage requirement. By June 1938, the naval leadership hammered out further specifics. (See Table 7.)

Without firsthand carrier experience, the Soviets looked elsewhere for inspiration, and essays at that time often referenced decisions and theories from France, Italy, and Germany. Italy had no aircraft carriers. Germany had begun construction but had no ships in service. France had a single inadequate carrier built on a leftover battleship hull. The major carrier powers received some attention, though much of it centered on smaller designs like Japan's *Ryujo* (8000 tons) and America's *Ranger* (14,000 tons) which allegedly offered increased efficiency but, unknown to the Soviets, disappointed their owners. While preference for smaller ships was not universal, by September 1938, when an army journal translated an Italian admiral's argument for large carriers even in the confines of the Mediterranean, the momentum of opinion had already placed the smaller ships to the fore.

New Carrier Designs

The first formal effort at carrier design, Project 71, evolved during 1938-1939 under the supervision of the head of TsNII-45, I. V. Kharitonov. (See Table 8.) It had the attraction of recycling the hull design of the Project 68 light cruiser *Chapaev*. While the Soviets never considered diverting existing cruisers into Project 71, there was considerable speculation abroad. The 1939 *Jane's* reported the completion of the 9000-ton carrier *Stalin*, converted from the *Svetlana*-class cruiser *Admiral Kornilov* (actually scrapped incomplete twelve years earlier) with twenty-two aircraft and 30 knots. *Jane's* also announced a new pair of *Krasnoye Znamya*-class carriers due for keel-laying by 1940,[3] which at 12,000 tons with twelve 4-inch guns, forty aircraft, and 30 knots were not far removed from Project 71.

Like *Chapaev*, Project 71 would have been largely riveted with combined longitudinal and transverse framing, but adapted with a 16m extension over the stern and round-downs at both ends. Flight-deck equipment included six arrester wires spaced 10m apart, but no crash barrier. Two compressed-air catapults could launch 4000kg aircraft at 110km/h from their 24m acceleration length. Crewmen could raise the windbreak, 18m wide and 3m high, just behind the catapults to shelter those on deck. The hangar was enclosed by 12mm sides and deck, with the wooden flight deck (60mm planks on 12mm steel) overhead. It could accommodate all thirty planes with wings folded, or eighteen fixed-wing fighters. Fire safety measures included three retractable steel curtains and inert gas to flood the avgas stores. The 13m x 12m cruciform elevators had electric drive to lift them from the hangar to the flight deck in 15 seconds. Designers anticipated launching the entire air complement in 25-32 minutes. Bomb storage showed a preference for smaller weapons: 20 of 250kg, 110 of 100kg, and 340 of 50kg.

The designed propulsion plant imitated *Chapaev*'s two-shaft turbine arrangement with six boilers (106 tons of steam per hour, 26kg/cm² pressure, 325° C). This provided good speed but inadequate range. Shipboard

TABLE 8: PROJECT 71

Displacement:	10,600 tons standard, 11,300 tons normal load, 13,150 tons full load
Dimensions:	195m wl, 215m oa x 18.7m wl, 24m max x 5.88m
Flight deck:	215m x 24m
Hangar:	148m x 18m x 6m
Machinery:	126,500shp = 33.75 knots
Bunkerage:	2550 tons oil, 4580nm at 18 knots
Guns:	eight 100mm/56 B-34 DP (8 x I), sixteen 37mm/63 46-K (4 x IV), twenty 12.7mm DShK mg
Aircraft:	ten reconnaissance-bombers, twenty fighters
Protection:	starboard belt 100mm, port belt 75mm, transverse bulkheads 75mm, armoured deck 50mm, conning tower 50mm

electricity came from four turbo-generators and two diesel-generators. The starboard-side island did not house the funnels, which instead were flared out from beneath the flight deck as in Japanese designs.

The fire control system included two directors containing B-20 rangefinders for the 100mm-guns and two MPEh-Eh-9,0 searchlights. As planned, the acoustics room would have housed Wolna, Dnepr, and Kama systems, though in fact none of these became operational. The radio outfit consisted of a Rul-U system (which also never entered service), plus a Reid station, Uragan and Skat transmitters, and Purga and Groza receivers.

The Scientific-Technical Committee approved the design in general but requested improvements, some practical (reduced bow trim, improved communications gear) and some less so (active roll stabilisation, 10-15 additional aircraft, sixteen 130mm guns). The flight-deck equipment apparently escaped criticism, and Project 71 would have displayed all her impracticalities as the Soviets taught themselves flight operations. Details of carrier equipment were among the many desired items for a naval committee that travelled to Germany in autumn 1939. The Soviets tried to purchase the plans of Germany's aircraft carrier *Graf Zeppelin* – they even tried to purchase *Graf Zeppelin*'s sistership, whose construction had ceased on 19 September 1939 when complete up to the armour deck—and managed at least to get a tour of *Graf Zeppelin*, roughly 90% complete at the time. Unfortunately, little good could come from such input as the Germans themselves were carrier neophytes. *Graf Zeppelin*'s catapult system, an effusion of over-complexity, added little to the launching process except to maximise vulnerability. A postwar American assessment found the landing equipment both awkward and dangerous.

Responding to the Committee's feedback, Kharitonov drew up an alternative (71b, *bolshoi* = large) with twice the tonnage, a size more in keeping with successful ocean-going designs in the major carrier fleets. (See Table 9.) The range factor alone – doubling 71's ability – made 71b the better choice for offensive operations on the high seas, not to mention her superior striking power and damage resistance. *Ranger* and *Ryujo* had demonstrated to their owners that size mattered when it came to providing a suitable platform for flight operations, especially in rough seas; this effectively undercut the theory of greater efficiency in small carriers. The 71b variant promised better sea-keeping for the northern Pacific. The advantage in an Arctic setting would have decreased in the extreme conditions there, where daylight could present a more restrictive factor than the sea state. These designs dated from a time before even the British had established night carrier capability, making an Arctic carrier useless for half a year.

The hull included a torpedo defence system. Protected by 20mm side plates, the two-storey hangar had enough space for seventy folding-wing aircraft. The Soviets don't appear to have considered using deck parks on the Americans pattern. The flight deck steel had a maximum 30mm thickness. It mounted two catapults and other equipment similar to that of Project 71. The propulsion plant included the popular Brown-Boveri turbines but in a two-shaft layout.

In the end, 71b had no chance of being built because it competed with battlecruisers for construction slipways

TABLE 9: **PROJECT 71B**

Displacement:	24,000 tons standard, 30,600 tons full load
Dimensions:	230m wl x 28m wl x 7.33m
Flight deck:	250m x 30m, two catapults
Hangar:	102m x 19m x 5m
Machinery:	154,000shp = 32.3 knots
Bunkerage:	8000nm at 18 knots
Guns:	sixteen 130mm/50 B-2LM (8 x II), thirty-two 37mm/63 49-K (8 x IV), thirty-two 12.7mm mg (8 x IV)
Aircraft:	forty torpedo-bombers, thirty fighters
Protection:	belt 100mm, armoured deck 50mm, flight deck 30mm, transverse bulkheads 20mm, hangar sides 20mm

The Project 71 carrier derived its hull and machinery design from that of the light cruiser Chapaev, *which actually reached completion – albeit postwar.* (Courtesy of the Lemachko Collection)

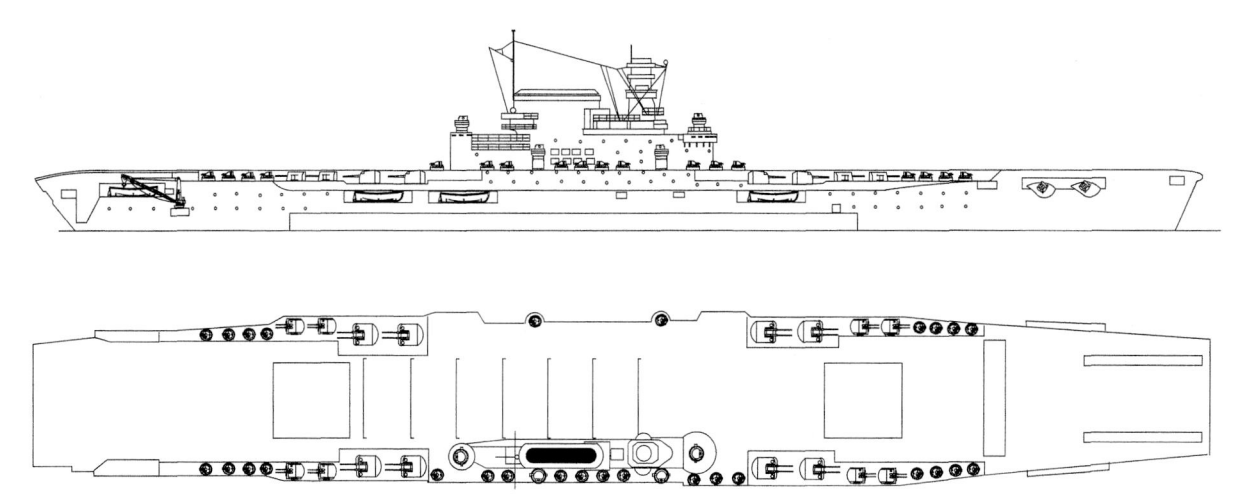

Estimated appearance for Project 72. (Drawing by Rob Lundgren)

and machinery, and no one doubted where Stalin's priorities lay. For 71, standardisation with the *Chapaevs* made an attractive selling point, leading to plans for two units to be built at Nikolaev.

This ambitious construction programme was being subjected to a cold dose of reality by the start of 1940, and the carrier hopes faded. Stalin's ocean-going fleet died in October with the order that no more large hulls were to be laid down. The diplomatic value of capital ships had lost relevance in wartime, and the Navy believed battle fleets had no role in a war that promised to last for years. Carriers seemed especially inappropriate, requiring the Soviets to master a new craft in the midst of a storm.

The Last Designs

The Commissar for the Navy, Admiral N. G. Kuznetsov, refused to abandon carriers. A 1941 effort to generate design requirements failed; the war was revealing the full extent of carrier capability and limitations, but the Soviets had none of this experience firsthand. Kuznetsov oversaw the compilation of available information on carrier battle experience and, in late 1942, directed the naval main staff to revisit carrier design. Rear-Admiral Yu. Pantele'ev supervised the initial study, which in January 1943 produced variants carrying thirty, forty-five, or sixty planes. These included a fighter/dive-bomber and a torpedo plane, with perhaps an additional pair of seaplanes; in the absence of available carrier aircraft, intelligence on foreign types provided the basis for planning. Specifications dictated an armament of eight to twelve 130mm DP guns, sixteen 85mm DP guns, twelve 37mm guns, and twenty-four 20-23mm guns. As in other navies, protection against guns continued as a major criterion for the armour scheme, leading to a planned immune zone of 11,000-25,500m against 130mm gunfire. Maximum speed would be 30 knots, and cruising speed would yield a range of 10,000 miles. An active anti-roll system would allow operations in Beaufort 9 conditions.

Design work began at TsKB-4, then transferred to TsKB-17. The project belonged to V. V. Ashik, a man so devoted to aircraft carriers that he made it the subject of his university dissertation in 1929 during the period of the carrier's exile from Soviet thought. B. G. Chilikin assisted with the work. Leisurely progress resulted in a trio of pre-sketches which were, however, not completed until November 1944. The variant with forty-five planes faded from consideration, replaced by a second large ('B') design, perhaps because expanding the second hangar from fifteen to thirty planes made few demands. (See Table 10.)

Flight-deck equipment generally resembled Project 71 but with rectangular lifts. Safety for the aviation fuel received special attention, with the storage tanks armoured and isolated by a cofferdam. The hull housed a Pugliese anti-torpedo system.

The leadership paid little attention to any of this. Apathy extended to the aviation element, so that requests for data on required deck area and arrester gear specifications went unanswered. Specialised carrier aircraft, required in limited numbers, presented an unwanted diversion from mass-production projects, especially given the unlikelihood of laying down a major warship in the middle of a war. It remains unclear if the Soviets completed any planes for the carrier role, or even if they started serious design work. Nevertheless, though official policy bypassed the aircraft carrier, it remained an object of study, and Project 72 survived into the postwar years as a starting point for discussions.

The outbreak of war with Germany had imposed a new perspective on naval planning as life-and-death realities reduced carrier design to an occasional plaything at most. With the end of the war in sight the subject found new relevance; warship hulls lying incomplete since 1941 would become available, a review of wartime developments spurred new design work, and *Graf Zeppelin*'s remains fell into Soviet hands. However, nothing credible took shape before Stalin's death created a comprehensive break into new naval policies.

Sources:

Morin, Arkadiy and Waluyew, Nikolai: *Sowjetische Flugzeugträger: Geheim 1910-1995*, Brandenburgisches Verlagshaus, 1996.

Westwood, J. N: *Russian Naval Construction 1905-1945*, Macmillan Press Ltd., 1994.

TABLE 10: PROJECT 72 VARIANTS

Project 72 I-B

Displacement:	30,215 tons standard, 36,100 tons normal, 39,850 tons full load
Dimensions:	250.7m wl x 31.4m wl x 8.57m
Flight deck:	273m x 33.5m, two catapults
Hangar:	130m x 20.5m x 5.5m
Machinery:	steam turbines, 30 knots
Range:	10,000nm at 18 knots
Guns:	sixteen 130mm/55 in B-2-U DP mounts (8 x II), sixteen 85mm/52 in 90-K DP mounts (16 x I), twenty-four 37mm in V-11 mounts (12 x II), forty-eight 23mm (24 x II)
Aircraft:	sixty-two
Protection:	belt 90mm, flight deck 30mm, armoured deck 55-80mm, hangar sides 30mm
Complement:	2113

Project 72 II-B

Displacement:	30,755 tons standard, 33,765 tons normal, 37,390 tons full load
Dimensions:	250.7m wl x 31.4m wl x 8.57m
Flight deck:	273m x 33.5m, two catapults
Hangar:	130m x 20.5m x 5.5m
Machinery:	steam turbines, 210,000shp = 30 knots
Range:	10,000nm at 18 knots
Armament:	twelve to sixteen 130mm in B-2-U DP mounts (6-8 x II), sixteen 85mm DP (4 x II, 8 x I), twenty-four 37mm in V-11 mounts (12 x II), forty-eight 23mm (24 x II)
Aircraft:	sixty-two
Protection:	belt 90mm, flight deck 30mm, armoured deck 55-80mm, hangar sides 30mm
Complement:	2290

Project 72 III-M

Displacement:	23,740 tons standard, 26,200 tons normal, 28,840 tons full load
Dimensions:	223.5m wl x 27.9m x 8.45m (full)
Flight deck:	241.75m x 32.5m
Machinery:	eight boilers; 4-shaft geared turbines; 144,000shp = 30 knots
Range:	10,000nm at 18 knots
Armament:	sixteen 130mm/55 in B-2-U DP mounts (8 x II), sixteen 85mm/52 in 92-K DP mounts (8 x II), twenty-four 37mm/67.5 in V-11 mounts (12 x II), forty-eight 23mm (24 x II)
Aircraft:	thirty
Protection:	belt 90mm, flight deck 30mm, armoured deck 55mm
Complement:	2000

Hudson, George E: 'Soviet Naval Doctrine under Lenin and Stalin', *Soviet Studies*, Vol. 28, No. 1, Jan. 1976, pp.42-65.

Silverlock, Gerard: 'British Disarmament Policy and the Rome Naval Conference, 1924.' *War in History*, Vol. 10, No. 2, April 2003, pp.184-205.

Åselius, Gunnar: *The Rise and Fall of the Soviet Navy in the Baltic 1921-1941*, Routledge, 2006.

Herrick, Robert Waring: *Soviet Naval Theory and Policy: Gorshkov's Inheritance*, US Naval Institute Press, 1989.

Rohwer, Jürgen and Mikhail Monakov: *Stalin's Ocean-Going Fleet: Soviet Naval Strategy and Shipbuilding Programmes 1935-1953*, Frank Cass Publishers, 2001.

McLaughlin, Stephen: *Russian & Soviet Battleships*, US Naval Institute Press, 2003.

Breyer, Siegfried: *Graf Zeppelin*, AJ-Press, 2004.

Philbin, Tobias R., III: *The Lure of Neptune: German-Soviet Naval Collaboration and Ambitions 1919-1941*, University of South Carolina Press, 1994.

Cernuschi, Enrico and O'Hara, Vincent: 'The Breakout Fleet: The Oceanic Programmes of the Regia Marina, 1934-1940', *Warship 2006*, Conway Maritime Press Ltd., 2006.

Layman, R. D. and McLaughlin, Stephen: *The Hybrid Warship*, US Naval Institute Press, 1991.

Kulagin, Konstantin: 'Razvitie sovetskikh avianesushchikh korablei 1925-1955', *Tekhnika i vooruzheniye*, No.7, 1999.

Platonov, Andrey Vitaleevich: *Nesostoyavshiesya 'avianosnye' derzhavy*, Saint Petersburg, 1999.

Greger, René: 'The Mysterious Fate of the *Poltava*', *Warship 1990*, Conway Maritime Press Ltd., 1990.

Spasskii, I. D. (ed.): *Istoriya otechestvennogo sudostreniya* (4 Vol.), Saint Petersburg, 1994-96.

Foreign Relations of the United States: The Soviet Union, 1933-1939, United States Department of State, pp.457-491.

Footnotes:

[1] The Navy had assumed command of coastal artillery just three years earlier.

[2] The Japanese factored significantly in Soviet naval planning at the time, prompting the formation of a Far Eastern Squadron in 1932, elevated to the title of Pacific Fleet in 1935.

[3] As late as 1966, *Warship International* printed an article titled 'The Soviet Navy in World War II' citing one ship of this class having started construction in Leningrad.

SECURING 'THE RIPEST PLUM':[1]

Britain and the South American Naval Export Market 1945-1975

Jon Wise looks at the attempts of British shipbuilders to secure warship orders in South America during the postwar era.

Many of Britain's traditional naval links with South America date from the 'decade of revolutions' (1810-1820), when a number of countries on that continent gained independence from Spain. By the outbreak of the First World War all the major warships of three of the four principal navies, Brazil, Chile and Peru, had been or were being constructed in Britain. The exception was Argentina.

Work Continuity and the Economy

There are two principal reasons why the UK Government was anxious to exploit the South American market again immediately after the end of the Second World War. Firstly, there was the need to maintain shipbuilding capacity and to preserve the skilled workforce, particularly in the privately owned 'mixed' yards. The Government therefore resorted to the tried and tested expedient of controlling construction in a *contra-cyclical* manner in order to compensate for the peaks and troughs in the naval and mercantile market and for what was expected to be a slump in merchant vessel orders following the war. What was not predicted was a sustained period of economic growth, often referred to as the 'Long Boom', which saw the size of the merchant fleet double between 1948 and 1965. The Royal Navy, on the other hand, beset with uncertainties as to its future role and to the composition of its fleet, saw numbers of orders dwindle alarmingly, with just 21 warships completed in British yards between 1945 and 1950. The winning of export contracts, particularly from countries which had been little affected by the war, therefore became an attractive proposition.

The second and more pressing reason related to the parlous state of the British economy, which had been crippled by six years of war. There was an urgent requirement to earn hard currency. With respect to South America it was recognised that there were no strategic reasons for stimulating the export of arms to the region, and it was conceded that US mutual defence arrangements were

ARV Aragua, *the third of the Vickers-built* Nueva Esparta *class destroyers for the Venezuelan Navy, completed in 1956. The external similarities to the RN's 'Battle' class are striking.* (World Ship Photo Library)

The Venezuelan *Nueva Esparta* class destroyer

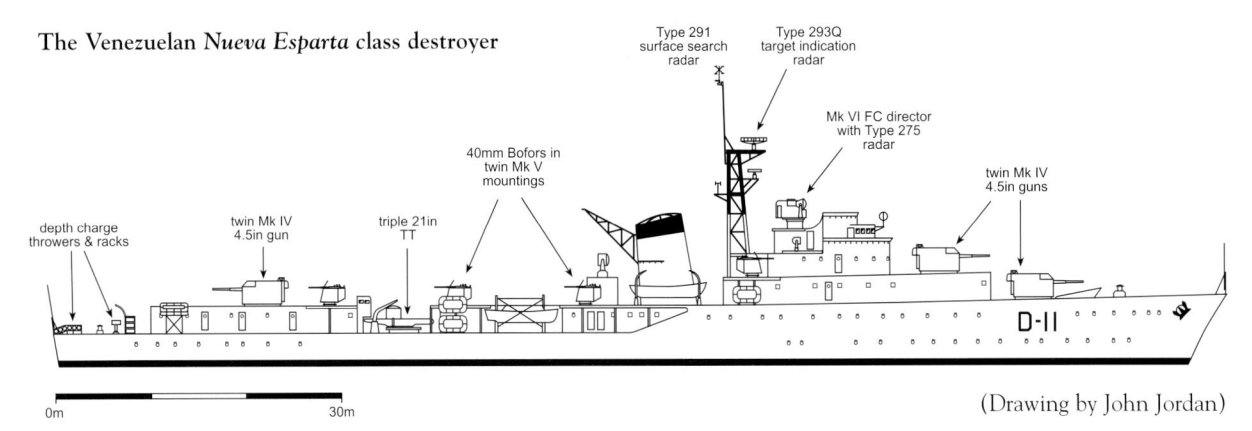

(Drawing by John Jordan)

already in place. Nevertheless, it was thought highly desirable to increase UK exports, particularly to dollar account countries on that continent. To do so strengthened political relations and presented the prospect of exploiting other markets, eg for the sale of civil aircraft. Exports to Bolivia, Colombia, Ecuador and Venezuela would yield the valued dollar, while Argentina, Brazil, Chile, Paraguay, Peru and Uruguay were in the sterling area. However, question marks were placed against Argentina – and to a lesser extent Chile – on account of the ongoing disputes over territories in Antarctica and also the Falklands.[2]

The Nueva Esparta *Class*

Britain had diplomatically courted Venezuela, described as being 'flush with dollars' from oil revenues, since before the end of the Second World War. The Royal Navy had sent the armed yacht HMS *Corsair* to attend the anniversary celebrations of a long-forgotten Venezuelan general in February 1945, a ceremony not attended by US warships. This gesture was later acknowledged by the President, and following protracted negotiations two, and later a third, modern destroyers were ordered to be built by Vickers-Armstrong at Barrow-in-Furness.[3]

The *Nueva Esparta* class drew comparisons with the contemporary RN *Daring* and 'Battle' classes, being almost identical in dimensions and displacement, and to an extent in their machinery and equipment. In appearance the Venezuelan destroyer could have been mistaken for a slightly bulkier-looking 'Battle' class. Internally the 50,000shp power-plant was slightly inferior (54,000shp in *Daring*), probably due to the less demanding sea conditions in which the ships were expected to operate. It was more obviously less capable in terms of electrical power, featuring 200kW turbo-generators as opposed to 350kW in *Daring*, and two 100kW rather than three 150kW diesels. However, *Nueva Esparta* was equipped with a powerful anti-surface armament comprising six 4.5-inch guns in Mk IV mountings, no fewer than 16 Bofors guns and a triple torpedo tube for the 21-inch Mk IX torpedo. The Mk IV gun mounting was comparable with the main armament chosen for the 'Battle' class, but the Venezuelans were prepared to accept a reduction in ammunition stowage in favour of superior habitability, particularly for the officers.

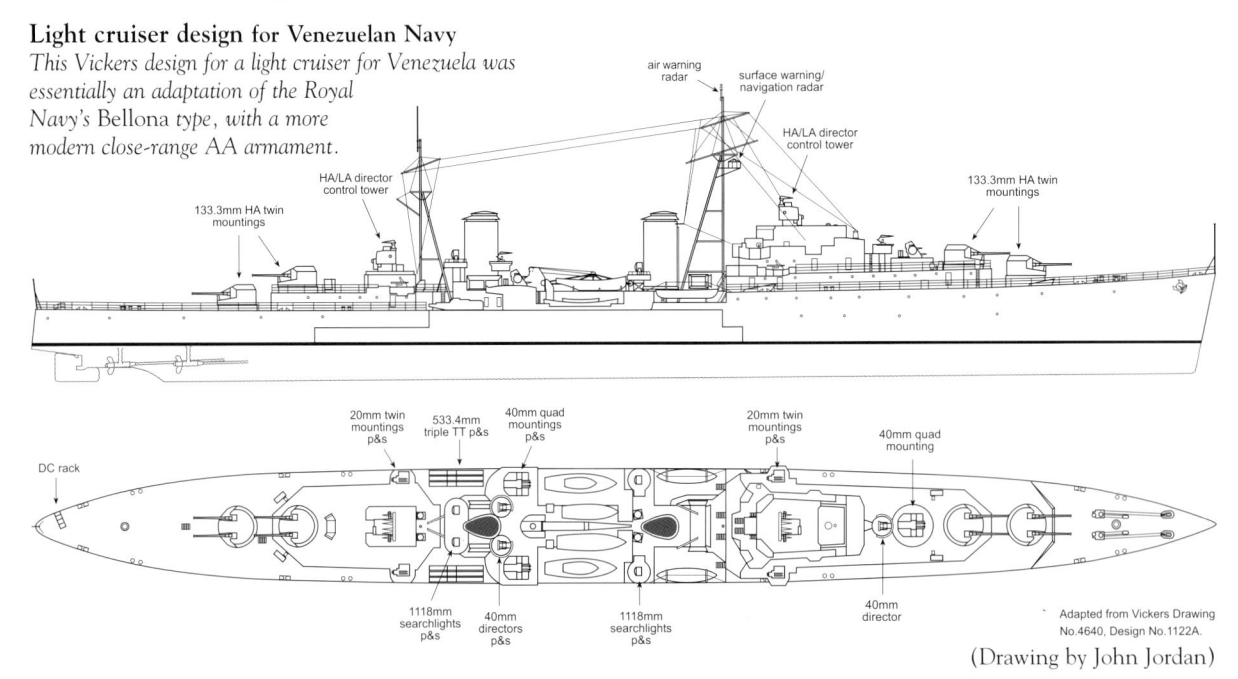

Light cruiser design for Venezuelan Navy
This Vickers design for a light cruiser for Venezuela was essentially an adaptation of the Royal Navy's Bellona type, with a more modern close-range AA armament.

(Drawing by John Jordan)

It took four years of vacillation and prevarication on the part of the Venezuelans, due in part to changes in government which included a military-backed coup in 1950, before the contract for the first two destroyers was signed. Initially, the purchase of various second-hand warships, firstly destroyers and then frigates, was discussed. By 1948 the Venezuelan Navy favoured a cruiser, and Vickers-Armstrong produced designs for such a vessel which closely resembled the war-time *Bellona* class. The Admiralty expressed profound misgivings as to the ability of the Venezuelans to man and to operate such a large warship. After construction had started at Barrow on the *Nueva Esparta* there were delays, due to the unexpected demand for skilled labour to cope with an increase in naval shipbuilding for the RN following the outbreak of the Korean War. This became the cause of considerable friction between the parties involved.[4]

The *Nueva Esparta* class formed only a part of the Venezuelan plan to strengthen and modernise its navy. Between 1950 and 1953 there was intense competition between the Italian firm Ansaldo and a British consortium comprising Thornycroft, Vickers and White to win a contract to build six destroyer escorts. In the end Ansaldo secured the work for Italy, much to the chagrin of the Foreign Office, who had invested a great deal of time and effort, and of the shipbuilding consortium, who argued that the British design was technically superior and only slightly more expensive.[5]

Chile and the 'Almirante' Class Destroyers

Historically, Chile was the South American country with which Britain had maintained the closest links since it gained independence from Spain in 1818. There was a great deal of respect and affection for the RN among senior officers, many of whom had trained in the UK and had even served aboard HM ships. By 1946, Chile was in talks with Vickers-Armstrong regarding replacements for its ageing cruisers. However, this project failed as did subsequent negotiations to acquire the iconic cruiser HMS *Ajax* second-hand, which ended in political and diplomatic farce in 1949, causing an unfortunate degree of estrangement between the two countries which was exacerbated by the deepening crisis over the future of contested Antarctic territories.[6]

Nevertheless, fears that Chile's eastern neighbour and bitter rival Argentina was about to acquire an aircraft carrier and develop a naval air arm prompted the opening of discussions in 1951 which were to lead to the building of two 'Almirante' class destroyers at Vickers-Armstrong. The contract was to be worth about £9 million, and these destroyers were to be equipped with a powerful anti-aircraft battery intended to counter the aerial threat.

At roughly the same time, a contract had been signed with Vickers-Armstrong to repair Chile's First World War-vintage battleship, *Almirante Latorre*, which had hitherto constituted the key element in countering the Argentine Navy's surface warfare threat. There had been a major engine room catastrophe in 1951 which had rendered the ship inoperable. Investigations into the damage determined that the ship would need to sail for the UK to be re-boilered, thus adding considerably to the costs involved.[7] In the event, the Chileans decided not to proceed with the battleship refit in order meet the cost of the new destroyers, even though this meant paying Vickers a hefty cancellation fee. This change of mind caused delays in the final signing of the 'Almirante' class contract; efforts were made to save money by reducing the specification of some of the machinery and equip-

*The competition: the ex-*Brooklyn *class cruiser USS* Philadelphia *purchased by Brazil from the United States, transferred in 1951 as part of the Mutual Defense Assistance Program and re-named* Barroso. [Author's Collection]

The Chilean Navy *Almirante* class destroyer

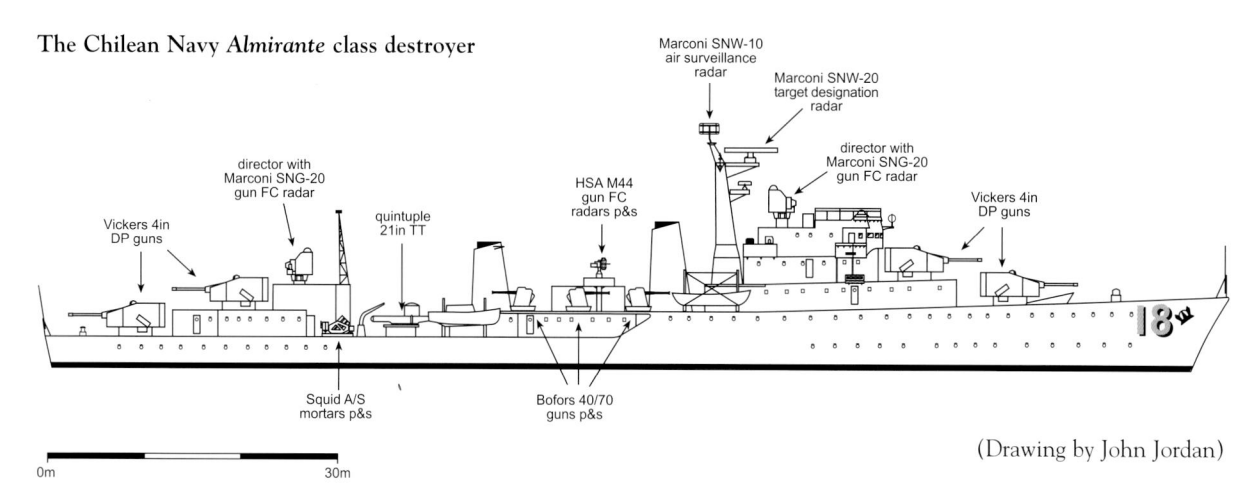

(Drawing by John Jordan)

ment without interfering with the ships' overall fighting efficiency.

Under the initial terms of the offer to the Chileans, the destroyers had been described as comprising a *Daring* hull and a 'Battle' arrangement with a 3,300 tons deep load displacement, making them superficially similar to the *Nueva Esparta* class. However, there were also notable differences and improvements between the two classes of destroyer which in part reflect the fact that the 'Almirante' class was designed some four or five years later than their Venezuelan counterparts, but also reflect Chile's status as a valued and trusted customer, thereby meriting the most up-to-date technology available.

The main gunnery armament comprised four automatic Mk N(R) single 4-inch guns. This was the first Vickers private venture of its kind undertaken since the war, and had only just been released for export in 1955 when the 'Almirante' design was first announced. The Mk N(R) had been developed from an earlier Army model and its medium calibre shell, which had direct hit or near-miss kill capability, was intended as a counter to the latest fast jet aircraft. The gun featured an elevation of 75 degrees

A close-up of the Chilean Vickers-built Almirante Riveros *returning from builder's trials at Barrow-in-Furness. Note the Vickers private–venture Mk N(R) single 4-inch gun and mounting and the Marconi-manufactured radars: SNW-10 for air surveillance atop the mast, SNW-20 for surface work, below, and the SNG-20 for gunnery control.* (Ken Royall)

Almirante Williams *at sea. The Sea Cat SAM missile launcher visible on the main deck on the starboard side replaced the after 40mm gun during a refit carried out at Talcahuano naval yard in 1964. Note the prominent identification 'W' on the bridge wing.* (Chilean Navy Official)

and a range of 12,500 yards. Although this automatic weapon had a higher rate of fire than a manually operated one, doubts about its sustained fire capability owing to the lack of a water-cooling arrangement was the principal reason why the gun was ruled out for possible service in the Royal Navy. It is interesting to note the internal Admiralty debate on the future of the AA gun at the time (1953). While the Director of Plans was convinced that this type of weapon would be obsolete in the long term, the Director Gunnery and Anti-Aircraft Warfare Division disagreed, stating that 4-inch gun calibre and below would never be superseded entirely by 'other devices', presumably by guided missiles.[8]

During the early design stage the Chilean naval staff pressed for specifications to be changed in order to improve the performance of the destroyers. Firstly, Vickers-Armstrong was requested to provide higher steam characteristics such as a boiler pressure of 650lbs per square inch at 850 degrees Fahrenheit at the superheater outlet from the boiler, as opposed to 440psi and a steam temperature of 650°F. This was intended to match the performance of ex-US destroyers which were being sold to other South American countries at the time under the terms of the Mutual Defense Assistance Program (MDAP).[9] Later in the same year (1955) there was an enquiry as to whether the Limbo ASW system could be fitted. This was rejected on account of the fact that this new weapon was only just being made available to the RN and Commonwealth navies.[10]

When the two warships first commissioned in 1960, they featured distinctive plated-in rather than lattice foremasts which were not evident in earlier sketch designs. These carried the latest Marconi export radars: SNW-10 for air surveillance, SNW-20 for surface work and the SNG-20 for gunnery control. The ships' closed-in bridges, air-conditioned Operations Rooms and specially designed heating and ventilation systems intended to cope with the extreme temperature variation of Chile's littoral all pointed to a well-planned, modern, albeit conventional destroyer design.

Later in the decade serious consideration was given to allowing Vickers-Armstrong, once again, to build submarines for both Chile and Venezuela. Although an updated 'T' class design was offered, both countries – and Chile in particular – wanted the latest *Porpoise* class boats. This presented a dilemma for the British government. HMS *Porpoise* was not yet in service with the RN, and security concerns were raised about key equipment such as propulsion, the torpedo tubes and radar. The Type 267 P/X band surface search set had yet to be released for export. Moreover, the English Electric propulsion equipment included components designed by Westinghouse, who had not granted permission for export. Most importantly, the design of the torpedo tubes had been configured exclusively to accept the new Mk 20(S) 'Bidder' torpedo, whose performance remained classified. On the other hand, as the total value of such an order was forecast to be in the region of £30 million, the Naval Arms Export Committee decided not to object to the request, and Vickers-Armstrong duly presented modified specifications. In an effort to disguise the fact that the design was based on the *Porpoise* class boat, some of the estimated performance figures were downgraded and other details were deliberately masked, although the Vickers team which prepared the brief admitted that it required only a cursory investigation to reveal the true identity of the design.[11] In the event, negotiations fell through as changes in government in South America introduced altered priorities.

Introducing Naval Air to South America

In March 1952 Brazil announced details of an ambitious naval building programme which included three light cruisers, one escort or light fleet carrier, six destroyer 'leaders', ten minelayers, three submarines, plus a survey vessel, a hospital ship and river gunboats. A direct approach was made to the British Government indicating that the Brazilians were particularly interested in receiving bids from UK private shipbuilding firms. It was estimated that if Britain was contracted to undertake the entire package, which included supplying a considerable number of naval aircraft and helicopters, the order would be worth in the region of £40-50 million spread over a five-year period, 1954-1959. Nevertheless, the government was under no illusion either that the entire programme would materialise or that the UK would be successful in competing with other countries. For example, the French T47 destroyer, then under construction for the *Marine Nationale*, was considered to be more modern and attractive to the Brazilians than the one being offered by the Thornycroft, White and Yarrow consortium, despite the French design being more expensive. Payment terms also favoured the French, as the Brazilians had a credit balance in francs while the British were anxious to be paid in dollars rather than in sterling.[12] Ultimately, the destroyers were not built either by France or by Britain, and it would be a further five years before Brazil acquired four ex-US *Fletcher* class vessels under the terms of the MDAP.

Unquestionably, the acquisition of an aircraft carrier represented the most attractive, but also the most contentious part of the programme. Brazil's desire to become the first South American country to have seaborne naval air power, and at the same time to steal a march on its rival Argentina, was complicated by internal dissent between the Navy and Air Force as to which should control the nascent fleet air arm. This particular issue was not resolved until 1965.[13]

In 1953 British hopes of winning this particular order seemed bright, as four light fleet carriers of the 1942 *Majestic* class programme, *Majestic, Powerful, Hercules* and *Leviathan*, had been lying in an incomplete state since 1946 – although three of the four ships were either earmarked for or about to transfer to Commonwealth countries, leaving *Leviathan* unallocated. It was felt that completing the ship in the United Kingdom would provide useful employment, and that she could be commandeered in case of an emergency at any time prior to delivery. In 1953, during one of the most dangerous periods of the Cold War, such considerations would have been uppermost in the minds of the naval staff.[14]

The UK's only foreign rivals were France, possibly Japan and the United States. Neither of the first two countries listed constituted a serious threat. In the case of the USA, the matter was complicated by the country's strategic plans for the continent. The Mutual Defense Assistance Act had finally been accepted by Congress in 1949 after much opposition. In terms of the Latin American navies this meant that they could acquire ex-US escort vessels and submarines at attractive prices. The intention was to make the continent's navies exclusively focused on ASW. The United States would provide the necessary training, and would encourage and lead multinational exercises.[15] Brazil's announcement of its intention to acquire an aircraft carrier, which was interpreted by the Americans as meaning an escort carrier, presented a dilemma for the northern superpower. On the one hand, Brazil had been a close ally of the USA during the Second World War, and had been the one South American country to have made a consistent, active contribution. Additionally, the Americans were concerned that the proposed missile tracking base to be sited on Brazilian soil should actually materialise. On the other hand, given opposition in the past, it was felt unlikely that the necessary legislation permitting the building or transfer of what amounted to a capital ship would be approved by Congress, as it would create an imbalance of naval power in South America.[16]

Thus Britain and Brazil entered a protracted period of negotiation, but could not agree a price for the completion and update of *Leviathan*. By 1956 attention had switched to acquiring HMS *Vengeance*, of the earlier *Colossus* class. Negotiations again stalled regarding the extent of the modernisation which a UK private shipyard could offer. The initial design of these war-built carriers had left little scope for the kind of modification which would keep pace with developments in the size and capability of the latest aircraft. Lift and accelerator capacity could not be increased, the flight deck could not be widened, and the fitting of the new arrester gear would reduce hanger height.[17] Therefore when HMS *Vengeance* was offered to Brazil, it was correctly advertised as being capable of functioning adequately as a trade protection carrier, an assessment of its essential limitations that had been realised as long ago as 1945.[18]

However, Brazil wanted a ship which would be capable of launching modern jet aircraft. This would require rebuilding the fore-end of the ship in order to incorporate an angled deck and a more powerful catapult. The latter requirement proved to be the sticking point. No British private firm was capable of undertaking this work before 1960, and Britain had to accept the political embarrassment of the contract for this radical modernisation being undertaken in a foreign shipyard, by Verolme of Rotterdam. The Dutch had recent and relevant experience to draw upon, being in the process of completing the re-building of another *Colossus* class vessel, HNlMS *Karel Doorman* (ex-HMS *Venerable*), at Wilton-Fijenoord.

When the two and a half year refit was completed in 1960, the Brazilian NAe *Minas Gerais* emerged with an 8.5° angled flight deck, a steam catapult, new lifts and strengthened arrester gear. She was armed with two quadruple 40mm gun mounts fore and aft the island with a third mount farther aft. Both the guns and the ship's SPS-12 air surveillance and SPS-8B fighter control radars atop the island were of US design. The initial purchase of the *Minas Gerais* from the British Government had been for $9 million. Her reconstruction at Verolme cost three times as much.

Predictably, as soon as Brazilian interest in gaining a naval air capability became known, Argentina began an urgent campaign to make a similar acquisition. Again, the purchase of an ex-RN light fleet carrier became the focus. Fortunately for the Argentines, the overthrow of the President Juan Perón in September 1955, rumoured to have been orchestrated by a cadre of senior naval officers, introduced a more amenable and politically predictable regime in Buenos Aires, with a consequent lessening of tensions over the disputed Falkland Islands and Antarctic territories. The British Government therefore approved the sale of the *Colossus* class HMS *Warrior* for an 'as lying' price of £1.75 million in July 1958, the ship being renamed ARA *Independencia*.[19]

Four years prior to the sale, HMS *Warrior* had entered a two-year refit at Devonport during which time the ship became the only *Colossus* class vessel to be fitted with an angled flight deck. Her hydraulic catapult was modified in order to handle 20,000lb, and she also was fitted with a mirror landing sight and the US SPS-6C air search set.[20] These improvements placed the Argentine carrier on an operational par with the *Minas Gerais*. In order to cover the cost of the purchase, the Argentine Navy had disposed of its 1911 vintage dreadnoughts *Moreno* and *Rivadavia* and its even more venerable armoured cruiser *Pueyrredón*, which had been launched in 1898.

The increased confidence in Anglo-Argentine relations brought about by the successful ARA *Independencia* deal was no doubt influential in the negotiations which took place during the 1960-1962 period, which nearly resulted in a contract worth £20 million being awarded to Yarrow to build four *Leander* class frigates and to J.S.White of Cowes for the construction of six minesweepers. The stumbling block proved to be the Export Credit Guarantee Department of HM Treasury, which refused to accept cover for 90%, as opposed to 75%, of the risk involved in allowing payment for the ships to be phased over seven years. With the Admiralty and Foreign Office ranked against the Treasury and the Board of Trade, it took a Prime Ministerial adjudication in favour of the latter before the issue was resolved in January 1962.[21]

Cruisers for Peru

The 1950s had been a highly successful decade in terms of British naval exports to South America, despite consistent opposition from the United States. It was to end on a high note too with the sale of two *Ceylon* class cruisers to Peru, a particular achievement as at the time the country was the most American-influenced of the South-West Pacific navies. HMS *Newfoundland* (re-named *Almirante Grau*) was transferred on 30 December 1959 and HMS *Ceylon* herself (re-named *Coronel Bolognesi*) raised the Peruvian ensign for the first time on the 9 February 1960. Both cruisers had originally been built under the 1938-1939 naval estimates, but both had received major refits in the early 1950s. HMS *Newfoundland* had been reconstructed with two new lattice masts, a new bridge and improved AA armament, while *Ceylon* received a newly-styled covered bridge and lattice foremast. Both cruisers had been fitted with Types 960, 274, 277 and 293 radar sets, most of which, however, were soon to be deemed obsolescent by modern standards. The torpedo tubes on both ships were removed.

The transfers cost Peru in the region of £1.25 million each and were completed in a very short period between August 1959 and February 1960. Although the acquisitions were ostensibly aimed at replacing two elderly 1905-1907 vintage cruisers, the true purpose of the purchases related to the country's rivalry with its neighbour Chile. Peru was anxious to rebuild its naval forces, which had been in decline over several years. It had been deeply disappointed not to have been offered two ex-US cruisers in 1951 as part of the MDAP, unlike the other major South American naval powers Argentina, Brazil and Chile.

The sale of the cruisers, and particularly *Ceylon*, was bitterly opposed by the United States and Peru's neighbours and erstwhile enemies Chile and Ecuador, on the grounds that it threatened a naval arms race between countries which could ill afford to spend extra money on defence at the expense of civil projects. Britain consistently refused to listen to such admonishments, contesting that nations had individual freedom of action in terms of defence spending, and if Britain was not prepared to supply arms, someone else would.[22]

This argument was carried forward into the next decade, although internal politics across the continent heralded changes which were to favour Britain still further, as will be discussed below. The last of these politically inflammatory sales of second-hand major warships concerned the light fleet carrier HMS *Centaur*. In 1966 a complex diplomatic crisis loomed over the sale of this ship, which had been declared surplus to requirements. It was reported that both the Chilean and Argentine Navies had expressed interest. The Argentines wanted to replace *Independencia* with the newer and more capable *Centaur* while the Chilean Navy, predictably fearful of its rival's increasing naval air superiority, also expressed an interest in buying the ship.[23] Diplomatic bungling resulted in both countries being given assurances that the carrier would not be sold to its rival and, perhaps fortunately at this point, the Foreign Office saw sense and negotiations collapsed.

A Fresh Approach to Naval Sales

The 1960s brought a radical overhaul in the way in which the UK approached defence sales; the formation of the Ministry of Defence in 1964 ensured that the civilian team that had formerly handled naval exports on behalf of the Admiralty, Finance Division 3, became part of a corporate Defence Sales Organisation. The employment of private business methods allowed the sales teams actively to seek export contracts rather than simply responding to enquiries from potential customers as had been the practice hitherto.[24]

As far as the newly named Naval Sales Division was concerned, there was also a shift in emphasis away from sales of second-hand vessels towards attracting customers to invest in new-build. Second-hand sales, although regarded as good 'bread-and-butter' business, reduced the potential market for new ships, and when these vessels became elderly, it was increasingly difficult to keep them supplied with spares. By 1971-1972, for the first time in many years, not a single ex-RN warship was disposed of to an overseas customer.[25]

To enter the new ship business in a modern, professional manner meant learning and utilising techniques related to research and promotion. Not only did this require the cooperation of the private building firms which had handled initial negotiations in the past, but also the assent of the Royal Navy, which was adamantly opposed to its sailors acting as salesmen. However, the success of three so-called 'Special Squadron' deployments to South America in 1962, 1964 and 1969 served to alter senior naval officers' perceptions, introduce new methods of demonstrating British naval equipment and, most importantly, resulted in a hugely successful series of naval sales to the continent.

The RN Special Squadron which circumnavigated South America between December 1961 and February 1962, visiting Brazil, Uruguay, Argentina, Chile, Peru and Colombia in the process, comprised HM ships *Lion*, *Dunkirk*, *Leopard*, *Londonderry* and RFA *Wave Prince* and proved 'ground-breaking' on three counts. Firstly, the size of the task group constituted the largest single concentration of RN warships in the region for thirty years, and signalled a renewed and serious commitment to the continent which had been diminished since the disestablishment of the America & West Indies Station in 1957. Secondly, the presence of two modern frigates in the squadron's number, including HMS *Londonderry*, which had been in service just over a year, and HMS *Leopard*, just over four, allowed the South Americans to inspect the latest RN designs in home waters. Thirdly, the offer of joint exercises during the visits permitted professional interchange, the opportunity to witness RN equipment in action, and the chance for participation in manoeuvres at sea as equals rather than as junior partners.

The 1964 visit followed a similar pattern. Even greater emphasis was placed on naval sales, with the presence in the squadron of the new 'County' class guided missile destroyer HMS *London*, the *Leander* class frigate *Penelope* and the submarine HMS *Odin*.[26] By the time of the 1969 deployment of the recently formed Western Squadron, which comprised HMS *Hampshire*, *Arethusa*, *Juno*, *Narwhal*, *Otus* and RFAs *Olwen* and *Lyness*, such was the realisation that the interested South American navies only wanted to see the latest technology that all participating vessels bar one had been completed in the course of the current decade.

This deployment included the utilisation of one of its number, RFA *Lyness*, as a floating exhibition for RN equipment. This innovation had been suggested by the ship's master Captain Averill, who pointed out that the large clearway on the vessel's main deck, which normally functioned as an assembly area for stores during replenishment at sea evolutions, constituted an ideal exhibition space. The experiment proved successful and subsequently was used extensively on other deployments. From a commercial point of view the provision of a floating exhibition served to confirm the special pulling power which ship visits can exert in comparison with conventional defence equipment shows ashore.[27]

The Navy also became convinced that the presence of civilian members of the Naval Sales Division aboard RFAs in harbour did not 'commercialise' ship visits or compromise what were regarded as traditional flag-showing naval deployments. Vice-Admiral Lewis, who commanded the 1969 deployment and whose post as Flag Officer, Flotillas (and later Second Sea Lord) placed him in a highly influential position within the upper echelons of the service, was reported to be 'completely converted … to the benefits of using the Royal Navy's influence to make good commercial impressions'.[28]

Export Orders

All this effort proved fruitful in terms of export orders. In the late 1960s major contracts were negotiated with Argentina, Brazil, Chile and Venezuela which were to lead to the construction of two destroyers, eight frigates, five submarines and six fast attack craft. Two ex-RN destroyers were also sold to Peru during this period.

The announcement made in May 1970 that two Type 42 destroyers were to be built for Argentina was an important milestone for the Southern Cone navy in two respects. Firstly, the ships would be the first new-build vessels to enter service since the Barrow-built training cruiser ARA *La Argentina* in January 1939. Secondly, one of its number, *Santísima Trinidad*, would be constructed under licence by Astilleros y Fábricas Navales del Estado, Río Santiago, with technical support provided by Vickers, who would build the first of class ARA *Hércules*. Although *Hércules* was laid down in 1971 and launched the following year – only the second Type 42 destroyer to be launched – the ship did not complete until 1976, and only reached Argentina for the first time in August 1977, owing to protracted sea trials in British waters. The completion date might have been postponed further had the Argentine Navy not agreed that the prefabricated stern section destined for *Hércules* could be used to repair HMS *Sheffield*, which had suffered a serious explosion in the ship's double bottom which split the hull. The welding accident which caused the damage had occurred just two months prior to *Sheffield*'s launch date, and the prompt decision by the Argentines meant that the

SECURING 'THE RIPEST PLUM': BRITAIN AND THE SOUTH AMERICAN NAVAL EXPORT MARKET 1945-1975

ARA Hércules *returning from her final builder's trials in May 1976. Note the prominent exhaust deflectors, nick-named 'Loxton Bends', on each side of her funnel. This device, intended to reduce the ship's infra-red signature, was unsuccessful and was fitted only in the two Argentine destroyers and HMS Sheffield.* (Ken Royall)

The second of Argentina's two Type 42s, Santísima Trinidad, *was built at AFNE, Río Santiago (Ensenada). She is seen here on work-up in the Solent in August 1981 during a brief stay in Portsmouth cut short by the impending invasion of the Falklands. This contract marked a new trend towards technology transfer with a view to upgrading the naval shipbuilding capabilities of the purchasing country.* (Mike Lennon)

building schedule was not delayed, as *Hércules* was due to take *Sheffield's* place on the slipway.

The completion of ARA *Santísima Trinidad* took much longer. This was partly due to problems with the transfer of technology between Britain and Argentina, and partly to damage caused by a terrorist attack on the ship in 1975. The second Argentine Type 42 finally commissioned in 1981. Both ships closely resembled the Batch 1 Type 42 destroyers which were entering service with the Royal Navy during the same period. It is interesting to note that prior to ordering the ships, for which Vickers prepared three different designs, the Argentine Navy had considered a different propulsion plant in the form of FIAT gas turbines instead of Tynes. As far as armament was concerned, the US 5-inch/54 calibre medium gun and two OTO Melara 3-inch/62 close-in weapons were considered, as well as the Norwegian Terne and the Bofors ASW launchers as alternatives for the British lightweight, fixed triple Mk 32 ASW torpedo tubes.[29]

The most notable difference between the British Type 42 and the Argentine version was the inclusion of the Aérospatiale MM38 Exocet missile, which fundamentally changed the function of the ship from an area defence anti-air warfare destroyer with limited ASW and surface-warfare capability to one with multi-purpose characteristics which included a modern and potent surface-to-surface weapon. Initially, the *Hércules* class was fitted with two Exocet canisters atop the hanger, *Santísima Trinidad* during build and *Hércules* retrospectively. During later refits, two more Exocet missiles were added and the four missiles were then re-sited either side of the funnels.

Both ships played an active role in the Falklands War. ARA *Santísima Trinidad* led the initial invasion of the islands with both the Army and the Navy Commanders embarked. The flagship put 90 Argentine marines ashore in inflatables on the morning of 2 April 1982 as part of the vanguard of the attack. British intelligence was well aware of the threat potential of these two destroyers. The surface fleet as a whole was considered to be vulnerable to air attack. The Argentines had been experiencing problems with Sea Dart, defects causing excessive miss distances during trials. *Santísima Trinidad* particularly was known to have suffered a major defect with her system, while *Hércules* could not fire the Batch 2 missile because of Missile Tuning Unit incompatibility. Although intelligence suggested that up to nine warships in the Argentine fleet were capable of firing the MM38 missile, with its 24-mile range, the surface threat was considered to be potentially less damaging, due in no small part to the weapon's relatively unsophisticated homing device.[30]

The Niteroi *Class*

Undoubtedly, the most lucrative of the deals secured by British shipbuilding companies during this period was for six frigates of the *Niteroi* class. The deal between the Brazilian Government and Vosper Thornycroft in 1970 to construct four of the vessels at their Woolston yard in Southampton and the other two at the Rio de Janeiro Naval Dockyard was worth in the region of £100 million.

The contract for this private, and untested design was won in the face of competition from West Germany and the USA who offered *Köln* and *Bronstein* class frigates respectively.

The Vosper Mk 10 design was immediately compared with its contemporary the Type 42, as both ships were markedly similar in displacement and overall dimensions. However, they differed considerably in all other respects, even to the extent that two of the Brazilian ships effectively constituted a sub-class, being equipped for an entirely separate role. Four of their number, *Niteroi*, *Defensora*, *Independencia* and *União* were specialist ASW frigates while the remaining two, *Constituição* and *Liberal*, were officially classed as General Purpose vessels, albeit with the emphasis on a powerful surface warfare capability.

Arguably, the most significant difference between the Type 42 and the Brazilian Mk 10 lay in the selection of the ships' machinery. Whereas the British chose a COGOG arrangement, the privately designed *Niteroi* class were provided with a twin-shaft CODOG installation: two Rolls-Royce TM3B gas turbines for maximum speed and four MTU 16V 956 TB91 diesels for cruising. This arrangement allowed the ships an endurance of 5,300 miles at 17 knots with two diesel engines coupled, 4,200 miles with all four diesels engaged, and a maximum of 28 knots and 1,300 miles with the Rolls-Royce gas turbines in use. Although the CODOG power-plant enabled operational flexibility throughout the speed range indicated above, it required a modern and sophisticated control system in order to secure the optimum response. Thus, the power-demand lever and push button control, considered innovative at the time, permitted the mode of propulsion – cruising diesel, gas turbine or a combination of the two – to be selected while complying with the safety control limits of the machinery.

The main ship-borne armament of the four ASW frigates was the Hawker-Siddeley Ikara missile system. Because the *Niteroi* class was designed to accommodate this system, rather than have it fitted retrospectively, the complicated split-level stowage used on the Ikara-armed RN ships, HMS *Bristol* and the eight *Leander* class conversions, was avoided, and the single-level magazine under the helicopter flight deck allowed a simple run aft through double doors to the launcher which was sited on the quarterdeck. The Ikara system was complemented by three other ASW weapons: a Westland WG13 Lynx helicopter with homing torpedoes, two sets of triple Plessey-Marine Mk 32 torpedo tubes and a close-range Bofors double-tubed 375mm rocket launcher sited forward of the bridge. The Ikara missile, the helicopter and the triple torpedo tubes all utilised the USA-manufactured Mk 46 active/passive acoustic homing torpedo.

The main surface armament comprised a single Vickers Mk 8 4.5-inch gun. *Constituição* and *Liberal* had a second Mk 8 fitted on the quarter-deck in place of the Ikara system. The two General Purpose frigates also received two MM38 Exocet missile canisters which were sited on the upper deck between the two masts. All ships of the class were equipped with close-range anti-aircraft defence in the form of a triple Short & Harland Sea Cat STA missile system and a pair of Bofors 40mm guns.

The name-ship of the Brazilian Niteroi *Class leaving Portsmouth on trials. Although comparable in size to the contemporary Royal Navy Type 42 destroyer, this private-venture design presented a radically different profile.* (John Jordan)

The radar fit included a Plessey AWS-2 E/F band air and surface surveillance array with associated Mk 10 IFF which was carried at the head of the mainmast. The foremast supported a ZW-06 I-band surface search radar together with one of two Selenia-Elsag conical-span pulse tracker radars (the other was sited abaft the funnel), together with ESM equipment. The main sonar comprised the hull-mounted EDO 610E, a medium-range set which used pre-formed transmitting and receiving beams.[31]

There can be little doubt that the *Niteroi* class frigates were modern, sophisticated warships fitted with a range of the latest British, European and US weapons and sensors, some of which were already in service with major navies and others, such as the sonar, relatively untried, private-venture equipment. They immediately rendered obsolete several of the Brazilian Navy's ex-USN vessels, particularly the two pre-war cruisers and the seven *Fletcher* class destroyers which were progressively discarded in the decade following the completion of the frigate programme in the late 1970s.

Shortly before the contract for the *Niteroi* class was signed, another deal was concluded in August 1969 with Vickers for the construction of three *Oberon* class submarines to be built at Barrow. These boats entered service during the period 1973-78. This contract was imaginatively linked to attractive financing arrangements for the surface warships being built. It meant that

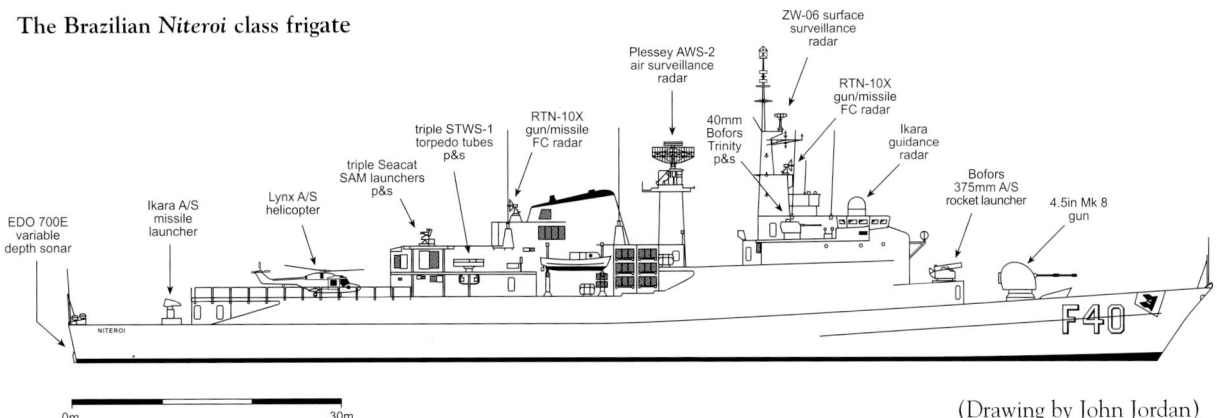

The Brazilian *Niteroi* class frigate

(Drawing by John Jordan)

The stern of Niteroi's sister Defensora, *showing the single-arm launcher for the Ikara A/S missile system and the EDO 700E variable depth sonar. In contrast to the installations in RN ships, the Ikara missiles were stowed horizontally behind the launcher.* (John Jordan)

Stern quarter view of the Brazilian frigate Constituição. *The 'General Purpose' configuration of this frigate and her sister* Liberal *included the fitting of a second 4.5-inch Mk 8 gun on the quarterdeck in place of Ikara, and Exocet missiles in canisters between the two masts.* (Mike Lennon)

The Brazilian submarine Riachuelo *lifted in Admiralty Floating Dock no.19 in Devonshire Dock, Barrow-in-Furness, on 7 September 1975. Presumably this was to check for any damage to the lower hull following the boat's dynamic launch the previous day. Ten years later, the skyline beyond AFD 19 would be unrecognisable following the construction of the gigantic Devonshire Dock Hall, where subsequent generations of nuclear-powered submarines have been constructed and then lowered into the water more safely, if less spectacularly, via a synchro-lift system. (Ken Royall)*

although the Vosper-built frigates and associated components were supplied by Britain, local cost credits were provided for the Brazilian part of the construction.

Unfortunately, disaster struck the second submarine, *Tonelero*, in October 1973 with the boat nearing completion when fire destroyed the control room centre section. The subsequent enquiry ruled that set procedures had not been followed and the fire started when an atomised spray of hydraulic oil was ignited by a welder's arc. Pressure of work at Barrow caused by the nuclear submarine programme meant that repairs to *Tonelero* had to be undertaken at Chatham Dockyard, thus seriously delaying the completion of the submarine.

Chile's British-built Frigates and Submarines

The acquisition of a naval air capability together with modern frigates and submarines of the latest design enabled Brazil to reassert its presence as the major naval power on the eastern seaboard of the continent. On the west coast, albeit on a smaller scale, Chile also sought to modernise its fleet by selecting British-built warships, a decision which was unquestionably influenced by the naval sales deployments of the 1960s described above.

However, progress towards this decision was not straightforward. Reluctance to commit was due, at least in part, to ongoing disagreements over policy direction between central government and the Navy. While successive Chilean administrations had exercised caution and often pragmatism with respect to the acquisition of naval *matériel*, the naval staff themselves frequently revealed extravagant and unrealistic plans to purchase the very latest in naval technology. On this occasion it was reported that they were considering having the two *Prat* class cruisers refitted by Vickers at an estimated cost of £30 million, perhaps with flight decks added on the ships' sterns to enable them to operate the latest Harrier vertical take-off (VSTOL) aircraft. This plan was no doubt prompted by the fact that Britain was in the process of developing VSTOL aircraft which could be adapted for use at sea.

The Chilean Navy wanted its two venerable heavy cruisers modernised in some form because of the threat of Argentine aggression that had been recently demonstrated during a series of incidents in the Beagle Channel, the international border between the two countries in the extreme south of the continent. By refitting the *Prat* class, Chile would retain the weight and range of gunnery it believed would be required.[32] Chilean naval thinking at the time still considered that a decisive naval battle with Argentine forces was likely to involve surface forces

SOUTH AMERICAN NAVIES: ACQUISITIONS FROM UK 1945-1975*

Purchaser	Class	Type	New/Second-Hand	Year	Number Acquired	Comments
Argentina	'River'	Frigate	SH	1948	1	Canadian built
Argentina	Colossus	Aircraft Carrier	SH	1958	1	ex-HMS Warrior
Argentina	'Ton'	Minesweeper	SH	1968	6	
Argentina	Sheffield	Destroyer	N	1976 & 1981	2	1 built in Argentina
Brazil	Colossus	Aircraft Carrier	SH	1956	1	ex-HMS Vengeance
Brazil	Niteroi	Frigate	N	1978-80	6	2 built in Brazil
Brazil	Oberon	Submarine	N	1973-77	3	
Chile	'Flower'	Corvette	SH	1946	3	Canadian built
Chile	'River'	Frigate	SH	1946	3	Canadian built
Chile	Almirante	Destroyer	N	1960	2	
Chile	Leander	Frigate	N	1973-74	2	
Chile	Oberon	Submarine	N	1976	2	
Ecuador	'Hunt'	Frigate	SH	1954	2	
Peru	Ceylon	Cruiser	SH	1959 & 1960	2	
Peru	Daring	Destroyer	SH	1969	2	
Venezuela	Nueva Esparta	Destroyer	N	1953-56	3	
Venezuela	Constitución	Fast Attack Craft	N	1974-75	6	

*Some of these vessels entered service after 1975. The year given denotes year in service or year acquired.

engaging in a heavy gun duel. Essentially, this future-war scenario had remained unaltered since the 1930s. Chilean fears at the time concerning Argentine aggression in the Beagle Channel did not materialise for a further decade until a crisis point was reached in 1978, when the two countries were on the point of declaring war. Although precise information about this incident is still scarce, there is evidence that the Chilean Navy had already carried out the planned offensive by the time an agreement was reached to suspend military action.[33]

In the event, having finally taken the decision to scrap the *Prat* class cruisers to allow the work on the two *Leander* class frigates and two *Oberon* class submarines to commence, the Navy still persuaded its government to enter negotiations and subsequently to purchase the cruiser *Göta Lejon* from Sweden; the latter had been laid down as long ago as 1943 and was last refitted in 1958. The subsequent building of the *Leanders* by Yarrow and the submarines by Scott-Lithgow later drew intense controversy following the military coup in 1973 which overthrew President Salvador Allende and introduced the dictatorship of General Augusto Pinochet. The British Labour Government became trapped between its socialist and moral principles and a growing unemployment crisis in the UK. In the end the building of the four vessels was allowed to continue. Unfortunately, the construction of the submarines, and the second boat *Hyatt* in particular, was also marred by shoddy professional standards and inept public relations in the Scotts yard on the Clyde.[34]

Conclusion

Vosper Thornycroft was responsible for the design and build of the six Venezuelan *Constitución* class fast attack craft which were constructed at Woolston between 1973-1975. These missile and gun armed vessels were fitted with Otomat surface to surface missiles at the stern and Oto Melara 76mm Compact guns forward. Cammell-Laird at Birkenhead extensively refitted the ex-RN *Daring* class *Diana* and *Decoy*, the generous size of these destroyers allowing a Plessey AWS-1 radar to be installed and a complement of eight Exocet missiles to be carried.

But this 'golden period' of warship new-build and second-hand sales and refurbishments did not last. Labour relations, demarcation disputes, over-capacity, a lack of visionary management, the inability to modernise and Margaret Thatcher's denunciation of shipbuilding as a 'sunset' industry have variously been blamed for its sad demise. Ironically, the withdrawal of the British from competition in the South American naval building market coincided with a period of greater commercial involvement by various European countries. The succeeding generation of new-build, major warships and submarines were built mostly by German or Italian companies or, increasingly, constructed under licence in the home countries. In the foreseeable future there seems little chance that the long tradition of UK naval shipbuilding in South America will be evident other than in a handful of second-hand vessels deemed surplus to requirements by an ever-shrinking Royal Navy.

Acknowledgements:
The author would like to thank WÖ Henk Visser, HNIMS Retd., Messrs. Ken Royall & Mike Lennon, and Dr. Carlos Tromben, official historian of the Chilean Navy, for the supply of some useful information and photographs for this article. He is indebted to John Jordan for his excellent drawings.

Editor's Note: An extended *Warship* Note on the Vickers 4-inch Mk N(R) gun mounting appears on pp.174-177 of this year's annual.

Footnotes:
[1.] The phrase 'the ripest plum' appeared in a Foreign Office

1. Internal Minute in 1945 which questioned the Admiralty's assumption that European Navies in the future would seek to buy British-built warships. The FO official argued that South America was 'the ripest plum among all markets for the products of naval shipyards', with ample demand together with an inability to construct their own vessels. See The National Archives (TNA), FO 371/44918 United States Naval Mission to Chile: proposed despatch to Chile of a British naval mission 1945.
2. TNA, PREM 8/766 Trade in Armaments with Latin America: Argentine Orders for naval vessels and aircraft from British firms 1947-1948.
3. TNA, FO 371/52221 British naval visit to Venezuela 1946; ADM 1/18038 Foreign Countries (52) Venezuelan celebrations at Cumaná: attendance of HMS Corsair and Venezuelan expressions of appreciation 1945.
4. TNA ADM 1/21140 Contracts (25): Ships for Venezuelan Government 1946-1949.
5. TNA, FO 371/97674 British offer to supply naval vessels to Venezuela 1952.
6. See *Warship* 2012 p.177.
7. Cambridge University Library, Vickers Company Archive Quarterly Reports 31 March & 30 June 1953.
8. TNA, ADM 1/25127 Design of 4 inch single naval gun by Vickers Armstrong for foreign sales: possible interest for service use 1953-1954.
9. TNA, ADM 116/6017 Naval Arms Export Committee: Minutes of meetings and related papers 1953-1954.
10. TNA, ADM 116/6018 Naval Arms Export Committee: Minutes and Papers 1954-1955.
11. TNA, ADM 116/6020, Naval Arms Export Committee: Minutes of meetings and related papers 1956. In the same year the Chilean naval authorities enquired about a 'small submarine' with comparatively low underwater speed. Vickers stated that the preliminary sketch design for this boat was based on the Admiralty 'S' class design, although the specifications provided show several similarities with plans for a small submarine design for the Royal Navy which was considered in the 1952-1955 period and given the provisional name of the *Boreas* class. (See D.K.Brown & George Moore, *Rebuilding the Royal Navy: Warship Design since 1945*, Chatham Publishing, London 2003, p.117.
12. TNA, ADM 116/6065 Scrapping of HMS Formidable and Brazilian requirements for warships 1952-1954.
13. Robert L. Scheina, *Latin America: A Naval History 1810-1987*, Naval Institute Press, Annapolis 1987, pp. 194-96.
14. TNA, ADM 116/6065, *op. cit.*
15. The inaugural UNITAS exercises took place in 1959 involving Argentine, Brazilian, Uruguayan, Venezuelan and US warships. Thereafter, an annual circumnavigation of South America by a US Task Group enabled multinational ASW tactics and skills to be practised with participating nations.
16. Foreign Relations of the United States 1952-1954 Vol.IV: United States Military Relations with Brazil July 1954.
17. Norman Friedman, *British Carrier Aviation: The Evolution of the Ships and their Aircraft*, Conway Maritime Press, London 1988, p.322.
18. TNA, ADM 1/26457 Proposal to sell HMS *Vengeance* to Brazil: Memo by First Lord 1956-1957.
19. TNA, ADM 1/26496 Sale of light fleet carrier to Argentina 1956; ADM 1/27019 Sale of light fleet carrier HMS *Warrior* to Argentina 1958-1963. The visit of the frigate HMS *Veryan Bay* to Buenos Aires in August 1956 was a significant step towards the albeit short-lived reconciliation between Britain and Argentina. (See FO371/119889 Visits by ships of the Royal Navy to Argentina.)
20. Friedman, *British Carrier Aviation, op cit*, p.231-32.
21. TNA, T236/6429 Export Credit Guarantee Department cover for export of goods to Argentina: frigates for Argentine Navy 1960-1962. Type 12 *Whitby* class and Type 14 *Blackwood* class frigates were also design options considered and then rejected by the Argentine Navy.
22. TNA, FO 371/126112 US attitude to sale of naval vessels to Latin America by UK 1957.
23. TNA, FO 371/179314 Chilean Navy interested in obtaining British warships 1965.
24. The Labour Government of 1964, perhaps contrary to expectations, positively encouraged the arms export trade. Denis Healey as Minister for Defence commissioned the head of British Leyland, Donald Stokes, to investigate the way in which arms exports were organised. The resulting Stokes Report (1965) introduced a unified system for the MoD based on private commercial practices.
25. John Peters, 'Defence Sales and the Naval Sales Division 1966-1970', in *The Naval Review*, LXII:3 1973, p.256.
26. TNA, DEFE 69/479 Visit of Special Squadron to South America 1964-1965.
27. Peters, *op cit*, p. 257.
28. TNA, FCO7/1511 Naval Sales from United Kingdom 1970-1971.
29. Norman Friedman, *British Destroyers & Frigates: The Second World War and After*, Chatham Publishing, London 2006, p.289.
30. Lawrence Freedman, *The Official History of the Falklands Campaign Volume II: War and Diplomacy*, Routledge, London 2005, pp.7,75-6.
31. Anon, Brazilian 'Niteroi class missile frigates', in *Naval Record*, April 1977, pp.57-63; Antony Preston, 'Niteroi Commissions', in *Navy International*, February 1977, pp.25-33; Antonio Ciampi, 'The Niteroi Class', in *International Aviation & Marine*, 1977, pp.51-58.
32. TNA, FCO 7/403 Sale of naval equipment 1967-1968.
33. Scheina, pp.185-87; James Garrett, 'The Beagle Channel Dispute; Confrontation and Negotiation in the Southern Cone', *Journal of Interamerican and World Affairs*, 27:3 1985, pp.81-109.
34. Lewis Johnman and Hugh Murphy, *Scott Lithgow: Déjà vu all over again: The Rise and Fall of a Shipbuilding Company*, International Maritime Economic History Association,

TOULON: THE SELF-DESTRUCTION AND SALVAGE OF THE FRENCH FLEET

Enrico Cernuschi and **Vincent P. O'Hara** look at the background to the scuttling of the French Fleet at Toulon in November 1942, and the efforts of the Italian *Regia Marina* to bring some of the key units back into service.

The scuttling of the French fleet at Toulon on 27 November 1942 was an event years in the making. It began in the chaotic days of June 1940. French sentiment for an armistice with the Germans was growing after the government fled Paris on 5 June. The Prime Minister of the United Kingdom, Winston S. Churchill, and some members of his government flew to France on 10 June to assess the situation and encourage continued resistance. During this trip Churchill met with Admiral François Darlan, the French Navy's chief of staff and supreme commander, and urged him to keep the fleet out of German hands. Darlan assured Churchill that Germany would never control the French Navy: 'It would be contrary to our naval traditions and to our honour.'[1] There was little else to cheer the prime minister on this trip, and on 17 June France's new premier, the 85 year *Maréchal* Philippe Pétain, announced it was time to stop fighting.

The terms of the armistice between France and the Axis powers that related to the fleet specified that ships other than those representing French interests in the empire would return to their home ports and be disarmed. Germany promised that it did not 'intend to use for its own purposes in the war the French Fleet which is in ports under German control, with the exception of those units needed for coastal patrol and for minesweeping.'[2] All of the home ports in metropolitan France save Toulon were, however, in the occupied zone, and the British considered this provision completely unacceptable.

The ruin of the Third Republic provided fertile ground for misunderstandings between the members of the crumbling alliance, both of whom felt betrayed. Nonetheless, the *Marine Nationale* signalled strongly that it intended to maintain its autonomy and discipline. Darlan authorised the defence of the channel ports through which the British evacuated nearly 200,000 men, even after they had been declared open cities. He ordered the incomplete battleships *Richelieu* and *Jean Bart* to safe havens in North Africa and the signing of the armistice on 24 June found nearly the entire navy concentrated in African, unoccupied, or British-controlled ports. Finally, the Navy had instructions and plans for ensuring that the Axis would not take over any French warships intact.

Great Britain meanwhile acted in what it perceived to be its best interests. Churchill and Admiral Dudley Pound, the First Sea Lord, distrusted Darlan's assurances and their suspicion led to the events of 3 July 1940 when French units in British ports were seized and a Royal Navy squadron opened fire on the French fleet at Mers el-Kebir while it was in the process of demobilising The British sank one French battleship and damaged two others along with a *contre-torpilleur*. Nearly thirteen hundred French sailors lost their lives at Mers el-Kebir between 3 and 6 July. Two days later *Richelieu* was attacked at Dakar by Swordfish aircraft and torpedoed.

Whether these actions advanced British security is debatable; what they did gain was Darlan's and the Navy's enmity. The battle fleet concentrated in Toulon, and the need for self-defence became an issue unanticipated by the armistice terms. On 3 July the Germans, angered that French naval units in British harbours had not yet returned to France, were threatening to reconsider the entire armistice.[3] However, after Mers el-Kebir Germany deferred the clauses relating to disarmament, and reopened negotiations about the status of French naval units. The unsuccessful British attack against Dakar on 23-25 September further demonstrated that the French were ready and able to defend their territory against their former partners. Following this attack Germany and a grudging Italy allowed France to retain in commission a battle fleet, the *Forces de Haute Mer* (FHM) or High Seas Forces, at Toulon. This comprised the fast battleship *Strasbourg*, five cruisers, and eight *contre-torpilleurs*; in addition coastal, escort, and submarine forces, the coastal and anti-aircraft batteries, and the squadrons at Casablanca, Dakar, Diego Suarez, the Antilles, and Indochina remained in service.

The major task of Great Britain's naval squadron at Gibraltar, Force H, was to support Malta, but it always considered the *Forces de Haute Mer* a menace – after

TOULON: THE SELF-DESTRUCTION AND SALVAGE OF THE FRENCH FLEET

A rare photo of the French battleship Dunkerque *during her return from Mers el-Kebir to Toulon 19/20 February 1942. The photo was taken from a German Ju-88 operating from Tripoli; the guns in the port-side quad 130mm turret are trained on the aircraft, probably as a warning not to approach too closely. Note the reinforcement bands on the port side of the bow section – the opposite side to the heavy damage inflicted when depth charges exploded alongside during the second British attack of 6 July 1940. Unusually, the tricolore recognition bands, which are crudely painted, extend down to the barbettes on turrets II and VII. The original close-range AA armament of 37mm guns appears to have been replaced by single mountings, probably the new Hotchkiss single 25mm gun. On her arrival at Toulon* Dunkerque *was docked in one of the Vauban Grands Bassins for more permanent repairs, which were in progress at the time of the scuttling. (Sincere thanks to Conrad Waters for allowing us to publish this photo from his personal collection)*

Dakar Admiral Somerville even worried about 'hav[ing] an Oran done on me' by the French.[4] Britain and France, in fact, were engaged in a *de facto* state of hostilities. This included periodic British attacks on French possessions: Dakar in September 1940, Syria in June 1941, and Madagascar in May 1942. Between July 1940 and October 1942, the Royal Navy seized 57 French merchant vessels at sea, and sank or damaged eleven. The Tunisian harbour of Sfax was raided from Malta three times in May 1941 and the Free Zone bombed on at least six occasions. In the meantime *Armée de l'Air* fighters shot down British flying boats and lone bombers on transfer missions any time they happened to encounter them along the African coast, and French aircraft twice raided Gibraltar.

Italy also lamented the return of a powerful French squadron to Toulon and regularly protested, usually in vain, whenever the Germans granted the *Marine Nationale* concessions. Rome was, in any case, able to delay the repair and refit in Toulon of the modern battleship *Dunkerque* once she returned from Mers el-Kebir in February 1942. The naval staff of the *Kriegsmarine*, in fact, harboured until November 1942 the illusion of an alliance with France, which they considered a more reliable and useful partner than Italy. The French officer corps and NCOs were sufficiently anti-British, but there was no possibility of an Axis continent at war supplying both the *Regia Marina* and the *Marine Nationale* with oil. In July 1940 the French had in the unoccupied zone about 300,000 tonnes of fuel including oil, diesel, and refined petroleum, both civilian and military. North and West Africa had a further 428,000 tonnes. The country's average consumption was about 20,000 tonnes a month. As the fuel bunkers of the *Forces de Haute Mer* alone required 25,000 tons it is easy to appreciate how a lack of fuel limited French opportunities for a general action. By January 1942, for example, the training of *Strasbourg* and her consorts was more theoretical than real.

This state of affairs induced Admiral Darlan to begin planning in February 1942 for a rapprochement with the United States, anticipating that this would occur in early spring 1943. He intended that the battle fleet should transfer from Toulon to North Africa, possibly bringing with it Marshal Pétain, as by that time a lack of oil put the whole fleet in danger of rusting away at its moorings instead of being Vichy's main asset.[5]

As an alternative – should it appear that the Axis had the upper hand – Darlan had a plan for a general action against Force H by the Toulon squadron in conjunction

135

with an air attack against Gibraltar. The plan, still valid in August 1942, could have been launched at any time as a retribution for the many offences suffered since Mers el-Kebir. Its major purpose, however, was political with the intent being to get a success – on the eve of a final European peace which many on the Axis side believed pending during the summer of 1942 – that could be used to improve the final terms with Germany.

In October 1942 Italian and French relations were at their lowest level, while the *Kriegsmarine* was still pursuing its wishful thinking regarding a possible naval collaboration and a future alliance with Vichy. In September the *Regia Marina*'s intelligence began signalling that an Allied landing in French North Africa was imminent. Despite Germany's refusal to believe such a possibility, *Comando Supremo* begun to organise forces from Tripolitania, Sicily, Sardinia, and Tuscany to be ready to seize Tunisia and Corsica.

The Allied Landings in North Africa

On 8 November 1942 American and British forces invaded Morocco, Oran, and Algiers. These landings provoked a violent reaction from the French squadrons based in Africa. The 2nd Light Squadron managed to

---

TABLE 1: ORGANISATION OF THE *FORCES MARITIMES FRANÇAISES*, 1 NOVEMBER 1942

Toulon

High Seas Forces
Battleship *Strasbourg* (fl)
1st Cruiser Division: *Algérie* (fl), *Dupleix*, *Colbert*
3rd Cruiser Division: *Marseillaise* (fl), *Jean de Vienne*
3rd Light Squadron:
    3rd Scout Division: *Guépard*, *Verdun*
    5th Scout Division: *Tartu*, *Vauquelin*, *Kersaint*
    6th Scout Division: *Volta* (fl), *L'Indomptable*
    7th Scout Division: *Gerfaut*, *Cassard*, *Vautour*
    10th Destroyer Division: *L'Adroit*, *Mameluk*, *Casque*

Metropolitan Police Division
1st Destroyer Division: *Bordelais*, *La Palme*, *Le Mars*
13th Torpedo-Boat Division: *Baliste*, *La Bayonaise*,
    La Poursuivante
3rd Escort Squadron: *Commandant Bory*, *Elan*, *La Batailleuse*,
    La Curieuse, *Chamois*, *L'Impétueuse*
1st Patrol Squadron: *D'Iberville*, *Yser*, *Les Eparges*
2nd class sloops: *Granit*, *Dédaigneuse*
Patrol Boat: *La Havraise*
Sub Chasers: *Chasseur I*, *Chasseur IV*
Minesweepers: *Cap Noir*, *Jean Bart II*, *Brin de Jonc*, *Moulinais*,
    Josette, *Claude*, *Altona 2*, *Caducée*, *Paon*, *Homard*,
    Roche bleu, *Calmar*, *Lennyan*, *Flèche*, *Blanche*,
    Chantereve, *Black Joke*, *Ariel*, *Pétrel 8*, *R4*

Tugs: *Coudon*, *Carquianne*
MFV: *Endurante*
Yacht: *L'Incomprise*
Tankers: *Durance*, *Garonne*, *Rance*
Transports: *Aude*, *Golo*, *Hamelin*, *Champlain*

Submarines (*groupe de relève*): *Casabianca*, *Redoutable*,
    Aurore, *Iris*, *Vénus*

Care & Maintenance (*gardiennage d'armistice*): 1 battleship,
    2 cruisers, 1 seaplane transport, 7 *contre-torpilleurs*,
    6 destroyers, 12 submarines, 1 netlayer (*Le Gladiateur*)

Bizerte
12th Torpedo-Boat Division: *La Pomone*, *L'Iphigénie*,
    Bombarde
3rd Patrol Squadron: *Commandant Rivière*, *La Batailleuse*
1st Minelayer Section: *Canard*, *Goëland*, *Grondin*, *Héron I*,
    Pen Men

2nd Minelayer Section: *Fracas*, *Gascogne*, *Ravignan*, *Penfret II*
25th Minelayer Section: *Chasseur 81*, *Saint-Antoine*, *L'Afrique*,
    Madone de Pompei, *Méduse*
Patrol boats: *Chien de Mer*, *Aigle de Mer*, *Loup de Mer*
Tugs: *Rhinocéros*, *Fort*, *Tenace*, *Vigoureux*, *Gabès*, *Sousse*

Care & Maintenance: 1 CT (*L'Audacieux*), 1 ML (*Castor*),
    9 submarines

Oran
7th Destroyer Division: *Tramontane*, *Typhon*, *Tornade*
CT *Epervier* (completing refit)
Sloop *La Surprise* (completing refit)
5th Patrol Squadron: *L'Ajaccienne*, *La Toulonnaise* (refit),
    La Sétoise (in transit)
Others: *La Bônoise*, (arrived 5 November)
12th Submarine Division: *Argonaute*, *Diane* (refit)
5th Submarine Division: *Actéon*, *Fresnel* (in transit, arrived
    7 November)
3rd Minelayer Section: *Tourterelle* (refit), *Pigeon*, *Chêne*
27th Minelayer Section: *Jean Argaud*, *Nadal*, *Joos*, *Anna*, *Lilias*
    (not operational)

Care & Maintenance: 4 submarines

Algiers
9th Submarine Division: *Caïman*, *Marsouin*
26 Minelayer Section: *Colonel Casse* (non-operational),
    Angèle Pérez, *Marsouin II* (operational but disarmed)

Others: *Engageante* (MS), 1 subchaser + *La Boudeuse* and
Sergent Gouarne in dock.

Dakar
Battleship *Richelieu*
4th Cruiser Division: *Georges Leygues* (fl), *Montcalm*, *Gloire*
10th Scout Division: *Le Fantasque*, *Le Terrible*
Sloops: *Dumont d'Urville*, *Annamite*, *D'Entrecasteaux*,
    Commandant Bory, *Gazelle*, *Calais*, *Air France I*,
    Air France III, *Air France IV*
3rd Submarine Division: *Le Centaure*, *Archimède*, *Argo*
17th Submarine Division: *La Vestale*, *La Sultane*, *Atalante*,
    Aréthuse
M/L submarine *Perle*

disrupt the landing at Yellow Beach near Casablanca, but the actions fought off Casablanca and Oran ultimately proved unsuccessful and costly. The Navy lost 462 men killed and suffered the sinking off Oran of the *contre-torpilleur Epervier*, the destroyers *Tramontane*, *Tornade*, and *Typhon*, and the sloop *La Surprise*. Off Casablanca light cruiser *Primauget*, the contre-torpilleurs *Milan* and *Albatros*, and the destroyers *Boulonnais*, *Fougueux*, *Brestois* and *Frondeur* were lost. Eleven submarines were also sunk or scuttled in North Africa. Nonetheless, such vigorous resistance encouraged observers in Berlin and Rome. At 1450 that afternoon Hitler and Mussolini tried to encourage a declaration of war by offering France a formal alliance. That evening Vichy accepted a German demand to use the airports and harbours in Tunisia. Before midnight the German MTB and motor minesweeper flotillas in Sicily were ordered to ferry to Bizerte as soon as possible the XXXV battalion of the 10° *Reggimento Bersaglieri*, the only unit immediately available, and several air-lifted units followed over the next few days.

Expectations raised in the Axis capitals by the *Marine Nationale*'s vigorous resistance was ultimately disappointed because of serious differences of opinion between hotheads like Admiral Jean de Laborde, the commander of the Toulon squadron who advocated war with the Allies, and moderates, like Rear-Admiral Paul Auphan, the Secretary of the Navy, who saw the invasion as an opportunity to escape the German yoke. Admiral de Laborde ordered the fleet to raise steam and was eager to intervene in the fighting. The afternoon of 8 November the Italian high command recorded a request from his command for German aircraft to cover a sortie by the *Forces de Haute Mer* which, it was claimed, were 'ready to sail in an hour.'[6]

When the expected orders did not arrive from the Admiralty in Vichy, de Laborde telephoned Admiral Auphan and urged a sortie that night, telling Auphan that he had all the necessary fuel and that 'my cruisers can cause decisive havoc on this armada.' Auphan, however, instructed de Laborde to wait. He explained that Darlan was in Algiers visiting a sick son, the situation was confused, and the cabinet would be meeting to discuss the situation. Next Rear-Admiral Negadelle, commander of a division of *contre-torpilleurs*, called Auphan urging him to take advantage of this 'unique opportunity to strike at the English'. Auphan pointed out that the fleet lacked air cover, modern anti-submarine equipment, and radar – indispensable for a successful night engagement.[7]

A close account of the political tug-of-war that followed in Vichy and Algiers over the next few days is beyond the scope of this article. In North Africa resistance continued, and mixed signals about cooperation with the Axis continued to emanate from metropolitan France. On 9 November, for example, *Comando Supremo* logged a request for a destroyer flotilla to conduct a raid from Toulon and then refuel at Cagliari or Palermo. The Italians agreed, but by the morning of 10 November the mood had changed. First, on the evening of 8 November, Admiral Darlan agreed to a ceasefire in Algiers after securing Pétain's authorisation to act freely in the Marshal's name.[8] Next, the admiral refused German military aid. Finally, at 1130 on 10 November Darlan ordered a general ceasefire throughout Africa, again in the Marshal's name. Although Pétain ultimately disavowed this declaration, it counted where it mattered most, in North Africa.

News of Darlan's action arrived in Munich, where Hitler and the Italian Foreign Minister, Galeazzo Ciano, were awaiting the French Prime Minister Pierre Laval, whom they had summoned to clarify French intentions. Hitler was already unhappy that Vichy had not immediately declared war and Darlan's action – not withstanding Pétain's disavowals – confirmed his belief that the French were not serious about resisting the western Allies. The next day ten German and six Italian divisions invaded the

---

Casablanca

Battleship *Jean Bart* (immobile)
CT *Le Malin* (under repair)
2nd Light Squadron:
Light cruiser *Primauguet* (fl)
    11th Scout Division: *Milan*, *Albatros*
    2nd Destroyer Division: *Fougueux*, *L'Alcyon*, *Frondeur*
    5th Destroyer Division: *Brestois*, *Boulonnais*
    6th Destroyer Division: *Tempête*, *Simoun* (under repair)
    6th Escort Squadron: sloops *Commandant Delage*, *La Gracieuse*, *La Grandière*
    6th Patrol Squadron: patrol boats *La Servannaise*, *L'Algéroise* (inactive), *Chasseur 2*, *La Sablaise* (inactive)
    5th SDO patrol boats: *Sentinelle*, *Bisson*, *Marie-Mad*, *Fructidor*, *Ros Braz*

Submarine Group of Morocco:
    4th Submarine Division: *Sidi Ferruch*, *Le Tonnant*, *Le Conquérant*
    16th Submarine Division: *La Sibylle*, *Amazone*, *L'Amphitrite*, *Antiope*
    18th Submarine Division: *Orphée*, *Méduse*, *La Psyché*, *Oréade*

Fédala

Minesweeper: *Abbé Desgranges* (arrived 7 November)

Indochina

Light cruiser *Lamotte-Piquet*
Sloops: *Amiral Charner*, *Marne*, *Tahure*
Submarine *Pégase*
River gunboats: *Francis Garnier*, *Tourane*, *Mytho*, *Cdt Bourdais*, *Avalanche*, *Vigilante*

Martinique

Aircraft carrier *Béarn*
Light cruisers: *Jeanne D'Arc*, *Emile Bertin*
Auxiliary cruisers: *Quercy*, *Barfleur*

Alexandria

Battleship *Lorraine*
2nd Cruiser Division: *Duquesne* (fl), *Tourville*, *Suffren*
Light cruiser *Duguay-Trouin*
3rd Destroyer Division: *Basque*, *Forbin*, *Le Fortuné*

free zone. On that same 11 November Italians landed in Corsica, while the Axis forces in Tunisia received continuous reinforcements by sea and air. Not a single shot was fired in defence of the free zone or Tunisia and the French metropolitan army was disbanded, surrendering a huge booty to the Axis. The Armée de l'Air – not sharing the Navy's principle of denying materiel to the Axis – recorded the seizure of 2,245 aircraft, most of them in the dépôts de stockage, including 303 fighters and 575 bombers.

As German tanks motored toward Toulon, Admiral Darlan invited the FHM to join him in North Africa. This would have seemed the best opportunity for the fleet to play a redeeming role in the war, but Admiral de Laborde refused to move unless Pétain so ordered. In fact, it is doubtful that Darlan believed de Laborde would sail. There was bad blood between the two admirals. They had reached a point where they communicated only in writing, even during Darlan's review of the fleet, and Darlan had been planning to replace de Laborde upon his return from Africa.[9] The Admiral's invitation was almost certainly intended to advance his negotiating position with the Americans.

After rejecting Darlan's invitation, de Laborde had to satisfy the Axis powers. That night the German command demanded to know whether he and Vice-Admiral Marquis, commander of the Toulon Naval District, would pledge to defend the base against attacks from the Allies and French 'dissidents'. After consulting with the French Admiralty the two admirals acceded to the German demand, and the German army stopped its advance 15 km short of the naval base, leaving Toulon an unoccupied French enclave on the continent. In fact Admiral Raeder had urged Hitler to leave Toulon unoccupied. He proposed instead that Berlin pressure the Vichy government to order the fleet into a state of co-belligerency against the Allies.

The Scuttling

The fleet's morale was unsettled after the occupation of the Free Zone. The apparent defection of Darlan caused confusion, and anti-German sentiment had become widespread. Demonstrations in favour of joining the Allies erupted on board some vessels, but de Laborde quickly suppressed these. He trusted the German pledge and considered the Allies the greater threat, fearing they would attempt another Mers el-Kebir against his ships.

This trust was misplaced. On 19 November Hitler order Operation 'Anton' – the occupation of the Toulon naval base and the seizure of the fleet. This involved a thrust by two armoured columns: one from the east would

The cruiser Dupleix, *which was operational with the FHM, was sabotaged with explosives with spectacular results, and burned for days. The numerous explosions aboard (notably the magazines and the torpedoes) resulted in casualties and a significant amount of damage to the dockyard area around the ship.* (Courtesy of Jean Moulin)

TOULON: THE SELF-DESTRUCTION AND SALVAGE OF THE FRENCH FLEET

The light cruiser La Galissonnière, *which was in one of the Missiessy docks for maintenance at the time of the German incursion into the dockyard, was partially floated out before the sea-cocks were opened in order to obstruct the dock gates and make salvage more difficult.* (Courtesy of Jean Moulin)

capture the command post at Fort Lamalgue and the naval dockyard at Mourillon; the western column would occupy the main dockyard and the Cepet Peninsula, which commanded the exit from the base. Aerial mines would block the outer exit from the port. 'Anton' commenced on 27 November 1942 without any forewarning to the Italians. At 0425 German tanks appeared at Fort Lamalgue and troops captured Admiral Marquis in bed. The Germans achieved surprise but their intelligence was inadequate. They were unable to immediately locate the communication centre and thus prevent a warning from being sent to Admiral de Laborde. The Admiral was sceptical about the threat, but nonetheless ordered crews to their stations and boilers lit. At 0520 German vehicles entered the Mourillon gate (Porte Nord), and tanks broke through the Castigneau gate to the west five minutes later. Upon learning of these penetrations de Laborde finally acted, sending out the order to scuttle by radio, flag, and signal light.

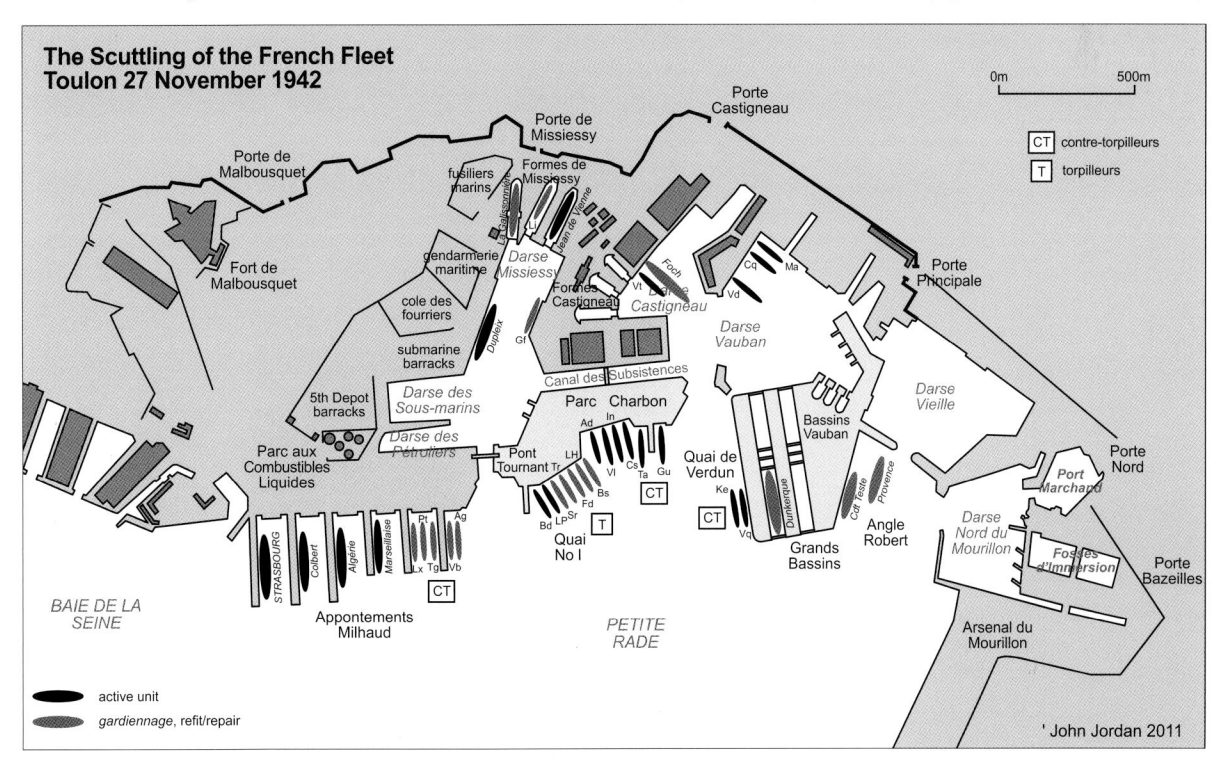

At 0550 the first German troops arrived at the Milhaud Piers where *Strasbourg*, *Colbert*, *Algérie*, and *Marseillaise* were moored, having taken twenty-five minutes to navigate the mile from the Castigneau gate. During this interval the crews had been energetically inserting explosives into the barrels of the main and secondary guns and sledge-hammering delicate equipment such as machinery dials, radios, rangefinders, and compasses. Teams destroyed the reduction gearing and turbines with oxyacetylene torches and hand grenades, and the boilers were starved of water. And, of course, the sea cocks were opened to flood the hulls.

Strasbourg appeared intact to the German soldiers when they arrived. A tank fired and hit a secondary turret, killing one officer and wounding six men. A 37mm gun returned fire, and the tanks retreated when a secondary turret trained on them. Then an officer emerged and called over a loud-hailer for the ship to surrender. Admiral de Laborde reportedly answered that the ship had already been scuttled. At 0620, after all men save a scuttling crew of 50 were ashore, explosions rocked the battleship and flames erupted down her length. *Strasbourg* eventually settled on an even keel with her upper deck four metres underwater.

Germans hailed the other ships along the pier and received similar replies to their surrender demands. The charges aboard *Algérie* began exploding as the Germans arrived. The cruiser burned for twenty days. *Marseillaise* settled with a 30 degree list – her captain ignored orders to sink the ship on an even keel – and burned for a week. Troops pushed aboard *Dupleix* in the Missiessy basin through crewmen abandoning ship. They even managed to find and close the sea cocks, but when the explosive charges began to blow, the German boarding party quickly disembarked, being showered with debris in the process. The cruiser's magazines exploded at 0830.

The scene was similar on the destroyers and smaller ships. Even the shore batteries were sabotaged. The only vessels to escape complete destruction were those in care & maintenance (*en gardiennage*) or undergoing refit. *Tigre* and *Panthère* had skeleton crews and were captured relatively intact. Five submarines got underway. Of these *Vénus* was scuttled in deep water, *Iris* was interned in Spain and three, *Le Glorieux*, *Marsouin*, and *Casabianca*, broke out and joined the Allies. Twelve Frenchmen died in the operation, and 78,888 were captured, although they were quickly released in exchange for a promise to have workers cooperate with the salvage operations.

It was no simple matter to render a battleship beyond economical repair in just a half hour, no matter how many sledgehammers, torches and explosives were employed. The long planned, well-practiced, and brilliantly executed destruction of the fleet demonstrated the *Marine Nationale*'s capabilities and loyalty. It was a pity that such competence was not exercised in a more rewarding task.

The Ships

The Germans had hoped to seize at Toulon a flotilla of modern destroyers they could use to attack Allied shipping, leaving the burden of convoy escort to the *Regia Marina*. The fleet's mass destruction converted this hope to ashes, and on 30 November the freshly arrived Italian Admiral Vittorio Tur wrote that he saw about 2,000 German sailors returning home by train due to the frustration of the *Kriegsmarine*'s anticipated flotilla programme. Instead, the German Navy had to content itself with forming a coastal force of auxiliary minesweepers and escorts with about a third of the crews French volunteers in German uniform. Everything else, except for about 40,000 tonnes of oil recovered in *Marine Nationale* depots, passed to the Italians, although most of this fuel was eventually used to supply traffic to Tunisia.

The greatest windfall was the merchant vessels found in Southern France and Tunisia. Not counting 161,042 GRT of foreign freighters requisitioned by the Germans in southern France in August 1942, the Italians received 306,711 GRT, the Germans 339,291 GRT and the French reserved about 50,000 GRT for their own purposes. The Axis merchant fleet in the Mediterranean totalled, on 10 June 1940, 2,305,004 GRT. Taking into account losses, new construction, and ships recovered from the Black Sea, Axis controlled tonnage was about 1,740,000 GRT on 1 November 1942. Of this traffic with North Africa

Toulon, December 1942: French sailors coming home after demobilisation. (Storia Militare)

The French cruiser Marsellaise *in January 1943.* (Storia Militare)

tied up about 250,000 GRT a month. The infusion of these French merchant vessels, which began to sail from mid-December 1942, gave the Axis a tonnage surplus, which on 8 September 1943 totalled 2,115,000 GRT in the Mediterranean (plus a further 100,000 tons in the Black Sea). This was effectively the same the Axis started the war with.

The warship situation was more complicated. In the eyes of the Axis powers the mass scuttling had reduced the fleet at Toulon from an 'immediate' asset to a potential 'long-term' asset that would require a great deal of time and effort to realise. Nonetheless, such a treasure trove of naval might could not be ignored, and within days German specialists were swarming the harbour's polluted waters assessing which ships could be salvaged, and which had to be broken up. They quickly confirmed that little could be profitably recovered, and Berlin reached an agreement with Rome on 3 December for the Italians to participate in the salvage and utilisation of the French fleet.

The Germans had found a few ships still afloat at Toulon because they had been in care and maintenance (*en gardiennage d'armistice*). These included the *contre-torpilleurs Lion, Panthère, Tigre*, and the destroyer *Trombe*. The Germans stripped out the immediately useful materiel and handed the four vessels to the Italians as soon as the *Regia Marina*'s sailors entered Toulon on 14 December. Hitler wanted the ships commissioned as

An Italian Navy diver conducts an initial hull inspection of La Galissonnière in December 1942. (Storia Militare)

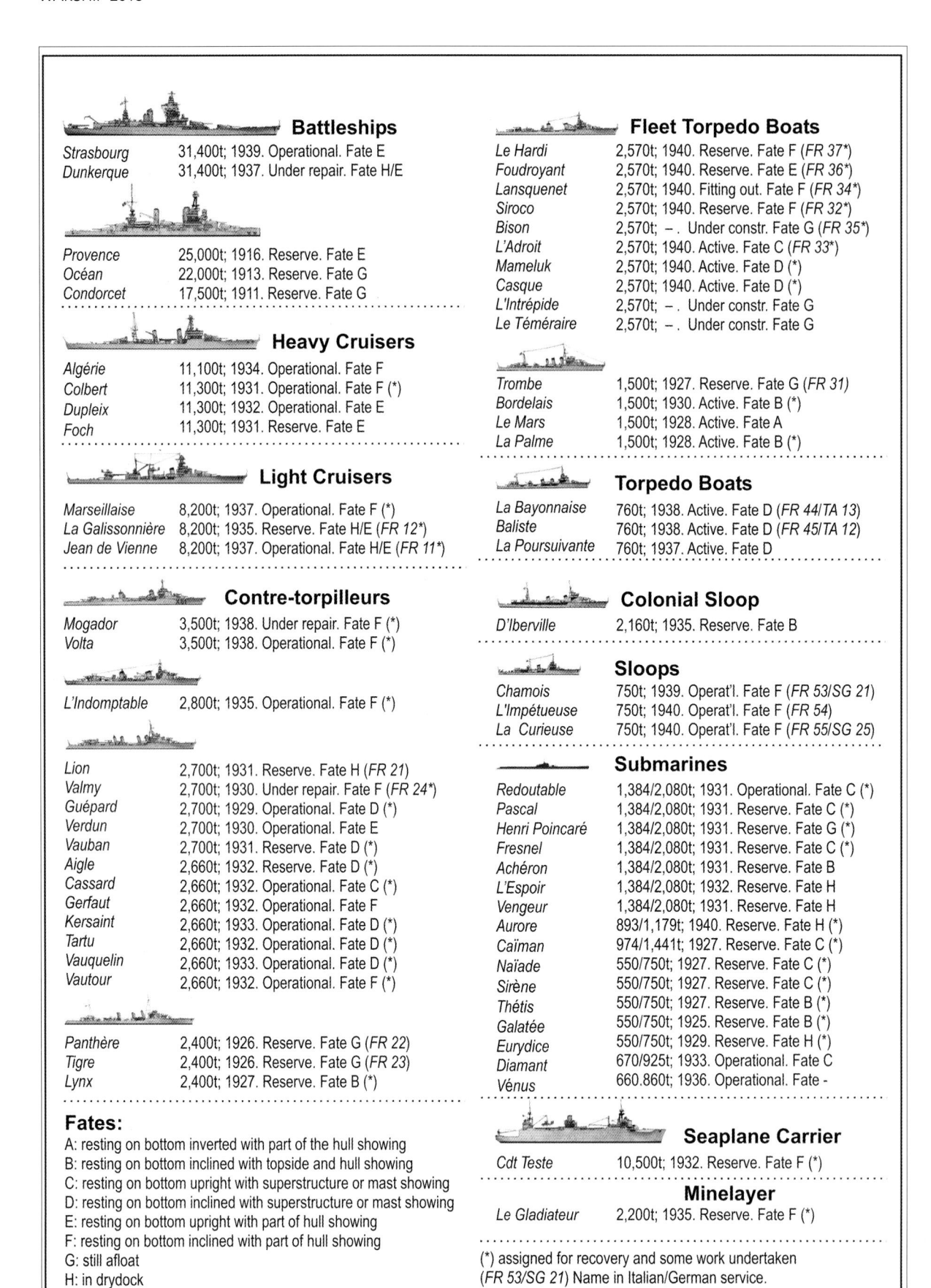

Battleships

Strasbourg	31,400t; 1939. Operational. Fate E	
Dunkerque	31,400t; 1937. Under repair. Fate H/E	
Provence	25,000t; 1916. Reserve. Fate E	
Océan	22,000t; 1913. Reserve. Fate G	
Condorcet	17,500t; 1911. Reserve. Fate G	

Heavy Cruisers

Algérie	11,100t; 1934. Operational. Fate F
Colbert	11,300t; 1931. Operational. Fate F (*)
Dupleix	11,300t; 1932. Operational. Fate E
Foch	11,300t; 1931. Reserve. Fate E

Light Cruisers

Marseillaise	8,200t; 1937. Operational. Fate F (*)
La Galissonnière	8,200t; 1935. Reserve. Fate H/E (FR 12*)
Jean de Vienne	8,200t; 1937. Operational. Fate H/E (FR 11*)

Contre-torpilleurs

Mogador	3,500t; 1938. Under repair. Fate F (*)
Volta	3,500t; 1938. Operational. Fate F (*)
L'Indomptable	2,800t; 1935. Operational. Fate F (*)
Lion	2,700t; 1931. Reserve. Fate H (FR 21)
Valmy	2,700t; 1930. Under repair. Fate F (FR 24*)
Guépard	2,700t; 1929. Operational. Fate D (*)
Verdun	2,700t; 1930. Operational. Fate E
Vauban	2,700t; 1931. Reserve. Fate D (*)
Aigle	2,660t; 1932. Reserve. Fate D (*)
Cassard	2,660t; 1932. Operational. Fate C (*)
Gerfaut	2,660t; 1932. Operational. Fate F
Kersaint	2,660t; 1933. Operational. Fate D (*)
Tartu	2,660t; 1932. Operational. Fate D (*)
Vauquelin	2,660t; 1933. Operational. Fate D (*)
Vautour	2,660t; 1932. Operational. Fate F (*)
Panthère	2,400t; 1926. Reserve. Fate G (FR 22)
Tigre	2,400t; 1926. Reserve. Fate G (FR 23)
Lynx	2,400t; 1927. Reserve. Fate B (*)

Fates:
A: resting on bottom inverted with part of the hull showing
B: resting on bottom inclined with topside and hull showing
C: resting on bottom upright with superstructure or mast showing
D: resting on bottom inclined with superstructure or mast showing
E: resting on bottom upright with part of hull showing
F: resting on bottom inclined with part of hull showing
G: still afloat
H: in drydock

Fleet Torpedo Boats

Le Hardi	2,570t; 1940. Reserve. Fate F (FR 37*)
Foudroyant	2,570t; 1940. Reserve. Fate E (FR 36*)
Lansquenet	2,570t; 1940. Fitting out. Fate F (FR 34*)
Siroco	2,570t; 1940. Reserve. Fate F (FR 32*)
Bison	2,570t; –. Under constr. Fate G (FR 35*)
L'Adroit	2,570t; 1940. Active. Fate C (FR 33*)
Mameluk	2,570t; 1940. Active. Fate D (*)
Casque	2,570t; 1940. Active. Fate D (*)
L'Intrépide	2,570t; –. Under constr. Fate G
Le Téméraire	2,570t; –. Under constr. Fate G
Trombe	1,500t; 1927. Reserve. Fate G (FR 31)
Bordelais	1,500t; 1930. Active. Fate B (*)
Le Mars	1,500t; 1928. Active. Fate A
La Palme	1,500t; 1928. Active. Fate B (*)

Torpedo Boats

La Bayonnaise	760t; 1938. Active. Fate D (FR 44/TA 13)
Baliste	760t; 1938. Active. Fate D (FR 45/TA 12)
La Poursuivante	760t; 1937. Active. Fate D

Colonial Sloop

D'Iberville	2,160t; 1935. Reserve. Fate B

Sloops

Chamois	750t; 1939. Operat'l. Fate F (FR 53/SG 21)
L'Impétueuse	750t; 1940. Operat'l. Fate F (FR 54)
La Curieuse	750t; 1940. Operat'l. Fate F (FR 55/SG 25)

Submarines

Redoutable	1,384/2,080t; 1931. Operational. Fate C (*)
Pascal	1,384/2,080t; 1931. Reserve. Fate C (*)
Henri Poincaré	1,384/2,080t; 1931. Reserve. Fate G (*)
Fresnel	1,384/2,080t; 1931. Reserve. Fate C (*)
Achéron	1,384/2,080t; 1931. Reserve. Fate B
L'Espoir	1,384/2,080t; 1932. Reserve. Fate H
Vengeur	1,384/2,080t; 1931. Reserve. Fate H
Aurore	893/1,179t; 1940. Reserve. Fate H (*)
Caïman	974/1,441t; 1927. Reserve. Fate C (*)
Naïade	550/750t; 1927. Reserve. Fate C (*)
Sirène	550/750t; 1927. Reserve. Fate C (*)
Thétis	550/750t; 1927. Reserve. Fate B (*)
Galatée	550/750t; 1925. Reserve. Fate B (*)
Eurydice	550/750t; 1929. Reserve. Fate H (*)
Diamant	670/925t; 1933. Operational. Fate C
Vénus	660.860t; 1936. Operational. Fate -

Seaplane Carrier

Cdt Teste	10,500t; 1932. Reserve. Fate F (*)

Minelayer

Le Gladiateur	2,200t; 1935. Reserve. Fate F (*)

(*) assigned for recovery and some work undertaken
(FR 53/SG 21) Name in Italian/German service.

Toulon, December 1942: the contre-torpilleur Lion, *which had been docked for maintenance prior to the scuttling.* (Storia Militare)

soon as possible so they could act as fast troop transports to Tunisia. It was one of the German Chancellor's many ideas based on paper assets rather than actual conditions. The first problem was caused by the naval dockyard's 13,000 French workers, who were willing to work for the Germans but not the Italians.

During December more than two thousand *Regia Marina* personnel arrived to survey the wrecks and to man the anti-aircraft and coastal batteries. The four ships were transferred to the Italian part of the dockyard on 22 December. Meanwhile, pressure was applied on Laval who, on 11 January 1943, grudgingly agreed to grant the four destroyers to the *Regia Marina* 'for the defence of Europe.' The French workers returned, but Italians had already completed the bulk of the quick repairs required for the *contre-torpilleurs* and the destroyer to sail to Italy for a complete refit. Renamed respectively *FR 21, 22, 23* and *31*, they raised the Italian flag on 19 January 1943, despite strong French irritation and protests.[10] They departed Toulon in February (*FR 31*), March (*FR 22*), and April (*FR 21* and *23*) for La Spezia, entering Italian service in April (*FR 31*), June (*FR 22*) and August 1943 (*FR 21* and *23*). Considered worn out and top heavy, they only conducted fifty missions, all in Italian waters. The most notable was *FR 22*'s 6 August 1943 transfer of the former Premier Mussolini from Ponza Island to La Maddalena in Sardinia.

The Italian plans, however, went beyond the recovery of just four warships. While the *Regia Marina* was surveying the harbour, Italian salvage enterprises in Genoa and Trieste formed a syndicate on 24 December 1942 with the acronym ERIT (*Ente Recuperi Italiani Tolone*) to conduct salvage work. By early January 1943 the privately owned salvage ships *Porto Edda*, *Raffio*, and *Dante* had arrived, beginning at once the recovery from that providential mine of the most precious items (bronze,

The Italian destroyer FR 21 (former Lion*) at La Spezia, August 1943.* (Rivista Marittima)

Toulon, January 1943: taken from an Italian floatplane. Centre picture: the French destroyer Bison, *still afloat as she had been under construction. From left to right: the scuttled destroyers* Bordelais, Siroco, Le Hardi, Foudroyant, L'Adroit, Volta, L'Indomptable, *and* Cassard. *(Family Gennari Collection from Storia Militare)*

copper, brass) which the Italian naval industry was eager to use in its 1943 and 1944 war programmes.

In the meantime a *Supermarina* document dated 14 January 1943 and a meeting of the *Comando Supremo* presided by Mussolini himself on 29 January both contemplated the recommissioning of the battleships *Strasbourg* and *Dunkerque* by the end of 1946 and of the cruiser *Foch*, as a light carrier, by spring 1946. More practical was the second phase of recoveries: the light cruisers *Jean de Vienne* and *La Galissonnière* and ten more destroyers designated to be raised, repaired, and commissioned in 1943 (including the *Bison*, not yet commissioned, but floating at Toulon, and the damaged *L'Audacieux*, found in a crippled state at Bizerte and finally sunk there by an air raid on 7 April 1943), ten in 1944 and five in 1945.

To understand such a programme it is necessary to add that after the 'Torch' landings the Italian naval staff appreciated that the arrival of American forces in the Mediterranean had effectively determined the outcome of the conflict, inducing the navy high command to inform the king that it was necessary to consider a political solution to the war, particularly as Mussolini's health was deteriorating. To balance this commonsense assessment the Germans countered strongly with much (correct) information about their new secret weapons, even commissioning spare parts for the V1 cruise missiles with Italian industry and promising, above all, new divisions and materiel for North Africa. At first Berlin seemed as good as its word, and in January 1943 *Comando Supremo* ceded the transport priority for Tunisia to the apparently constant flow of new German divisions (three within three months supported by two infantry brigades, two paratroop brigades, one Tiger tank group, and an armoured reconnaissance battalion). At the same time

Toulon, January 1943: the French cruiser Foch *during her recovery by the Italians. She would be refloated on 16 April 1943. (Famiglia Gennari collection from Storia Militare)*

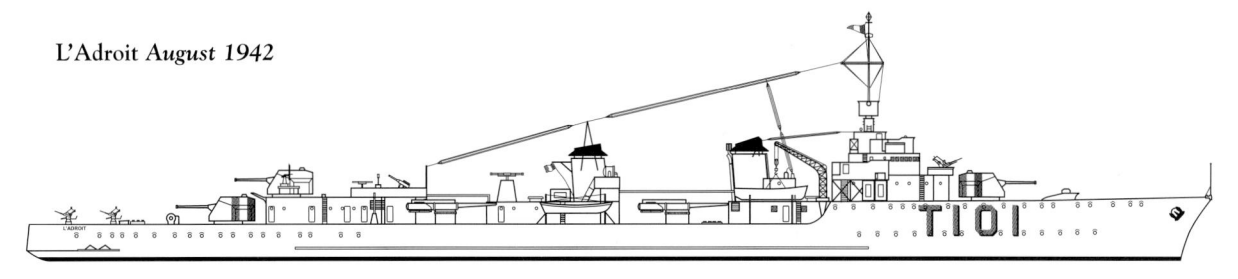

TOULON: THE SELF-DESTRUCTION AND SALVAGE OF THE FRENCH FLEET

L'Adroit August 1942

Both the Germans and the Italians coveted the modern torpilleurs d'escadre *(lit. 'fleet torpedo boats') of the* Le Hardi *class, of which three were operational, three in reserve and a seventh (Lansquenet) in the final stages of fitting out at the La Seyne shipyard opposite the dockyard. These were large, powerful ships capable of 38-40 knots, with an armament of three twin 130mm guns and seven 550mm torpedo tubes in one triple and two twin mountings. This is L'Adroit, the division leader of the three operational ships, as she would have appeared in November 1942. She had been completed with a 3-metre stereo rangefinder in an open mounting aft as a temporary measure, but had received the most modern close-range armament available: two of the new single 25mm Hotchkiss guns forward of the bridge, a twin 37mm Mle 1933 mounting atop the after deckhouse, and single 13.2mm Browning MG on platforms at the sides of no. II 130mm mounting, while the original twin 13.2mm Hotchkiss MG mountings had been relocated to the stern. (Drawing by John Jordan)*

Russian feelers to Rome for a separate peace with the Axis along the 1941 borders were renewed from November 1942 until late spring 1943. This promoted an optimistic vision of a summer 1943 offensive towards Gibraltar from Tunisia and Spain to be followed, most probably, by a general peace. It was only in February 1943 that the sudden halt in the flow of new German divisions and the delayed shipping of the last battalions of the units already despatched to Tunisia revealed suddenly that the German barrel was empty and that the Reich had given up any serious hope for a strategic decision in Africa, deciding, instead, from March 1943 to reduce by half the ordinary supplies to the German troops in anticipation of an imminent retreat from that continent.

By March 1943 plans to recover the two modern French battleships were shown to be unrealistic, and the next month an evaluation of the newly raised *Foch*'s poor condition persuaded the *Regia Marina* to abandon any further hope for that ship, even in her original cruiser role, and workers immediately began to demolish the hulk.

The Italian attention was thus concentrated on the destroyers: the modern *Siroco*, *L'Adroit*, *Lansquenet*, *Bison*, *Foudroyant*, and *Le Hardi* (FR 32, 33, 34, 35, 36 and 37). The *contre-torpilleur Valmy* (FR 24) was originally scheduled to be scrapped, but found to be in better condition than expected after being raised. She was towed to Genoa in July 1943. These new additions needed to be modified and fitted according a scheme devised by the Ansaldo company. *Siroco* (towed to Genoa on 10 June 1943) was to be the prototype. According to a 31 August 1943 programme for 1944, these ships were to be completed beginning in early 1944. The remainder of the programme to recommission the remaining French destroyers was, by that time, considered unlikely after the disappointing experience and the many breakdowns suffered by the first four ships put into service.

The second important group of French vessels seized were the ones at Bizerte, which the Germans agreed to cede to the Italians on 9 December 1942 for lack of *Kriegsmarine* personnel to man them. The two small sloops, *La Batailleuse* and *Commandant Rivière* (FR 51 and 52), sailed from Bizerte to Italy on 19 December 1942. Refitted at Spezia and considered of modest efficiency, they were used from 28 January 1943 in the Upper Tyrrhenian Sea and along the French coast on 72 missions.

The three torpedo boats *Bombarde*, *La Pomone* and *L'Iphigénie*, named *FR 41, 42* and *43*, sailed for Palermo on 22 December 1942 and were refitted later at La Spezia. By March 1943 they began training with their new crews, but on 6 April 1943 they were loaned to the German Navy

The destroyer FR 32, former Siroco, at Genoa on 23 August 1943, during her refitting. (Aldo Fraccaroli via Storia Militare)

The corvette FR 51 *(former* La Batailleuse*) at La Spezia on June 1943.* (Rivista Marittima)

Rapallo roads, March 1943: the trials of a former French torpedo boat seized at Bizerte and just commissioned by the Italian Navy. (Enrico Cernuschi collection)

upon Hitler's request. Under the Italian flag they conducted 29 missions, 11 of them training sorties.

The *Regia Marina* showed little interest in the French submarines. Nine were found at Bizerte (*Phoque*, *Saphir*, *Requin*, *Espadon*, *Dauphin*, *Turquoise*, *Circé*, *Calypso*, and *Nautilus*). The first seven were renamed *FR 111, 112, 113, 114, 115, 116,* and *117* on February 1943; the remaining two were sunk by a USAAF raid on 31 January 1943. Of this group *Phoque* and *Saphir* were considered in good condition. They sailed to Italy on 6 January 1943 followed on the 20th by *Requin* and *Espadon* and, on 23 February, by *Dauphin*. Only *Phoque* was actually commissioned in February 1943 while the others, too old and worn out, were used as pontoons to charge the batteries of other boats. An additional boat, *Henri Poincaré*, recovered at Toulon, sailed to Italy on 2 September 1943 where her

Some Italian sailors aboard the ex-French minelaying submarine Saphir, *seized at Bizerte in December 1942.* (Aldo Fraccaroli via Storia Militare)

The French submarine Diamant, *a sister of* Saphir, *just refloated by the Italians on March 1943 ready for scrapping.* (Storia Militare)

The 330mm main guns of the French battleship Dunkerque, *which had been sabotaged during the scuttling, are cut by the Italians in June 1943.* (Storia Militare)

fate would have been similar of the others, as a programme to convert some of these submarines into underwater transports had already been abandoned. Although many sources state that these boats were towed to Italy, in fact they all sailed under their own power.

The biggest disappointment was caused by the modern light cruisers *Jean de Vienne* and *La Galissonnière* (*FR 11* and *12*). On 22 May 1943 they raised the Italian flag, but their condition was worse than originally believed and the engineers determined they would require a long refit in Italy before commissioning in 1945, at best, as anti-aircraft cruisers. Their tow to Genoa was however delayed in July 1943 following a German request, as such an initiative would cause an uproar among the French workers. In August the *Regia Marina* staff, which had accelerated since July the despatch to Italy of all the materiel and ships present in Toulon which could be utilised or scrapped at home, decided to go ahead anyway. The 8 September 1943 armistice, however, stopped the departure which had been scheduled for the following week.

Many other ships from various locations entered Italian service. The 3,150-tonne minelayer *Castor* (*FR 60*), found at Bizerte with her machinery in poor condition, was used as a depot ship before being scuttled on 7 May 1943, despite efforts made to refit her on site to lay some defensive minefields using French and Italian weapons. The minesweeper *La Coubre* (120t, renamed *FR 70*), the only *Marine Nationale* ship in Corsica, surrendered at Ajaccio on 11 November 1942 to the destroyer *Pigafetta* and was immediately put in service under the Italian flag. Six further minesweepers (*CH 81*, *Madone de Pompei*, *Méduse II*, *Ravignan*, *Héron I* and *Pen Men*), all considered in good condition, were seized in Tunisia becoming *FR 74, 75, 76, 77, 78,* and *79*. The tanker *Le Tarn* – damaged by the Italian submarine *Dandolo* on 4 November 1941 – was found at Bizerte and was transferred to Italy on 16 April 1943 under the name *FR 85*. *FR 71* (ex-*Pétrel III*) was seized at St. Raphaël while *FR 72* (ex-*Aigrette*) and *FR 73* (ex-*Georgette*) were taken in Provence as were the eight tugs *FR 91–98*. Seventy-four yachts (*FR 201-207, 21 219, 221, 230-259, 260-285,* and *307*) were pressed into service along the Riviera as subchasers (*211-219*), coastal minesweepers (*230-259*), sail training vessels for the Naval Academy (*201-207*) and auxiliary patrol vessels. These tiny ships greatly increased the efficiency of the Axis coastal system along the southern French coast which hitherto had consisted of a few similar German auxiliary vessels and some scattered *Regia Marina* units.

The two cruisers FR 11 (on the right) and FR 12, formerly Jean de Vienne *and* La Galissonnière, *on March 1943 after they had been both refloated by the Italians. Note the oil stains on the hull, which show the extent of their submersion following the scuttling.* (Collection Aldo Fraccaroli, via Storia Militare)

While the salvage work and the scrapping were proceeding, the Italian Navy manned the French coastal and anti-aircraft batteries in Provence and Tunisia with its own personnel. By early March 1943 eleven of the fifteen planned anti-ship and seven of eight anti-aircraft batteries around Toulon had been commissioned, often using recovered weapons. For example, the twelve 100mm AA guns of the seaplane carrier *Commandant Teste* and the eight single 90mm guns from *Foch* were used in these batteries. The most important Toulon gun emplacements were the two twin 340mm turrets mounted on Cap Cépet. As the original guns had been sabotaged Admiral Tur recovered with utmost urgency two similar weapons from the battleship *Provence*, which was in the process of being scrapped.

The unexpected armistice between Italy and the Allies signed on 8 September had major ramifications. That same night *Supermarina* ordered its Toulon command to scuttle the MTBs *MAS 424* and *437* and the survey ship *Ferdinando Marsigli* (342t). The fate of French warships remaining in Italian hands after the German occupation of northern Italy was debated by the *Regia Marina*'s chief of staff Admiral Raffaele de Courten and the Allied Mediterranean commander-in-chief Admiral A. B. Cunningham on 23 September 1943. On that same day they agreed that the ex-French, -Greek, and -Yugoslavian ships still in the *Regia Marina*'s inventory would be returned in exchange for Italian vessels recovered by the Allies in Italian harbours during their advance. The pact was respected by both sides and the final result was that between October 1943 and March 1945 the *Regia Marina* handed back to their original owners two destroyers, two torpedo boats, four gunboats, one subchaser, five minesweepers, four tugs, two depot ships, and nine patrol boats. In turn Italy recovered two midget submarines, three MTBs, one MA/SB, four minesweepers, five minelayers, four tugs, two landing ships, one landing craft, and thirteen tankers.

The last French prize to be returned was the minesweeper *FR 71* on 30 September 1944, but the first were obviously the most important: the destroyers *FR 23* and *31*, alias *Tigre* and *Trombe*, which were returned at Bizerte on 28 October 1943. A witness on board the destroyer *Riboty* (which was to take home the skeleton crews of the two ships that were being returned) remembered: 'During the changing of the flags, while a band was playing the Marsellaise, there was an accident as a group of French soldiers on the mole boarded the *FR 23* trying to grab the Italian flag. A huge tussle erupted for about five minutes and the poor French band was involved, with its instruments floating in the channel before American military police arrived, restoring order with a liberal use of their night-sticks.[11]

The later damage to *Trombe* in an attack by a fascist republic navy MTM explosive boat on 17 April 1945 in the Ligurian sea did not advance the spirit of cooperation between the two navies. In May 1945 Admiral De Courten proposed to settle the *Marine Nationale*'s claims for the warships seized and commissioned by the *Regia Marina* during the war with the offer to recover and restore for the French Navy the destroyer *Lansquenet*. That vessel was, in fact, the most advanced (and in the best condition) of the *Le Hardi* class wrecks, as the *Kriegsmarine* had tried until April 1945 to commission her at Genoa. Paris, however, declined, making further substantial demands. The 10 February 1947 Treaty of Peace dictated, in fact, the delivery to the French by the Italian Navy of three cruisers, four destroyers, two submarines, one sloop, six MTBs, three MA/SBs, five landing craft, six tankers, one transport and twelve tugs. Only two cruisers, four destroyers, one sloop, two MTBs, four tankers and six tugs were actually delivered in 1948, while the remaining ships remained commissioned by the *Marina Militare* following a bargain which settled the old quarrel that originated six years previously at Toulon, in Corsica and at Bizerte.

Footnotes:

[1.] Anthony Heckstall-Smith, *The Fleet that Faced Both Ways* (London: Anthony Blond, 1963), p.15.

[2.] Ibid, p.40. 'Supervision' would have been a better translation of the French word *contrôle*

[3.] Ibid, p.58.

[4.] Michael Simpson, *The Somerville Papers: Selections from the Private and Official Correspondence of Admiral of the Fleet Sir James Somervile, G.C.B., G.B.E., D.S.O.* (Aldershot, England: Scolar, 1996), p.154.

[5.] Vezio Vascotto, 'L'enigma Darlan,' supplemento della *Rivista Marittima*, (February, 2002), p.84-86.

[6.] Antonello Biagini and Fernando Fratolillo, *Diario Storico Comando Supremo*, Vol VIII (Rome: Ufficio Storico dello Stato Maggiore dell'Esercito, 1999), 670.

[7.] Jean-Jacques Antier, *Les grandes Batailles Navales de la Seconde Guerre mondiale: Le drame de la Marine française* (Paris: Omnibus, 2000), p.644.

[8.] George F. Howe, *Northwest Africa: Seizing the Initiative in the West* (Washington DC: USGPO, 1970), p.251. There is speculation that Darlan had, in fact, planned to engineer a reconciliation with the Anglo-Americans from the beginning.

[9.] Antier, *Les grandes batailles navales de la Seconde Guerre mondiale: Le drame de la Marine française*, p.635.

[10.] Ugo Foschini, *La mia guerra in mare 10 giugno 1940 – 2 maggio 1945* (Rome, GB Editoria, Rome, 2008), pp.56-57.

[11.] Giacomo Scotti, *I disertori*, (Milan, Mursia, 1980), pp.234-35.

RUSSIA'S COLES 'MONITORS':
Smerch, Rusalka and Charodeika

These three vessels marked an important step forward in Russian shipbuilding, introducing both the Coles turret and the double bottom. Moreover, the latter pair were the first ironclads built with Russian iron, armour, and engines. **Stephen McLaughlin** describes their origins, design and construction.

The Genesis of the Coles Turret

Although they owed nothing to the ideas of Swedish-American inventor of the *Monitor*, John Ericsson, the three vessels covered in this article were often referred to as 'monitors' by the Russian navy because of their low freeboard and turret-mounted guns. In point of fact they reflected the ideas of Captain Cowper Phipps Coles, a British naval officer. During the Crimean War Coles had built a raft, the *Lady Nancy*, for use in the Sea of Azov, that featured a centrally-mounted 32pdr.[1] Coles subsequently elaborated on this basic pattern, developing the idea of an armoured, low-freeboard vessel for attacking the Kronshtadt fortresses. This vessel was to feature a 68pdr gun mounted in a non-rotating turret provided with multiple ports, so that it could be brought to bear on almost any point of the compass. The polymath engineer I.K. Brunel suggested to Coles that it would be far better if the gunhouse itself were made to rotate by mounting it on a railway-type turntable. Coles adopted this suggestion, and was soon aggressively promoting his rotating 'cupolas' as the ideal method of arming warships – not without reason, for his turret was fundamentally different to that of Ericsson, and ultimately proved superior. Unlike the Ericsson turret, which rotated on a single massive column, the Coles turret rested on a series of rollers below the deck, leaving the interior uncluttered by the column and braces necessary in Ericsson's version. Moreover, by recessing the base of his turret in the deck, Coles reduced its target area and lowered the vessel's centre of gravity. The Admiralty eventually adopted Coles' invention, laying down the *Prince Albert*, an iron-hulled turret ship, in April 1862; the same month it began the conversion of the first-rate wooden battleship *Royal Sovereign* into an ironclad turret ship. Other vessels based on Coles' ideas soon followed.

The Russian Naval Ministry was following these developments, and sometime in the latter half of 1862 asked its attaché in Britain, Captain 1st Rank S.P. Shvarts, to make enquires about the Coles cupola. In response, Shvarts sent drawings of the turrets and their mechanisms; he also asked the Thames Iron Works, then building the ironclad battery *Pervenets*, whether it was willing to build such a turret, but the firm replied that, due to its unfamiliarity with the device, it could do so only if it were provided with detailed drawings. Moreover, the cost would be quite high. When this discouraging information reached St. Petersburg, the Shipbuilding Technical Committee decided that a wooden 'experimental cupola' should be built in Russia as cheaply as possible and mounted aboard an old ship, or even ashore, to test the mechanisms involved.

And there matters ground to a halt, presumably due to lack of money even for a wooden prototype cupola. It was only when the threat of war arose over the Polish rebellion that shipbuilding money suddenly became available on a far greater scale than ever before, presenting the Naval Ministry with an opportunity to compare the competing turret designs of Coles and Ericsson. As a result, the emergency programme approved on 11/23 March 1863 included, in addition to the ten Ericsson-type monitors of the *Uragan* class, a vessel to be equipped with two Coles turrets.[2]

Smerch: Design and Construction

At this point Charles Mitchell enters into the story. In March 1862 Mitchell, an experienced Tyneside shipbuilder, had been invited by the Russian Naval Ministry to modernise its shipyard on Galernyi Island, and in January 1863 he had already begun building the ironclad broadside battery *Ne tron menia* there.[3] With the adoption of the emergency programme in March 1863, Mitchell was asked to design a vessel with Coles turrets, and by May his proposal had been accepted by the director of the Naval Ministry, Admiral N.K. Krabbe. Mitchell was to build:

> an amoured iron gunboat like the vessel Napier's of Glasgow are building for Denmark, at a price of 55,000 pounds, with turrets and everything necessary, applying to this construction contemporary improvements and making use, in the preparation of the turrets, of the assistance of Captain Cowles [*sic*].[4]

The Danish vessel referred to was the *Rolf Krake*, a two-turreted, shallow-draft, low-freeboard vessel ordered on 28

TABLE 1: *ROLF KRAKE* AND *SMERCH*

	Rolf Krake	*Smerch*
Displacement:	1,360 tons	1,460 tons design; 1,560 tons actual
Dimensions:	183ft 9in pp, 187ft x 38ft 2in x 10ft 6in	185ft pp, 188ft 8in wl x 38ft 2in x 12ft max
	56.0m pp, 57.0m x 11.63m x 3.2m	56.4m pp, 57.5m wl x 11.63m x 3.66m max
Armament:	4 x 68pdr smoothbores (2 x 2)	four 60pdr (7.72in/196mm) smoothbores (2 x 2)
Protection:	wrought iron armour	wrought iron armour
	sides: 4.5in (114mm)	*sides*: 4.5in (114mm), reducing to 4in (102mm)
	turrets: 4.5in (114mm)	*turrets*: 6in – 4.5in (152mm – 114mm)
	deck: 0.25in (6.35mm)	*deck*: 1in (25.4mm)
		conning tower: 4.5in (114mm)
Machinery:	700ihp	Two rectangular boilers, two horizontal direct-acting engines, 700ihp
Speed:	8kts	8.3 knots
Endurance:	135 tons	110 tons coal; 600-800nm at ?kts
Complement:	150	1867: 11 officers, 122 enlisted
		1875: 12 officers, 143 enlisted

August 1862 from Robert Napier & Sons, Glasgow (see Table 1).[5] Mitchell's initial proposal seems to have copied *Rolf Krake* very closely, but over the next months it was subjected to numerous modifications by the Shipbuilding Technical Committee; other alterations were made during construction, the end result being a vessel differing in many details from its original model.

The new ship, eventually named *Smerch*, was built at Galernyi Island in St. Petersburg, and was assigned Mitchell's hull number 117. The work was supervised by Mitchell's brother-in-law Henry Frederick Swan,[6] while Colonel A.F. Sobolev of the Construction Corps represented the Shipbuilding Technical Committee.

General Features

The *Smerch* was in many ways typical of an emerging type: the relatively small, low-freeboard Coles turret ship. Other examples of this breed were the Prussian *Arminius*, the Dutch *Schorpioen* and the Peruvian *Huáscar*.[7] Mitchell's initial proposal had called for a ship of 1,400 tons, but various modifications demanded by the Shipbuilding Technical Committee increased this to 1,461 tons by the time the design was approved; at this displacement she was to have a draught of 10ft 6in (3.2m), with a freeboard of only 2ft 6in (0.76m). By 1875 her actual displacement had grown to 1,560 tons, giving her a draught of 11ft (3.35m) mean, leaving a freeboard of only about 2ft (0.61m).

Although Mitchell had followed the pattern set by the *Rolf Krake*, numerous changes had been introduced by the time the *Smerch* entered service. For example, at the time of her launch the ship had a small permanent bulwark at the bow, and it was also intended to fit her with false bulwarks which could be folded down in action to clear the turrets' fields of fire, but the permanent bow bulwark was removed before she entered service, and the folding bulwarks were probably never fitted. The conning tower was also altered; originally it was much like that of *Rolf Krake*, elliptical in plan and no higher than the turrets; in *Smerch* it was changed to a cylindrical shape (4ft 6in/ 1.37m internal diameter) and, at the suggestion of Rear-Admiral I.F. Likhachev, commander of the Baltic Fleet's ironclad squadron, it was raised slightly so that its occupants could see over the forward turret. The actual steering position was on the lower deck directly below the conning tower, with another on the upper deck for use when not in action. Other differences from her Danish model included a double bottom and twin screws.

Another major change was the result of *Rolf Krake*'s own battle experience. On 6/18 April 1864, during the Schleswig-Holstein War, the ironclad engaged a Prussian shore battery near Gammelsmark. Although the ship's 4.5in (114mm) side armour was for the most part proof against the Prussian artillery, the deck, covered only by 0.25in (6.4mm) plates, was penetrated by a 24pdr shot, killing or wounding 21 men.[8] Mitchell therefore provided 1in (25.4mm) armour on the deck; this led to a 20-ton weight increase, which increased the draft by 2in (51mm). The turrets' rollers were also strengthened as a result of the examination of *Rolf Krake*'s wartime performance.

In addition to introducing the Coles turret, the *Smerch* was the first Russian ship built on a version of the 'bracket-frame' system first used by Edward Reed in HMS *Bellerophon*. Reed had used unbroken longitudinal girders with the frames being fitted between as intercostals, then plated over the whole structure to form a watertight double bottom. But in *Smerch* the frames were continuous and the stringers inserted as intercostals.[9] The frames were 21in (533mm) between centres. It was also possible to flood the double bottom spaces to reduce the ship's above-water target area – although given her overweight condition, this

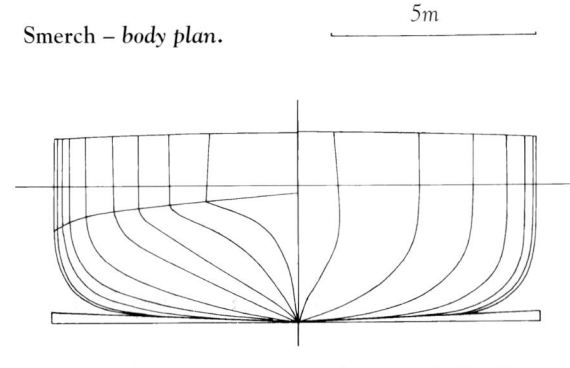

Smerch – body plan.

(Drawing by Ian Sturton)

RUSSIA'S COLES 'MONITORS': *SMERCH, RUSALKA* AND *CHARODEIKA*

Smerch – *external profile and deck plan.*

10m

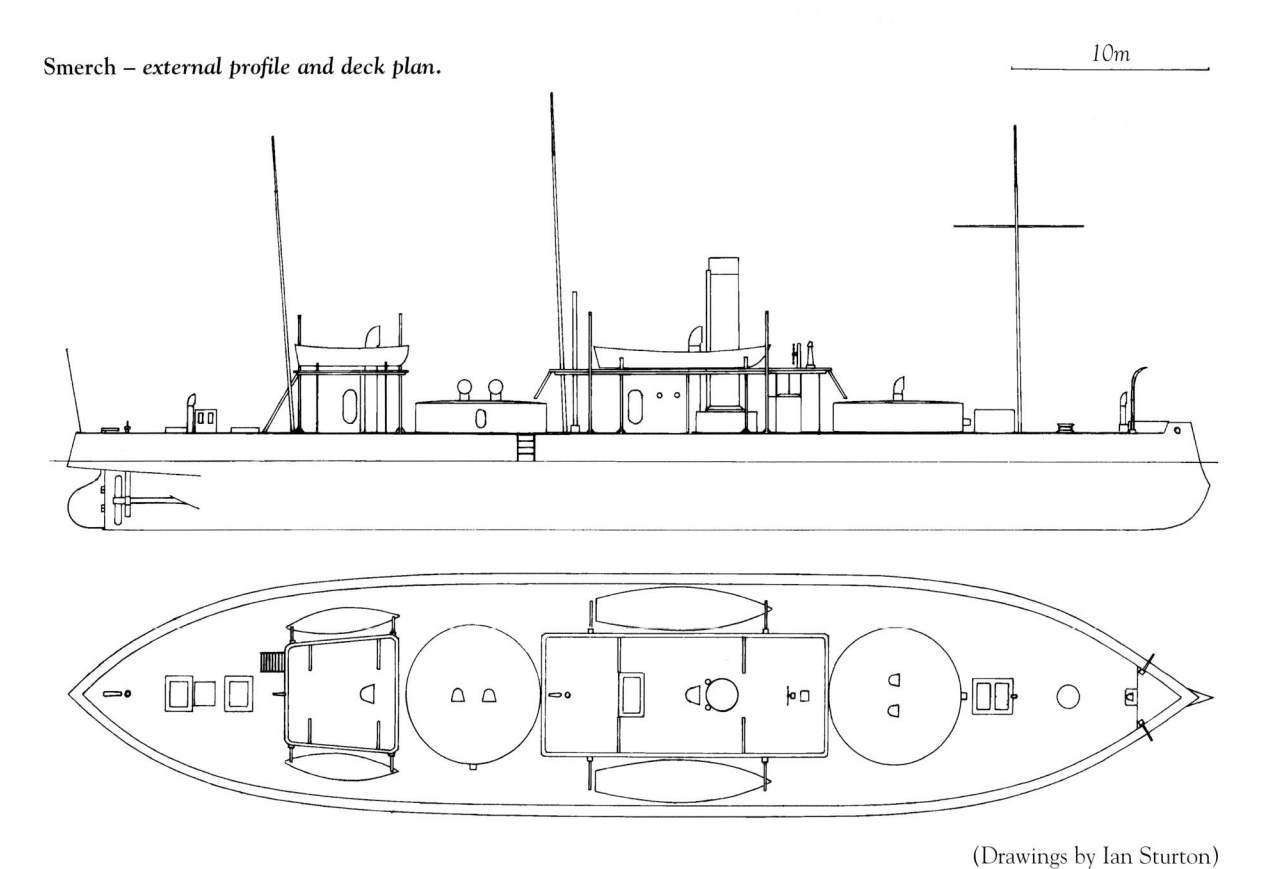

(Drawings by Ian Sturton)

Smerch *immediately after her launching. Although somewhat dark, the small bulwark forward and the after turret can be discerned.* (Courtesy of the late Boris Lemachko)

Smerch – *hull lines.*

10m

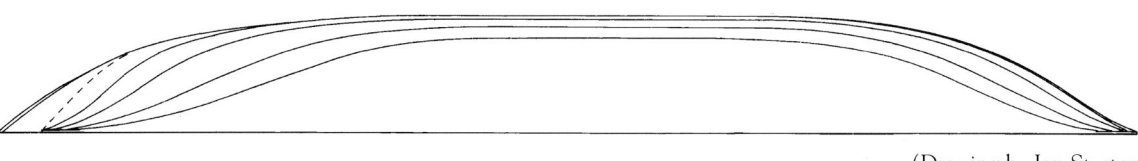

(Drawing by Ian Sturton)

151

TABLE 2: CONSTRUCTION DATES

	Smerch	*Charodeika*	*Rusalka*
Ordered:	13/25 June 1863	14/26 Jan 1865	14/26 Jan 1865
Added to List:	26 Aug / 7 Sep 1863	29 May / 10 Jun 1865	29 May / 10 Jun 1865
Construction begun:	1/13 Aug 1863	May 1865	May 1865
Laid down:	19 Nov / 1 Dec 1863	25 May / 6 Jun 1866	25 May / 6 Jun 1866
Launched:	11/23 Jun 1864	31 Aug / 12 Sep 1867	31 Aug / 12 Sep 1867
Entered Service:	1865	1869	1869
Builder:	Mitchell & Co., Galernyi Island St. Petersburg	Mitchell & Co., Galernyi Island St. Petersburg	Mitchell & Co., Galernyi Island St. Petersburg
Constructors:	A.F. Sobolev	K.G. Mikhailov	A.A. Svistovskii, N.A. Samoilov
Cost (hull and machinery):	554,100 rubles	762,000 rubles	762,000 rubles

Notes:
Added to List: The date a ship was officially added to the list of the fleet and given a name.
Construction begun: The date when the first iron was laid on the slipway.
Laid down: The date of the ceremonial keel-laying, not necessarily corresponding to an important stage in the ship's construction.

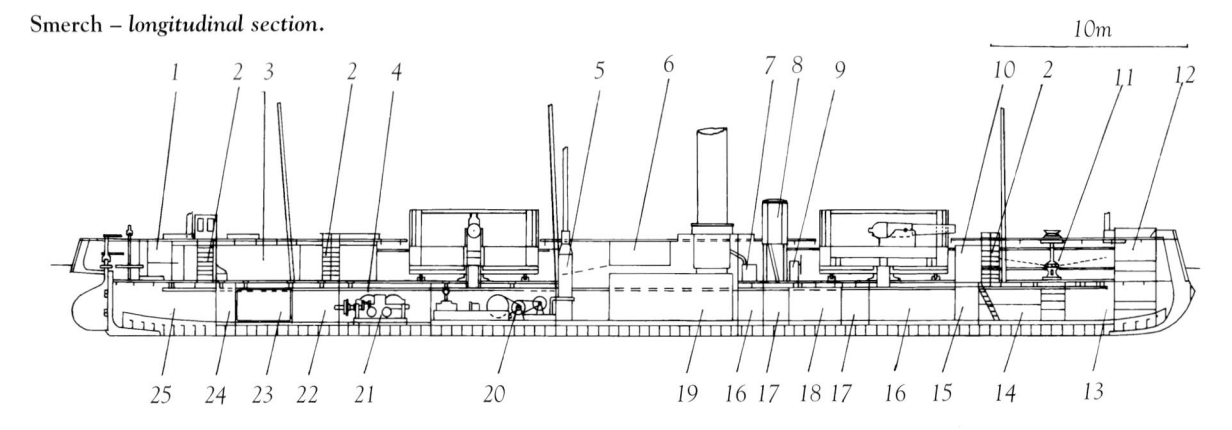

Smerch – *longitudinal section.*

Smerch – *hold plan.*

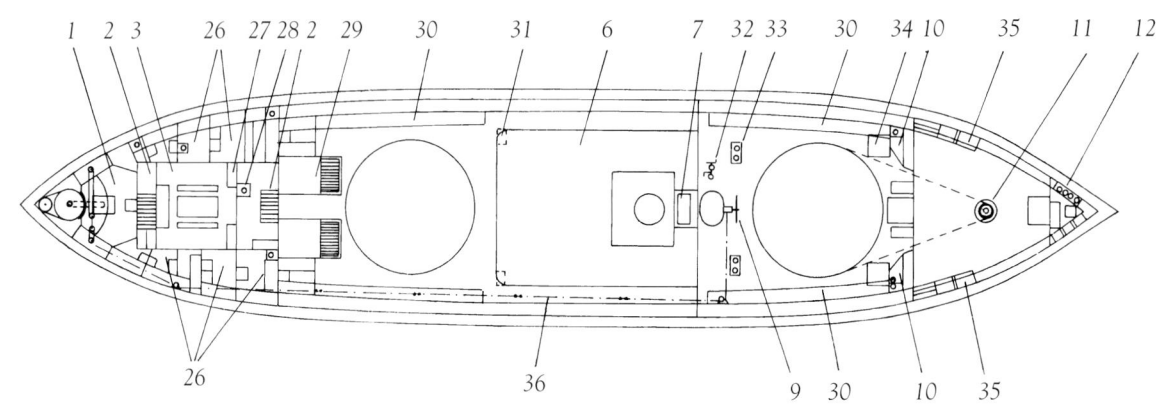

(Drawings by Ian Sturton)

Key:
1. Captain's cabin
2. Ladder
3. Wardroom
4. Ventilation main
5. Cupola furnace for heating up iron filling of Martin shells
6. Coal bunkers
7. Galley
8. Conning tower
9. Steering wheel
10. Boatswain's cabin
11. Hand windlass for the capstan
12. Heads
13. Storeroom
14. Boatswain's stores
15. Chain locker
16. Storeroom for gunnery equipment
17. Water tanks
18. Powder magazine
19. Boiler
20. Auxiliary steam engine
21. Main engine
22. Provisions locker
23. Shell magazine
24. Magazine for solid shot
25, 26, 27. Officers' quarters
28. Hatch for passing shells
29. Skylight
30. Racks for baggage
31. Coal scuttle
32. Pump
33. Hatch for passing powder
34. Gangway hatch
35. Crew's lockers
36. Tiller rope with guide rollers from tiller to steering wheel

Smerch riding at anchor somewhere in the Baltic early in her career. Her turrets are turned to face the camera, each showing a single embrasure. (Courtesy of the late Boris Lemachko)

would probably have been both unnecessary and unwise.

And indeed, when put to the test her double bottom proved less watertight than it should have been. On 23 July/4 August 1865 *Smerch* struck an uncharted rock in the Finnish skerries. The ship was holed forward, and although the bulkhead doors were promptly closed and the ship's steam-driven pump (150 tons/hour capacity) was set to work, the valves intended to close off the ventilation ducts either were not properly secured or failed to work, and water was able to penetrate throughout the ship. *Smerch* sank in shallow water within two hours.[10] She was raised on 20 August / 1 September 1865 using 'soft' (rubber) pontoons invented by the submarine designer I.F. Aleksandrovskii, and returned to service soon after.

Armament

Smerch's armament was carried in two Coles turrets, which provided for wide arcs of fire. Despite her flush-deck, however, she could not fire directly forward or aft because of a variety of small deckhouses and hatches. Her captains reported her arcs of fire to be 146-148° on either beam for the forward turret, and 147-158° for the after one, the variations probably being due to the addition or removal of fittings over the course of her career.

The turrets had diameters of 22ft (6.7m), and their designed armament was two 60pdr (7.72in/196mm) smoothbore muzzle-loaders each. These were replaced in 1867 by two Krupp 8in (203mm) breach-loading rifles; only one of these larger guns could be accommodated in each turret, so the old gunports were plated over and new ones cut; also necessary was an aperture in the rear turret wall for the handle of the ramrod. In 1870 the Krupp guns were replaced by Obukhovskii 9in (229mm) rifled guns. Finally, in 1876 the ship was rearmed again with a new, longer pattern of 9in Obukhovskii gun. Ammunition supply was 120 rounds per gun.

An interesting feature of the ship as built was the cupola furnace between the turrets for Martin molten iron shells.[11] These were similar in theory to the red-hot shot of the sailing-ship era. Molten iron was poured into the hollow shell, the idea being that the shell would shatter when it hit an enemy ship, so that the liquefied iron filling would be splattered over a wide area and start fires that would be almost impossible to extinguish. After filling with molten iron, the shell was good for about an hour before the iron cooled too much to be effective. Molten iron shell were safer to handle aboard ship than red-hot shot, and they enjoyed a brief vogue, but they were most effective against wooden ships; as ironclads proliferated their usefulness decreased, and they were eventually abandoned.

In the 1870s *Smerch* was fitted with a variety of light anti-torpedo boat guns. Four 4pdr (3.4in/87mm) guns were mounted, and a 0.65in Gatling gun and a 45mm Engström quick-firing gun were also added to her armament. At an unknown later date four Hotchkiss 37mm revolving cannon were mounted, two atop each turret; they probably replaced the old, slow-firing 4pdrs.

Protection

As Russian firms were still unable to supply solid plate of the requisite thickness, Mitchell was allowed to obtain the 360 tons of armour required for the *Smerch* from British companies.

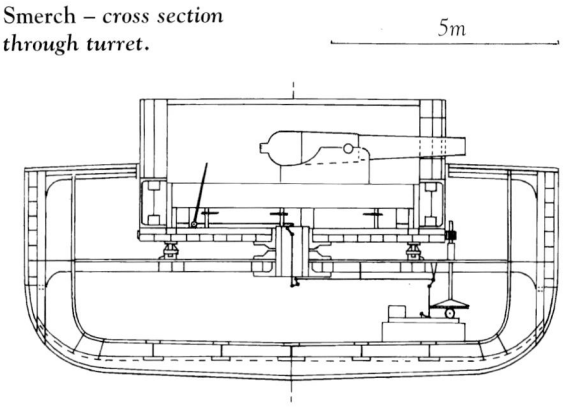

Smerch – cross section through turret.

5m

(Drawing by Ian Sturton)

153

A fine shot of Smerch *later in her career. Aside from the pairs of 37mm revolving cannon on top of the turrets and a small structure on the bridge abaft the funnel – possibly a wheelhouse – the ship seems little changed from her original appearance.* (Courtesy of Sergei Vinogradov)

The ship was completely protected above water. The side armour had a height of 7ft (2.13m), 4ft 6in (1.37m) of which extended below the waterline as designed. It was 4.5in (114mm) for most of the length of the ship; about 15ft (4.5m) from the bow and stern it was reduced to 4in (102mm). It was backed by 8in (203mm) of teak. The turrets were also protected by 4.5in plate, increasing to 6in (152mm) near the embrasures. The conning tower was originally to be protected by 3.5in (89mm) armour, increased to 4.5in during construction.

Two features may have been borrowed from the *Uragan* class: there was a slight overhang aft that served to protect the propellers and rudder from enemy fire; and the lower portion of the funnel had an armoured casing of four layers of 1in (25.4mm) plate, extending 4ft (1.22m) above the deck.

The deck was protected by 1in over the entire length of the ship, while the thickness of the hatch covers was 1.45in (37mm).

Machinery and Trials

Whereas *Rolf Krake* had a single propeller, *Smerch* had twin screws, making her the first Russian ship so equipped; they were 7ft 10in (2.39m) in diameter. Her engines were made by the British firm of Maudslay, Sons & Field; they were horizontal direct acting engines with cylinder diameters of 36in (914mm) and an 18in (457mm) piston stroke. These engines were rated at 200 nominal horse power (nhp) each, a measurement calculated from the engine dimensions and steam pressure in the cylinders; as one historian has noted, nhp 'bears no real relationship to the actual power developed by an engine but was an early method by which engines could be compared.'[12] Indicated horse power (ihp) was the power an engine actually developed, and was generally two to three times greater than the nhp rating.

The boilers were of the fire-tube type working at a pressure of 1.7 atmospheres, grate surface was 140ft^2 (13m^2) and heating surface was 4,100ft^2 (381m^2). A small railway was installed from the coal bunkers to the furnaces, to make moving the coal easier. The funnel was telescoping, and was fitted with blowers to increase the draught.

Trials were run from 31 May/12 June to 5/12 June 1865. The ship drew 9ft 9in (2.97m) forward and 10ft 4in (3.15m) aft; with a total of 800ihp, revolutions came to 100-116rpm and speed was about 8.3kts; this was probably measured by log, and so likely to be very approximate.

A third boiler was provided for powering a 6nhp engine, which drove the main water pump, the ventilation system, and also turned the after turret. The forward turret was apparently rotated by its own small steam engine.

In 1882 the ship was re-boilered, and in 1889 the bottom plating was replaced. By this time the speed of the ship did not exceed 6.5kts.

Rig and Ground Tackle

There were three pole masts of the Coles telescoping type. These are usually described as signal masts, but they also supported a light sailing rig, probably consisting of fore-and-aft sails only, although photographic evidence is lacking for its exact form. These were probably intended more to steady the ship than to propel her; the early ironclads lacked the heavy topweight of fully-rigged ships, so they tended to roll quickly due to excess stability; but the constant pressure of the wind on the sails would give a ship a more or less constant heel, reducing the ship's tendency to roll.

There were two anchors, each weighing 2.3 tons, plus one of 0.2 tons and one of 0.15 tons. There was also a warp-anchor of 0.35 tons.

Rusalka and Charodeika: Design and Construction

With the emergency shipbuilding programme underway, in the autumn of 1863 the Naval Ministry turned its attention to the next generation of ironclads. On 31 October/12 November 1863 it issued requirements for a coast-defence vessel offering a 'small target' – probably meaning a low freeboard; nevertheless it was to be capable of sailing throughout the Baltic. It was to be armed with 15in Dalgren smoothbores, protected by armour up to 6in (152mm) thick (although it could be laminated), and driven by two screws. Proposals were due by 1/13 April 1864.

In March 1864, while this competition was still in progress, the Naval Ministry approved a building programme of eight ironclads of several different types, including sea-going ships.[13] Although Mitchell was the favoured designer, he was allocated only one ship, with the other seven to be distributed among Russian builders to foster the domestic ironclad shipbuilding industry. Mitchell submitted his proposals, probably in May or early June; he outlined four designs for differing types of ironclads, designated C to F[14] (for details, see Table 3):

C: A fully-rigged sea-going 'corvette' that evolved into the Kniaz Pozharskii and Minin (although the latter was extensively altered during construction);
D: A two-turret monitor, considerably larger than Smerch;
E: Submitted in two versions (E with a single hoisting screw and E' with 2 fixed screws), these was intended as improved versions of the Pervenets class broadside ironclads, but eventually emerged as the 'turret frigates' Admiral Lazarev, Admiral Greig, Admiral Chichagov and Admiral Spiridov;
F: Dubbed 'the tortoise' (cherepakha) by Mitchell because it was 'slow, but reliable', this seems to have been an improved Smerch.

In the early summer of 1864 these designs were reviewed by a Special Advisory Council, which then submitted its comments to the Shipbuilding Technical Committee (chaired by Major-General S.I. Cherniavskii). Still another set of comments was received from the commander of the ironclad squadron, Rear-Admiral I.F. Likhachev, on 28 June/10 July. The general tenor of the comments seems to have been that the ships were too small for their armament, and that they would need more powerful engines. Moreover, Admiral Likhachev believed that, due to advances in artillery, the proposed protection of the designs was inadequate; he also felt that it would be better to concentrate on fewer types.

The results of all these deliberations were passed on to the director of the Naval Ministry, Admiral N.K. Krabbe, and on 23 August/4 September 1864 he handed down his decision: Design D was eliminated entirely, and two of each of the remaining four designs (E and E' being considered separate designs) were to be built.

Perhaps because it was the simplest type, it was decided to lead off the programme with the two ships of Design F, now modified and designated F[2]. The contract with the intended builder, an enterprising merchant named S.G. Kudriavtsev, was signed on 14/26 January 1865; it called for the two ships to be handed over to the navy by 15/27 May 1867. In addition to providing facilities at the state-owned Galernyi Island shipyards (the ships were built on the same slipways where the Ericsson monitors Edinorog and Strelets had been built), the Naval Ministry undertook to provide the armament, armour, machinery, masts and rigging, boats, anchors, and a variety of minor gear. Kudriavtsev was to build the hulls from Russian-made iron 'of the best quality', and the contract price for each hull was 539,000 rubles.

Construction at first went along briskly, but soon there

TABLE 3: IRONCLAD DESIGNS, SUMMER 1864

Designation:	C	D	E	E'	F
Type:	Broadside	2 turrets	Broadside	Broadside	2 turrets
Displacement:	2,563 tons	2,105 tons	2,185 tons	2,185 tons	1,316 tons
Length:	265ft/80.8m	240ft/73.2m	240ft 10in/73.4m	240ft 10in/73.4m	200ft/61m
Beam:	45ft/13.7m	43ft/13.1m	43ft/13.1m	43ft/13.1m	38ft 3in/11.65m
Draught:	18ft 3in/5.57m	15ft 6in/4.73m	15ft 6in/14.73m	15ft 6in/14.73m	13ft 1.5in/4m
Armament:	8 guns	4 guns	4 guns	4 guns	4 guns
Machinery:	450nhp	350nhp	350nhp	350nhp	250nhp
Propellers:	1 hoisting	2 fixed	1 hoisting	2 fixed	?
No. of Ships:	2	1	2	1	2
Proposed Builders:	1 by Semianikov & Poletika; 1 by Charles Mitchell	New Admiralty	Semianikov & Poletika	Karr & Makferson	S.G. Kudriavtsev

Note: The displacement figures in these tables were not actual displacements but Builder's Old Measure (BOM), which was calculated based on the dimensions of a ship, and generally gave a smaller 'tonnage' figure than water displacement.

were delays – for example, the drawings of the machinery arrangements did not reach the builders until 17/29 August 1865, holding up work. That same month Kudriavtsev died. A special commission under the authority of the director of the Shipbuilding Department, Rear-Admiral N.V. Voevodskii, reviewed the state of the work; it found that a considerable part of the framework and deck beams were already in place, as was some of the hull plating. In December the contract was transferred to Charles Mitchell, who was granted an additional 77,165 rubles due to changes in the design that would increase the cost of the ships.

In addition to the delays caused by the transfer of the contract, there were other problems. The armour was late in delivery, and some of the internal arrangements remained unsettled until late in the construction. The stem-posts, cast by the Izhorskii Works, were delivered only in the autumn of 1866. The ships' commanders insisted on a number of minor alterations, as did the successive commanders of the armoured squadron, Rear-Admirals I.F. Likhachev and G.I. Butakov.

When the ships were finally launched on 31 August / 12 September 1867 they still lacked machinery, armour, turrets and guns, conning towers and masts. Work continued until the spring of 1869, when they were finally ready for trials – two years later than stipulated by the original contract.

General Characteristics

The configuration of the ships was very similar to that of *Smerch*: two Coles turrets, each with two guns, with a small conning tower abaft the forward turret and a single funnel. A light bridge was installed between the turrets, about 12ft (3.6m) wide, with wing platforms extending to the width of the ship for navigation and lights; the wings also provided a convenient perch for leadsmen when taking soundings. The coamings of the hatchways were led up to the level of the bridge, providing a little more security against flooding in rough weather. The boats were suspended on davits from the bridge. Over time the bridgeworks grew more elaborate, a feature common to all the turret ships; eventually there was a small wooden pilothouse above the conning tower, and light anti-torpedo boat guns were mounted on the bridge and the upper deck.

The freeboard amounted to only 2ft (0.6m), and the ships were designed with small raised forecastles and poops and were to be fitted with folding bulwarks to improve their sea-keeping, but the bulwarks were eliminated in 1867, before the ships entered service; the forecastle and poop were also deleted at some point. Not surprisingly, the decks were generally awash with any sort of sea running, and the ships reportedly rolled heavily.[15] They also did not

TABLE 5: WEIGHTS, RUSALKA AND CHARODEIKA AS COMPLETED

Hull:	625 tons (29.8%)
Conning tower and turrets without armour:	270 tons (12.9%)
Bridges, wood fittings:	101 tons (4.8%)
Teak backing of armour:	105 tons (5.0%)
Armour:	399 tons (19.0%)
Armament (including mountings and ammunition):	120 tons (5.7%)
Coal:	150 tons (7.1%)
Machinery (inc. boiler water):	180 tons (8.6%)
Crew, boats, rig, provisions:	150 tons (7.1%)
Total:	2,100 tons

Rusalka – *body plan*.

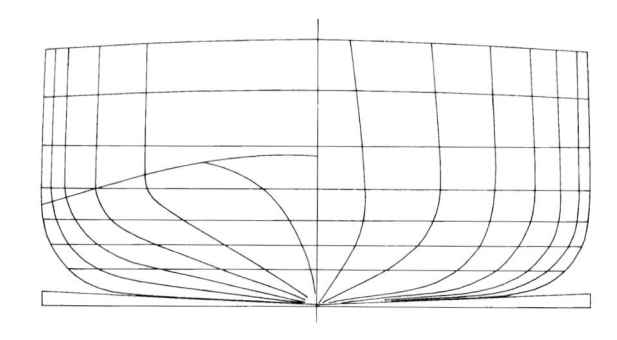

(Drawing by Ian Sturton)

TABLE 4: CHARACTERISTICS OF *RUSALKA* AND *CHARODEIKA* AS DESIGNED AND COMPLETED

Displacement:	1,881.7 tons designed; 2,100 tons normal
Dimensions:	206ft wl x 42ft x 11ft (designed), 12ft 7in (actual)
	62.8m wl x 12.80m x 3.36m (designed), 3.84m (actual)
Armament:	As designed: four 9in (229mm) steel rifled guns (2 x 2)
	1869: two 9in (229mm) (1 x 2), two 15in (381mm) smoothbores (1 x 2)
Protection:	Wrought iron armour
	sides: 4.5in (114mm) amidships, 3.75in (95mm) forward, 3.25in (83mm) aft
	turrets: 5.5in (140mm)
	conning tower: 4.5in (114mm)
	deck: 1in (25mm) amidships
Machinery:	Two rectangular boilers, two horizontal direct-acting engines, 875ihp
Speed:	8.5 knots
Endurance:	150 tons coal normal, 250 tons maximum; ?nm at ?kts
Complement:	1877: 13 officers, 171 enlisted

Rusalka – *external profile and hull lines.*

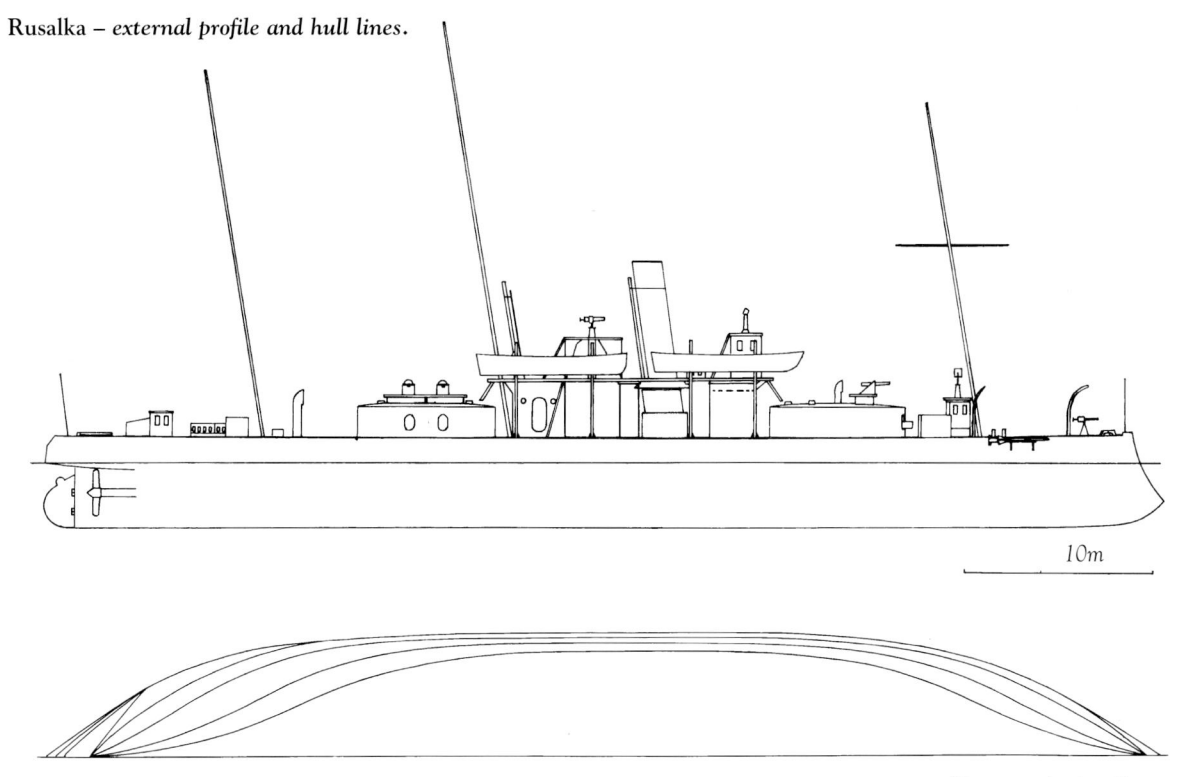

(Drawings by Ian Sturton)

manoeuvre well, often not responding to the helm until given more than 20° of rudder. Steering was laborious, and in 1871 another wheel was added to the upper steering wheel in an attempt to alleviate this problem.

Like the *Smerch*, the vessels were built on the bracket-frame system, with double bottoms. The keel was assembled from 9/16in (14mm) plate, and the frames were spaced 2ft (0.6m) apart. The hull plating was 13/32in (10mm) to 3/4in (19mm) thick. The hull was divided into twenty-five compartments by watertight bulkheads. The ram was 6ft 6in (1.98m) below water and projected 4ft 7in (1.4m).

Rusalka ran aground in June 1869, and her watertight integrity proved no more effective that *Smerch's* had been four years earlier; despite the double bottom, water leaked into the inner hull, and the ship had to be grounded to prevent her sinking. The incident led a young *michman* (sub-lieutenant) named Stepan Osipovich Makarov to publish a study on the survivability of warships, but the full realisation of his recommendations would have to wait forty years, when major improvements were finally introduced following the loss of the small battleship *Gangut* in June 1897. As for *Rusalka* and *Charodeika*, they were subjected to a variety of minor alterations, and it was only in 1874 that the ships were considered fully effective.

Charodeika *early in her career; note the bow of what appears to be a wooden frigate in the right background.* Charodeika *and her sister* Rusalka *had the same basic configuration as the earlier* Smerch. *Important distinguishing features include the raked funnel, the turrets with their two embrasures each, and the lack of the small platform abaft the after turret seen on* Smerch. *(Courtesy of the late Boris Lemachko)*

Rusalka – *longitudinal section.*

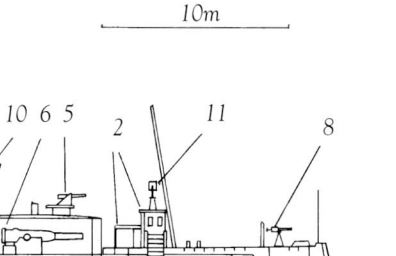

Rusalka – *deck plan.*

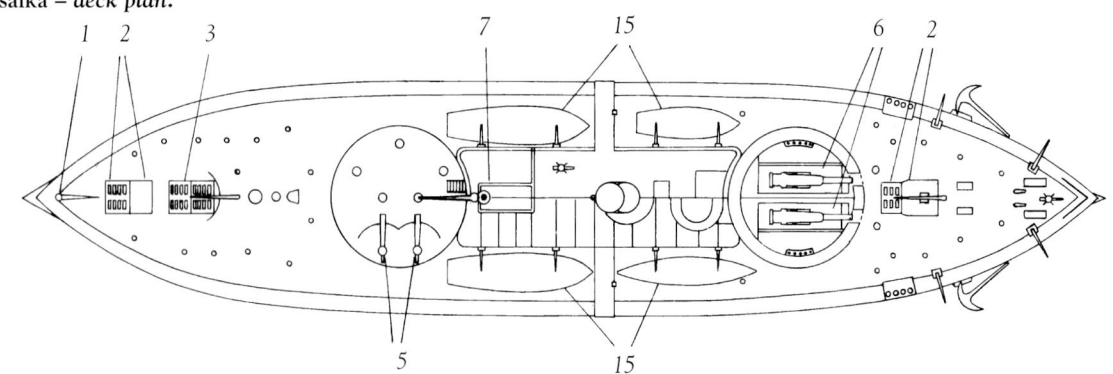

(Drawings by Ian Sturton)

Key:
1. Tiller
2. Skylight and capstan drum
3. Skylight
4. Officers' cabins
5. 87mm gun
6. 9in (229mm) gun
7. Boiler room hatch
8. 37mm Hotchkiss gun
9. Main compass
10. Conning tower
11. Search light
12. Boiler
13. Steam pump
14. Engine
15. Boats

Armament

The two turrets were of the Coles type, with an external diameter of 26ft (7.92m) and an internal diameter of 22ft (6.71m). As in *Smerch*, their fields of fire were obstructed on forward and after bearings by a number of small structures; they were generally credited by their captains with arcs of fire of about 150° on either beam.

The designed armament was four 300pdr 9in/229mm steel rifled guns, but the introduction of this gun was delayed due to manufacturing difficulties, so in 1867 it was decided to arm the ships with four 15in/381mm American-pattern Rodman smoothbores cast at Olonets; similar guns were being installed in the *Uragan* class single-turret monitors at the time. The new gun required an increase in the width of the embrasures, to 30in (762mm). However, by the time the ships actually entered service in 1869 they were armed with two 9in/229mm model 1867 rifles in the forward turret and two 15in smoothbores in the after turret. The *Rusalka*'s smoothbores were replaced by 9in rifles in 1871, and soon after *Charodeika* also received a uniform battery of four 9in rifles. In 1878-1879 these were replaced by longer guns of the same calibre. The axes of the guns were only 4ft 2in (1.27m) above the waterline; they could elevate to 7°, for a maximum range of 3,000 yards. The magazines held 75 rounds per gun.

In common with other Russian ironclads, during the 1870s the *Rusalka* and *Charodeika* were fitted with light anti-torpedo boat guns, but their numbers, calibres and locations are uncertain. *Charodeika* carried four 87mm guns, two on each turret top, while *Rusalka* had only one on the after turret, for a total of three. At various times their light armament also included 45mm Engström guns, Hotchkiss 37mm five-barrelled revolvers and 47mm single-barrelled guns, and 1in (25.4mm) Palmcrantz-Nordenfelt guns. Some of these were carried on the bridgeworks, others on the upper deck.

Protection

These were the first ships protected by Russian-made armour, manufactured by the Izhorskii and Votkinskii works. There were delays in delivery, as Russian firms were still mastering the rolling of the thicker armour plate required for these ships.

The 4.5in (114mm) side armour amidships had a total height of 7ft 6in (2.28m), of which about 5ft 6in (1.70m) was submerged at the design displacement. Forward the armour thinned to 3.75in (95mm), and aft it was reduced to 3.25in (83mm). The armour was backed by teak 12-18in (305-457mm) thick. The turrets were protected by 5.5in (140mm) plate on teak backing, while the conning tower had 4.5in (114mm) armour.

An interesting view of Rusalka in drydock, perhaps following her grounding in June 1869. The location may be Helsingfors. (Courtesy of the late Boris Lemachko)

In the central portion of the hull the deck was 1in (25.4mm) thick, thinning fore and aft to 0.25-0.5in (6.35-12.7mm). It was covered with pine planking, but near the turrets the pine was replaced by oak, better to withstand the blast of the guns.

Machinery and Trials

The machinery was manufactured by the Russian Berd (Baird) Works, under a contract signed on 2/14 May 1866. As in *Smerch*, the shallow hull meant that the engines had to be very compact, and therefore two small engines were used in place of a single larger one. The two rectangular boilers worked at a pressure of 1.6 atmospheres, providing steam to two horizontal direct-acting engines, with cylinder diameters of 38in (965mm), and piston strokes of 18in (457mm). Each engine drove a four-bladed propeller of 8ft 6in (2.59m) diameter.

The contract called for each engine to have an output of 200nhp, with a total of 900ihp for the entire plant. These targets were not achieved; on trials in 1869 the

Rusalka, probably in the 1880s. Among the new features visible in this photograph are the enclosed wooden wheelhouse and the platform immediately abaft the funnel, with what looks like a 37mm Hotckiss revolving cannon on it. Another 37mm gun can be seen on the after turret between the two ventilators, pointing at the camera. Both 37mm guns are under protective coverings. (Naval History and Heritage Command, NH 84755)

TABLE 6: GUNS

	60pdr smoothbore	15in smoothbore[1] (old drawing)	8in Rifle[2]	9in/17.3 Rifle[3] (old drawing)	9in/20 Rifle[4] (new drawing)
Calibre:	7.72in/196mm	15in/381mm	8in/202.3mm	9in/229mm	9in/229mm
Dates:	1855	1864	1867	Entered service 1869	1867
Weight:	?	~19,900kg	9,009kg	12,711kg	15,070-15,225kg
Barrel length:	3,460mm/17.6 cal	?	4,273mm/21 cal	3,962mm/17.33 cal	4,572mm/20 ca
Bore length:	N/A	9 cal	2,832mm/14 cal	3,353mm/14.66 cal	3,873mm/16.9 cal
Rate of fire:	?	?	1 round in 5 min	?	?
Projectiles & Performance					
Weight:	26.2kg	199.8kg	79.9kg	122-124kg	122-124kg
Charge:	6.56kg	?	10.2kg	19.45kg	30.7kg 'battle'
MV:	471m/sec	360m/sec	375m/sec	386m/sec	447m/sec
Range:	3,519m @ 18.25°	?	?	?	?
Ships mounting:	Smerch 1865-1866	Rusalka 1869-1870 Charodeika 1869-1871	Smerch 1867-1869	Smerch 1870-1875 Rusalka 1869-1877 Charodeika 1869-1878	Smerch 1876 onward Rusalka 1878 onward

Notes:

1. Cast at the Olonets Works. Adopted from the American Rodman gun, with the bore cast with the gun, not drilled, and the bore was water-cooled after casting. Trials were started on 27 June/9 July 1865. The gun successfully passed trials, surviving over 500 shots. Proving ground trials indicated that these guns, when firing the steel shot, could 'demolish' 6in armour at ranges up to 740m.

2. These began as Krupp-made steel muzzle-loading smoothbores ordered in 1863; the next year it was decided to rifle some of these barrels. Originally a charge of 12.9kg was used, but after a Krupp-made 11in gun burst in September 1871, the charge was reduced to 10.2kg, with the 12.9kg charges to be used 'only in wartime and only against ironclads.'

3. Conversions from the steel-barrelled, cast-iron-reinforced 9in smoothbores ordered by the Naval Ministry from Krupp in 1863. In March 1865 Krupp offered to convert these barrels to rifles, and nineteen guns were sent back to Germany for this work; in addition to being rifled, the original cast-iron jackets were removed and replaced with two layers of steel bands.

4. Twenty-two 9in rifles of a new design were ordered from Krupp, and the Obukhovskii Works subsequently manufactured more guns to the same design. Many of these barrels were subsequently converted to 9in model 1877 guns, which had similar dimensions and weights, but were lengthened by adding an extension to the barrel; these guns had a higher muzzle velocity. It is possible that Smerch, Rusalka and Charodeika were rearmed with the 1877 model guns later in their careers.

Charodeika managed only 786ihp for a speed of 8.5kts, while the *Rusalka* developed only 705ihp, but somehow managed 9kts. These speeds were probably recorded using logs, rather than on a measured mile, and are therefore likely to be very approximate.

In addition to the main engines, there was an auxiliary engine to run the pumps and ventilation system. In 1869 an auxiliary boiler was installed on the *Rusalka*; this was probably done to reduce the drop in steam pressure caused by steam being bled from the main plant for the auxiliary engine. The *Rusalka* was re-boilered in 1878 and 1891.

Rig, Boats and Ground Tackle

The ships had three light iron masts and carried a rig similar to that of *Smerch*, although its exact form is uncertain. Their complement of boats included a ten-oared cutter, a six-oared whaleboat, and four-oared and two-oared pinnaces. The boats were stowed between the turrets, suspended on davits from the light flying bridge. In 1871 *Charodeika* was equipped with a steam cutter (32ft 7in/9.93m x 10ft 9in/3.28m), built by the Finnish Kreiton shipyard.

They each carried two 1.52-ton and one 1.36-ton anchors.

Loss of the Rusalka[16]

The *Rusalka*, under the command of Captain 2nd Rank V.Kh. Ienish, put to sea from Revel (now Tallinn, Estonia) on the morning of 7/19 September 1893; her immediate destination was Helsingfors, whence she was to proceed to Kronshtadt for the winter lay-up. When she had left port the wind was freshening, and after a few hours the ship found herself being battered by a northeasterly gale blowing at Force 8. The accompanying gunboat *Tucha* (Captain 2nd Rank N.M. Lushkov) lost contact with the *Rusalka* around noon, and the ironclad was never seen again; twelve officers and 166 men were lost. The only traces found of her were a body that washed ashore on the Finnish island of Kremare in a dinghy and a few life buoys; an extensive search of the sea bed failed to discover the wreck.

In January 1894 a commission appointed to investigate the loss judged that Rear-Admiral P.S. Burachek, commander of the detachment, should never have

TABLE 6: GUNS, CONTINUED

	4pdr/3.4in[5]	Engström[6] single-barrelled	Palmcrantz[7] (Nordenfelt) 4-barrelled	Hotchkiss[8] 5-barrelled	Hotchkiss[9] single-barrelled
Calibre:	3.42in/86.87mm	1.75in/44.45mm	1in/25.4mm	37mm	47mm
Dates:	1867	1876	1879	1879	?
Weight:	?	100kg	203kg	209kg	230kg
Barrel length:	1,713mm/19.7 cal	1,041mm/23.5 cal	980mm/38.6 cal	740mm/20 cal	?
Bore/Rifled length:	1,182mm/13.6 cal	897mm/20.2 cal	860mm/33.8 cal	616mm	?
Rate of fire:	?	20rpm (5-6rpm aimed)	140rpm	32rpm	19rpm
Projectiles & Performance					
Weight:	5.74kg	1.013kg	0.298kg	0.5kg	1.5kg
Charge:	0.615kg	0.081kg	0.034	0.08kg	0.75kg
MV:	306m/sec	310m/sec	447m/sec	442m/sec	701m/sec
Range:	3,294m @ 14.13°	915m @ 3.03°	1,200m max	2,778m @ 11°	4,575m @ 10.4°

Notes:

5. A standard field artillery calibre adopted for shipboard use. These short, low-velocity guns were used in cases where armour penetration was not the primary consideration. They were manufactured by the Obukhovskii Works and Krupp; the steel tube was not reinforced. The mounting was of the carriage type.

6. Designed by the Swedish naval officer, Carl Christian Engström. Called the 'Engstrem' gun in Russian service.

7. Another gun of Swedish origin, invented by Helge Palmcrantz, but more commonly known by the name of Palmcrantz's financial backer, Thorsten Nordenfelt. The Russians called it the Palmkrants gun.

8. One of the most widely used quick-firing anti-torpedo guns of the 1880s, developed by Benjamin B. Hotchkiss, an expatriate American who established the firm of Hotchkiss et Cie at Saint-Denis, a suburb of Paris.

9. In addition to the guns listed in this table, *Smerch* mounted one 0.65in Gatling gun early in her career.

A fine view of Charodeika. *Two 87mm (4pdr) guns on carriage mountings can be seen atop the forward turret, and there appears to be a searchlight just abaft the foremast. On the upper deck amidships it is possible to make out a 37mm Hotchkiss gun against the white funnel base.* (Courtesy of Sergei Vinogradov)

A photograph of Rusalka's quarterdeck late in her career, probably not long before her loss. The gun atop the after turret appears to be a single-barrelled 47mm Hotchkiss QFG. (Courtesy of the late Boris Lemachko)

allowed *Rusalka* go to sea in such weather; Captain 2nd Rank Lushkov of the *Tucha* was also held to be at fault for losing contact with the *Rusalka*. A monument to those lost aboard the *Rusalka* was erected in Reval in 1902.

In 1932 the wreck was reportedly discovered by divers from a Soviet government agency, EPRON (*Ekspeditsiia podvodnykh rabot osobogo naznacheniia* – the Expedition for Underwater Work of Special Purpose); but EPRON's task was to locate and recover underwater items that might be of value to the cash-starved Soviet government, and *Rusalka's* wreck was of no interest to it. It was only in July 2003 that an expedition led by Vello Mäss of the Estonian Maritime Museum in Tallinn rediscovered the wreck – or discovered it, since the location reported by EPRON did not match the wreck's actual site. The ship rests in 240ft (73m) of water in an almost vertical position, with her bow buried in the sea bottom; her stern rises 108ft (33m) above the bottom, covered in snagged fishing nets.

The evidence provided by the discovery of the wreck has led to a new theory regarding what happened in the ship's last hours. The 1893 commission believed that either water penetrated to the boiler room through hatchways, extinguished the fires, and left the ship without power, or the steering gear failed. Either event would have left the ship helpless in the face of the sea; she would have been turned broadside to the waves, the light superstructure would have been smashed, flooding would have followed and, given her small reserve of buoyancy, she would soon have been swamped or capsized. But this does not account for the wreck's near-vertical position. Mäss and Kaido Peremees, the lead diver of the Estonian expedition, have proposed instead that the ship began taking on water forward, perhaps through a poorly repaired leak; water was also coming in through the ventilation intakes. Being about only one-third of the way to Helsingfors, Captain Ienish apparently decided to return to Reval – the ship's rudder is set to starboard, indicating that she was turning when she sank. Caught by the waves during her turn, the ship capsized, and her turrets fell out. Already bow-heavy and with her engines still running she was driven down to, and then into, the bottom.

The exact location of *Rusalka's* wreck has not been made public in order to prevent casual diving on the gravesite of her crew.

Careers

Smerch ('Waterspout'): The ship ran her trials in May/June 1865. On 23 July/4 August 1865 she sank in shallow water in the Finnish skerries as a result of striking an uncharted rock. She was raised on 20 August/1 September 1865 using pontoons. She underwent major repairs in 1882 and 1889, including the replacement of much of her bottom plating. On 1/13 February 1892 she was reclassified as a 'coast defence armourclad' and served as a school ship. On 20 December 1903/2 January 1904 she was turned over to the Port of Kronshtadt and stricken on 7/20 February 1904. She was redesignated Blokshiv (hulk) No. 2 on 14/27 October 1909 and converted for use as a mine storeship. She continued in this role during the First World War, and was abandoned at Helsingfors by retreating Red forces during the evacuation of Finland in April 1918. She was returned to the Bolshevik government in May 1918 as a result of the Treaty of Brest-Litovsk and resumed her duties as a mine storeship. From 1923 she was redesignated Blokshiv No. 3, and from 1 January 1932 she was known as Blokshiv No. 1. On 7 October 1941 she sank in Kronshtadt harbor as a result of German artillery fire; she was again stricken on 6 March 1942, but raised in the summer of that year and on 8 December re-entered service. She was renamed BSh-1 on 16 May 1949; she was finally stricken on 2 April 1959 and subsequently broken up.

Charodeika ('Sorceress'): She ran her trials in 1869 and was later attached to the Mine (Torpedo) Training Detachment. She was reclassified as a 'coast defence armourclad' on 1/13 February 1892. After an uneventful career she was turned over to the Port of Kronshtadt on 18/31 March 1907 for disposal, stricken on 25 March/7 April 1907, and broken up in 1911-1912.

Rusalka ('Mermaid'): She ran her trials in 1869. In June 1869 she struck an uncharted rock in the Gulf of Finland; her outer plating was damaged from frames 11 to 25, an extent of 28ft, and she had to be deliberately run aground to prevent sinking. In March 1870 she was attached to the Artillery Training Detachment. She was re-boilered in 1878 and 1891. Reclassified as a 'coast defence armourclad' on 1/13 February 1892, she was lost with all hands on a voyage from Revel to Helsingfors on 7/19 September 1893 (for details, see above); she was officially stricken on 14/26 October 1893.

Acknowledgements:

I would like to express my gratitude to Sergei Vinogradov for providing much of the material used in this article; to the late Boris Lemachko for photographs; to Ian Sturton for help with the drawings; and to Ian Buxton and David Saunders, who generously shared information. Also of great help were Lars Ahlberg, Rob Brassington, Ed Rudnicki and Terry Sofian who helped sort out the anti-torpedo boat armament of these ships. As always, my wife Jan Torbet provided invaluable help as an editor.

Sources:

Two Russian articles are the main sources for this article: R.M. Mel'nikov, 'Dvukhbashennaia bronenosnaia lodka "Smerch"' (*Sudostroenie*, 1985, no. 4, pp. 59-63) and V.Iu. Gribovskii, 'Bashennye lodki "Rusalka" i "Charodeika"' (*Sudostroenie*, 1985, no. 6, pp. 64-66). These are supplemented by 'The Russian Ironclad "Smertch"' (*Engineering*, 12 October 1866, p. 285), V.Iu. Gribovskii and I.I. Chernikov, *Bronenosets 'Admiral Ushakov'* (St. Petersburg: Sudostroenie, 1996), pp. 30-36 and I.P. Spasskii, editor, *Istoriia otechestvennogo sudostroeniia* (5 vols.; St. Petersburg: Sudostroenie, 1994-1996), vol. II, pp. 28, 31-36. The careers of these ships are known only sketchily; S.S. Berezhnoi, *Lineinye i bronenosnye korabli – kanonerskie lodki: spravochnik* (Moscow: Voennoe izdatel'stvo, 1997), pp. 81-82, provides the basic data.

For the armament of these ships I have relied on L.I. Amirkhanov, *Artilleriia rossiiskikh monitorov* (St. Petersburg: Gangut, 1998).

Footnotes:

1. Oscar Parkes, *British Battleships: 'Warrior' 1860 to 'Vanguard' 1950: A History of Design, Construction and Armament* (revised edition; London: Seeley Services & Co., 1957), pp.44-5; Andrew Lambert, 'Coles, Cowper Phipps', in: Spencer C. Tucker, editor, *Naval Warfare: An International Encyclopedia* (Santa Barbara: ABC-CLIO, 2002), vol. 1, pp.238-9.
2. For the *Uragan* class, see Stephen McLaughlin, 'Russia's "American" Monitors: The *Uragan* Class', *Warship 2012* (London: Conway, 2012), pp.98-114.
3. For Mitchell and the *Ne tron menia*, see Stephen McLaughlin, 'Russia's First Ironclads: *Pervenets*, *Ne tron menia* and *Kreml*', *Warship 2011* (London: Conway, 2011), pp.112-129.
4. David Saunders, 'Charles Mitchell, Tyneside and Russia's First Ironclads' (*Northern History*, vol. XLVIII, no. 1 [March 2011], pp.75-95), p.88. I am grateful to Ian Buxton for drawing my attention to this very important article and putting me in contact with its author.
5. See Arnold A. Putnam, '*Rolf Krake*: Europe's First Turreted Ironclad' (*Mariner's Mirror*, vol. 84, no. 1 [February 1998], pp.56-63).
6. Russian sources give the name as 'A. Svan', which, despite the discordant first initial, was certainly Henry Frederick Swan, who had the management of all Mitchell's affairs in Russia from 1862 to 1865. See D.F. McGuire, *Charles Mitchell 1820-1895: Victorian Shipbuilder* (Newcastle upon Tyne: Newcastle upon Tyne City Libraries & Arts, 1988), pp.13, 73.
7. The *Schorpioen* and *Huáscar* still exist, at Den Helder in the Netherlands and Talcahuano, Chile, respectively.
8. Borgenstam, Curt Jr., et al., 'Question 20/93: Armor Penetration in Various Warships' (*Warship International*, vol. XXXII, no. 2 [1994], pp.202-203), p.203.
9. Spasskii, editor, *Istoriia otechestvennogo sudostroeniia*, vol. II, p.32. Note, however, that Gribovskii and Chernikov, *Bronenosets 'Admiral Ushakov'*, p.31, say that the frames were inserted as brackets between continuous stringers.
10. This incident is the source of a story in the London *Times* of 5 September 1865 that the ship had 'foundered and sank', which has occasionally been repeated in subsequent western publications.
11. Andrew Lambert, *HMS Warrior 1860: Victoria's Ironclad Deterrent* (Annapolis: Naval Institute Press, 2011), p.108; Ernest F. Slaymaker, 'The Armament of HMS Warrior', part 1 (*Warship*, vol X, no. 37, pp.44-52), p.50.
12. Denis Griffiths, *Steam at Sea: Two Centuries of Steam-powered Ships* (London: Conway Maritime Press, 1997), p.232.
13. The evolution of the 1864 ironclad construction programme is somewhat confusing; I have reconstructed its progress from Gribovskii and Chernikov, *Bronenosets 'Admiral Ushakov'*, p.32, *Istoriia otechestvennogo sudostroeniia*, pp.34-36, and Saunders, 'Charles Mitchell, Tyneside and Russia's First Ironclads', p.90.
14. Designs A and B were presumably the *Ne tron menia* and *Smerch*, already under construction at this point.
15. Paul H. Silverstone, *Directory of the World's Capital Ships* (London: Ian Allan Ltd., 1984), p.358.
16. Some details on the loss of *Rusalka* can be found in D. Fedotoff White, *Survival Through War and Revolution in Russia* (Philadelphia: University of Pennsylvania Press, 1939), pp.8-9; for her recent discovery, see James P. Delgado, 'The Wreck of the Mermaid: Hunting for *Rusalka*, the Czar's Lost Ironclad' (*Archaeology*, vol. 61, no. 5 [September/October 2008], pp.20-26).

WARSHIP NOTES

This section comprises a number of short articles and notes, generally highlighting little known aspects of warship history.

PHOTOGRAPHY AT CLYDEBANK SHIPYARD

Ian Johnston, author of the recent book *Clydebank Battlecruisers* (Seaforth Publishing, 2011), which traces the story of the building of these ships using contemporary construction photographs, describes the background to the remarkable visual archive from which these images came, and which is now in the care of the National Records of Scotland.

For over one hundred years, ships great and small built at Clydebank shipyard were routinely photographed from keel laying to trials. Between the years 1899 and 1968, the shipyard was owned by John Brown & Co Ltd and it was during this period that many of the most significant ships to be built in Britain, including the Cunard liners *Lusitania*, *Aquitania*, *Queen Mary*, *Queen Elizabeth* and *QE2* and warships such as *Hood* and *Vanguard* were completed there. However it was not just the famous ships that received photographic treatment; all vessels built at Clydebank from the 1880s onwards were covered, including merchant vessels, yachts, paddle steamers and a tug.

My first encounter with this collection was in 1971 when I visited the photographic department at Clydebank as an art student with a growing interest in shipbuilding. The department was tucked away at the top of a winding stairway and along a corridor in an old building adjacent to the main office, and was complete with a studio, processing labs, printing rooms and an office filled with grey filing cabinets. I was amazed to find images of ships such as *Asahi*, *Repulse*, *Queen Mary*, *QE2*, and many others lying around as if by some curious quirk of time they were still in the yard. It was the sheer quality of the images, pin sharp and in many cases beautifully framed that impressed me most. In my naivety I did not believe that photographs of such quality could have been taken in the early years of the last century. The collection of glass plate negatives were located separately in a dingy basement room with no windows and one bare light bulb. On a subsequent visit I felt like a kid in a sweet shop left in this room to sift through the negatives and make a selection of images.

Progress of construction photographs, as they were known, were taken by many shipyards to record and demonstrate progress over what could be a build time of several years as well as for publicity purposes. The photographs generally followed a similar pattern, starting with an image of the keel on the building berth followed by general shots of the hull on the berth with details such as a stern frame or shaft brackets. Launching was covered with a series of shots, while fitting-out included overall and detail shots showing machinery, gun mountings and various superstructure elements being added until completion. Departure from the yard and trial views completed the series. Sensitivities as well as the Official Secrets Act surrounding warship contracts did not restrict photography, although very few – if any – internal shots were taken of completed warships.

Work in the shipyard shops was not usually covered, although completed machinery, turbines, boilers and condensers etc., were often photographed where they were manufactured. Periodically, the photographers would take general shots of the yard, and from time to time record ships built elsewhere on the Clyde passing by the yard. Inevitably, the presence of an in-house photography department resulted in the occasional passport photo for senior management.

While other shipbuilders also photographed ships under construction, many did so by contracting local photographers to do the work while others, as at Clydebank, established their own departments. What seems to set Clydebank apart is the scale of the operation. From the company's records, the first mention of photographers is on 29 June 1887, when two men are recorded in the wages books under photography; J Stuart, paid £6 fortnightly and D Wallace, presumably an assistant or apprentice, paid ten shillings fortnightly. The employment of photographers at this date coincided with the company winning the orders for the Inman liners *City of New York* and *City of Paris*, then among the most prestigious liners to be built. By April 1904, five persons were entered into the wages book:

D Lindsay, £4. 10s
T Berry, £2. 6s
P Forbes, £2
W McCreadie, £1. 8s
J Butters, £1.

This suggests a senior photographer, a photographer and three assistants. By November 1919, nine people were on the books, with Lindsay receiving £5. 15s 6d and Berry £3. 15s 6d per week. None of the others earned over £1. 5s per week. From this it seems certain that the photographs reproduced in *Clydebank Battlecruisers* were taken by D Lindsay and T Berry, and to them due acknowledgement must be made for such a fine record of these ships. At the height of the depression in May 1932, only Lindsay and Berry were on the books at £5. 1s and

WARSHIP NOTES

As well as ships built at Clydebank the photographers sometimes took pictures of vessels passing by that had been constructed elsewhere on the river, making use of the splendid 153ft viewpoint offered by the 150-ton cantilever crane. These two images, both from 1916, show the Fairfield-built AMC Avenger *and the battleship* Valiant *heading down river. In the right background can be seen Beardmore's Naval Construction Works at Dalmuir. (National Records of Scotland, courtesy of Ian Johnston)*

£2. 14s 6d respectively, which says something about their worth to the company, as the *Queen Mary* was suspended with no other work in the yard.

The very first images taken at Clydebank were recorded onto glass plates 12 x 10 inches in size although 15 x 12 as well as 10 x 8-inch plates were used frequently. Large plate cameras continued to be used until after the Second World War, when half plate and 5 x 4 (and subsequently 2¼ square) celluloid negatives come into use.

The first warship to be systematically photographed, albeit sparingly, was the battleship *Ramillies* launched in 1892. According to a list of photographs kept by the shipyard, the following images were captured of the ship: ten of a model (some of which depicted a working model); two of the hull on the stocks; four of her launch; seventeen deck details; four showing panels in the Admiral's cabin; two showing the electric turning gear in the barbette and eight of the ship on trials.

Subsequent coverage of warships was even more complete, as this selection from the catalogue suggests:

Barham, battleship, 281
Repulse, battlecruiser, 359
Hood, battlecruiser, 502
Australia, cruiser, 229
Fortune, destroyer, 45
Southampton, cruiser, 104
Duke of York, battleship, more than 600
Indefatigable, fleet carrier, 441
Bermuda, cruiser, 209
Barrosa, destroyer, 119

Passenger vessels faired better in overall numbers of photographs taken, largely because of interior shots:

Lusitania, 76
Queen Mary, 1016
Caronia, 1131
Carinthia, 650

When the last ship left Clydebank in 1972 following the collapse of Upper Clyde Shipbuilders, of which John Brown & Co had become a division, the records of the Clydebank company including the photographs were saved for the nation. There are 23,000 glass plate negatives and at least another 20,000 celluloid negatives plus an additional number of uncatalogued celluloid and small glass plate negatives. Many of the negatives were printed to make bound photographic volumes at the time, and these also form part of the collection. Today, the negatives reside with the National Records of Scotland in Edinburgh who have taken on the task of conserving, re-cataloguing and scanning the collection for posterity.

The photographic archives of other well-known shipbuilders have not fared as well as those of Clydebank, and in some cases very few images remain to mark the earlier years of such well-known yards as Palmers, Fairfield, Armstrong. Much of this loss can be attributed to the casual disposal of company records when firms closed – tales abound of glass plate negatives and other important documents dumped in skips or thrown on bonfires. As it is, the photographic collection from Clydebank shipyard remains as an outstanding record of British shipbuilding achievement.

SHIPS FOR SOUTH AMERICA: POST-WAR PROPOSALS FROM FAIRFIELD'S

Kenneth Fraser continues his research in the Glasgow City Archives, and has turned up a number of interesting proposals for warships to be built for foreign navies.

The surviving records of the Fairfield Shipbuilding Company are (with one exception) held by Glasgow City Archives, and although details of many foreign inquiries that look potentially interesting have not survived, there are several files of post-war date which may be worth describing.

In October 1958 the company received an inquiry from the Peruvian Navy[1] for the possible construction of two light cruisers of 8000 tons with a speed of 35 knots, and three destroyers of 2650 tons. An anonymous official of the shipyard writes that the cruisers would cost about £15m each, and *Daring* class destroyers £5m each. He expresses doubts that Peru could afford such expenditure, and considers that the company would not be justified in undertaking design work unless there was a reasonable chance of an order. In the event, Peru contented herself with second-hand ships, the cruisers HMS *Ceylon* and *Newfoundland*.

Much less ambitious was a request in the same year[2] from the navy of the Dominican Republic for between three and six patrol vessels. A design was prepared, and drawings (unfortunately not present) were made. The particulars were:

Maximum length: 185 feet
Maximum breadth: 25 feet
Maximum depth: 15.5 feet
Maximum draught: 9 feet
Full load displacement: 550 tons
Propulsion: diesel engines for a speed of 22 knots
Armament: 1 x 4in gun (forward), 2 x 40mm, 4 x 20mm
Complement: 60

It is stated that the ships were to have a 'destroyer type outline': one might envisage a shorter version of the pre-war corvettes of the *Kingfisher* class. However, nothing came of the inquiry, nor does it appear that the Dominican Navy acquired any ships with similar characteristics from elsewhere.

A substantial file[3] refers to possible orders for patrol vessels from Turkey. In July 1960 the agent of a British firm in Istanbul reports that a friend with contacts in the new government (there had just been a military coup) informs him that they wish to order eight motor torpedo boats, to a design (which he describes) drawn up by a Dutch firm. They were to be 34m long and carry an armament of two 520mm torpedo tubes, one 57mm, one 40mm and two 20mm. guns. Fairfield's replied that the yard had recently been working on similar vessels for another government, of which plans (not in the file) were enclosed. An exchange of correspondence follows over the next two months, in which Fairfield's refer to the main particulars of their design, which were radically different from those above:

Waterline length: 200 feet
Beam: 25 feet
Displacement: 550 tons
Propulsion: diesel engines on two shafts for a speed of 26 knots

Nothing is said about the armament, but a few days later the agent refers to patrol vessels, supposedly ordered from a German yard, with one 47mm gun and depth-charge throwers. They are 25m long with a speed of 25 knots, but the Turks are now considering larger vessels of 30-35m length, 4.5-5m beam, 1.3-1.8m draught, with a speed of 32 knots.

Some days later, Fairfield's respond that their design is evidently very different from those that are being submitted by others (this is putting it mildly!), that the yard's facilities are not suitable for small vessels, and that it would be better for them not to tender. The Turkish Navy was to acquire numerous patrol vessels in the late 1960s, but none seem to correspond exactly to those quoted, although the MTBs of the *Jaguar* class from Germany were broadly similar to the design from the Netherlands.

Dated from a few years later, there is a tantalising file[4] in which the plans have survived, but not the related correspondence. To make matters more mysterious, the inquiry (which seems to date from 1964) is referred to in the index to the papers as 'Frigate for Libya' while the plans themselves are endorsed 'Malaysian frigate'. One may conjecture that the same design had been offered to both governments. From the plans, a sketch of which is reproduced here, the ship's main characteristics can be observed:

Length: 330 feet
Breadth: 40 feet
Depth: 26.5 feet
Displacement: not stated, but the dimensions are similar to those of the Royal Navy Type 41 frigates (*Leopard* class), of 2520 tons full load
Armament: 2 x 4.5in guns (twin)
  2 x 40 mm (single, p&s)
  1 x Seacat SAM missile launcher
  1 x Limbo anti-submarine mortar
  1 small helicopter (that shown on

Fairfield Frigate for Malaysia (1964?)

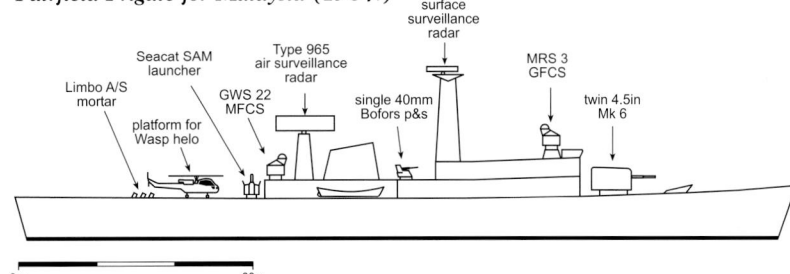

The diesel-powered frigate proposal for Malaysia had weapon systems based on the RN's Leander. *There was a landing pad for a Wasp A/S helicopter forward of the Limbo A/S mortar, as in the latter, but no hangar. (Drawn by John Jordan using material supplied by the author)*

the plan appears to be a Wasp)
Complement: 17 officers and 200 men
Propulsion: diesels, of which no details are available

Thus the design (worked out in detail) might be considered a diesel-powered (and presumably slower) equivalent of the *Leander*. Its armament is comparable (apart from the twin 4.5in mounting) to Yarrow's smaller Malaysian frigate *Hang Jabat* completed in 1972. However, no order resulted.

Perhaps the most interesting files[5] originated from another enquiry from Peru, received in December 1966. It involved a specification for two destroyers, as follows:

Dimensions: as necessary
Full load displacement: about 3000 tons
Speed: 35 knots
Range: 4000 to 6000 miles at 15 knots

Propulsion: either steam turbines, CODAG, COSAG or diesels
Armament: 4 x Bofors 120mm guns in single mountings (2 forward, 2 aft)
  3 x Bofors 57mm or 75mm guns (the replacement of some of these guns by missiles of unspecified type was referred to as a possibility.)
  1 x 375mm. Bofors anti-submarine rocket launcher
  2 x anti-submarine torpedo launchers
  depth charges

The Peruvians wanted 'a versatile ship, with capacity against surface ships, submarines, and aircraft' which would be 'the best possible compromise within the limitation of about 3,000 tons of full load displacement'. We may speculate that the ships were intended as a counter to Chile's *Almirante Williams* class built by Vickers.

Work on a preliminary design

Fairfield Destroyer for Peru: Project A (1967)

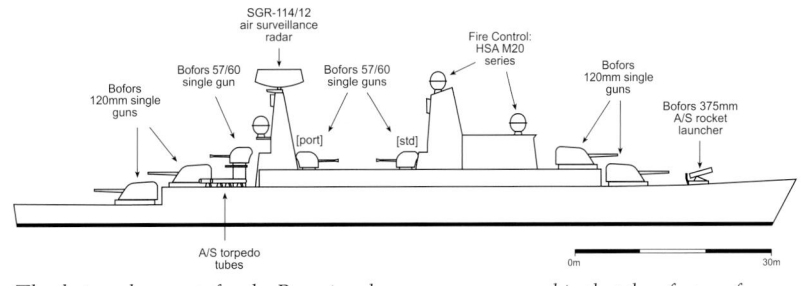

The designs drawn up for the Peruvian destroyers are unusual in that they feature few weapons systems of British design and manufacture. The radars of Design A are of Dutch origin, while the weaponry is almost exclusively from Bofors. A 'Vickers' annotation was appended (in-house) next to the A/S torpedo tube requirement on the original specification from Peru, so it is possible that the single tubes would have fired the torpedo developed as a private venture by VSEL during the late 1960s from the failed RN Mark 22 (a wire-guided successor to the Mark 20 Bidder). (Drawn by John Jordan using material supplied by the author)

began immediately. In March 1967 Fairfield's naval architect reported that he had told the Peruvians that their requirements would require a ship of 3500 tons, and advised them that a reduction of speed to 32 knots would be necessary to bring down the tonnage. A reduction in the armament was also being considered. It was believed that the ships would take five years to design and build. He was basing his design on the *Daring* class. Later correspondence refers to a complement of 237 and a full load displacement of 3150 tons in a hull 375 feet long at the waterline, 390 feet overall and 43 feet in beam – the same as the *Daring*.

Four designs of the same dimensions, with slightly different characteristics, were prepared. Proposal A (a sketch of which is reproduced here) followed the specification in its armament (except that the number of A/S torpedo launchers was increased to four). It should be noted that the foremost 57mm mounting is offset to starboard and the midships one to port. There were to be two gas turbines of 21,500shp each, and two diesels of 2,300bhp each, for a speed of 32 knots. The engines are described as similar to those in the Danish *Peder Skram* class.

Proposal B removes the third 120mm turret and the after 57mm mounting but was otherwise similar to proposal A. Proposal C substitutes guns from OTO Melara, which Fairfield's considered to be cheaper and lighter than the Bofors weapons; there would have been three 127mm and two 76mm guns, mounted in the same positions as Proposal B. Proposal D has the same armament as Proposal C, but steam turbines of 66,000shp replace the CODAG plant, giving a speed of 34 knots.

In June it was reported that although these proposals had been well received, Fairfield's were competing with several leading British and European yards and that a decision would be made in the following month. However, in September a financial crisis in Peru caused the decision to be postponed, and in the event, her navy had again to make do with second-hand vessels, the former HMS *Decoy* and *Diana*.

This Peruvian proposal may possibly represent the final attempt to build destroyers with an all-gun armament; it is noteworthy that the design is dominated by anti-aircraft and anti-submarine capabilities, whereas the conventional anti-ship torpedo tubes which were traditionally the major weapon of the destroyer have fallen into disuse.

It should also be mentioned that the collection includes a complete set of Admiralty plans[6] for the proposed icebreaker *Terra Nova* described in the 2010 volume.[7]

Footnotes:
1. Glasgow City Archives, UCS2/101/17.
2. UCS2/101/18.
3. UCS2/101/100.
4. UCS2/121/151/1.
5. National Archives of Scotland, UCS2/101/143-148: I am grateful to Dr. David Brown, of the National Archives, for allowing me to see these files.
6. Glasgow City Archives, UCS2/121/149.
7. Jon Wise, 'The Royal Navy's icebreaker project', *Warship* 2010, pp.183-186

THE FRENCH 13.8CM GUN IN BRITISH COAST DEFENCE SERVICE

Jeff Dorman and John Guy describe the wartime fates of the secondary armament of the battleships *Courbet* and *Paris*.

The French *Courbet* class of battleships were authorised under the 1910 naval estimates. The class comprised four ships, *Courbet* (named after the celebrated admiral), *Paris*, *Jean Bart* (named after the seventeenth century corsair) and *France*, and all were completed just prior to the First World War. These powerful dreadnoughts carried as their main armament 12 x 30.5cm (12in) guns in six twin turrets, and as secondary armament 22 x 13.8cm (5.4in) Model 1910 guns in armoured casemates.

By the start of the Second World War *Courbet* and *Paris* had been relegated to training roles, *Jean Bart* had been disarmed, while *France* had foundered in 1922 after hitting uncharted rocks in Quiberon Bay. Both *Paris* and *Courbet* were in action against German land forces in June 1940 before being ordered to British ports, *Paris* to Plymouth and *Courbet* to Portsmouth, where they were interned.

In November 1940 it was agreed with Vice-Admiral Muselier, Commander-in-Chief Free French air and naval forces, that the 13.8cm guns on both ships could be removed. He requested that nine of these guns, together with fire control equipment and 180 rounds of ammunition per gun be dispatched to Douala and Libreville in French West Africa for coastal defence. By March 1941 this order had been complied with, leaving 27 serviceable guns and mountings for disposal.

Since June 1940 and the threat of a German invasion, Britain's defences had undergone a tremendous expansion of both emergency coast batteries and Royal Artillery defence batteries, fixed and mobile. The weapons to arm these batteries were

Detail of the port battery of 13.8cm guns on on the French battleship Paris *just prior to the First World War. (Authors' collection)*

Courbet anchored at Portsmouth. Note the false painted bow wave. (Authors' collection)

supplied from the naval reserve stocks and in January 1941 comprised:

6in – 140
5.5in – 20
4.7in – 30
4in – 230

Unfortunately, the Admiralty was by now lobbying the War Office for the return of the 4in and 4.7in guns for the arming of merchant ships. At first reluctant to release the guns, the War Office had agreed by January 1942 that all 4in guns employed by the defence regiments would be returned to the Navy, replacing these guns where it was deemed necessary with 75mm guns.

Now it would be the turn of the coast batteries to come under scrutiny. In December 1941 there were ninety-six 4in and 4.7in guns in coast defence service, and the Commander in Chief Home Forces viewed their withdrawal with grave concern. However, concessions had to be made, so a list of criteria was drawn up with a view to evaluating the status of each battery concerned. Also the question was asked as to what guns could be offered as replacements when the 4in and 4.7in were withdrawn. The Admiralty replied that it had at its disposal 26 x 13.8cm French guns and 8 x 6in naval equipments, the French guns having only 70 rounds of ammunition per gun. The CinC was not too impressed with the French guns and was only 'prepared to install 12 with 150 rounds per gun, and then only if nothing better can be found'. Nothing better was found, so the evaluation process began, and was to be completed by the end of January 1942.

The criteria for battery selection were:

1. Guns that must be retained now but could be released as replacements become available:
23 batteries, 26 x 4.7in, 20 x 4in guns.
2. Guns which cannot be replaced for structural reasons:
7 batteries, 4 x 4.7in, 14 x 4in guns.
3. Guns which can be replaced by 12 x 13.8cm and 8 x 6in guns:
10 batteries, 20 x 4in guns.
4. Guns which can be withdrawn when required and for which replacements are less urgent:
6 batteries, 12 x 4in guns.

The above programme was approved by the Chief of General Staff on 27 January 1942, who called for its immediate implementation. The number of batteries allocated 13.8cm guns was increased to seven: at Dawlish, Hayle, Padstow, Par, Sidmouth, Port Talbot and Whitehaven. All batteries were to be ready for action no later than 1st August 1942.

It was hoped that the existing emplacements in these batteries could be modified to accommodate the French guns, but due to their size this proved impracticable, and new gunhouses as close as possible to the present batteries were required so as to utilise the existing war shelters, magazines, and other buildings. It appears that this course of action was adopted, except at Sidmouth where the battery was re-located to a new site, and at Par where the existing emplacements were connected to the new ones.

The first battery to be completed was Hayle, which was ready for action in April 1942, the rest of the batteries following by the middle of May. Given wartime restrictions and shortages, it was quite an achievement to build new gunhouses, lay cable runs and dismount the 4in guns in just a few months.

A French 13.8cm QF gun at Whitehaven Battery; note the counterweight needed to balance the weight of the new gun shield to allow smooth traversing of the mounting. (REME)

Detailed photo of a 13.8cm gun soon after removal from Courbet. *(JDJG Archive)*

The French 13.8cm M1910 gun must be unique in that it was used by both Britain and Germany's coast defences in WWII. (JDJG Archive)

Whitehaven Battery: inside the shield showing the breech mechanism. To the right is the line layer's position and to the left the elevation layer; the telephone on the inside of the shield is for gun no.1. (REME)

It can be imagined that at first the gunners approached their task with some apprehension, but this was unfounded. A Fire Control and Drill book was issued, which was virtually the same (save for the cover) as for the 6in Mk 7 coast gun. In correspondence Captain Roberts, who served at both Port Talbot and Whitehaven, recalls the 13.8cm equipments as being: i) very accurate, ii) very 'sweet' to operate, iii) the shells easy to handle, and iv) the breech shoot guide was particularly useful. If there was one complaint it was about the lack of ammunition for practice, some batteries having not had full calibre practice since the guns were installed. Although a 37mm sub-calibre barrel was available, this was no substitute, especially as many of the batteries were manned by the Home Guard.

To illustrate the case it was not until March 1943, nearly a year after the guns were installed, that Sidmouth, Par and Hayle were allowed ten rounds per gun for practice. Notwithstanding the ammunition problem the 13.8cm performed well in its new role until the end of 1944 when, in common with most emergency coast batteries, the guns were placed in 'care and maintenance' or closed down.

With victory in sight it was agreed to return the 13.8cm guns to France, so by March 1945 the regimental armament withdrawal parties were busy at their work dismantling the equipments. These were dispatched to Falmouth, and then in September 1945 to Cherbourg, so ending a unique chapter in British coast defence history.

And what of the ships? Both were inspected and found unfit for sea service and beyond economical repair. *Paris* was commissioned in June 1941 as a base ship for auxiliary vessels in Plymouth. Returned to the French Navy in July 1945, she was towed to Brest in August and finally sold for scrap in December 1955. *Courbet* was transferred to the Free French Navy in July 1940 and served as an Anti-Aircraft Guard Ship. She was in action during the 'blitz' on Portsmouth, claiming five enemy aircraft shot down with her 75mm AA guns. When her AA ammunition was expended she became a depot and training ship. On 9 June 1944 she was scuttled as part of a breakwater for the Mulberry harbours off the Normandy coast.

The French 13.8cm M1910 gun

In the *Courbet* class of battleship the 13.8cm guns were in single mountings as anti-torpedo boat batteries, 18 at Upper Deck level and four on the Main Deck aft. They were mounted in armoured casemates on central pivot mountings, and when the ships were reconstructed during the 1920s maximum elevation was increased from 15° to 25°, giving a range of 16,100m (17,600 yards).

The gun itself was of built-up construction with a screw breech, designated in British service as a quick-firer because it used separate loading ammunition, the propelling charge being contained in a brass case 900mm (35.4in) long. Shells issued for British service were either the 31.5kg (69.4lb) high explosive (HE), or the 39.5kg (87.1lb) semi-armoured piercing (SAP); rate of fire was 5–6 rounds per minute.

Surprisingly, once dismounted the guns and mountings required very little work to make them suitable for coast defence service. Nevertheless two major items had to be fabricated. One was a new enveloping gun shield, as the original one was inadequate for coast defence use. The second item was a holdfast; this was hexagonal in shape measuring 44.5in across the flats with a circle of 24 x 1.25in bolts 7in high on a diameter of 38.5in.

What remains of the batteries today:
Dawlish Battery: NGR SX96167619.
When visited the two gun emplacements were extant and in good condition, being used as shelters in a park. An engine room and searchlight emplacement were also extant in the area below the cliffs.
Padstow Battery:
NGR SW91857676.
There are remains of this battery north of the harbour, overlooking the mouth of the river Camel, including the holdfasts and ready-use ammunition lockers.
Par Battery: NGR SX07165314.
The searchlight emplacements can be seen on the shore line in front of a factory. The battery is quite a long way behind the searchlights, and much of it remains (albeit covered by the vegetation). The two gun emplacements can be seen complete with bolt rings, magazines and an observation post and other buildings. It is possible to see where the gun emplacements were extended when the 13.8cm guns were installed.
Hayle Battery (St Ives):
NGR SW52423988.
This battery was sited next to the railway line. All that remains is one building next to the railway bridge. The base of one searchlight emplacement can be seen lower down, just above the shore. Nothing else could be found.
Sidmouth Battery:
NGR SY12098695.
The 13.8cm guns were installed in Connaught Gardens; there is a small plaque in the wall to record the battery. The gun emplacements could not be located; all that could be found was an engine room and the double-deck searchlight emplacement. The original 4in battery was at a different site which could be identified by two mounds in the area to the west of Connaught Gardens. The Battery Observation Post was used for both batteries and was to the west of the gardens.
Port Talbot Battery:
NGR SS75268845.
This battery was sited just to the east of the harbour entrance and pier, it was extant for many years but has now been bulldozed into the sea. Large lumps of concrete in the sea can be seen, but nothing else remains.
Whitehaven Battery:
NGR NX97351943.
Whitehaven battery was extant until fairly recently: the two gun emplacements with ammunition storage at the rear on the top of the cliff and below the cliff, two searchlight emplacements, the engine room and two Lyon Light emplacements. Demolition work has removed the two gun emplacements; it is uncertain if the buildings at the bottom of the cliff have been affected.

Editor's Note: This article was originally published in the May 2011 issue of *Casemate* (no.91), the newsletter of the Fortress Study Group (www.fsgfort.com). It is reproduced here, in edited form, with the permission of the editor, Charles Blackwood, and of the authors.

THE TORPEDO-BOAT *TAIAROA*

In response to Mark Briggs' article on the Tasmanian torpedo-boat *TB 191* (*Warship* 2012, pp.33-39), **Chris Scott** and **Bruce Hall**, Archivist and Information Support officer respectively for Dunedin City Council, have written in with information regarding the torpedo-boats built by Thornycroft for New Zealand.

Like its Australian counterparts, the government of New Zealand purchased Spar torpedo-boats as a response to perceived threats from Russia. Four were purchased from Thornycroft in 1882, at a unit cost of £10,000.

The two boats for the cities of Christchurch and Dunedin were delivered to Port Chalmers, on the Otago Harbour, in 1884. Number 169, known as the *Taiaroa* after a noted Maori chief, operated from a base at Deborah Bay, a short distance

The torpedo-boat Taiaroa *at her moorings in Deborah Bay.*

from its point of delivery. The best-known image of the vessel[1] shows it moored at Port Chalmers, which was probably the boat's initial base. A purpose-built wharf was built to service the boat by 1887. The vessel saw use in manoeuvres at Oamaru harbour, where a target vessel filled with 229 pounds of gun cotton was blown up; the result was spectacular, but the explosion was not actually detonated by the spar torpedo.[2]

The photographs shown here were taken at what may have been the *Taiaroa*'s last major outing. These images were produced by Thomas Rawson, who was the Engineer for the Otago Harbour Board from 1889-1902. A set of four images is held by the Dunedin City Council Archives,[3]

Looking forward on board the SS Kent.

Taiaroa *alongside SS Kent prior to the latter's departure for South Africa.*

WARSHIP NOTES

Another view of Taiaroa *alongside* SS Kent *prior to the latter's departure for South Africa.*

Taiaroa *leaving the* SS Kent *having disembarked General Babbington.*

and the glass-plate negatives of three are held in the Hocken Collections.[4]

The departure of the Ninth Contingent for the Boer War from Dunedin, on March 12 1902, was attended by the Premier Richard Seddon, and General Babington, the Commander of the New Zealand Defence Force. The troops arrived at Port Chalmers by train, and embarked on the SS *Kent* in disorderly scenes, women and men alike fainting in the crush surrounding the gangways.

The *Kent* slipped its moorings at 15.30 and proceeded to Deborah Bay, where General Babington was able to board the vessel from the torpedo boat. The newspaper accounts do not mention the *Kent* pausing, but the photographs indicate that the vessels appear to be stopped. If so the stay must have been brief, as the *Kent* was beyond the harbour mouth within the hour. The still waters of the harbour were ideal for the operation of the unstable torpedo-boat, which most likely did not accompany the *Kent* beyond the Harbour entrance.

It is noteworthy that the *Taiaroa* was stripped of its spar for this occasion at least. The limited utility of the weapon was recognised by this time, and other boats in New Zealand service had been fitted with Whitehead torpedoes. It seems that the *Taiaroa* had only a few months left. A recorded testimony that the vessel was broken up at a slip near its base in 1902[5] seems likely. Uncertainty in some accounts as to whether the boat met her end in 1901 or 1902 is resolved by the dates associated with Rawson's photographs.

Some of the *Taiaroa*'s plates were allegedly used to support a garden, and the engine was stored at the university in Dunedin before going to the Canterbury University School of Engineering Library. The engine is now in the Lyttleton Torpedo Boat Museum, along with fragments of the Christchurch boat.

Footnotes:
[1.] Hocken Collections, University of Otago Ref: c/n E2828/27a.
[2.] *Otago Witness*, 30 April 1886.
[3.] Photographs 512-515.
[4.] I.J. Farquhar Collection, POO-021/1/136-40, 149.
[5.] *Deborah Bay*, by Norman Ledgerwood, pp.88-9 (privately published) 2006.

THE VICKERS 4-INCH MK N(R) MOUNTING

Four of these mountings were fitted as the main armament in the two *Almirante* class destroyers built for Chile during the mid-1950s (see Jon Wise's article pp.119-133). **Peter Marland** describes the gun and its associated fire control system, and compares it with contemporary weapons in service with the Royal Navy.

The Vickers 4-inch Mk N(R) was a successful export gun that built on an Army prototype. It was offered to the Royal Navy in late 1953 as part of the approval for export to Chile but was turned down, largely on grounds of 'Not Invented Here', but also because of the large stockpile of 4-inch Mk 19 and 4.5-inch single mountings already available. The Navy Department objected to its out-of-balance elevating mass and through-trunnion loading, and felt that it did not offer a significantly better rate of fire than the established manually-loaded twin Mk 19.

In actual fact, Vickers produced a very sound design with a 62-calibre barrel (called the Mk Q gun) for better range than the wartime 45-calibre Mk 19. The gun mounting was fed from twin hoppers, allowing one man to conduct up to three burst engagements at 40-50 rounds per minute without an exposed crew on the upper deck, and the feed system was much less complex (and hence more reliable) than either the contemporary 3-inch or the 6-inch guns. It would have made a very capable RN weapon, and presaged many of the later improvements, save for both hoppers being loaded with one type of round, and no method of selectively switching to other single rounds like starshell or radar echo. However, in the Chilean ships this was not a problem, as there were four mountings available, allowing one for illumination.

Development

Some websites link the Vickers 4-inch Mk N(R) with the UK Green Mace AA gun system for the Army. The relationship is slightly more complex. Green Mace was a 4-inch prototype (to become 5-inch service) weapon using fin-stabilised discarding sabot shells. It was fed alternately from left and right feed drums (with 13 rounds each) which elevated with the cradle and were closely coupled. The gun was water-cooled and achieved circa 96 rounds per minute; the feed arrangements had a number of technical similarities with the Vickers 3-inch and 6-inch naval mountings. The decision not to take it through to production was made in 1956, but the prototype was fired for trial purposes until 1958.

The 4-inch Mk N(R) was actually derived from the X1 model Medium AA (MAA) gun built by Vickers Armstrong Elswick, which was fired at Eskmeals in 1956. The Vickers proposal to the Admiralty in late 1953 clearly follows the X1 drawings held by the *Firepower* museum at Woolwich, and the covering letter stated that the proposal (using a naval 4-inch Mk 16 barrel) was based on the MAA equipment developed 1950-53

TABLE 1: GUN MOUNTING FEED SYSTEM STRESS

Gun/Mounting	4.5-inch Mk 6	4.5-inch Mk 8	4-inch Vickers	3-inch Mk 6	6-inch Mk 26	5-inch Mk 1
All-up round weight (lb)	55+38.5	81	66	38	130+77	130
Rounds/min (per gun)	18	24	50	90	20	60
Feed system lb/min	1683	1944	3300	3420	4140	7800
loadton/min	0.75	0.87	1.47	1.52	1.85	3.48
Rd+Ctge Transfer points	2+2	4	2	7	5+5	4

that achieved 48 rounds per minute. The so-called Vickers Universal Mount included a through-trunnion feed system using alternate trays that shuttled between left and right hoppers. The only changes during the final development were the tilting of the 23-round hoppers to 38½° (the mid-point of the -7° to +85° elevating range), the simplification of the feed arrangement to two transfer points (via tilting loading trays), and the substitution of a new 62-calibre barrel, *vice* the original 45-calibre proposal.

The mounting used a pneumatic rammer, hydraulic (on mounting) RPC with short stiff drives, and had a seated Captain of the Turret with a secondary gyro gunsight inside a single window. The gun fired HE or starshell rounds, with either: Fuse Time Mechanical No 211 (TM for AA fire), Bofors VT Fuse (VT for AA fire), Fuse SAP/D/DA for surface fire with direct action or direct action delayed modes, and Fuse Time Mechanical No 215 (for Starshell); there were automatic fuse setters between the hoppers and the loading tray. There was no gunbay, and the hoppers were replenished by an upper-deck crew using an endless chain hoist from the deep magazine.

The accompanying table shows the feed system throughputs (round weight x rate of fire) for the post-war British gun mountings, as an indication of the relative stresses involved. The shading reflects stress factors due to mass, feed velocity, or complexity that influenced overall reliability: white (low), light grey (intermediate), darker grey (high).

Overall Weapon System

The overall system integrator was Vickers (supported by Marconi for the radar aspects). The key components of the system were as follows:

Combat Information Centre (CIC):

A comprehensive ops room featured displays grouped by functional area or role (see illustration). Video distribution was relatively simple, and display integration and interlaced markers were not up to contemporary RN standards.

Principal Control Officer (PCO):

The PCO had a 'pod' above the bridge in place of the traditional RN

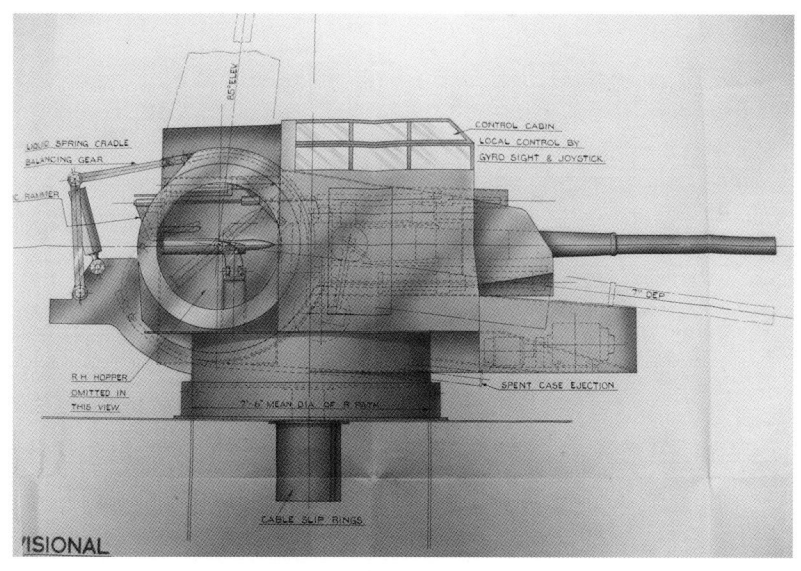

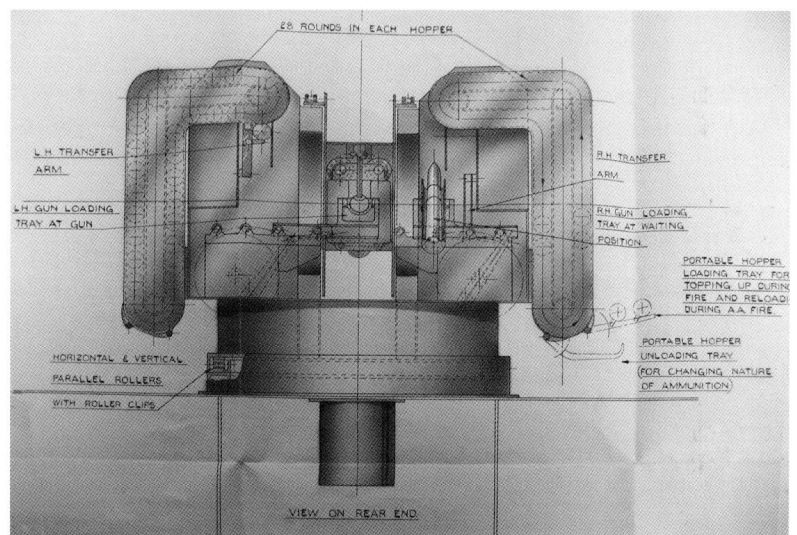

Above: The mounting as originally proposed. In the original design the two ammunition hoppers, each holding a total of 28 rounds, were 'wrapped around' the gun mounting (see rear view). There were hinged loading trays (for topping up/reloading) and unloading trays (for changing the nature of the ammunition) at the base of each hopper.

The mounting in its final configuration with the hoppers inside the gunhouse. Note the seat for the Captain of the Turret inside a single window; this replaced the greenhouse control cabin shown in the early sketch. The photo was taken at Viña del Mar, Valparaíso in 2004. (Peter Marland)

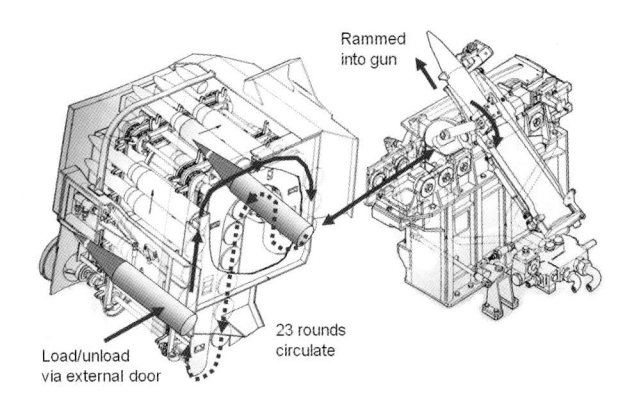

One of the two 23-round feed hoppers of the mounting in its final configuration. The round was picked off by the loading tray, which then slid across to the centreline of the mounting and tilted in line with the gun. The left and right hoppers fed the gun alternately.

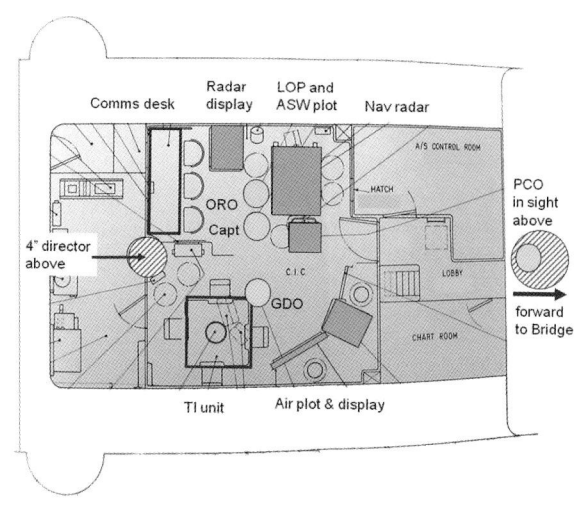

The CIC layout, with its displays grouped by functional area or role.

gun direction position. The PCO was seated and was able to work 'head out' with his sight, a radar display and weapon designation pushes, all under an 'astrodome' cover, allowing him to fight the ship's armament in all weathers (see illustration). The concept was reminiscent of RN cruiser practice for night action at the end of the Second World War, and would suit surface action in Chile's southern fjord country, as far south as the Magellan Straits.

Fire Control System (FCS): The Vickers proprietary system was based on the carcase of the new Mk 6M director (for Flyplane 5) but with a single Marconi SNG20 tracking radar – at this time the RN was mulling altering its existing type 275 twin-radome radar to a single aerial to reduce tracking errors. The below-decks Transmitting Station equipment included an array of single-purpose boxes (AA computer, Surface computer, gyro level stabiliser, stabilisation correction unit, and gun correction panel) reminiscent of RN destroyer practice at the end of the Second World War, in which a disparate range of boxes each attempted to fix another's shortcomings. The mechanical units were built by Vickers Crayford, and did <u>not</u> draw on contemporary RN fire control (either the Admiralty Fire Control Box Mk 10 or the Ferranti electric predictor in Flyplane), nor did it relate to research work on Medium Range System Mks 4 and 5 in which Vickers and Elliott's were engaged. The fire control system allowed the use of either No 1 gun or No 4 gun with starshell ('A' and 'Y' mountings in RN parlance), and also had surface, AA and Bombardment roles. The AA fire control predictor was tachymetric, whilst the surface computer was goniographic.

Evaluation

The *Almirante* class weapon suite did not simply mirror British practice. The key differences are outlined below.

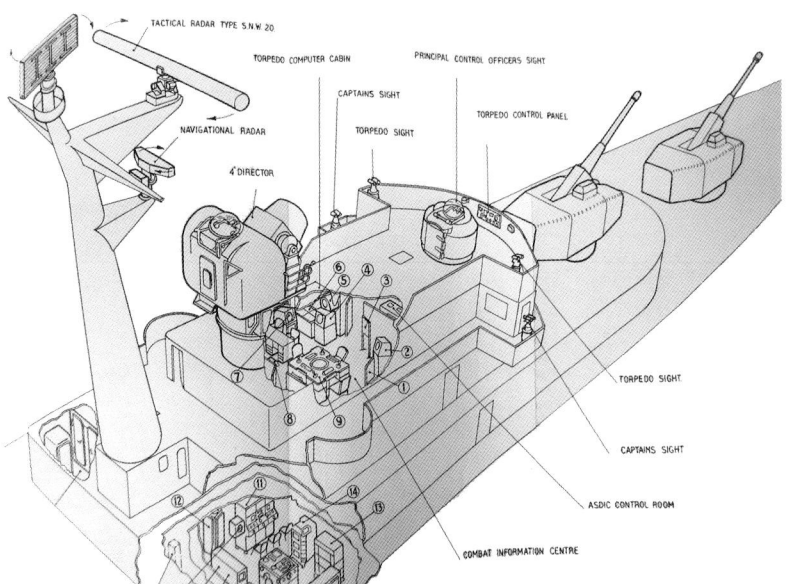

Overall schematic of the weapon system.

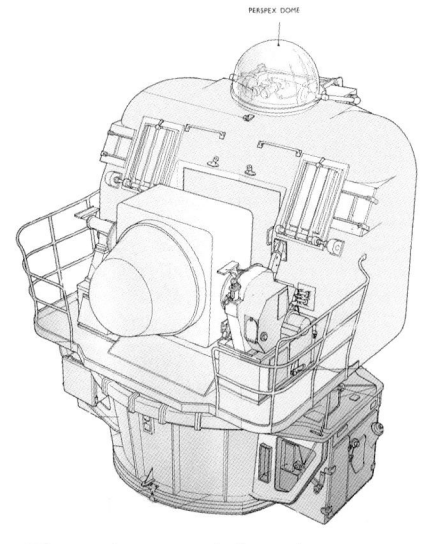

The gun director, with the single antenna for the Marconi SNG20 tracking radar on its face.

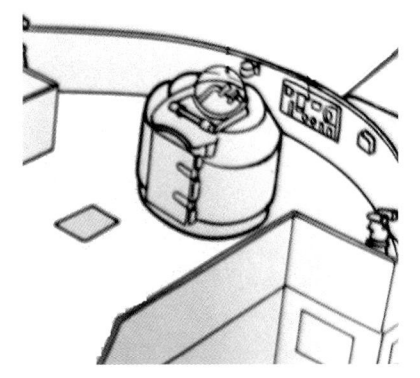

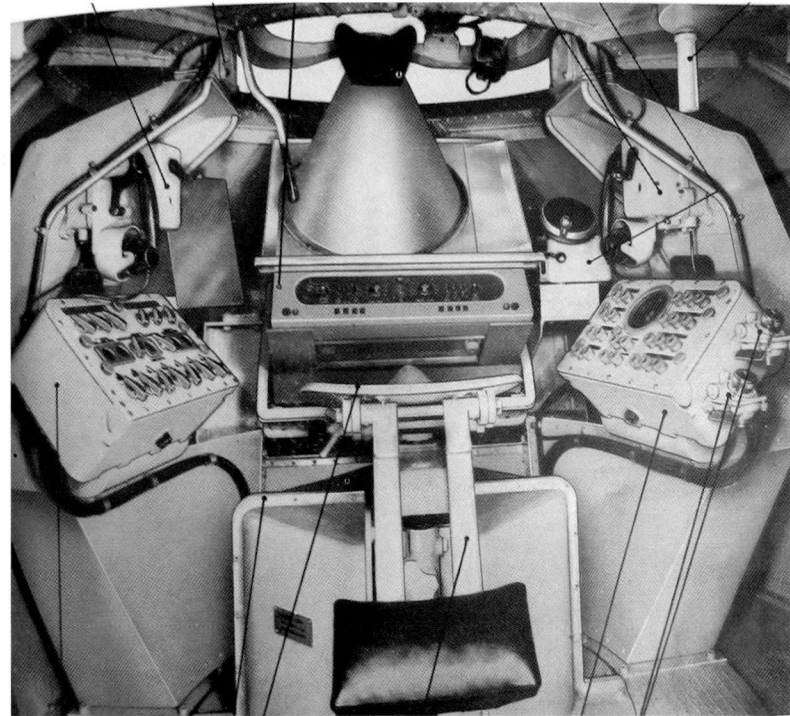

WARSHIP NOTES

The PCO 'pod' atop the bridge. The view on the right shows the inside of the pod looking forward.

The Action Information Organisation (AIO) and supporting ops room system was adequate. The reason not to 'push the bounds' further may have been to limit development cost within a competitive marketplace. As such the displays, markers and overall architecture reflect RN late war practice, but with better ergonomics, given the ability to take a 'clean sheet of paper' approach to the compartment layouts.

The PCO fighting the ship 'head out' did not mirror contemporary practice, since the RN had moved to 'below control' with the Command in the ops room, against complex environments; the Chilean interest in the PCO marks the ship for offensive surface action.

The gun mountings exploited prior work on the MAA gun for the Army, but were significantly better than RN practice in terms of firing a pre-loaded hopper of ammunition with only a single crew member closed up, a reliable feed system, and the stiff servo drives. These were more balanced features than the RN implemented in its contemporary 3-inch, 5-inch and 6-inch mountings.

The fire control system was relatively pedestrian and did not draw on RN developments, implying that Vickers maintained a clear demarcation between their National work and their export proposals. This may also reflect their Company bidding process or unwillingness to carry a pro-rata share of MoD's intramural development cost, with the commercial risk that the end-system might then not be released for export.

It is hard to make a direct comparison with equivalent UK designs. The *Almirante* class were later than the *Daring* and superior to the Venezuelan *Nueva Esparta*, but by the late 1950s RN attention had shifted towards the 'County' class DLGs with Seaslug and 'Tribal' class general-purpose frigates, and away from traditional gun-armed destroyers.

Primary Sources:
ADM 1/25127 and handbooks held at HMS *Excellent*'s museum at Whale Island, plus archive material at *Firepower* Woolwich.

Note on the Author: Peter Marland is a former RN Weapon Engineer Officer with sea jobs in HM ships *Blake*, *Bristol* and *Euryalus*, and postings ashore in research and in procurement. He now works as an Operational Analyst.

HOLLAND 5 (1902-1912)

Jamie Smith, Chairman of the Tunbridge Wells Sub Aqua Club (TWSAC), writes about a recent dive on the historic wreck of one of Britain's first submarines.

The *Holland 5* is designated as a Protected Wreck under the Protection of Wrecks Act 1973. She is the most intact example of the 'Holland' class submarines and in 2011 was placed on the at-risk register. TWSAC has very kindly been granted a visitor's license by English Heritage to dive on this historic wreck. On 8 August 2012, TWSAC enjoyed the unique opportunity of marking the centenary of the submarine's loss by diving on her, in the company of English Heritage and the Nautical Archaeology Society.

Brief History and Description
Holland 5 and *3* were the first submarines to be commissioned by the Royal Navy. (*Holland 1*, *2* and *4* were still being built at the time). Designed by the American John Philip Holland, they were the first to use electric motors while submerged and gasoline engines while on the surface. The 'Holland' class submarines were very much experimental craft. Many improvements to submarine design were made with the knowledge gained from operating them, and the 'A' class which followed consisted of thirteen boats of this improved design.

Designed to withstand pressures

WARSHIP 2013

Detail of the conning tower hatch, showing one of the hinges, the window, and some of today's residents.

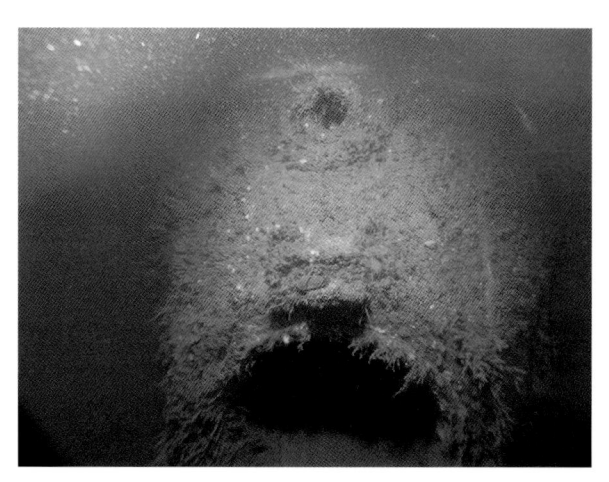

Above and below: *The missing torpedo hatch, showing where the lever bar, locking bolt and hinge pin have been broken off.*

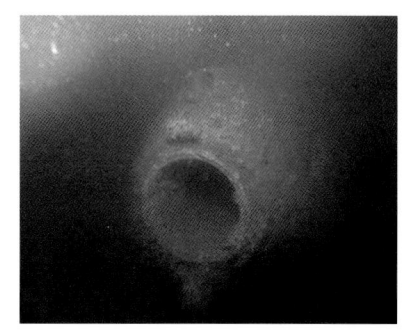

not exceeding 100 feet, the five boats built for the RN displaced 122 tons, and had a length of 63ft 10in (19.23 metres) and a beam of 11ft 9in (3.62 metres). They were powered by a 4-cylinder, 160bhp Otto gasoline engine and were driven by a single screw, giving a surface top speed of 8 knots and a range of 250 miles. When submerged, a 74hp electric waterproof motor was engaged, giving a submerged speed of 7 knots for a duration of three hours at 120 volts and 500 amps. Eight crew were carried, in rather cramped conditions.

The submarines were armed with three 18-inch (or five short) Whitehead torpedoes. These were 11ft 8in long, and were capable of 30 knots for a range of 2000 yards. They carried a charge of 200lbs of gun cotton and benefited from the addition of a gyroscope, to give greater accuracy.

Navigation was an issue as the compass could not be kept inside the all-steel hull of the submarine. Instead, it was mounted on the outside of the hull, positioned abaft the hatch, which was made of bronze to minimise compass deviation. When submerged, or in rough seas, the compass could be viewed by a small periscope with the compass card illuminated by an electric bulb. While running on the surface, the boat could be steered and navigated from the outer casing, by attaching a wheel into a slot in the hull. This was a somewhat precarious arrangement given the very low freeboard, making it suitable only for inshore waters on calm days.

Holland 5 was built at a cost of £35,000 by Vickers, Barrow-in-Furness, under licence from the Holland Torpedo Boat Company. She was built of the same high grade steel as the Forth Railway Bridge. She was launched on 10 June 1902 and commissioned on 19 January 1903.

Part of the damaged after part of the submarine.

WARSHIP NOTES

Two views of the submarine's propeller. (All photographs by Jamie Smith and Derrick Scott of TWSAC)

At the time of her launch *Holland 5* sported the first periscope in the Royal Navy, which was of British design. This early periscope needed some refining: when looking forwards the object in view was seen upright; when observed beam on the object was seen on its side; and when the periscope was trained astern the object was inverted.

Holland 5 was considered obsolete even before her completion. She had a fairly uneventful short life, apart from running aground off Fort Blockhouse during trials. On 8 August 1912 she was being towed to Sheerness to be scrapped. While off the Sussex coast near Eastbourne she foundered, sinking in 30 metres of water. It is thought that the torpedo hatch was left ajar, causing her to take on water and sink; there was no loss of life. The sinking is being investigated by the *Time Team* television programme, and their conclusions will be broadcast in due course. The final resting place of *Holland 5* is a few miles east of the Royal Sovereign Lighthouse and 10.5 miles due south of St. Leonards.

The Holland 5 Today

The wreck of *Holland 5* was discovered in 1995, and is now protected and managed by English Heritage. She is sitting bolt upright in 30 metres of water, still looking very submarine-like and in remarkable condition considering the time she has been on the sea bed. The propeller guard has fallen away to the starboard side, probably knocked off by trawling activity. The wreck was festooned with nets when it was first dived, as it lies in scallop ground. These nets were removed by divers from the Nautical Archaeology Society in 2005 and 2006. There is some damage aft, around the engine exhaust, and the compass has gone, possibly removed before she sank. The hatch (conning tower) window is still clearly visible, making it possible to peer into the control room below. Moving forward over the torpedo loading bay and then on to the bows, the torpedo hatch is missing. This was present when the submarine was first dived on, but was lost sometime in the 18 months prior to August 2010 when its loss was discovered. The cause of its loss is not known: it may have been stolen by divers or torn from its mounting by a trawl.

Overall the submarine still looks almost ready for action, just in need of a good exfoliation from marine growth and a lick of paint. However there is some concern that the loss of the hatch will accelerate the deterioration of the interior. She will continue to be monitored and watched over by English Heritage, TWSAC and the Nautical Archaeology Society.

Tunbridge Wells Sub Aqua Club

Tunbridge Wells Sub Aqua Club (http://www.twsac.org/) was founded in 1962 and is a very active diving club. Its members have a keen interest in archaeology and naming un-named wrecks in the English Channel. As far as the club is concerned, a wreck with no name has no history. If a wreck can be given a name, then it has both name and history, and can then be given the respect it deserves, especially if it is a war loss. Members of TWSAC have so far named seven wrecks. In 2001 they raised the 10.5cm gun of *UB-130*; it is now on display at Newhaven Maritime Museum.

The Nautical Archaeology Society

The Nautical Archaeology Society (http://www.nauticalarchaeologysociety.org/) is a registered charity based at Fort Cumberland, Portsmouth, and is dedicated to advancing education and techniques in nautical archaeology and in promoting public awareness of Britain's underwater heritage.

Sources:

Fyfe, Herbert C: *Submarine Warfare*, Grant Richards, 1902.

Tall, Commander JJ & Kemp, Paul: *Submarines in camera 1901-1996*, Blitz Editions, 1998.

Akerman, P: *Encyclopaedia of British Submarines 1901-1955*, Periscope Publishing Ltd, 2002.

Web links:

http://en.wikipedia.org/wiki/Holland_class_submarine

http://www.battleships-cruisers.co.uk/holland_class.htm

http://www.english-heritage.org.uk/discover/maritime/map/holland-no-5/

http://www.twsac.blogspot.co.uk/search/label/Holland%20v

http://www.youtube.com/watch?v=q5F7PvZhsN0&feature=youtu.be&hd=1

Thanks to Maxine Clement and to Mark Beattie-Edwards, MA, MIfA, NAS Programme Director.

A's & A's

Building the Grand Fleet: 1906-1916 (*Warship* 2012, pp.8-21)

Former *Warship* editor John Roberts has written in to point out that the boilers of the battleship HMS *Conqueror* in the photo published on page 16 were of the Babcock and Wilcox, not the Yarrow type as stated in the caption.

British Cruisers: Two World Wars and After (Naval Books of the Year, *Warship* 2012, pp.184-185)

The Editor apologises for ascribing the name 'David Baker III' to the artist responsible for many of the drawings in the book. This should have read A D Baker III, a name which will be familiar to many readers.

TB 191: A Tasmanian Torpedo Boat (*Warship* 2012, pp.33-39)

Regular *Warship* contributor Colin Jones has written in with the following additional information:

The torpedo boat *TB 191* 'disappeared from Tasmanian records', to use the words of the author, because she was transferred in 1900 to the books of the colony of South Australia and towed to Adelaide in 1905 by the *Protector*, arriving there via Portland on 3 May. South Australia had a stock of torpedoes but no boat to operate them up to this time. As I stated in my article on p.62 of *Warship* 2001-2002, she was out of service by 1910 and the hull was sold in 1917. The photo in my article was the same as that on p.38 of the latest edition. The paddle steamer can be identified as the *Monarch*, thus placing the location of the photo firmly in Hobart.

John Brown's in Search of South American Orders (*Warship* 2012, p.169)

Subscriber John Reid writes as follows:

Unicorn had 8 – 4in guns (4xII), not 4.5in, so the weight available to replace this armament with a 4.7in low angle (LA) armament was quite small, had Argentina persisted with that request. Using data from John Campbell's authoritative *Naval Weapons of World War Two*:

4in Mk XIX twin mount: 14-15.5 tons depending on shield, etc.

There are three quite different 4.7in mounts to consider:
4.7in Mk IX in CP XXII single mount with shield (as in 'S'–'W' classes): about 13.3 tons;
4.7in Mk XII in twin CP XIX (as in 'J', 'K', 'N' classes): 25.5 tons;
4.7in Mk XI (62lb shell) in twin Mk XX (as in 'L' and 'M' classes): 37.3 tons.

Thus, in terms of weight of mounting, a 4in twin HA is roughly equivalent to a 4.7in single LA, but ammunition stowage could also be heavier depending on the allowance of rounds per gun. Since the proposal was not worked through in detail, it is not possible to assess the impact on the design.

HMS *Curacoa* (*Warship* 2012, pp.173-174)

At the end of the Warship Note on HMS *Curacoa* in *Warship* 2012 it states that this will be the first of a pair, to be followed by one looking into the discrepancies in the published figures for how many of the ship's crew lost their lives in her sinking. The research for this side of the story was at the time incomplete, and the aim was to have it finished and written up for this edition of *Warship*. However the timing of the Ministry of Defence's programme of reviewing and then releasing Second World War naval casualty files to the National Archives (formerly the Public Record Office), which began in May 2012, meant that these files only started to become available for public consultation just as *Warship* 2013 was going to press. With no idea whether the relevant files would appear in this initial batch or not, the editorial team made the decision not to set space aside for a Warship Note which then might not be able to be completed. It is the intention of the MoD to complete the release of the files by the end of 2013.

In addition, reader Tone Lovell has written in to point out a spelling mistake in the same Warship Note: on p.173 and in footnote no.1 on the following page it should be 'B E Domvile', with a single letter 'l'. This is particularly ironic given that the article was about incorrect spelling! Having checked in a few volumes of *The Navy List*, the Assistant Editor admits his error, and offers by way of explanation the fact that the copy of the ship's log held in the National Archives (ADM53/39086) that covers *Curacoa*'s commissioning, compiled by the ship's navigating officer, has, in the space marked 'Approved' on the cover, just the captain's signature, which as well as being far from a neat and clear affair, also happens to have the later part of the surname so badly smudged as to be illegible.

Russia's 'American' Monitors: The *Uragan* Class (*Warship* 2012, pp.98-112)

Warship subscriber Charles Schedel has written in with the following comments on the article on the Russian *Uragan*-class monitors:

A combination of factors led to the loss of USS *Weehawken* in Charleston harbor on 6 December 1863. The *Passaic*-class monitors had a waterway in the keel with an arc of 16 inches and a depth of only 3.75 inches. Since the centrifugal bilge pumps were located aft, a trim by the stern was necessary to drain bilge water from the forward part of the ship.

These monitors also had insufficient shell storage space for extended operations and as a result shells were often stored in the 'hold' located below the removable floor plates of the berth deck. This practice reduced both their freeboard and the trim by the stern by about 12 inches.

At the time of her loss, *Weehawken* was anchored in 30 feet of water off Morris Island during a moderate gale. She had recently taken on board a considerable number of shells that drastically decreased her forward freeboard. This allowed water to enter through an open hawse pipe and reduce the forward freeboard even further. As the sea became heavier, more water entered via the windlass room hatch. This water could not flow to the pumps aft and soon the increasing trim by the bow brought this hatch under water, resulting in her sinking by the bow with the loss of four officers and 27 enlisted men.

Source: Amen, *The Atlantic Coast*, pp.114, 142-144.

It is doubtful that the *Uragan*-class monitors were armed with copies of US Army 15in Rodman guns. When the US Navy considered the possibility of using these guns to arm the *Passaic*-class monitors they were found to be too long to fit within their 21ft inside diameter turrets.

A great deal of confusion exists with regards to Dahlgren and Rodman guns, some sources even claiming that they are identical and were just given different names by the US Army and Navy. Although both guns have a similar 'soda bottle' shape, a 15in Rodman is significantly longer and heavier than a 15in Dahlgren. The easiest way to differentiate between them is the shape of the breech face. Rodman guns have an almost flat breech face cut with notches for an elevating ratchet. Dahlgren guns, on the other hand, have a hemispherical breech face ending in a protruding cascabel drilled vertically for a threaded elevating screw and horizontally for a breeching rope.

When Captain Dahlgren was ordered to produce a 15in gun for the USN, he swallowed his pride and had it made using the Rodman method of casting it hollow around a water-cooled core. All previous Dahlgren guns had been cast as solid cylinders and then bored out and lathe turned to shape. Accordingly, all 15in, 20in and some late 11in Dahlgren guns were cast by the Rodman method. Dahlgren lacked confidence in the Rodman method and went out of his way to disassociate himself from these 'hybrid' guns. As a result, many high USN officials began referring to them as 'Rodman' guns although they were actually Dahlgren guns cast with the Rodman method. When these 15in guns proved to be reliable and particularly effective against Confederate ironclads, Dahlgren tried to reclaim the credit for them, resulting in confusion that persists to the present day.

Source: Amen, Ripley, *Artillery and Ammunition of the Civil War*, pp.98-99.

A scale drawing showing the differences between 15in Rodman and Dahlgren guns can be found in *Arming the Fleet* by Spencer Tucker, (NIP, 1989) p.224.

HMS *Talbot* (*Warship* 2012, p.141)

On the final page of the article about *Talbot* class cruisers we published a photograph from the collections of the National Museum of the Royal Navy showing the name ship of the class, which was captioned as depicting her at 'Suvla Bay, Sept.16th, 1916.' This date prompted an immediate enquiry from regular *Warship* contributor Ian Sturton, wondering what the ship was doing at Suvla Bay, and firing her guns, some nine months after the evacuation of allied forces from the Gallipoli peninsular.

A check of the ship's logs for the months of September 1915 and 1916 reveals two possible answers. *Talbot*, under the command of Captain Fawcett Wray, and part of the 3rd Cruiser Squadron, spent September 1915 operating in support of the allied landings at Suvla Bay, mainly to provide fire support but also making extensive use of her ship's boats to ferry troops. She was at Suvla from the start of the month until Sunday 12 September, when she departed for Mudros for repairs and provisioning. She returned to Suvla on Friday 17 September, and remained there for the rest of the month. She fired against the enemy on 2, 5, 6, 8 and 10 September, usually with her 6in guns though also on at least one occasion with her 12pdrs as well. No.1 starboard 6in gun was dismounted at Mudros, for reasons not given. On Thursday 23 September she was hit once by enemy fire, on the foretop, but damage appears not to have been significant.

By September 1916 *Talbot* was off the coast of East Africa, largely engaged in routine operations, patrols and exercises. However, she did once open fire, and this happens to have been on Saturday 16 September, while off Lindi Bay, in support of the ongoing operations against German forces. The precise sequence was: 06.05, stopped, let go starboard anchor in 6¾fms, veered, opened fire on beaches. 06.45 ceased fire, troops and embarkation party landed, returned at 11.20. 16.00 landed relief Maxim gun crews. The ship remained on the East Africa Station on into 1917.

So, either the date is correct and the location is wrong – i.e. the ship is pictured firing on 16 September 1916, but off East Africa – or the location is correct and the date is wrong – i.e. it is Suvla Bay, but during September 1915, though not on the 16th. If any readers can offer further clarification we would be glad to hear from them.

Sources:
ADM53/62204 – HMS *Talbot*, ship's log, September 1915.
ADM53/62216 – HMS *Talbot*, ship's log, September 1916.
Burns, Lt.Cdr. KV: *Devonport Built Warships*, Maritime Books, 1981.
Corbett & Newbolt: *Naval Operations*, Longmans Green, 1922.
Van der Vat, Dan: *The Dardanelles Disaster*, Duckworth, 2009.
The Navy List. Various editions.

NAVAL BOOKS OF THE YEAR

R A Burt
British Battleships 1919-1945
Seaforth Publishing, Barnsley, Yorkshire, 2012; hardback, 432 pages, illustrated with B&W photographs and line drawings; price £45.00.
ISBN 978-1-84832-130-4

Official secrecy restrictions greatly limited the length and scope of the final chapters of *British Battleships 1860-1950* by Oscar Parkes, published in 1957; his treatment of the *King George V* class and *Vanguard* was sparse and austere. Comprehensive details of the capital ship story from 1912 to 1960 had to wait for the release of official records under the thirty-year rule and the 1976 classic *British Battleships of World War Two*, by Alan Raven and John Roberts. The existence of this book meant that, like the biblical Ahab, Ray Burt had to tread delicately to avoid duplication when describing the evolution of the British battleship between the wars. His book, first published in 1993 with the title *British Battleships 1919-1939*, was a fascinating volume, freestanding and full of fresh material from the Public Record Office and the National Maritime Museum, different drawings and new photographs. Each capital ship class from the *Queen Elizabeth* to *King George V* was covered in detail, with complete data, particular attention (including diagrams) being paid to war damage to the older ships. It resembled Raven and Roberts only in format and general layout, and complemented it in information. Both books are now out of print and very expensive in the second-hand market.

It is therefore excellent that Burt's book is back after nineteen years, and doubly excellent that it reappears as a second edition, with some 75 additional photos, a larger page size and a complete redesign to take full advantage of the new images. Drawings and text are unchanged apart from short footnotes on the recent (and inconclusive) inspection of the wrecks of *Hood*, *Prince of Wales* and *Repulse*.

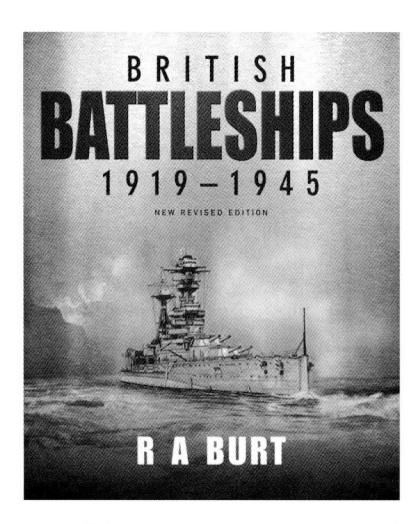

Although the title dates have changed to include the six war years, regrettably no attempt has been made to add the four *Lions* or *Vanguard*. As before, a separate chapter of almost forty pages deals very thoroughly with *Courageous*, *Glorious* and *Furious*, three aircraft carriers converted from large light cruisers, but the *Eagle*, also a former capital ship, receives scant attention. The omission of this somewhat irrelevant chapter, fascinating though it is, would have allowed space for the missing battleship quintet.

This reservation aside, the result is a magnificent monument to the Royal Navy's golden years that can be recommended for pride of place on any bookshelf. Notably, and very commendably, the price has only increased by £5.00 since 1993. In addition, new editions of the author's other two volumes, *British Battleships of World War One* and *British Battleships 1889-1904*, will be published shortly.

Ian Sturton

Matthew S Seligmann
The Royal Navy and the German Threat 1901-1914: Admiralty Plans to Protect British Trade in a War Against Germany
Oxford University Press, 2012; hardback, 196 pages, extensive bibliography & footnotes; price £60.00.
ISBN 978-0-19-957403-2

The conventional wisdom tells us that while the major threat to Britain's maritime security during the latter part of the 19th Century was posed by the fast cruisers built by France and Russia to attack her trade, the early years of the twentieth century saw a direct German challenge to Britain's naval supremacy in the form of the ambitious programme of capital ship construction driven by Admiral Tirpitz. Matthew Seligmann, in this new book, postulates that this view is simplistic, and that not only did the Germans contemplate and plan for an assault on Britain's trade using auxiliary cruisers converted from fast Atlantic liners, but that the British Admiralty was well aware of this threat – even to the point of overestimating German intentions and capabilities – and expended considerable energy attempting to counter it.

A number of key points emerge from the author's research. Germany did indeed subsidise the series of fast transatlantic liners, which held the blue riband between 1897 and 1906, with a view to their possible use as *Hilfskreuzer* in time of war, when numerous heavy guns (initially 10.5cm, then 15cm) would be fitted. These ships had military features which included a double bottom, twin screws, machinery spaces beneath the waterline, and seatings for the heavy guns. Reserve naval personnel would have been embarked at overseas bases by drawing on the crews of locally-based gunboats, and the cargo holds would have been used as supplementary coal bunkers to give them the necessary radius. With their excellent sea-keeping qualities and an average speed of 23.58 knots they could have outrun any existing regular cruiser in the North Atlantic.

The British were confused as to how best to respond to this threat. Initially it was envisaged that the Royal Navy would meet like with like, and in 1903 'speed subsidies' were agreed with Cunard for the construction of the liners *Mauretania* and – ironically – *Lusitania* with a view to their requisitioning as Armed Merchant Cruisers in time of war. However, when Admiral Fisher became First Sea Lord in 1904, this policy was revoked. Like many senior naval officers, Fisher disliked the idea of vulnerable merchantmen being used for this task and was unhappy with the diversion of naval funding to subsidise their construction; the result (according to the author) was the turbine-powered large armoured cruisers of the *Invincible* class, which would have the necessary firepower, protection and capability for sustained high speed to hunt down and destroy the German raiders. However, when completed these ships and their immediate successors of the *Indefatigable* class were promptly commandeered to serve as a 'fast division' for the battle fleet, a role for which their design – and in particular their light protection, designed to keep out the 15cm shells of the German surface raiders – made them fundamentally unsuited (with later consequences which are well known).

Attention then turned to securing the prohibition of the arming of merchant ships under international law, but the British case at the Second Hague Conference of 1907 and the London Naval Conference of 1908-09 was undermined both by German obduracy and by the historical precedents Britain had herself created in the arming of merchantmen. The proposed solution was the creation of a network of intelligence centres at the major intersections of the trade routes tasked with the monitoring of friendly and potentially hostile mercantile traffic, to enable British shipping to be re-routed in the event of a threat and Royal Navy cruisers to be summoned by wireless to deal with it. Despite a major setback when Fisher chose to obstruct the implementation of these provisions during his 'war' with Admiral Charles Beresford, this system was in place by the outbreak of war in 1914, by which time substantial numbers of Defensively Armed Merchant Ships (DAMS) – an idea promoted by Churchill during his time as First Lord of the Admiralty – were also plying the trade routes.

All of these developments are examined in detail by Matthew Seligmann with extensive use of primary sources. Much of the information in these has had to be carefully pieced together due to the number of files which are known to have been 'culled' or have simply disappeared. It is a methodical study with particular insights into the divisions within the German naval hierarchy, in which the Imperial Navy Office (headed by Tirpitz and responsible for budgetary matters and construction) was frequently at loggerheads with the Admiralty Staff (responsible for operational doctrine, and the prime mover behind the *Hilfskreuzer* policy), and into the origins of the battle cruiser. Since the rationale for these ships was never formally declared – Fisher's 'I never in all my life have ever yet explained, and I don't mean to' says it all – there remains some doubt about their primary mission, but the author makes a convincing case for their use as 'raider killers'.

The great puzzle in all this is why, having expended so much money and planning effort on the *Hilskreuzer* concept, the Germans failed to make more use of these ships when war was declared – of the fast liners only the *Kronprinz Wilhelm* had any great success as a raider. Seligmann suggests a number of reasons for this. However, it is clear that the British Admiralty consistently over-estimated the threat – for many years it remained convinced that the German ships carried their guns broken down in the holds at all times, despite a total lack of evidence that this was true – and that the Germans showed a lack of conviction and determination in implementing their long-standing plans, instead falling back on a grand Mahanian strategy which was always doomed to failure.

John Jordan

William P. Althoff
Arctic Mission, 90 North by Airship and Submarine
Naval Institute Press, 2011; hardback, 284 pages, illustrated with 125 B&W photographs and illustrations; price £25.00.
ISBN 978 1 61251 010 1

This book tells the story of the US Navy's two attempts to reach the North Pole in 1958, by the USS *Nautilus* and by a non-rigid airship (or 'blimp') later known as *Snow Goose*. The voyage of the USS *Nautilus* is well known, the journey of the blimp rather less so.

The eight main chapters interweave the two journeys with useful background information such as the technical and diplomatic scenarios, an insight into the politics surrounding these events (the Soviet Union had just beaten the USA in the race to launch the first satellite), and the very different fates of the two types of vessel involved. Things are rounded off by a short chapter on the careers of the *dramatis personae*, followed by various appendices, some very helpful chapter notes, a bibliography and index.

The book is well-written and at times reads like an adventure story, particularly the author's account of the flight of the blimp, technically a US Navy ZPG-2, and its travails against inclement weather. Despite subsequent developments – the nuclear submarine went on to become an essential component of the world's major navies whereas the airship disappeared from the military inventory soon after – the author's sympathies appear to lie with the lighter-than-air craft.

Other things that stand out include: the comparative youthfulness of *Nautilus*' commanding officer, Cdr Anderson, who looks to be the youngest man present in the photo of the boat's sail-top conning position which is used as the cover illustration; the resolution of the people involved in both voyages and their determination to overcome various obstacles; and the key involvement of experts. Modern thinking often seems to deliberately exclude expertise on the basis that it pre-determines the outcome, whereas the *Nautilus* would not have succeeded without Dr. Waldo Lyon, who had already spent a lifetime studying the Arctic ice and who continued to do so after this voyage. In a similar vein the *Snow Goose* probably would not have succeeded without the expert arctic navigation of the RCAF's Wing Commander Greenaway, who knew well the region to be overflown and navigated the craft almost singlehandedly.

Also of note is the author's ability to refer to both the absurdities and paranoia, as well as the achievements, of the Cold War era; his references to Russian research successes and achievements in the Arctic are even-handed and informative.

This is a fascinating narrative, thoroughly recommended.

W B Davies

John D Grainger
Dictionary of British Naval Battles
The Boydell Press, 2012; hardback, 588 pages, 8 maps; price £95.00.
ISBN 978 1 84383 704 6

Like any dictionary, this is not a book to be read cover to cover. It is a large, straightforward reference book, to be turned to as and when necessary.

Grainger, who has written and edited books for the Navy Records Society, begins with a brief introduction in which the criteria for inclusion are discussed, and in particular the problematic nature of the words 'battle' and 'British'. The actions of dominion navies are included, as are those of the Anglo-Saxon kingdoms, the Vikings, and the East India Company; those involving the Romans are not. Some of Drake's more debatable activities appear as well; as Grainger explains, setting too rigid a set of boundaries would have been too 'exclusive'.

The immense quantity of information is presented in a clear, readable manner, with each entry followed by its source references. However, the organisation of the material is idiosyncratic, to say the least. Jutland and Trafalgar are where you would expect them to be, but the placing of other battles is more problematic. For example, the October 1944 action when the light cruiser *Charybdis* was sunk by German torpedo boats off the Channel Islands does not appear in 'C' where one might expect it to be – there is only an earlier *Charybdis*' action against a slave ship in 1834. The index is little help, as the name *Charybdis* has four entries but with no indication of the type of ship or the date; this means that the reader has to try each in turn to find the right entry. (In fact the 1944 *Charybdis* action turns out to be deeply buried within the 1942-44 sub-section of the five-and-a-half page 'Hitler's war' sub-section of the 13-page 'English Channel' section under the letter 'E'). There are similar problems with the Battle of Sluys, which is within the eight-page 'North Sea' sub-section under 'N'. These difficulties are compounded by there being no initial capital letter – 'A', 'B' etc. – in the running heads at the tops of the pages, making the book difficult to navigate. Grainger does explain his reasoning for these geographical/ thematic sections, but the layout of the book and the inadequacies of the index, which makes cross-referencing difficult, do not help his cause.

Unfortunately, there are also numerous small factual errors. The German 'battlecruiser' *Moltke* makes an appearance on p.162, but crops up again just three pages later as a 'battleship'; during the Falklands conflict of 1982 it was the *Ardent*, not the *Antrim*, which was sunk. Such errors, while minor on their own, tend to undermine the overall authority of the text.

Despite these shortcomings, this is a useful reference book which many will wish to own. However, the purchase price of £95 will deter many potential readers, and it is to be hoped that Boydell will consider publishing a more affordable paperback edition.

Stephen Dent

John Jordan
Warships After Washington
Seaforth Publishing, 2011; hardback, 338 pages, many B&W photos and line drawings; price £30.00.
ISBN 978-1-84832-117-5

The series of naval armaments agreements that commenced with the Washington Treaty of 1922 had a major impact on international politics during the inter-war period; equally, they had a key influence on the technical capabilities of many of the warships that were ultimately tasked with fighting the Second World War. The political and technical aspects of naval arms limitation have both been subjected to much individual analysis, but less effort has been devoted to exploring the links between the two factors. *Warships After Washington* essentially aims to close this gap by combining a review of the political and economic imperatives influencing the 1922 agreement with an analysis of how these – and the legal terms of the treaty – fed through to the design solutions adopted by the five contracting powers.

The book begins with an overview of the principal navies and warship programmes underway at the time of the Washington Treaty. An examination of the agreement itself and its impact on the five signatories is followed by a detailed analysis of the warships built in the period between the signing of the treaty and the London agreement of 1930. Each principal category – capital ship, cruiser, aircraft carrier, submarine, and destroyer – is accorded its own separate chapter, together with an additional one on types such as the Italian *esploratori* and French *contre-torpilleurs* that reflected the distinct operating environment found in the Mediterranean. The book concludes with a summary of the abortive Geneva Conference of 1927 and the partially successful London Treaty of 1930, which aimed to resolve some of the unintended consequences of the original agreement, such as the displacement of the previous rivalry in capital ship construction to other warship types.

The scope of the task the author has set himself is immense but he rises admirably to the challenge through a combination of clear structure, concise prose and insightful analysis. The book also benefits from a series of standardised schematic drawings of many of the designs described as well as numerous tabularised data summaries. These facilitate comparison between the different design paths the five leading naval powers decided to pursue. Whilst photographic coverage provides little that has not been seen before, the images are linked to the text with excellent captions that further enhance overall understanding. Given that many previous books on the inter-war naval arms limitation agreements have focused on their influence on capital ship and cruiser forces, the extensive coverage *Warships After Washington* gives to other categories such as destroyers and submarines is particularly welcome. Whilst the so-called 'Washington cruiser' was one of the major consequences of the limitation of capital ship construction during the 1920s, the extension of the naval arms race to other types has often been overlooked. The book is also relatively strong in analysing the factors influencing naval developments in France and Italy, fleets which have previously suffered from comparatively limited coverage in English language publications.

Warships After Washington is not without its flaws. Whilst it is difficult to dispute the logic underpinning most of the author's conclusions, one or two of the book's premises are open to dispute, such as the statement that the United States was '...a colonial power only by default...'. It would also have been interesting to see some design concepts and the factors driving them explored in more depth, particularly with regard to the Imperial Japanese Navy. Both of these criticisms are a reflection of the difficulty of conducting a thorough analysis of a hugely complex subject whilst maintaining sufficient focus on the major salient points to draw meaningful conclusions. Despite these reservations, *Warships After Washington* is generally successful in achieving this balance, and represents essential reading for anyone with an interest in twentieth century naval history.

Conrad Waters

Thomas J Cutler
The Citizen's Guide to the U.S. Navy
Naval Institute Press, Annapolis, 2012; softback, 318 pages, illustrated with B&W photographs, charts, diagrams, colour plates and a map;
price £14.99/$22.95.
ISBN 978-1591-141570

This book comes in two parts. In the first, the history of the U.S. Navy and its current missions are neatly and usefully summarised. Chapters on ships (25 pages) and weapons (31 pages) then provide brief – and generally data-free – general information; however, the aviation chapter, nineteen pages of which the primary focus is on organisation and aircraft nomenclature, is disappointing. The author directs readers interested in greater detail to other Naval Institute Press publications, although surprisingly not to their *Combat Fleets*.

The second part of the book is a very different affair: naval procedures and customs are explained to civilians or foreign naval personnel visiting U.S. ships or shore installations. The treatment of uniforms, badges, emblems, flags, saluting and procedural form is exhaustive, and the niceties of rank recall the Habsburg court in old Vienna. For instance, a senior naval officer customarily closes a memo to a junior officer with 'Respectfully', a junior to a senior with 'Very Respectfully'; these may be abbreviated to 'R' and 'V/R', or, in e-mails, 'r' and 'v/r'. The abbreviation for a Master Chief Petty Officer of the Navy is MCPON, and he or she should be so addressed in writing ('Dear MCPON') or verbally (pronounced 'mick-pon'). Navy personnel in certain circumstances may salute with the left hand, Army and Air Force personnel never.

The author, a retired American lieutenant-commander, notes that the book is a condensed version of his *NavCivGuide: A Handbook for Civilians in the United States Navy*; many of his other publications are from the same stable (*The Bluejacket's Manual, Dictionary of Naval Abbreviations, A Sailor's History of the U.S. Navy, Command at Sea*). This particular title, although informative and very readable, is probably not one for the average bookshelf.

Ian Sturton

Colonel Roy M Stanley II, USAF (Retired)
Looking Down on War: Axis Warships
Pen & Sword Maritime, 2011; hard cover, 256 pages, numerous B&W photos and line drawings; price £25.00.
ISBN 978-184884-471-1

Written by a retired US Air Force intelligence officer, *Axis Warships* provides an unusual insight into Allied wartime knowledge of their opponents' fleets during the Second World War, through an analysis of contemporary photo reconnaissance images retrieved from retired Department of Defense files. The vast bulk of material examined comprises aerial photography, much of it new to the reviewer. However, there is also reference to surface imagery, maps and recognition silhouettes to provide a comprehensive indication of what was available to Allied photographic interpreters at the time.

Colonel Stanley provides analysis of all three main Axis navies, as well as France's *Marine Nationale* – described here as 'The Axis Fleet That Might Have Been'. However, it is the *Kriegsmarine* that predominates, with a lengthy 119-page chapter that incorporates separate sections on the principal warship types, including virtually ship-by-ship coverage of the major surface units. This is supplemented by a separate chapter focusing largely on German naval bases and harbours. By way of contrast, photographic evidence of the much larger Imperial Japanese Navy is rather less comprehensive. As the author explains, this is partly due to the success of Japanese efforts to thwart Allied intelligence in the pre-war period. The difficulty of implementing reconnaissance of principal enemy facilities once conflict commenced, due to the long ranges involved, was another factor. Consequently, most images in this section were taken during combat operations.

The author's experience as a photographic interpreter and intelligence analyst allow him to provide an interesting appreciation of how reconnaissance photos might have been used, as well as saying something of their limitations. There is also some indication of how other intelligence sources might have been used to produce a more complete picture. To give just one example, it is suggested that an aerial RAF image that purportedly shows a Japanese submarine off Brest would have resulted from a special reconnaissance flight triggered by 'Ultra' intelligence.

However, the submarine is not the Japanese *I-34* claimed by the book as this boat was sunk by the Royal Navy's *Taurus* on departing the Far East. It is this lack of attention to detail that is one of the main drawbacks of Axis Warships, as there are numerous other minor errors, inconsistencies and spelling mistakes, all suggesting a far from diligent editorial process. This absence of rigour is also evident in the book's overall design and layout, which has a haphazard, half-finished appearance that makes poor use of the undoubtedly interesting material that has been assembled. Whilst some allowance has to be made for the inevitably variable quality of the original imagery, it is hard to escape the conclusion that little has been done to mitigate this in the design and production process.

In conclusion, Axis Warships provides an interesting insight into the wartime sources and uses of photographic naval intelligence. Unfortunately, its value is significantly diminished by a lack of care or attention to detail that seems at odds with the author's former career.

Conrad Waters

Richard Worth
Thunder in Its Courses: Essays on the Battlecruiser
Nimble Books, Ann Arbor, USA, 2011;
51 pages, 25 B&W illustrations and diagrams; price £19.00
ISBN:978-1-60888-101-7

Thunder in its Courses comprises seven short essays on the battlecruiser, one of the most controversial, arguably least successful but most frequently discussed, of warship designs. Richard Worth deals successively with the genesis of the type, the first battlecruisers, design failures along the way, the type's demise, an extended examination of the lengthy career of the Japanese *Kongo*, and finally, in 'The Mightiest Might-Have-Been', speculates that the Russian *Izmail*, had she ever been completed, could have become 'the most dominating dreadnought', superior even to the *Hindenberg*, which is often referred to as the best battlecruiser of the First World War.

The first couple of essays illustrate perfectly one of the major problems associated with any discussion regarding these vessels, namely the difficulty of arriving at a consensus about what actually constituted a battlecruiser. For that matter which was the first one? After citing the Japanese *Asama* and *Tsukuba* designs, Worth offers other contenders including the German *Blücher* and the French *Edgar Quinet*. He concludes that in all of these their 'cruiser-caliber' weaponry precluded any pretentions to battlecruiser status, which left the 'battleship-caliber' *Invincible* as the first true ship of its kind.

Predictably, Worth is critical of Fisher's involvement in the design of the three *Courageous* class ships, finding it difficult to comprehend the rationale behind these heavily armed but lightly armoured vessels, even though they ultimately found useful secondary careers as pioneer aircraft carriers.

Thunder in its Courses is well illustrated with both photographs and line drawings, but at just 50 pages is a very short book and thus an expensive purchase. As the 'Further Reading' section illustrates, there are probably more theories on this subject than there were battlecruisers actually built. Therefore the book, written in an informal, often conversational style, should be regarded as a contribution to an on-going debate; useful material perhaps for a discussion over dinner or a pint rather than the definitive word on the matter.

Jon Wise

Henri Landais
Les Avisos Coloniaux de 2000 tW (1930-1960) Tome 01
Lela Presse, Outreau, 2012;
large format hardback, 416 pages, copiously illustrated with plans, maps and B&W photographs; price €65.00.
ISBN 978-2-914017-64-0

The *avisos coloniaux* were 2000-tonne colonial sloops intended for the local defence of remote colonial stations. Powerfully armed, but with a moderate speed of 15 knots, they were designed to operate in the tropics, with insulated and well-ventilated crew spaces and with a shelter deck amidships which extended to the ships' sides. Laid down from the late 1920s, they were extremely influential when the provisions of the 1930 London Treaty came to be framed, their characteristics forming the basis for the qualitative limits imposed on the 'treaty exempt' category of warship. Eight units had entered service by June 1940; a ninth unit was 70% complete and was sabotaged at Bordeaux, and a tenth cancelled.

When this book was announced, the intention to publish in two volumes occasioned some surprise. The warship monographs published in France over the previous two decades have generally been single, often slim volumes, whereas the first of the two volumes on the colonial sloops weighs in at a massive 416 pages. It is easy to see why. The compilation of these two volumes clearly constitute a labour of love for the author, Henri Landais, who appears to have spent a considerable part of his life collecting the necessary material.

The first volume covers the technical aspects of the class, the many modifications and modernisations extended to the first four ships completed (A1-A4), and the service history of these same ships. A second volume, presumably slightly less bulky, will cover the modernisations and service life of the remaining four ships (A5-A8).

The technical study comprises the customary textual description of all aspects of the design, based on the offical specifications, together with a comprehensive set of data tables. It is profusely illustrated by official plans and line drawings by the author. Every aspect of the ships is detailed, from military hardware down to anchors, boats and deck furniture, and illustrated by well-chosen close-up photographs, many of which have not been published previously. The modifications section includes seven pages of specially-commissioned colour artwork by Bertrand Magueur showing the ships at various key points of their respective careers. The quantity and quality of the illustration is astonishing; for example, the comparatively rare Hotchkiss single 25mm Mle 1939 mounting, which is accorded only a single line of description in Campbell (*Naval Weapons of World War II*), is illustrated by no fewer than three line drawings (including one perspective view) and four close-up photos.

The historical section is divided into four parts: peacetime service 1932-39, wartime service 1939-45, postwar service 1945-56, and the end of their careers 1956-57. It is copiously illustrated by maps and contemporary photographs, many of them from private collections. The wartime section includes an extended account of the tragic fratricide which occurred when the FNFL-manned *Savorgnan de Brazza* (A3), aided by FAFL aircraft, attacked and disabled the Vichy French *Bougainville* (A1) off Libreville in West Africa, with the loss of eleven men.

Nineteen appendices cover a variety of operational and technical matters. These include radars, the explosives used in anti-submarine weaponry, detail differences between the ships, badges and naval ranks (with illustrations in colour) and camouflage schemes.

This first volume is a cornucopia of information and illustration. There is no pretension to modern book design; the layouts are extraordinarily 'busy' and the structure of the book is sometimes confusing, despite the colour-coded name tabs which decorate the page edges of the sections dealing with specific ships. It could be argued that there is almost too much here, and that the book would have benefited from some judicious pruning by the author, as there are many instances where several drawings of a single item of equipment from different sources are juxtaposed despite discrepancies in scale, quality and detail. However, this is work which radiates energy and enthusiasm, and it will be welcomed by naval enthusiasts and ship modellers alike.

John Jordan

John Asmussen & Eric Leon
German Naval Camouflage, Vol. I, 1939-1941

Seaforth Publishing, 2012; hardback, 192 pages, illustrated with 300 colour profiles, plans and detail views, plus photographs in colour and B&W; price £35.00/$74.95.
ISBN 9781848321427

This is a book which makes a strong initial impact on the reader: facing the title page is a reproduction of a colour photograph of *Lützow* and *Köln* sporting 'Baltic' style camouflage schemes, accompanied by a lengthy caption covering such issues as modern digital restoration of the often murky and inaccurate colour of such images, deceptions that can be caused by the original colours, as well as points of interest in the actual image itself. The book maintains this level of analysis throughout, with no detail too small, no aspect too obscure if it helps to pin down exactly what a ship looked like at a certain time.

The sub-title, while understandable, is actually slightly misleading, in that a lot of pre-1939 peacetime colour schemes are also included, as well as those worn by *Kriegsmarine* vessels during their involvement in the Spanish Civil War. There is even some background information on identification markings worn by ships of the Kaiser's navy. Short textual chapters examine types of camouflage, aerial identification markings, the evolution of *Kriegsmarine* camouflage patterns, and 'scale effect', the latter being of particular interest to model makers.

The main body of the book is an impressive collection of plan, profile and detail drawings, plus photographs – mostly black and white, but with some colour – illustrating the paint schemes worn by German warships during the first half of the Second World War. These are accompanied by detailed captions explaining the purpose of the scheme shown, its effectiveness, modifications, any areas of uncertainty, and issues to do with the reliability and/or completeness of the surviving/known visual record. The openness with which the authors are prepared to discuss these issues is to be commended, and serves to reinforce the authority of the work.

The book has a similar page size to *Warship* but turned on its side, and this 'landscape' format is used to display the illustrations to good effect. The quality of the photographs varies considerably; some have clearly been chosen primarily for what they show rather than for their intrinsic merit. The two authors, both graphic artists, are responsible for all the drawings in the book; these are superb, although they are not always reproduced as sharply as might be expected. The appearance of the artist's copyright and byline on, as opposed to next to, many of the drawings, is slightly off-putting.

The emphasis is on the paint schemes of the major warships, with just a short chapter covering destroyers; there is nothing on U-boats, S-boats or other vessels, which hopefully will be dealt with in the second volume. Details such as crests and name boards, ships' boats and aircraft, and even *Graf Spee*'s various disguises are also covered.

All in all, a highly impressive book.

Stephen Dent.

Douglas Ford
The Elusive Enemy: US Naval Intelligence & the Imperial Japanese Fleet

Naval Institute Press, Annapolis, 2011; 320 pages, 5 maps, Notes, Bibliography, Index; price £18.95.
ISBN 978-1-59114-280-5

Elliot Carlson
Joe Rochefort's War: The Odyssey of the Codebreaker who Outwitted Yamamoto at Midway

Naval Institute Press, Annapolis, 2011; 624 pages, 46 B&W photos, 2 maps, Notes, Bibliography, Index; price £25.00.
ISBN 978-1-61251-060-6

The Pacific campaign of 1941–1945 revolutionised not only the tactics of engagement at sea but also the very methods of operation: opposing fleets no longer needed to be in sight of one another in order to fight; battleships were superseded as the key strike weapon by aircraft carriers; power projection on a grand scale could be targeted ashore from distances of thousands of miles; and new methods of providing logistical support enabled fleets to become predominantly self-sufficient for long periods of time.

Much has been written about the campaign but, as Douglas Ford in *The Elusive Enemy* remarks, the role played by intelligence has been under-researched. He suggests that records of such activities understandably tend to be kept secret for longer than other strategic issues and that the relative shortage of information has served to deter academics, although this has been mitigated to some extent in recent years through Freedom of Information legislation.

The Elusive Enemy and *Joe Rochefort's War* approach the same subject in contrasting ways. Ford provides a chronological overview and analysis of naval intelligence gathering, making exhaustive use of primary sources to support his findings, while Elliott Carson's biography concentrates on the role played by a single person and principally, though not exclusively, on what is considered to be *the* key event of the campaign, the Battle of Midway in June 1942.

Both writers demonstrate in the clearest terms the nature of the formidable challenge facing American intelligence in early 1942. Ford notes that the US Navy had a tradition of systematically analysing the capabilities of potential enemies; the Office of Naval Intelligence had been established as long ago as 1880. However, at the outset of war there was an acute shortage of accurate information about the capabilities of Japan's military hardware and its likely tactics, the Japanese having paid close attention to stringent security. Moreover, the USN had adhered to the accepted notion that Japan was a backward nation both in terms of economic advancement and technological expertise. Both writers concur that elements of racial prejudice also served to cloud perceptions, and that these may have contributed to incorrect assumptions being made regarding the threat level prior to Pearl Harbor.

Ford argues that US naval intelligence continued to face problems after the fighting had started owing to the on-going paucity of information. Much reliance had to be placed on combat experiences and reports, but these took time to analyse. For example, US deficiency in radar and communications equipment was eventually diagnosed as an acute problem but the necessary countermeasures could not be immediately addressed. More famously, tactics to counter the agility of the Zero aircraft and the technological prowess of the fabled 'Long Lance' torpedo were hindered by the lack of hard data regarding the capabilities of these weapons. Thus it was a measure of American resourcefulness, organisation and determination that from virtually a 'standing start' US naval intelligence was able to make vital inroads and contribute significantly to the ultimate defeat of a formidable opponent.

Joe Rochefort, the subject of Elliott Carlson's brilliant biography, which rightly won the Theodore and Franklin D. Roosevelt Naval History Prize 2011 for outstanding contribution to American naval history, was in every sense the modern, complex hero. Although a fiercely loyal and highly professional career officer, he could be difficult and off-hand to the point of insubordination. Possessed of a brilliant mind and an intolerance of inferior intellect, he was both revered and hated. His grasp of signals monitoring and the mysteries of cryptographic intelligence, his first-hand knowledge of Japan and his mastery of its language all contributed to make him the ideal yet still controversial choice to head Station Hypo at Pearl Harbor. Here Commander Rochefort's team of codebreakers worked round the clock to unlock enough of the impossibly complex Japanese signals code to convince themselves by late May 1942 that Midway was to be the target for the most powerful Japanese task force yet assembled. In the face of fierce opposition from other intelligence units, and particularly from a cadre of enemies in Washington, Rochefort persuaded Admiral Nimitz, the C-in-C Pacific, of his convictions and a disaster potentially far more serious than Pearl Harbor was averted.

Carlson's book builds inexorably to the climactic moment in this Rocherfort's career. The author is meticulous in charting the life of a man who left school without qualifications, joined the navy and rose rapidly through the ranks. The fact that he was a 'mustang', a former enlisted man who never attended the prestigious Annapolis Naval College, inevitably worked against him. Surprisingly, for a nation which prides itself on its meritocracy, we learn the extent to which patronage, petty likes and dislikes and downright snobbishness helped shape the careers of its naval officers. The plotters in Washington managed to get Rochefort re-assigned immediately after Midway. Application for the award of the Distinguished Service Medal he so richly deserved was vetoed by Admiral King, a decision which was finally reversed in 1986, by which time Rochefort was dead.

Both of these books contribute much to the fascinating subject of intelligence which always lurks in the background of any campaign account. A possible criticism of Ford's book is that he attempts to cover too much ground, and the less knowledgeable reader might get lost in the detail of this unashamedly academic study. On the other hand Rochefort's biography, in the experienced hands of journalist Carlson, is instantly accessible and a real 'page turner'.

Jon Wise

Jean Moulin
Les Contre-Torpilleurs Type *Aigle*

Marines Editions, Rennes, 2012; large format softback, 176 pages, many plans, maps and B&W photographs; price €39.55.
ISBN 978-2-357430-96-9

The last in a series of monographs about the French interwar *contre-torpilleurs* published by Marines Editions, this is a particularly welcome addition to the canon. Jean Moulin has effectively taken over the mantle of Jean Lassaque, producing first the volume on the six four-funnelled CT of the *Guépard* class (2010), and now this volume on the four-ship *Aigle* class. (*Milan* and *Epervier*, originally belonging to this group, were completed to a different design and were the subject of one of the earlier volumes.)

The book follows a broadly similar format to the earlier volumes in the series. There is a general introduction putting the design into its proper context, a historical section detailing the service lives of each of the four ships from cradle to grave, a technical section with comprehensive data on the ships as completed and as later modified, a useful set of appendices which include the organisation of the French fleet in peace and war with a particular focus on the three-ship *contre-torpilleur divisions* (DCT), and a *Schémas* section which includes both official plans of the ships as designed and line drawings by the author and others showing subsequent modifications. One of the most interesting topics covered is the conversion of *Albatros* to a gunnery training ship following the Second World War, when she was fitted with new guns which included the German 10.5cm SKC/33 (subsequently fitted in the ex-Italian cruisers *Châteaurenault* and *Guichen* – see *Warship 2005*) and the prototype of the 100mm twin Mle 1945 (to be embarked in the battleship *Jean Bart*), together with their associated fire control directors and radars.

The book is well-illustrated with photographs, maps and plans and is produced in an attractive large-format soft cover format. The design is strikingly more 'modern' than that of the earlier volumes in the series, and is generally successful. The reviewer's only reservation concerns the contents page and the double-page spreads which introduce each section, which feature reverse printing (light grey on black), a combination of large heads with a small typeface for the detailed contents, prominent (and slightly bizarre) bracketing and thumbnail-size photos, many of which do not appear elsewhere. This simply does not work well from the reader's point of view, and fails to enhance the admirable clarity of the layouts in the main body of the book.

These, however, should be considered minor criticisms considering the overall quality of the book, which is comprehensive in its coverage, superlatively illustrated and one of the best in the series.

John Jordan

Philippe Caresse
Le Cuirassé *Bismarck*
Lela Presse, Outreau, 2012; large format hardback, 192 pages, profusely illustrated with plans, schemas and B&W/coulour photographs; price €55.00.
ISBN 978-2-914017-73-2

Le Cuirassé Bismarck, Philippe Caresse's first published book, appeared in 2003. It quickly sold out, and has now been reprinted by Lela Presse in a revised edition which includes many new images.

Following a brief introductory section which deals with the ship's name, a history of previous ships bearing the name, and the design process, there is a particularly comprehensive technical section detailing all aspects of the ship, including paint schemes, illustrated by line drawings, official plans, colour artwork and close-up photographs of gun mountings and other equipment. The chapter which deals with the ship's completion and subsequent trials in the Baltic is excellent , and concludes the first part of the book. The second part is devoted to a full account of *Bismarck*'s first and final operational sortie, Operation 'Rheinübung'. Appendices include a list of the 116 survivors (including the ship's cat, who was subsequently aboard the destroyer *Cossack* and the carrier *Ark Royal* when they in their turn were sunk!), an account of the dives on the wrecks of *Hood* and *Bismarck*, and the fate of the other warships (British and German) which took part in the operation.

Given the plethora of books published on *Bismarck* and 'Rheinübung' in English, readers of *Warship* will wish to know what makes this book stand out from its competitors. Firstly, as a Frenchman Philippe Caresse has the advantage of writing from an 'independent' perspective, without the considerable cultural burden which weighs down British authors writing about the Royal Navy's pursuit and sinking of the *Bismarck*. He has made extensive use of the official archives of the *Kriegsmarine* in researching the book, and this has resulted in some interesting insights into the planning of the operation and the preparations which preceded it. The drawings and plans, most of which are of high quality, are unusually comprehensive, and the specially drawn situation maps which illustrate every phase of 'Rheinübung' are uniformly excellent. However, if there is one feature of this book that really stands out it is the photographs, of which there are approximately 320, including some colour views. The close-ups and on-board shots are superb and cover virtually every item of equipment and every corner of the ship, while the general views of the ship on trials, preparing for break-out in the Norwegian fjords, in action in the Denmark Strait, in the North Atlantic and during the final gunnery action are unusually comprehensive. Many of these photographs are from private collections, and many are previously unpublished. For the reader who has only rudimentary French, the book is worth purchasing for the photographs alone.

John Jordan

David Kahn
Seizing the Enigma: The Race to Break the German U-Boat Codes, 1939-1943 [Revised Edition]
Naval Institute Press, 2012; paperback, 387 pages, 39 B&W photographs; maps, appendices, bibliography; price £16.00/$27.95
ISBN 978-1-591-114-807-4

The war-time achievements of the code-breakers of Bletchley Park are now common knowledge. Over the past forty years, the work of an assortment of scientists, mathematicians and linguists including Alan Turing, who has been dubbed 'the father of the modern computer', has been revealed, mulled over and sometimes glamourised in the fashionable manner in which the achievements of 'geeks' are now celebrated. Alternative mythologies have been promoted by films made on both sides of the Atlantic.

David Kahn's book sets out to refute these often blatant inaccuracies by providing a thorough account of the history of British attempts to penetrate German naval codes. The author is well qualified for the task having balanced a career in journalism with lecturing in Intelligence at Yale and Colombia universities. His 1997 history of cryptology *The Codebreakers* is regarded as the seminal work on the subject. One senses that in the future *Seizing the Enigma* will be regarded in the same vein.

The requirement to read the intelligence reports despatched in encrypted code messages sent to U-Boats deployed across the North Atlantic convoy routes became crucial as the Second World War entered its second and then third year, and Britain and its people became ever more dependent on this vital supply route. However, the German Enigma cryptosystem used by all three services was highly sophisticated and thus very difficult to penetrate. The Enigma machine had three (later four) code-wheels for encipherments. A key task for the code clerk was to select at random the three letters which in turn set the code-wheels, thus producing the coded message. For the *Kriegsmarine*, which insisted on far stricter security than either the *Luftwaffe* or the *Wehrmacht*, the settings to be used were issued as a series of random three-letter groups indicated by letter groups that bore no relation to the setting groups. These 'indicators' were converted to their secret forms according to a table in a book. The message was sent to the recipient who, with the aid of the codebooks, was able to decipher the message.

Thus it was the capture of the codes themselves rather than just the Enigma machine which provided the best chance of overcoming this hugely complex problem. Two operations conducted against isolated German weather ships stationed in the Arctic by RN task groups, together with the dramatic and perhaps fortunate discovery of a weather code book onboard a sinking U-Boat in the Mediterranean, gave the code-breakers the information they needed.

Kahn's book does not limit itself to the events of the Second World War and the achievements at Bletchley Park. The story starts with the capture by the Russians of the Imperial German Navy code book and cipher key from the wreck of SMS *Magdeburg* in the first month of the First World War. This vital information was secretly passed to the British. Subsequently, German High Command refused to believe their codes had fallen into the hands of the enemy and it was three years before it made fundamental changes to its system. The author calls this delay 'one of the greatest communications security failures in history'. It proved to be a lesson learned, however, as the *Kriegsmarine* demonstrated a quarter of a century later.

Kahn tells a long and technically demanding story with all the skills of a professional journalist. He deftly mixes intricate accounts of the workings of the Enigma machines themselves and their accompanying codes with useful pen portraits of the principal characters involved. It is only in his descriptions of Royal Navy operations that unfamiliarity with British naval terminology occasionally grates – but this is a small shortcoming in what is otherwise an absorbing and thoroughly well documented account. Kahn avoids making extravagant claims for the significance of this exclusively British achievement, arguing that the capturing of the code books 'greatly helped' the winning of the Battle of the Atlantic and thus the war itself, but, significantly, contending that if the codes had not been solved the war would not have been lost altogether, only prolonged with the loss of even more lives.

Jon Wise

Siegfried Breyer and Miroslaw Skwiot
German Capital Ships of the Second World War
Seaforth Publishing; hardback, 432 pages, many B&W photos and line drawings; price £45.00.
ISBN 978-184832-143-4

Produced by two of the most respected authorities on the *Kriegsmarine*, this large format, high-quality book lives up to its subtitle of being 'the ultimate photograph album' of Germany's capital ships of that era.

The book commences with a brief overview of German capital ship development from the end of the First World War. This is followed by separate chapters on the *Panzerschiffe* and on the *Scharnhorst* and *Bismarck* classes. Within these chapters, each individual ship is afforded its own, lengthy subsection of largely photographic content laid out in broadly chronological order. There is also a brief appendix on the never-completed aircraft carrier *Graf Zeppelin*.

Whilst *German Capital Ships of the Second World War* has sufficient text to provide a satisfactory context for the photographic content, it does not pretend to provide either a detailed technical or operational history of the ships that it illustrates. This is a sensible approach, as it provides sufficient space for the photographic material to be used to best effect. Images have been reproduced to a large size and as clearly as the originals allow, with many occupying a full page or more. The result is visually stunning, allowing even small details to be observed. Although many of the photographs have been published before elsewhere, the combined number and quality of images presented is probably unprecedented.

There are, nevertheless, some imbalances in the photographic coverage. For example, the 44-page section on the first *Panzerschiff*, *Deutschland* (later *Lützow*), devotes around fourteen pages to her construction, trials and commissioning but only six to her wartime service. A similar, if less-pronounced bias is evident in the sections illustrating other ships of this type. In broader terms, there seems to be more limited use of photographs from the later period of the war despite the increasing availability of material for this period from private collections. The book is, perhaps, strongest when dealing with the battleships *Bismarck* and *Tirpitz*. No fewer than 120 pages are allocated to recording the two sister-ships' short careers and the result is both balanced and comprehensive.

Other minor criticisms include one or two questionable statements in the text – for example, the assertion on p.317 that *Bismarck*'s war diary and film footage were picked up by U-boat prior to her final destruction. Although the author has attempted to provide dates for most of the images, which will be of considerable benefit to naval historian and ship modeller alike, more detail could have been provided in some of the captions. However, these are minor complaints about an interesting and well-produced book that provides a fitting memorial to the work of Herr Breyer, who regrettably died just before it was published.

Conrad Waters

Capt. Robert B. Workman Jr., USCG (Ret.)
Float Planes and Flying Boats: The U.S. Coast Guard and Early Naval Aviation
Naval Institute Press, 2012; hardback, 324 pages, illustrated with 270 B&W photographs; price £27.50/$41.95.
ISBN 978 1 61251 107 8

This is a history of early naval aviation in the United States, during which time the US Navy, Marines and Coast Guard fought to get their respective aviation elements properly established. In the case of the USCGS a variety of hurdles had to be overcome before it was able to establish its air arm as the very useful service of the present day.

The author has chosen to illustrate the story with the lives of the early pioneers who made it all possible, and finishes his book with the death of one of the most important of these, Cdr. Elmer F Stone, Coast Guard Aviator Number One. Despite his key involvement in early aviation developments, Stone is largely unknown on both sides of the Atlantic. His reputation also seems to have suffered by virtue of establishing flying pay for the USCGS, much to the dismay of the non-flyers!

Each of the book's eleven chapters is on a clearly defined topic. An account of the early days is followed by the growth brought about by the First World War (when the Coast Guard was put under Navy command), then the transatlantic flight of the NC flying boats, followed by separate chapters on the Naval Aviation Test Organisation, Marine Corps and USCG developments to 1938, carriers and catapults and finally the growth of the USCGS air arm.

This format does have the disadvantage that the reader is forced to jump backwards and forwards in time during the course of the book and it also necessitates some repetition of facts and events, but is actually eminently sensible. There are a few other idiosyncrasies that need to be accepted: rank titles and abbreviations are capitalised throughout as in some other US publications, and short sentences are sometimes interjected into the prose as if the author were addressing the reader directly.

Cdr. Stone was clearly a very farsighted individual who set up acceptance testing for all three services, designed a gunpowder catapult and then a carrier catapult, designed an early form of arrester gear and was specifically requested by the US Navy to evolve these into service equipment for *Saratoga* and *Lexington* during their conversion. The Navy also requested his presence on the meticulously planned transatlantic flight of the three NC flying boats in May 1919, his own aircraft being the only one to reach the Azores before flying on to Europe and England. Surprisingly, Alcock and Brown's successful non-stop transatlantic flight only a month later is omitted from a narrative that carefully notes each of the other competitors' failures in the race to be first.

The chapters on the growth of the services include a comprehensive guide to the great variety of aircraft used by the USCG in these early days, not a few being seized from drug or rum runners. Well illustrated where photographs exist, these and other chapters also include facsimiles of important documents where appropriate alongside the occasional copy of an original drawing of an aircraft.

This is an important book which for the reviewer filled in quite a few of the blanks about early naval aviation. It also brings home the difficulties faced by early flyers in staying in the air or, in the case of the aircraft of the title, just getting airborne! More than once the reproductions of test reports simply state 'will not take off' in a certain wind or sea state.

W B Davies

Edward C Raymer
Descent into Darkness

US Naval Institute Press, 2012;
paperback, 214 pages, illustrated with B&W photographs;
price $18.95/£11.99.
ISBN 978-1-59114-724-4

This book tells the story of the wartime service of one of the US Navy's salvage divers who worked on the wrecks of the ships sunk in the Japanese attack on Pearl Harbor. Edward Raymer, like so many, had originally joined the Navy simply because it represented a proper job during the Depression; after failing in his initial application to train as an airman he became a diver.

Unusually, rather than adhering to a strictly chronological treatment, Raymer begins his narrative with a dramatic, deeply unsettling account of getting trapped inside the sunken USS *Arizona*, surrounded by the disintegrating corpses of her crew, his air supply running out, panic and terror taking hold as he struggles to escape. He survived this particular ordeal, but some of his comrades were less fortunate. The official record tends to gloss over the hazardous and unpleasant nature of these activities, and Raymer's declared purpose in writing this memoir is to set the record straight. Raymer writes well, and his description of Pearl Harbor immediately after the attack has a real immediacy about it, although he does tend to assume a certain level of knowledge of diving and underwater working techniques on the part of the reader.

The majority of the divers' early work was connected with the removal of useful, easily removable or repairable fittings such as guns and ammunition, as well as the occasional piece of unexploded enemy ordnance. It was carried out in conditions of often complete darkness with the divers, on the ends of their long air lines and communications chords, working entirely by touch, from memorised plans, or by way of instructions from the surface. Later on came the task of repairing enough of the damage for the ships to be raised prior to going into dock for full repairs. In the case of the *Nevada* this was relatively straightforward, but the extent of the damage sustained by the *West Virginia* leaves the reader amazed that salvage was even attempted, let alone carried out successfully.

Another key job was the recovery of the bodies of crewmen, which was undertaken as a result of political pressure from Washington but had to be abandoned in the face of the sheer awfulness of the task. Considerable time and effort was also expended on salvaging the personal possessions of one particular officer from the capsized USS *Utah*, together with the ship's safe. Raymer and his colleagues were not above such clandestine activities themselves, eventually resulting in one of them being arrested and charged by the FBI.

After another application for flying training was rejected Raymer volunteered for front-line service in the South Pacific, and soon found himself amidst the hell-in-paradise of the Guadalcanal campaign. Here he worked repairing ships damaged in action, survived the sinking of his own vessel, the salvage tug *Seminole*, by Japanese destroyers, went on to serve in the horrific land campaign, and was finally invalided home after contracting malaria.

While Raymer never openly dwells on it, he grows up a lot during the course of the events described in this book: the brash, self-confident young man of 1941 is slowly tempered by experience, from witnessing the deaths of friends and comrades to meeting the First Lady and finding her not to be the monster that his staunch Republican upbringing had led him to believe. He becomes a wiser, more reflective soul, as likely to ponder on the beauty of the undersea world as to indulge in foul-mouthed joking with his fellow divers.

This is an impressive book written by an impressive individual.

Stephen Dent

Norman Friedman
Naval Weapons of World War One: Guns, Torpedoes, Mines and ASW Weapons of All Nations
Seaforth Publishing, 2011; large format hardback, 408 pages, copiously illustrated with many plans and B&W photographs; price £45.00.
ISBN 978-1-84832-100-7

We have had to wait a long time for this 'prequel' to John Campbell's classic encyclopaedia *Naval Weapons of World War Two*. It has been well worth the wait; Norman Friedman's new volume is everything we would have expected of the author: comprehensive, authoritative and exhaustively researched.

The starting point for the book was a manuscript left by John Campbell. However, this proved to be incomplete; the only surviving material was that covering British naval guns and German guns of 17cm calibre and above. Dr. Friedman has therefore had to delve deep into the various national archives in order to complete his study. He has also put his own stamp on the book by adopting a revised structure in which the weaponry is divided into categories, and only then subdivided by nationality. This enables him to introduce each section by writing in general terms about the developments in that category of weapon. The author has also broadened the scope by including lengthy sections on tactics. This has led him into areas which are controversial – there is, for example, still considerable debate among scholars about the ranges at which the British and (more particularly) the German fleets intended i) to open fire, and ii) to settle on a parallel course to fight their respective battle lines – and there will inevitably be those who disagree with some of the author's conclusions. However, the benefit of this broader approach becomes readily apparent in the sections on torpedoes and mines, where tactical (and, in the case of mines, even strategic) considerations effectively drove development. For those of us who grew up believing that the war at sea in 1914-18 was centred on large fleets of dreadnoughts which rarely caught more than a fleeting glimpse of each other, these sections are a revelation. The comprehensive introduction to the 'Guns' section has an overview of naval gun construction and shell/propellant development which is also notable for its insights and clarity.

Much of the naval hardware featured is illustrated by plans and photographs. In a departure from Campbell's earlier book the author has used plans from original documents and plates from weapons manuals alongside drawings and schemas from well-known and authoritative artists such as Ian Buxton, Bill Jurens and Erwin Sieche. All are beautifully presented. Much of the labelling on the original plans is too small to be legible, but the author has generally been able to compensate for this by providing lengthy informative captions.

The book is not without its faults, and the sections on some navies are inevitably stronger than others. The section on French Guns is littered with spelling errors, and while the descriptions of the early major-calibre guns cannot be faulted, the author's attempts to avoid duplication in his description of the turrets of the later guns gets him into serious difficulties. There are confusions and inaccuracies in the descriptions of both the 30cm and the 24cm turrets of the *Danton* class, and on p.218 the author states that two of the six 24cm turrets were on the centreline(!).

These errors are unfortunate, and it is to be hoped that they will be corrected if/when the book is reprinted. They are untypical of the book, which is clearly the result of considerable careful and detailed research, despite the uneven quality (and quantity) of the data available from the various national archives. When I first opened it, I had intended to read just sufficient to enable me to write a fair and detailed review; I ended up reading most of the book. For a work purporting to be an 'encyclopaedia' of weapons systems, this is praise indeed.

John Jordan

Jim Bresnahan (ed.)
Refighting the Pacific War; An Alternative History of World War II
Naval Institute Press, Annapolis, 2011; hardback, 275 pages, illustrated; price £18.99/$29.95.
ISBN 978 1 59114 079 5

This is not a book to read if you're expecting a counterfactual account of the Pacific War, with the Japanese storming ashore on Oahu after a third air strike on Pearl Harbor, or sinking the US carriers at Midway. Jim Bresnahan is a broadcast journalist who has previously authored 'what-ifs' on the American Civil War and American baseball. He also has a self-confessed fascination with the Pacific War, and in this book he aims to try to resolve some of the questions he has often asked himself about the latter: 'Was the war inevitable?' and 'Could Japan have won it?'.

In his preface Bresnahan states that '...the key to counterfactual history is maintaining a short-term focus...' and this is how he has tackled his subject. There is no detailed narrative of the Pacific war; instead, he has limited himself exclusively to American naval actions, with no attempt to cover actions involving British, Commonwealth, and Netherlands forces. Rather than attempting to construct a completely alternative narrative for the war, he has instead set a series of questions, which are addressed by a panel of historians, writers and experts. There are some well known names, such as HP Willmott, Anthony Tulley and Jon Parshall, as well as less well-known contributors such as 'Dusty' Kleiss, a dive bomber pilot at Midway, and Sumner Whitten, a USMC Second Lieutenant who fought on Guadalcanal.

The book starts with an interesting and detailed introduction written by Vice Admiral Yodi Koda of the JMSDF, describing Japanese pre-war naval aspirations and giving an outline of the war. Following this, ten chapters take the reader though the well-known timeline of the Pacific war. Each consists of short, narrative sections interposed with questions. So for example, 'December 7: Pearl Harbor' has a page-length narrative, setting the scene, before asking the first question: 'What if the Americans had heeded potential warnings in advance of the Pearl Harbor raid?' This is followed by short sections written by four of the contributors, in this case Donald Goldstein (himself the author of books on Pearl Harbor), Jon Parshall (co-author of *Shattered Sword*, about the Battle of Midway), Keith Allen (a defence analyst and amateur historian of WWII) and Stephen D Regan (ex-US Navy, university professor and author), in which they give their own answers and the reasons behind their conclusions. Subsequent short narratives and questions follow, for example: 'What if the Japanese had targeted oil tanks and ship repair facilities in their second wave or had launched a third wave to hit those targets?', 'What if the US carriers had been at Pearl Harbor on December 7', and 'What if Nimitz had been C-in-C, Pacific Fleet before December 7? What if someone else had been appointed C-in-C, Pacific Fleet after December 7?' Each chapter in the book follows the same style. The result isn't quite what some readers may expect from an 'alternative narrative history' of the Pacific war, but it does provide diverse answers to specific questions.

Initially sceptical, I found that the more I read the more I began to enjoy the contributors' varying opinions, especially when they disagreed in their interpretations and answers. Many of the contributions are genuinely interesting and thought-provoking, and may inspire or challenge readers' own opinions on key issues. However, I would have preferred a more complete narrative, and felt that Bresnahan's criteria had limited the scope of his work. Bresnahan does not attempt to provide a link between the sections, and stands back from the conclusions and interpretations of his contributors. On a more practical note, some maps would have been useful, and possibly some photographs that were more closely linked to the text.

Despite these limitations, the book has much in its favour, and is inexpensive enough to recommend to anyone wishing to extend their library of books on the war in the Pacific.

Andy Field

Wolfgang Hirschfeld and Geoffrey Brooks
Hirschfeld; The Secret Diary of a U-boat
Frontline Books, this edition 2011; paperback, 255 pages, 21 B&W photographs and one line drawing; price £12.99.
ISBN 978 1 84832 622 4

A detailed account of life aboard a U-boat during the Second World War first published in 1996, this edition includes additional material released on the death of the German author, an NCO during the period 1940–1946. Much is made of the fact that keeping a diary was a serious crime in Nazi Germany and whilst the result is an immediacy of narrative, the author's motives for keeping such a clandestine document go largely unexplored. Geoffrey Brooks also attempts to make something out of the apparent need of Herr Hirschfeld to obtain 'clearance' for the release of some information.

The book comprises ten chapters progressing through to the war's end, followed by an appendix relating specifically to *U 234* and its cargo; there are comprehensive chapter notes and an index. It is an extremely readable book, moving swiftly through the author's naval career, first above water and then with the U-boat arm of the *Kriegsmarine*. The main body covers the deployments of *U 109* (Type IXB), its successes and its failures. There is both detachment and humanity in the writing, a dilemma that most submariners must have suffered from when presented with the human cost of their victories. The author's feelings for his fellow NCOs are often warmer than for the officers, and it would have been interesting to have an account of how the survivors amongst his colleagues managed to rebuild their lives after the war. As with other U-boat memoirs, Hirschfeld's account demonstrates how the *Kriegsmarine* tried to maintain a training and advancement programme for the individual similar to that in place in peacetime right up to the end, despite increasingly fraught circumstances,

The final part of the book deals with the author's service in *U 234*, a cargo-carrying Type XB (a converted minelayer). This vessel set out for Japan just before the end of the war and finally surrendered to the Americans. The cargo comprised a consignment of radio-active material, a crated Me 262 jet fighter, and various other items of war materiel intended for Japan, and was accompanied by two Japanese Officers and eight German specialists. When the author found a Japanese officer labelling the boxes of radio-active material *U 235* and queried this, he was informed that they were originally intended as cargo for *U 235*, but that she was no longer going to Japan; this resulted in speculation that *U 235* was the number assigned to a mystery boat intended for export. However, the reviewer suspects that the Japanese officer may have simply been describing the contents of the boxes (U-235 is an isotope of uranium), and possibly having a joke at the expense of the author in the process. Interestingly, whilst the uranium was certainly of interest to the American Manhatten Project, and its presence is recorded in the report on the boat's cargo, no mention was made of the jet fighter. Despite the speculation of the author on the possible reasons for this omission, as well as his apparent need to refer to some higher authority before publication, no plausible evidence is presented for any conspiracy to hide the truth.

W B Davies

Bryan Perrett
North Sea Battlegound: The War at Sea 1914-1918
Pen & Sword Maritime, Barnsley, Yorkshire, 2011; hardback, 152 pages, illustrated with B&W photographs, maps and diagrams; price £19.99.
ISBN 978-1848-844506

The recipe for this volume is clear: digest a number of existing books, including several on the tip-and-run raids on East Coast ports, simplify into a number of 'set pieces' and publish. The result is a brisk canter through the basics of the North Sea war, and an account which is particularly idiosyncratic in its coverage. There are two pages on the first Battle of Heligoland Bight, three pages for Dogger Bank, seven on Jutland, and twenty on the shelling of Scarborough, Whitby and Hartlepool. Two whole chapters are devoted to the Zeppelin and Gotha raids on England.

The British blockade was at the heart of North Sea operations but its legality, its effect on neutral states and the activities of its Prize Courts are not probed. Proper space has been allocated to British seaplane and aircraft carriers, to the activities of British submarines in transit to the Baltic and to Sir Reginald (not Francis!) Bacon's monitors off the Belgian coast. The consequences of full, unrestricted submarine warfare from February 1917 are hardly mentioned. The tragic death of Captain Fryatt surely merits a place. Claims to 'provide complete operational background information within the area' are misleading, as Room 40, which provided invaluable advance information of German movements (and often-ignored operational advice), receives cursory attention.

Checking and proof reading are poor. The irritating absence throughout of the umlaut or the equivalent additional 'e' means that names like *König* and *Grosser Kurfürst* are consistently misspelt (and an erroneous comma makes two battleships out of the latter). Beatty became First Sea Lord in 1919, not 1921, and the rank of Grand Admiral did indeed have a Royal Navy equivalent: Admiral of the Fleet. The author appears to be unaware that the large British light cruisers *Courageous* and *Glorious* mounted 15in (38cm) guns. This book cannot be recommended.

Ian Sturton

Dale E Knutsen
Strike Warfare in the 21st Century
Naval Institute Press, Annapolis MD, 2012; hardback, 208 pages, 30 illustrations; price $27.95 / £17.50.
ISBN 978-1-61251-083-5

A number of publications give details of the ships, submarines and aircraft that make up the contemporary US Navy, but few of them list the range of strike weapons that these platforms are capable of embarking. Fewer still explain in layman's terms not only how those weapons are used but also how they are procured and designated. This concise book, written by an expert who worked at the USN airborne weapons establishment at China Lake for thirty years, fills that gap rather well.

The author discusses target types ashore and afloat, explains their defences and the types of weapon needed to strike them, describing the full range from 'dumb' bombs to the most advanced stand-off guided munitions and explaining the advantages and disadvantages of each. Airborne strike support measures such as electronic warfare and decoys are also discussed. The book is well indexed and there are a number of useful appendices which contain a glossary of terms, design criteria, weapon characteristics and places where additional information can be found. The text is clearly written with the addition of flow diagrams to explain development projects, drawings of the various weapons and an example of a typical strike operation.

This is a thoroughly professional but readable book that explains the US Navy's current arsenal of strike weapons and their specialised uses. I thoroughly recommend it to anyone with an interest in contemporary naval operations.

David Hobbs

Maurice Cocker
Royal Navy Destroyers: 1893 to the Present Day
The History Press, this edition 2011; softback, 159 pages, illustrated with 199 B&W photographs and 15 line drawings; price £16.99.
ISBN 978 0 7524 6159 5

A new edition of a book first published in 1981, this book sets out to catalogue all the vessels in the Royal Navy to which the designation 'destroyer' has been applied, starting with the earliest right up to the latest Type 45s. It comprises a group of introductory notes, the main body of the catalogue, seven appendices, a bibliography and an index of ships names. The main body of the text addresses each class of destroyer in chronological sequence. There are complete data tables, together with an appropriate picture (or pictures) and service notes. The appendices cover such topics as destroyer armament, builders, losses and details of vessels sunk by destroyers.

Much of this information is presented in a straightforward manner. However, some of the phraseology is idiosyncratic, to say the least, and there are a few serious errors. A flotilla of destroyers is described as a 'school', and the term 'utility classes' the author ascribes to the emergency flotillas of the Second World War may be technically accurate, but is not custom and practice. He further states that the Batch III Type 42 is 'larger in all respects than the Type 45' and that the Sea Dart magazine was expanded to hold double the number of missiles – in reality the expansion comprised empty steel work only.

As a catalogue of destroyers this book has some value, but the vagaries of some sections means it should never stand alone as a definituve reference.

W B Davies

John Gordon
Fighting for MacArthur
Naval Institute Press, 2011; hardback, 371 pages, illustrated with B&W photographs and maps; price $32.95.
ISBN 978 1 61251 062 0

This fine book tells the story of the part played by the US Navy and Marine Corps in the desperate defence of the Philippines during 1941-42, an undeservedly little known aspect of a famous, doomed campaign. The author contends that this comparative obscurity is down, at least in part, to a deliberate campaign by the titular general and his supporters to deflect attention from his own disastrous performance. The evidence presented here may not be quite as conclusive as Gordon would like us to believe, nevertheless the tale he tells is one of ingenuity, determination and tremendous courage against near impossible odds; moreover he tells it very well.

MacArthur, despite his prominent position in the book's title, actually features only intermittently, not least because he seems to have had little time for, and equally little to do with, his naval comrades in arms. (He was also evacuated from the Philippines long before the end of the campaign; inter-service co-operation seems to have significantly improved once he was gone.) On the occasions when the general does make an appearance Gordon misses few opportunities to stick the boot into this cherished national icon, portraying him as naive, out of touch, delusional, relentlessly self-publicising, arrogant, irrational, vindictive and possibly even a bit mad. MacArthur has never been an historical favourite of this reviewer; nevertheless while the Philippines would probably still have fallen even without his blundering, objectivity is lacking here, perhaps because of the author's desire to give the USN and Marine Corps their undoubted due. Gordon does not, however, hold back from criticising the over-cautious use of naval forces and the rather un-American overall defensive strategy in general.

There is a somewhat narrow focus on events in and around Manila Bay. On the one hand this serves to emphasise how isolated the defenders of Corregidor and Bataan were, but it can also on occasion leave any reader without a thorough background knowledge feeling a little lost. Gordon is also far more interested in facts than in giving a sense what it was actually like. This is a book full of dates and places, the names of units and of individuals, rather than the impressions of the participants; for example, the reader really doesn't get much idea of the realities of jungle warfare when experienced by sailors who had perhaps trained in it for just a couple of days.

Despite all the advantages that the Japanese held, their initial landings on Bataan were a disaster, and those on Corregidor very nearly had the same result. In both cases their casualties were horrific. The US Marine Corps units and the extemporised ones of Navy personnel acquitted themselves impressively alongside regular US and Filipino forces units. During the former landings, in a foretaste of the grimness of the coming years, just six men out of some three hundred were captured, the remainder of the isolated, confused invaders being killed in action or choosing suicide. Ironically Japanese records showed that the complete inexperience of the USN men when it came to jungle warfare produced amongst their foes the impression of special units made up of personnel possessing a near-suicidal level of bravery.

The famous 'concrete battleship', Fort Drum, with its pair of 14in gun turrets, was actually manned by the army, and as such appears relatively little here, though it seems to have been the most successful of the defences of Manila Bay, harrying the invaders with near impunity and only finally surrendering when ordered to at the conclusion of the campaign.

As the story progresses it becomes more and more about the land campaign, as the small collection of gunboats, PT boats, minesweepers and armed yachts are one by one sunk, irreparably damaged, run out of fuel and/or ammunition or, finally, scuttled. The ships and their crews were regarded as expendable – even before Pearl Harbor some had been ordered to in effect go looking for trouble (which fortunately for them they didn't find).

Gordon keeps the narrative ripping along. As the tale unfolds it is hard to avoid a growing sense of the terrible, shocking fruitlessness of it all. It was, of course, a story which would be repeated, albeit in reverse, time and time again across the Pacific in the years to follow.

Stephen Dent

Jim Crossley
The Hidden Threat:
The Story of Mines and Minesweeping by the Royal Navy in World War I
Pen & Sword Maritime, 2011; hardback, 165 pages, 8 photographs, 16 figures and 4 charts; price £19.99.
ISBN 978-1 84884-272-4

This book, which includes a chapter on the Gallipoli campaign, is a short history of minesweeping and of minelaying, both offensive and defensive, by the Royal Navy during the First World War. The author declares that 'British mines and minesweeping techniques had to be rapidly developed from a shamefully poor base' and that the mine menace was eventually contained by 'a courageous body of fishermen and a few determined naval officers' He further states that in 1914 the British stock of mines – about 4,000 – was 'pathetically small' and that the mines tended to drag their moorings and often failed to explode, though other sources suggest that they were liable to explode prematurely; most were of the Naval Spherical type, which were fired by a rotating arm. In contrast, Germany is credited with having a large (though unquantified) stock of efficient mines (fired by Hertz horns) and with having immediately mounted an 'aggressive mine-laying offensive'. Britain did not have her own Hertz-horn mine, the H.II, in quantity production until the end of 1917.

As the dominant naval power, before the war Britain had had no reason to advance mining technology and she had tried to have mines banned by the 1907 Hague Conference. However, after their successful use in the Russo-Japanese War, the Royal Navy developed the Naval Spherical Mine, while following a favourable report by Lord Charles Beresford in 1907, the Royal Naval Minesweeping Reserve was established; as soon as war was declared, some 200 fishing vessels were enrolled in the RNMR. At the beginning of hostilities, there was concern in both Britain and Germany that extensive minelaying would seriously impede the freedom of movement of the battlefleets, as neither country had done much to equip its navy with special vessels for mine warfare. Both would continue to rely on merchant and fishing vessels, and both only began to build specialist naval vessels for minelaying (these included submarines) and for fleet minesweeping after the war had started. Germany had fitted most of her more modern light cruisers for minelaying, but this book gives only a single example of one being used for this purpose while, at Jutland, the only vessel carrying mines was the British *Abdiel*. The initial German minelaying offensive, though not without effect, laid only 840 mines by the end of 1914. As for the often-derided British mines, *Seydlitz* and *Ostfriesland* were severely damaged by Naval Spherical Mines in 1916:

and in 1917 mines were the most effective weapons in the ever-increasing war against the U-boats.

Thus there are grounds for suspecting that Crossley's sweeping criticisms of British mine warfare may be exaggerated. Regrettably, he provides no bibliography, let alone footnotes, so the reader had no means of knowing how his conclusions were reached. It is hard to understand why either the author or publisher begrudged the time or effort to include one; either way, it is a great pity. The text is interspersed with a good number of vivid personal accounts of the mining war. However, the rest of the book will really satisfy only those readers who are prepared to accept its conclusions without question and have no interest in pursuing its subject any further.

John Brooks

Shawn T Grimes
Strategy and War Planning in the British Navy, 1887-1918
The Boydell Press, 2012; hardback, 278 pages, 3 maps, extensive bibliography & footnotes; price £65.00.
ISBN 978-1-84383-698-8

Based on the author's doctoral dissertation, this book aims to redress the gap in the historiography of the Royal Navy's strategic development by analysing naval planning during the years 1887-1918. Grimes attempts to show: that the Service's planning followed a discernible developmental path which originated with the Naval Intelligence Department's work in the late 1880s, when the potential threat to British interests was posed by an alliance between France and Russia; that the plans developed during the period 1887-1905 influenced later plans for a potential war against Germany; and that planning after 1902 was a reaction both to the European balance of power struggles and to questions surrounding Scandinavian neutrality and the *status quo* in the Baltic.

Two personalities stand out in this account: Admiral John ('Jacky') Fisher, who was First Sea Lord 1904-10 and then again from late 1914 until the summer of 1915; and Admiral George Ballard, Assistant Director and later Director of the Naval Intelligence Department and a key figure in much of the pre-war planning.

Fisher, mercurial and dynamic – his distinctive written memos are a heady mix of poorly-formed sentences and CAPITALS – believed that the Navy should utilise its numerical and qualitative superiority to take the offensive to the enemy in any future European war, and that the Army should be merely the 'Navy's projectile', causing havoc wherever it could be usefully landed. He deplored the 'continental' strategy which was gaining increased momentum towards the end of his first tenure, and his choice of Admiral Arthur Wilson as his successor was dictated not by the latter's intellectual capabilities – and certainly not his 'people skills' – but, according to Grimes, because Wilson could be trusted to keep the Navy's plans from the Committee of Imperial Defence (CID)! In the event it was Wilson's conspicuous failure to present the Navy's case at the CID meeting on 23 August 1911 which fostered the belief that the Admiralty lacked credible war plans: even the normally mild-mannered Prime Minister, Herbert Asquith, described the Navy's strategy as 'puerile'.

Ballard, on the other hand, is viewed as a very capable officer with an excellent grasp of the strategic realities who was capable of putting a brake on some of Fisher's wilder schemes. Fisher appointed him Director of Naval Intelligence in 1906 and accorded him all the powers necessary to draw up full sets of alternative plans for a naval war against Germany. The plans developed during 1906-07 were to become the basis of the Navy's future planning; the war plans formally adopted in late 1912 repeated virtually every detail of the Ballard Committee's Plan A/A1, which prescribed a distant blockade comprising a northern patrol line of armoured cruisers between the Orkneys & Shetlands and Norway and the Norwegian coast, together with destroyer/submarine patrols to block the Dover Straits, support for the northern cordon being furnished by a main British fleet based in Scotland while the southern line was supported by the Channel Fleet.

Grimes details the close relationship between war plans and manoeuvres during the period, and the influence of the Naval War College course and the officers associated with it. He also makes some interesting and informed observations about the extent to which the plans influenced the Navy's construction programmes, and in particular the characteristics of the destroyers and 'scouts' built during the early 1900s. Although he does not decry the creation of a fully-fledged naval staff during the immediate pre-war period, he holds strongly to the view that it was in a number of respects inferior as a planning tool to the Department of Naval Intelligence which had until 1912 been largely responsible for the Navy's strategy. If there is a criticism to be made of Grimes account, it is that he is perhaps too indulgent towards Fisher, who not only regarded the Navy's strategy as the Navy's private business but who, during his second coming, attempted to subvert the Navy's entire 1915 construction programme in order to provide the necessary ships for his hare-brained and implausible 'Baltic Project'.

This book, while expensive, provides a valuable complement to other recently published works on the same period. The author's case is well argued and backed with solid evidence. There is no illustration beyond the three maps at the front, but these are clear, well-drawn and appropriate. The text is printed clearly on good-quality paper, and the integration of the jacket with the hard cover is a welcome step.

John Jordan

Marek Krzysztalowicz
Type VII: Germany's Most Successful U-boats
Seaforth Publishing, 2011; hardback, 256 pages, over 320 photographs, 100 3D computer graphics images; price £40.00
ISBN 978-1-84832-141-0

This book was originally published in two parts in the author's native Poland but has now appeared in the UK in a single large volume. The Type VII U-boat has received extensive coverage over the years, but what really sets this book apart from its competitors is the astonishing collection of photographs and illustrations, including many three-dimensional line diagrams and computer renderings. The page format (approximately 300mm x 250mm) allows the visuals to be reproduced at a size and scale which makes them that much more useful as reference images for artists, illustrators and modellers.

The first section covers the seven different variants of the Type VII (Type VIIA to VIIF plus the Type VIIC/41) and includes many technical details, drawings and photographs of each variant. The second section details the production of the Type VII, including specifics of the different construction yards and the manufacturing process. The third section explores the various compartments of the Type VII and looks in detail at the technological components: hydrophones, engines, sonar, periscopes, radar, snorkel, guns and torpedoes. As with the first section, the text is complemented by some excellent technical diagrams and photographs.

The fourth section of the book – Volume II of the original publication – is the largest, and gives an operational history of the Type VII boats from the beginning of the war until the German surrender. It includes a selective year-by-year account of the U-boat war and ends with a table which shows where and how each Type VII boat was lost.

The addition of two sections containing three-dimensional drawings of the Type VII, firstly of the early models and then of the Type VIIC/41, provides a fine visual reference for modellers and includes a fascinating photographic tour of *U-995*, the only Type VIIC/41 to survive to this day and which is now preserved as a museum at Laboe, Germany.

Marek Krzysztalowicz clearly knows his subject; he writes well and the illustrations – many previously unpublished – have been carefully chosen; The large 3D diagrams help to show the different boats from a variety of angles and are a very useful visual reference alongside the photographs. The book provides an excellent introduction to this most iconic U-boat type, and the unusual wealth of visual sources are sufficient to make it a worthwhile investment.

John Peterson

Ken W. Sayers
Uncommon Warriors: 200 Years of the Most Unusual American Naval Vessels
Naval Institute Press, 2012; hardback, 292 pages, 50 B&W photographs; price £27.95.
ISBN 978-1-59114-760-2

It is often easy to forget that the success of a navy is as much attributable to the support it receives as it is to the fighting power of the front-line combat vessels. Over the years the United States Navy has utilised a vast assortment of craft to fill niche support roles. Classified as Auxiliary, General (AG) or Miscellaneous, Unclassified (IX) it is this rich assortment of ships that are the subject of *Uncommon Warriors*, a unique study by former naval officer Ken Sayers. The topic is inevitably broad, with the classification covering a range of vessels: some like the *Glomar Explorer* developed for a single specific task; others that found new uses when no longer capable of fulfilling their original purpose, often frugally converted to make use of solid hulls for new roles very different from those for which they were designed.

Following an informative introduction in which Sayers explores the origins of hull classification in 1920, the book is split into two main parts. The main section is the most interesting, being given over to the concise histories of 46 of the most interesting vessels, including for example *Wolverine* and *Sable*, two coal-fired Great Lakes paddle steamers converted into training aircraft carriers on Lake Michigan during the Second World War. The final third of the book consists of a comprehensive list of the 470 vessels that have held an AG or IX classification, with each ship being provided with a brief bulleted synopsis of its history.

Much of the book's value comes in the detail of the secondary careers of major units, often glossed over in contemporary reference works. One example is the Spanish unprotected cruiser *Reina Mercedes*, which was salvaged by the US Navy in 1899 following the Spanish-American War and served as station ship *IX-25* at Annapolis. Her main function was to quarter the enlisted personnel assigned to the Naval Academy; she also provided a home for the Commander of the naval station and his family before being finally decommissioned and broken up in 1957.

Sayers adopts a chatty, colloquial style which makes for an easy read but eventually becomes quite irritating. Whilst this collection of operational histories is undeniably informative, the superficial approach and lack of technical information is disappointing. Primary sources seem to have been little consulted, the book drawing heavily on the *Dictionary of American Naval Fighting Ships* and official ship websites, and there is little insight into the background and decision-making processes which underpinned the conversions. However, whilst the style of writing will not be to everyone's taste, the book does provide an unusual perspective on the history of the US Navy.

Phil Russell

Conrad Waters, Ed.
Seaforth World Naval Review 2013
Seaforth Publishing, 2012; hardback, 192 pages, many B&W and colour photographs, line drawings; price £30.00
ISBN 9781848321564

This is the fourth year of the publication of Seaforth's *World Naval Review*. Editor Conrad Waters is to be congratulated for maintaining exemplary standards throughout, despite having to work to an extremely tight time-scale in his efforts to keep the Review right up to date. The layouts, aided by some stunning photographs on practically every page, complement the overall quality evident in the text.

As in previous annuals, the editor's introduction is followed by sections entitled 'World Fleet Reviews', 'Significant Ships' and 'Technological Reviews'. What emerges from this year's review of the fleets is the progressive decline in warship numbers in the old Western European navies, the irresistible rise of Indian and Chinese naval power, the struggle by Russia to regenerate its fleet and regain its status, and some 'downsizing' in the mighty US Navy.

An interesting trend can be detected in several articles, namely that many smaller navies are developing their 'blue-water' capabilities in order to undertake expeditionary missions, for example in support of anti-piracy patrols off the Horn of Africa and in the Red Sea. Inherent in what Geoffrey Till has described as the 'post-modern' navy is the understanding that single countries with limited defence budgets cannot solve their security problems alone and that a collective effort is required. Of equal, topical relevance is the rise in importance of Ballistic Missile Defence. This capability, which is mentioned in passing by several contributors, is placed in context during the course of a short but excellent article on the subject by Norman Friedman.

It is in the nature of an annual publication about navies that much will remain the same year on year; warships take time to build and enjoy a comparatively long 'shelf-life'. The structure of the annual has likewise remained largely unaltered over the past four years; the contributors are by and large the same individuals, and there is a danger that their approach to their subject matter may become predictable. The other potential problem with this otherwise excellent publication lies in the very nature of the subject matter. Most of the 'significant ships' are either in the process of building or in the very early stages of their service. Inevitably, the contributors have to draw heavily on the evidence of official bulletins, defence journals, press releases and internet articles. There is therefore a real danger of the text reading like a glossy promotional handout provided by a navy or construction company.

These, however, are minor complaints given the generally high standards of the publication. The relevance of navies to the prosperity and ambitions of the emerging as well as the established countries of the world is evident on every page of this annual. The *Seaforth World Naval Review* fulfils an important function in faithfully presenting a genuinely world-wide perspective on the subject. Long may it continue to do so.

Jon Wise

Robert C Stern
The US Navy and the War in Europe
Seaforth Publishing, 2012; hardback, 320 pages, many B&W photographs, appendices; price £35.00.
ISBN 978-1-84832-082-6

The US Navy's campaigns in the Pacific have been exhaustively chronicled by naval historians, but its efforts in the Atlantic have received little attention. This book aims to redress that balance, and in the process turns up a surprising amount of new information.

Robert C Stern writes well, and his observations on the development of the 'special relationship' between Britain and the USA are particularly astute. As is well known, it was Churchill who made all the running in the period between the fall of France in June 1940 and the formal entry of the United States into the war in December 1941. The despatch of Harry Hopkins, a trusted friend of the American President, to London in January 1941, was neither expected nor anticipated by the British. Stern makes it clear that Hopkins' initial (and unspoken) mission was to assess the likelihood of Britain's survival with a view to informing any response Roosevelt might make to Churchill's urgent pleas for material assistance. British historians have perhaps underestimated the extent to which Roosevelt used Hopkins to distance himself from Churchill's attempt at a personal embrace. Roosevelt needed to demonstrate that his primary concern was to serve American, not British interests, and after 1942 both powers were looking towards a postwar world where they would again be competitors. It appears that Churchill was hurt by this, but it should have been unsurprising.

Fortunately for Britain, Roosevelt quickly grasped that a victory for Hitler's Germany posed a very serious threat to US security, and he went much further than might have been expected in providing industrial and economic assistance to Britain and in putting the US Navy on a war footing in the North Atlantic, to the extent that the United States was virtually a co-belligerent in the months which preceded Pearl Harbor.

One of the most striking themes of this part of the book is how unprepared the US Navy was for the active convoy escort role imposed on it. US naval forces in the Atlantic were essentially the rump of the fleet, comprising a few old battleships, the second-line carrier *Ranger*, a division of modern cruisers, and a few divisions of 20-year-old 'flush-deckers'; the only modern battleships and carriers were those working up before deploying to the elite Pacific Fleet. Admiral Ernest King (C-in-C Atlantic) constantly protested that his force was not ready for the new assignment. Anti-submarine warfare was not a discipline the US Navy had readily embraced; the ships available were poorly suited to escort duties in the stormy waters of the North Atlantic, and the crews had not trained for this mission. Having transferred 50 flush-deckers to Britain under Lend-Lease – the ships proved to be of dubious military value – the US Navy was then compelled to 'import' British-built 'Flower' class corvettes and ASW trawlers in early 1942 in an attempt to stem the devastating German U-boat offensive off the US East Coast (Operation *Paukenschlag*).

The book proceeds with a blow-by-blow account of the campaign against the Axis powers, beginning with the aerial resupply of Malta by the carrier *Wasp* and the reinforcement of the Home Fleet by US Navy battleships to neutralise the threat of *Tirpitz*, followed by the landings in North Africa, Sicily and the Italian mainland, and culminating in the landings in Normandy and the South of France. The relationship between the Americans and the British was not always smooth, and there were disagreements regarding the timing of the landings in mainland France – the Americans pushed for an early date whereas Churchill wanted to prioritise the Mediterranean – and the handling of the forces deployed to northern waters – King was furious about the PQ17 debacle and pushed for the withdrawal of the US TF99 from Home Fleet control. Nevertheless, the combined achievements of the Allied forces were impressive, despite regular setbacks against determined German opposition. For a time the German glide bombs (the Fritz X and Hs293) presented a serious threat in the Mediterranean, but by June 1944 the Allies had honed their amphibious capabilities and had achieved complete aerial superiority. The major opposition during the landings in Normandy was arguably provided by the weather, which delayed the initial sailings and broke up one of the two Mulberry harbours.

Stern's account is illustrated by an impressive selection of contemporary photographs, not all of the highest quality but providing a newsreel-like commentary on the proceedings. The book is well-produced on high-quality paper. There are two useful appendices, on the 'Reverse Lend-Lease' ships and the various types of landing ships/craft employed respectively. Some theatre maps would have been useful, but the book is otherwise everything one would expect.

John Jordan

Helen Doe & Richard Harding (editors)
Naval Leadership and Management, 1650-1950: Essays in Honour of Michael Duffy
The Boydell Press, Suffolk, 2012;
206 pages, no illustrations;
price £60.00.
ISBN 978-1-84383-695-7

Michael Duffy was Director of the Centre for Maritime Historical Studies at the University of Exeter between 1991 and 2007: there can be no finer testament to his influence and to the affection and regard in which he is held both at Exeter and elsewhere that almost all the contributions in this book are by current and former pupils and colleagues.

As Richard Harding claims in the Introduction, the notion that it was 'happenstance' that brought the genius of Horatio Nelson to the Battle of Trafalgar at exactly the right moment has long been discounted. Indeed, it is now acknowledged that the Royal Navy's famous victory in 1805 towards the end of the 'Long Eighteenth Century' was founded on a sophisticated system of naval administration and management which in turn is being increasingly recognised as a key building block of the 'bureaucratic development of the modern state in Europe'. The essays in this excellent publication explore this fascinating 'hinterland' of infrastructure, organisation and logistics which, if these vital assets are to succeed, demand high quality leadership and management. Successive sub-sections are entitled 'Leadership: The Place of the Hero', 'Leadership and Organisational Frictions: Contested Territories, Management Capability and the Exercise of Naval Power' and 'The Evolution of Management Training in the Royal Navy, 1800-1950'. However, this is not a celebratory story of unremitting achievement; rather it plots an evolutionary process which, rejecting a strictly chronological format, starts with an account of the extraordinarily autonomous nature of Admiral Rainier's East Indies Command at the end of the 18th Century and finishes with an examination of midshipmen training at Dartmouth during the interwar years.

Amongst the other attributes of Admiral Rainier highlighted by Peter Ward was a far-sighted and 'modern' attitude towards man management, a philosophy based on the adoption of a humane approach towards those under his command. If the fact that the Admiralty was able to leave the immense responsibilities of the East Indies Command almost entirely in the capable hands of Rainier demonstrates fine leadership judgement in itself, the same could not be said in the early 1740s when the First Lord of the Admiralty, the Earl of Winchelsea, presided over a period described by Richard Harding as 'perhaps the nadir of British naval power'. Although at the time it was the individual leadership qualities that bore the blame, Harding demonstrates that the real cause lay in a systemic failure of the leadership *network*.

Roger Morriss's contribution concerns the work of the Transport Agents and the creation of a naval Transport Board in 1794, and emphasises the importance of this little-regarded service to the efficient bureaucratic structure supporting the Navy's day-to-day operations. If this recognition implies a close attention to detail, the same could not be said of the poor career prospects, pay and morale suffered by RN junior officers of the early inter-war period. Mike Farquharson-Roberts's study of the root causes of the Invergordon Mutiny in 1931 suggests that junior officers had more than adequate grounds to share the discontent of the lower deck, even if they did not express this by mutinying. Once again, leadership failure at the highest level, from a distanced cadre of Admiralty Board Members as well as First Sea Lords Beatty and Madden, proved inadequate in the years leading up to Invergordon. In a fascinating passage, Farquharson-Roberts draws on the work of occupational psychologist Frederick Herzberg regarding employee motivation. Herzberg's 'two factor' theory determines that so-called 'hygiene' aspects are essential to morale/productivity. For the junior officers at Invergordon 'Pay and Benefits, Company Policy/Administration, Physical Environment and Relationships with co-workers' were aspects of their working environment which all fell way short of adequate.

Other contributions include Gareth Cole and Britt Zerbe examining the problems of integrating land-fighting men with sailors, looking at respectively the manning of bomb vessels where artillerymen and naval personnel mixed unhappily under two quite separate commands, resulting in the introduction of The Royal Marine Artillery; and the position of the British Marine Corps officers in relation to their Royal Navy counterparts. David J. Starkey looks at the organisational structure which lay behind privateering during its heyday in the 18th Century. In conclusion, Elinor Romans describes the education given to the cadets who entered Dartmouth at the age of thirteen during the early interwar period, and the change following the Invergordon mutiny from a heavily academic curriculum to a primarily practical one which accentuated the importance of leadership training. To this end, 'Boat Work' which involved the cadets taking responsibility for a small group of men became 'arguably the most important subject on the Dartmouth curriculum' and helped instil the leadership qualities which were to be demanded of these young men during the Second World War.

Jon Wise

WARSHIP GALLERY

HMS *Pandora* and the 1st Submarine Flotilla, 1921-22

In this year's Warship Gallery **Stephen Dent** and **Ian Johnston** present a series of photographs showing units of the 1st Submarine Flotilla during the early 1920s, a time when even though the Royal Navy was once again at peace, the flotilla was still actively engaged in a full programme of training and exercises along with the rest of the Atlantic Fleet.

The 1st Submarine Flotilla was, as the name suggests, the Royal Navy's first, initially formed of the five 'Holland' type boats in the summer of 1902. By the start of the 1920s it was made up of a collection of submersible leviathans that few if any could have imagined eighteen years earlier.

The steam-powered 'K' class submarines were mostly commissioned during 1916-17 and formed the 12th and 13th Submarine Flotillas; they acquired a famously appalling reputation for accidents and disasters, and by the end of the war four had been sunk, with horrendous loss of life. With the submarines intended to operate with the main battle fleet, each flotilla had as its flagship a light cruiser. The completion of the 'M' class meanwhile was delayed, ostensibly out of fear that the Germans might copy the concept of a 'submarine monitor', though uncertainty as to what they were supposed to do may well have been a more important reason.

With the end of the war, after a brief interlude when the 'K' class boats made up both the 1st and 2nd Submarine Flotillas, in October 1919 seven of them formed the 1st Submarine Flotilla (part of the Atlantic Fleet – the post-war successor to the Grand Fleet; in turn it became the Home Fleet in 1932), the remainder being used for trials work or being placed in reserve. The flotilla was led by the light cruiser *Inconstant*. By 1921 numbers were down to five 'K' class: K2, K6, K12, K15 and K22 (ex-K13), but they had now been joined by M1, together with *Pandora* as depot ship and the drifter *Silhouette* as tender. The other surviving 'K's were in reserve or had been paid off, while M2 and M3 had only recently been completed and were not yet in full commission.

In wartime the 'K' class had not operated with a depot ship, being regarded as large enough to function as independent warships. This cannot have done much to alleviate their unpopularity, for while they were much longer than earlier submarines they were still very cramped inside, due to the size of the propulsion plant as well as the great quantity of other equipment squeezed into their hulls. With wartime pressures lifted, a depot ship became essential, and this role fell to HMS *Pandora*. She had begun life as the SS *Seti*, built by Palmers for the Moss Line and completed in 1902. Purchased by the Admiralty in 1914, she was renamed *Pandora* in November. For most of the war she served as depot ship to the 9th Submarine Flotilla, based at Harwich, before being assigned to the Rosyth-based 1st Submarine Flotilla in August 1919. She underwent a major refit at Devonport during 1920-21, recommissioning on 4 January 1921.

Although the flotilla was officially based at Rosyth, an idea of its actual field of operations (and hence the need for a depot ship) can be gained from *Pandora*'s movements during 1921-22:

09.00, 4 January 1921: commissioned from refit, Devonport, for 1st Submarine Flotilla, Atlantic Fleet.
January: Portland, Devonport.
February: Pembroke.
March: Torbay, Portland, Chatham.
March-August: Chatham & Sheerness.
August-September: Rosyth.
September-October: Invergordon, Fortrose.
November: Rosyth, Fortrose, Sheerness & Chatham.
December: Chatham.

January 1922: Chatham, Portland, Arosa Bay (N.Spain).
February: Portland.
March: St Helens Roads, Chatham.
April: Chatham, Spithead, Portland.
May: Portland, Chatham.
June: Chatham, Invergordon, Burghead, Lossiemouth.
July: Torbay, Portland, Sheerness, Chatham.
August: Chatham, Sheerness, Invergordon, Nairn.
September: Nairn & Invergordon.
October: Invergordon, Burghead, Toerbermorey, Oban, Campbeltown.
November: Oban, Campbeltown, Milford Haven, the Nore & Chatham.
December: Chatham.

The spells at Chatham were mostly spent alongside, undergoing routine maintenance, taking on stores and suchlike, with the submarines of the flotilla also present and doing much the same. The most notable event seems to have been the disciplining of an officer for exceeding his monthly wine bill! Stores were embarked both for the ship herself and for the submarines that she supported (see accompanying plans). The journeys down river to Sheerness were to take on coal from the hulk C109 (ex-*Agincourt*). At Rosyth, in contrast, *Pandora* alter-

WARSHIP GALLERY

A fine view of Pandora *lying peacefully at anchor in the Firth of Forth. Her origins as a merchant ship are evident. At 4550 tons, she was 300ft long and 23ft in the beam; with three coal-fired boilers her triple expansion engines produced 2200hp to give a top speed of 11 knots. A Chatham-manned ship, her crew totalled 318, consisting of 16 officers, 112 seamen, 31 Marines, 98 Engine Room Establishment, and 61 other non-executive ratings. (All photographs courtesy of Ian Johnston)*

nated between time alongside in the dockyard itself, and being tied up to a buoy out in the Firth of Forth, with submarines departing and arriving all the time. This was the repetitive but vital lot of the submarine depot ship, something which became much more important when she was at Invergordon, where permanent facilities were very limited.

The January voyage to northern Spain was an annual affair, with the fleet carrying out extensive war exercises on the way. For the 1st Flotilla it was not altogether a happy business: in January 1921 *K5* disappeared with all hands during the exercises; the following year, as *Pandora* arrived back at Portland, her whaler capsized and a crewman was drowned. Mock attacks and other exercises were also carried out regularly during passages between the various bases.

The flotilla was assigned to the Atlantic Fleet with a view to its submarines operating in between the cruiser

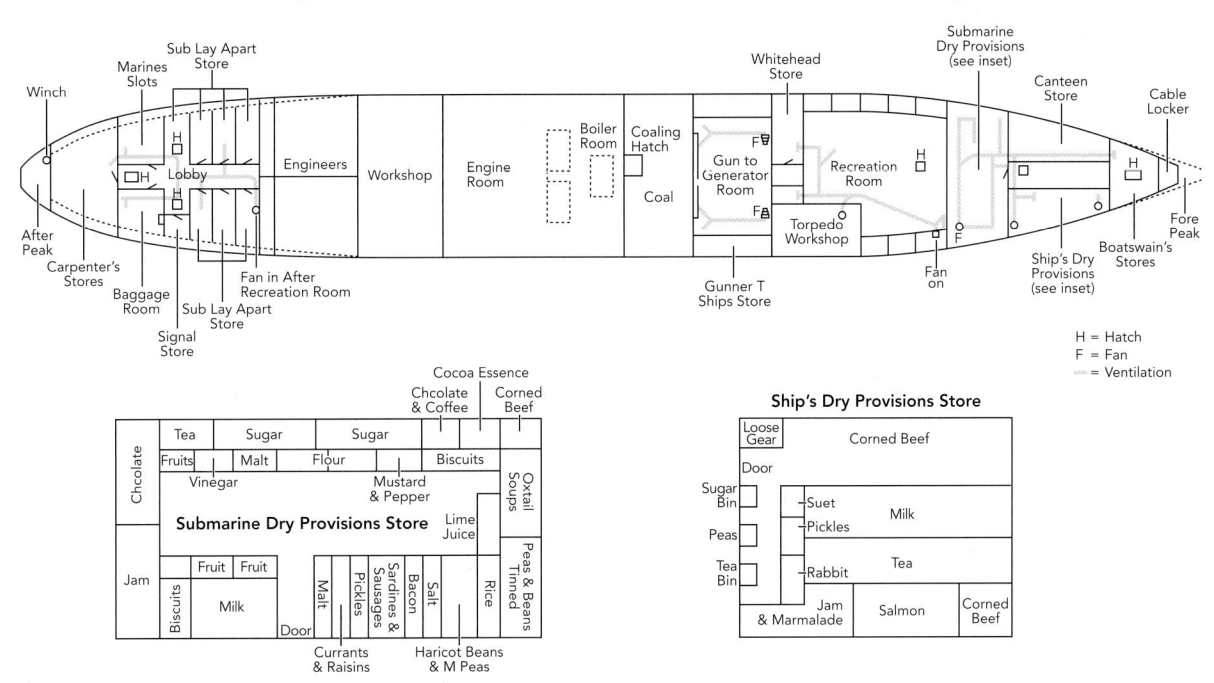

Plan (not to scale) of HMS Pandora, *based on sketches in ship's log, showing general layout of the ship and her store rooms. Note that some of the annotation is tentative only, being taken from hand-written labelling. (Drawings by Stephen Dent, based on ADM53/81521 – HMS* Pandora, *Ship's Log, 18 December 1921 to 4 December 1922.)*

201

A magnificent view of K2 (Lt.Cdr. F H Taylor DSC) at Invergordon, with the stern of another 'K'-boat visible in the left foreground. Beyond are the battleships Warspite and Malaya, of the 1st Battle Squadron (1st Division) with a drifter and pinnaces in attendance. Note the aircraft platforms on Warspite's 'B' and 'X' turrets, and the submarine's extended bridgework and positioning of her 4in guns on the superstructure. There also appears to be a structure of some sort atop Malaya's armoured director hood, the purpose of which is not known. K2 had actually been placed in reserve at Rosyth, and in December 1920 was earmarked for scrapping. The following month K5 disappeared with all hands during fleet exercises in the Western Approaches, and K2 was reprieved from the scrapyard to take her place in the flotilla. After a couple of months in dockyard hands she recommissioned on 8 March 1921.

K12 at Invergordon, photographed at much the same time. Note the very different disposition of the gun armament, with one 4in gun on a streamlined cutwater forward of the bridge structure, and a 3in AA forward of the funnels. In between these can be seen the hinged covers for the boiler room vents, in the raised position – note that they bear the submarine's pendant number. Close examination of the photographs reveals that although the submarine is running her diesel engines – note the exhaust, aft – she also has some steam up in her forward boiler. Another detail of note is that in the superstructure of K2, the site of the twin revolving torpedo tube mounting can still be seen, below the forward gun, while in K12 it has been fully plated over. The third battleship, in the distance to the right, is either Valiant or Barham.

K6, this time at Portland, with Chesil Beach and the tanks of the naval fuel depot (today the site of the National Sailing Academy) in the background. Note the longer funnels compared to the other two photographs, also that the wireless masts are not extended. Awnings are rigged to give some protection to the forward and after main hatches, likewise the covers to the two guns. Portland was a major base for submarine and anti-submarine training throughout the inter-war period.

screen and the main battle fleet: in the event of imminent action they were to spread out and dive, then attack the enemy using torpedoes and, in the case of the 'M's, their massive guns firing at short range in the 'dip-chick' manoeuvre – surfacing, firing and then quickly diving to make their escape. The superior surface speed of the 'K's would meanwhile enable them to pursue and destroy any enemy units seen to be retiring. It was these kind of tactics that were practised on the annual manoeuvres, as evidenced by the activity of *M2* during January 1922:

9 January: in company with *Pandora*, departed Chatham for Portland, arrived 10 January.
11 January: exercised 12in gun drill, otherwise 'usual routine'.
12 January: 08.30 cast off for exercising, proceeded at

A slightly poorer-quality shot of one of the 'K' class under steam, passing a light cruiser of the Caroline class. The diesel engines of the submarine also appear still to be running, most likely for battery charging.

11 knots. 10.06 dived, to 30ft, 'fired water shots and exercised dip chick firing'. 11.33 surfaced, blew externals. Back in harbour by 13.00, alongside HMS *Assistance* (repair ship, Atlantic Fleet).

15 January: hands attended divine service on board *Pandora*.

16 January: patrolling off Casquet light.

17 January: 07.15 dived, to 27ft, 07.30 surfaced. 08.00 'Strategical Exercise commenced'. M2 was part of the Blue Fleet, opposing the Red Fleet. 13.40 sighted mast of warship, dived. 14.35 surfaced, 15.34 sighted Red Fleet and convoy. 16.55 surfaced and reported Red Fleet's position, composition and speed by WT, then shadowed.

18 January: off Ushant. 13.45 sighted warships, 15.00 Red Fleet, dived. 15.48 attacked HMS *Queen Elizabeth*.

19 January: similar to above, made submerged attack on HMS *Royal Oak*. Speed when travelling on the surface normally 11-13 knots. Arrived at Arosa Bay.

21 January: trimmed down by stern to examine bow caps and shutters, hands employed unshipping WT mast.

22 January: cast off from *Assistance*, alongside *Pandora*.

23 January: re-embarked WT mast, which was then re-fitted on 25 January.

24 January: 12in gun drill, cleaning ship.

26 January: torpedo tube drill. During this period various minor items such as paint brushes and cooking utensils were lost overboard due to the heavy weather, suggesting that the bay was actually not all that sheltered.

27 January: 12in gun drill.

30 January: left Arosa Bay, in company with M1.

(A regular part of the routine throughout was one or other engine being used to charge the submarine's batteries, usually for a period of an hour or two.)

The photographs here of the 'K' class submarines clearly illustrate the various modifications carried out as a consequence of the type's disastrous early service: the raised bow to improve seakeeping, extended bridge structure for better navigation and keeping lookout, and re-positioned gun armament. Even so, the 'K's continued to spend considerable amounts of time in dockyard hands; by their very nature they were still pushing the submarine technology of the day to its limits, and remained accident-prone throughout their careers. The 'M' class, in contrast, seem to have been successful, despite their somewhat unconventional appearance and dubious role. Then in November 1925 M1 was lost with all hands in a collision with a merchantman; the 1st Flotilla was disbanded shortly afterwards and the remaining 'K' class were sent for scrapping. M2 was converted to carry aircraft and she too was lost in an accident, again with everyone on board, in January 1932.

Pandora meanwhile ended up alongside at the submarine base at Fort Blockhouse, Gosport, functioning as both a depot and a school ship. She took the name *Dolphin* from the old sloop she replaced, a name which ultimately came to apply to the establishment as a whole. In December 1939, having been sold for disposal, she was sunk by a mine off Blyth.

Note:
The photographs in this Warship Gallery were acquired by a friend of regular contributor Ian Johnston in a car

M2 *and one of her two sister boats, probably* M1, *and two 'K' class, alongside* Pandora, *with the latter two submarines 'lighting up'. The volume of smoke, especially from the nearer of the two 'K' boats, is noteworthy, and a clear indication of the trouble that the submarines had with their oil-fired boilers – in cold conditions the oil tended to become 'waxy' and there were also problems with sea water contamination, both of which would have an adverse affect on combustion.*

WARSHIP GALLERY

The interior of M1's 12in gun mounting, showing part of the elevation mechanism. This compartment was outside the pressure hull, and remained free-flooding: unsurprisingly this occasionally caused problems with water getting into the breech mechanism. The 12in guns fitted were originally 40-calibre Mk IX weapons as used in battleships of the King Edward VII class; it seems that these were later replaced by slightly lighter 35-calibre Mk VIIs from the Majestic class.

boot sale – proof (if any were needed) of the sort of treasures that can be found in such places. Apart from the occasional annotation on a few of them there was no accompanying information. All the text and captions that comprise the rest of the feature have been compiled by the Assistant Editor using assorted primary sources

M1 (Cdr. C G Brodie) coming alongside Pandora at Fortrose, sometime during September–November 1921. Pandora made two visits to Fortrose, on the Moray Firth, during this period. On the first of these occasions she embarked a detachment of Royal Marines for exercises; when she returned to Invergordon the latter marched back overland, a distance of perhaps six miles as the crow flies but the best part of thirty by road. She also landed her ship's running team for similar activities.

M1 coming alongside at Rosyth, some time between 15 and 30 August 1921. Clearly visible aft is the 3in gun, the submarine's secondary surface armament. Also intended for anti-aircraft use if necessary, it was fitted on a high-angle disappearing mounting, hydraulically raised and lowered. This did not prove to be a great success, taking two and a half minutes to raise and lock into position for use, and only half a minute less to retract again. The light cruiser in the distance appears to be of the Arethusa class, so may well be Inconstant.

M2 coming alongside at Portland, with a deck party at the ready. Of interest is the different form of the front of the submarine's bridge compared to M1.

M2 on a placid sea at Invergordon with two light cruisers in the background. The nearer cruiser is of the Caledon *class, the further of the earlier* Arethusa *or* Caroline *classes (so could be* Inconstant*). The submarine's 3in gun is retracted, but the radio mast is rigged.*

(mainly logs, operational reports, and *The Navy List*) as well as some published works. In addition the invaluable help of John Roberts, John Jordan and the staff of The National Archives (formerly the Public Record Office) in Kew, London, is gratefully acknowledged. If any readers can add anything to that which is presented here, *Warship* would very much like to hear from them. In particular, the identity of the photographer, C Gladwill (or Gladwell), poses something of a mystery. He appears to have been on board HMS *Pandora*, but there is no record of anyone of that name serving in the RN at the time, nor of a commercial or press photographer. This suggests a private individual, which prompts the question as to why he was taking photographs on board one of HM Ships?

HMS Royal Oak (Captain PH Hall-Thompson CMG), part of the 2nd Division of the 1st Battle Squadron, crossing the Bay of Biscay, Thursday 19 January 1922. During exercises that day and the previous one the ship had engaged the 'enemy' battlecruisers Repulse *and* Hood. *She also had to take action to avoid a steamer while on passage.*

HMS Argus (Captain AJB Stirling) 'taking things easy' while crossing the Bay of Biscay, Thursday 19 January 1922. Note the chart house and masts, in the raised position. Argus was at that time attached to the Atlantic Fleet and, as the Navy's only fully operational aircraft carrier, was extensively used for deck trials of a wide variety of types of aircraft. Three days previously experimental landing trials had taken place at Spithead using Nieuport Sparrowhawk fighter and Fairey Pintail reconnaissance aircraft. The former was rated as 'satisfactory' for landing, but less good when it came to taking off; the latter as 'impossible… totally unsuitable for deck landing' with the pilot unable to see the deck at all during the actual landing, it being in the 'blind spot' of the aircraft, which was only arrested when the starboard wing tip caught in the arrestor wires, the aircraft slewing over to starboard and coming to rest at right angles to the ship's axis! Things did get better, however: by 9 February, with the ship now off Malta, five machines flew off and made a torpedo 'attack' on the 'enemy' Red Fleet at sea.

Looking forward on the port side of Pandora as she crosses the Bay of Biscay, 20 January 1922.